GRADE 3

McGRAW-HILL

Language Arts

TAAS Study Guide and Practice

Pages T2-T32

TAAS

Study Guide and Practice

This TAAS study guide and practice tests will help you get ready for the TAAS test.

Purpose and Audience

The student will respond appropriately in a written composition to the purpose/audience specified in a given topic.

When you take the TAAS test, you will be asked to write for a certain purpose. Your purpose is your reason for writing. You may be asked to write for the purpose of **informing**, **influencing**, or **entertaining**.

Purpose: Writing to Influence

Persuasive Writing Persuasive writing tries to make people think or act a certain way.

Prompt

Write a letter to your parents. Give your opinion about why you want a pet. Support your opinion with convincing reasons.

Look for words or phrases that name your audience.

This sentence tells you what to include in your letter.

Look for clues that tell you the purpose of your writing.

TAAS

Purpose: Writing to Inform

Informative: How-to Writing Explanatory writing gives directions or explains how to do something.

Prompt

Think about how to make your favorite sandwich. Write directions for your teacher in which you explain how to make it. Be sure to give step-by-step instructions.

Look for clues that name your audience.

Read the prompt carefully to find the purpose of your writing.

This phrase tells you how to organize your ideas.

Informative: Classification Writing Writing that compares looks at two things and describes how they are alike and how they are different.

Prompt

Think about what you like and don't like about tests. Write a composition explaining what you like about tests and what you don't like about tests. Include specific details.

Are you writing to entertain, inform, or influence your audience?

Look for words or phrases that tell you what information to include in your writing.

- **What phrases would you use in each composition to make it flow?**
- **What would you say as an introduction in each of your compositions?**

Purpose: Writing to Entertain

Sometimes you write stories to entertain people and make them feel a certain way. You can write about something that really happened or something that you have made up in your mind.

Narrative Writing A story can be make-believe or real.

Prompt

Imagine that one day your dog got loose on a school field trip. <u>Write a story</u> about what might happen if you took your dog on <u>a school field trip.</u>

Look for words that tell you the purpose for writing.

This phrase tells you the setting of the story.

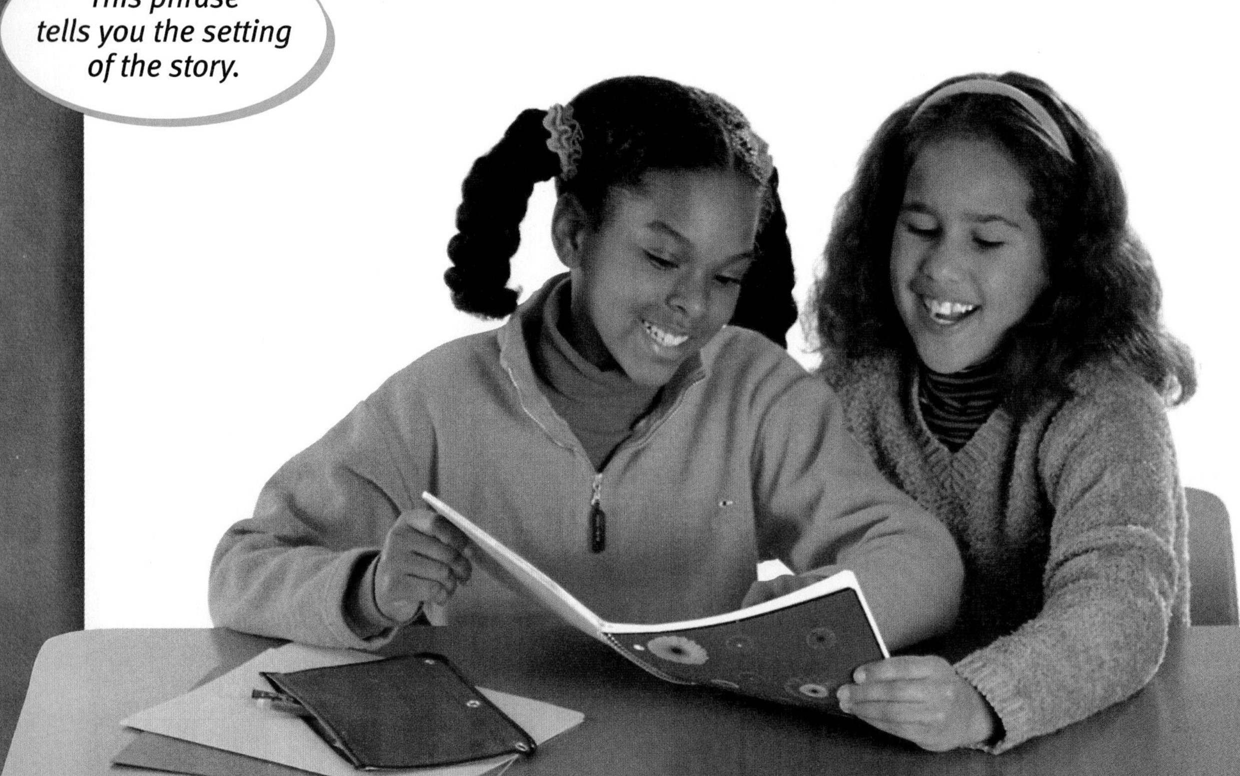

Audience

When you take the TAAS test, you will be asked to write to a certain audience. Your audience is the people who will read your composition.

Formal	Informal
letter to a teacher	note to a friend
writing for a test	telephone message
paper for school	your diary/journal

Here is a sample of **formal** writing.

The Comanches lived on the plains of West Texas. They rode fast horses and chased buffalo across the plains. Comanches lived in teepees, which were easy to take apart and put back together. When they followed the herds, it was easy for them to take the teepees along.

Here is a sample of **informal** writing.

Sara,

Mom called and said to pack for the trip to Harlingen. I'm at Daniel's house, but I'll be home for dinner by six.

Juan

- **What type of letter would you write to your grandfather? Explain why.**
- **Will you use formal or informal writing in a report about the Texas flag? Explain how you know.**

Organize Ideas

The student will organize ideas in a written composition on a given topic.

The **Prewrite** and **Revise** steps of the writing process give you the chance to organize ideas.

Below is a graphic organizer used in the **Prewrite** step. It will help you decide what you will write about and the order in which you will write it.

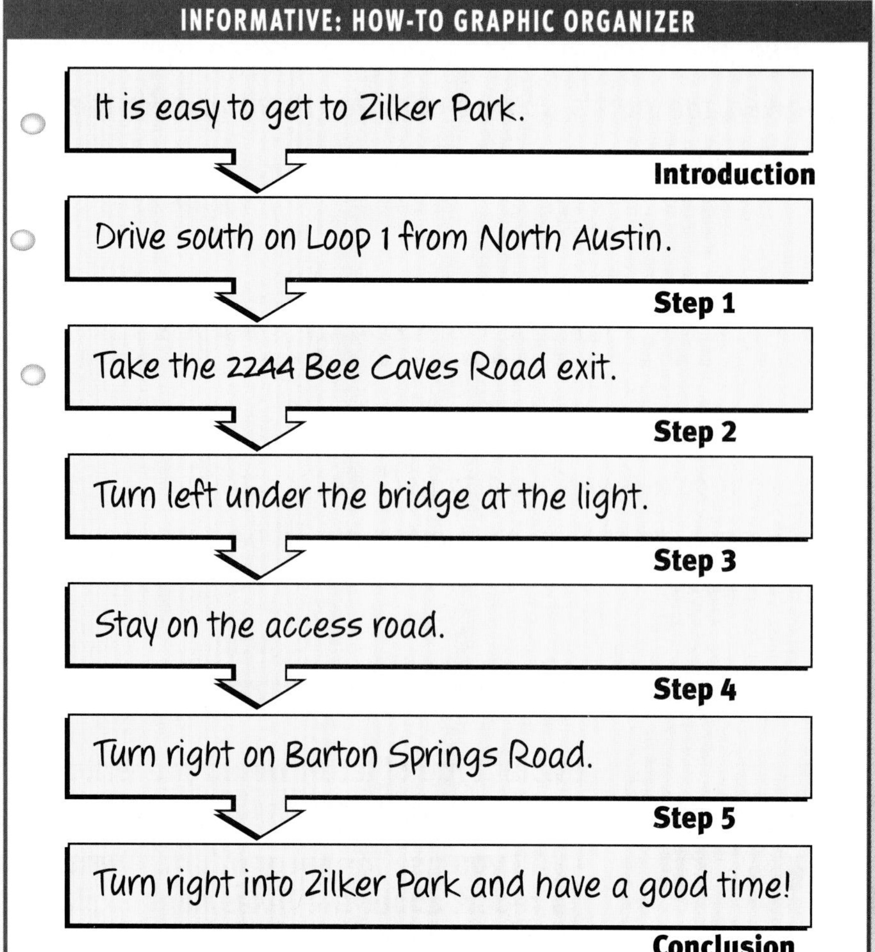

INFORMATIVE: HOW-TO GRAPHIC ORGANIZER
Here is the main idea.
Here are some supporting details.
It is easy to get to Zilker Park.
Introduction
Drive south on Loop 1 from North Austin.
Step 1
Take the 2244 Bee Caves Road exit.
Step 2
Turn left under the bridge at the light.
Step 3
Stay on the access road.
Step 4
Turn right on Barton Springs Road.
Step 5
Turn right into Zilker Park and have a good time!
Conclusion

TAAS

Revise Here is Jack's persuasive letter urging his teacher to consider Zilker Park for the next field trip.

140 Allen Street
Dallas, Texas 75200
March 5, 20__

Mrs. Rita Martin
West End School
600 Park Lane
Dallas, Texas 75230

Dear Mrs. Martin,

I think we should go to Zilker Park for our field trip. It is not very far from our school. Please listen to my reasons, and maybe you'll agree with me.

My first reason is that it is close to our school. We could walk to the park. This would save money.

My next reason is that Zilker Park has so many different things for us to do. There is a fun playground. The ball field is great. We can ride the train. Going to Zilker Park would give us more time to play since it wouldn't take long to get there.

Barton Springs is in Zilker Park. You can play sports. We could study about this spring before we go and see it!

By now you must be thinking Zilker Park is a great place for a field trip. It won't take much planning. Just say yes to Zilker Park.

Yours truly,
Jack

This sentence should be moved to support the next paragraph.

This sentence should be combined with the second paragraph.

This sentence is off topic. It should be deleted.

Good organization of paragraph.

- **What else does Jack need to rearrange to make sure his paper is in logical order?**
- **How else can Jack improve the organization of his paper?**

OBJECTIVE 3

Language Control

The student will demonstrate control of the English language in a written composition on a given topic.

Rebecca decided to write a story about a giant armadillo.

Use correct spelling.

Write in complete sentences. This fragment can be combined with the previous sentence.

Capitalize first word in sentence and proper nouns.

Use an apostrophe in a contraction.

Use quotation marks.

It was late, but I was reading about armadillos for a report. It was interesting, but I was so tired. Zzzzzzz.

I woke with a start. The lite was so bright. Where was I? I looked around. I was not in my room!

Then I heard a voice, "Quick, come with us." I looked around. And saw an odd-looking person. She was extremely tiny and had a tail like a cat.

"Who are you?" I demanded.

"i'm stella, but there's no time for small talk," she said.

"Whats wrong?" I asked.

"A giant armadillo is out to get us and we must hide!" Stella cried. Off she ran with me following.

Suddenly, I tripped and fell. The giant armadillo was coming my way. I closed my eyes.

Rebecca! Rebecca! It's time to wake up." I heard my mother's voice and slowly I opened my eyes.

- **Why is it important to use correct grammar in a narrative?**
- **How are quotation marks used in the story?**

Elaboration

The student will generate a written composition that develops/supports/elaborates the central idea stated in a given topic.

Look at Joshua's paper about the Caddo and Jumano tribes. Notice how the use of elaboration could make his paper more interesting to the reader.

> Both the Caddo and Jumano tribes lived in Texas long ago.
>
> Jumanos lived close to the Rio Grande near what is now the city of El Paso. Caddoes lived along creeks and rivers in the lush forests of East Texas.
>
> Jumanos made their homes from adobe because the climate was hot and dry. Caddoes made their homes from tree limbs, grass, and mud.
>
> Jumanos farmed for most of their food. When farming was difficult, they had to find other things to eat. Caddoes farmed and hunted for food. Food was plentiful in East Texas, and the Caddoes always had more than enough to eat.

How long ago?

Explain why the homes were made from adobe. More detail needed.

Why was farming difficult?

- **What descriptive words and phrases could you use to make this paper more interesting?**
- **What other ways can Joshua use elaboration to make his paper more interesting?**

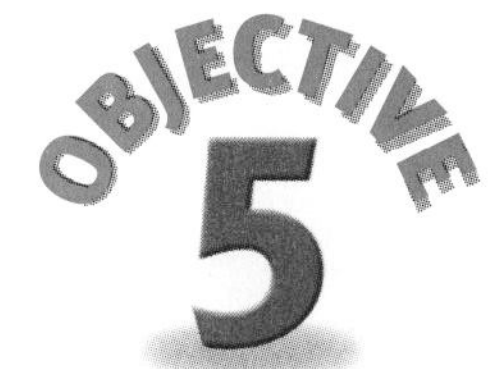

Sentence Construction

The student will recognize appropriate sentence construction within the context of a written passage.

The English language has rules for sentence construction. We follow these rules so our writing will be clear to the people who read it.

Complete Sentences Complete sentences help the reader understand what you have written and what you mean. A complete sentence must contain a subject and a verb. The sentence must state a complete thought.

- For help with rules for writing complete sentences see Handbook pages 502-504.

Sentence Fragments A sentence fragment is a sentence with a missing subject or predicate. Sentence fragments can confuse the reader because part of the sentence is missing.

- For strategies on how to avoid writing sentence fragments see Handbook pages 502-504 and Troubleshooter pages 488-489.

Run-on Sentences In a run-on sentence, sentences are incorrectly joined either with a comma or with no punctuation.

- For strategies on how to avoid writing run-on sentences see Handbook pages 502-504 and Troubleshooter pages 490-491.

Below is a sample TAAS page.

TAAS

Read the passage. Some sections are underlined. The underlined sections may be one of the following:

- **Incomplete sentences**
- **Run-on sentences**
- **Correctly written sentences that should be combined**
- **Correctly written sentences that do not need to be rewritten**

Choose the best way to write each underlined section. If the underlined section needs no change, choose "No Mistake."

Sample

It was almost dark in downtown Austin. (1) LaDonna watched as thousands of bats flew from the spaces inside of the Congress Avenue bridge. The bats flew out. To find insects. (2) They would fly back in the morning. They would return to the bridge. (3)

A complete sentence has a subject and a predicate.

You can correct a sentence fragment by adding a subject.

Use the word and *to join sentences.*

1 ○ It was almost dark.
○ It was almost dark. In downtown Austin.
○ In downtown Austin was almost dark.
○ No Mistake

2 ○ The bats flew out. Find insects.
○ The bats flew out. Insects to find.
○ The bats flew out to find insects.
○ No Mistake

3 ○ They would fly back in the morning and return to the bridge.
○ They would fly back. They would return to the bridge in the morning.
○ They would fly back in the morning and they would return to the bridge in the morning.
○ No Mistake

Usage

The student will recognize appropriate English usage within the context of a written passage.

Pronouns Pronouns have different forms depending on how they are used in a sentence. A pronoun can have a subject, object, or possessive form.

- For help with subject, object, and possessive pronoun forms see Handbook pages 515-516.

Subject-Verb Agreement When you write a sentence, you must choose the verb that agrees with the subject. You must decide if your subject is singular or plural.

- For a list of specific rules for subject-verb agreement see Troubleshooter pages 494-495.

Verb Tense You must be sure to use the correct tense in your writing. Is the action happening in the past, present, or future?

- For help with verb tense see Handbook pages 509-510 and Troubleshooter pages 496-497.

Adjectives and Adverbs You can make your writing more interesting when you use adverbs and adjectives. Adjectives can be used to compare nouns, while adverbs can be used to compare verbs and other adverbs.

- For help with correct forms of adjectives and adverbs see Handbook pages 518-521 and Troubleshooter page 500.

TAAS

Below is a sample TAAS test page. You will be asked to apply what you have learned about correct word usage.

Here is a sample page from a TAAS test. Read the passage and choose the word or group of words that belongs in each space. Choose the best answer.

Sample

Many people think that a coral reef is the __(1)__ sight they've ever seen. A coral reef is like an underwater garden teeming with hundreds of colorful sea animals Most coral reefs __(2)__ naturally. However, off the coast of Texas, there are many artificial reefs. Some have __(3)__ on sunken ships.

Use an adjective to tell about a coral reef.

Make sure that a plural verb agrees with its plural subject.

Be sure that the tense of your verb is correct.

1 ○ more beautiful
○ beautifuler
○ most beautiful
○ beautifulest

2 ○ grows
○ were growing
○ grown
○ grow

3 ○ forms
○ formed
○ forming
○ form

Spelling and Mechanics

The student will recognize appropriate spelling, capitalization, and punctuation within the context of a written passage.

The English language has rules for spelling, capitalization, and punctuation. We follow these rules so our writing will be clear to the people who read it.

Spelling

Correctly spelled words help readers understand which word you have written and what you mean.

- For help with spelling rules and strategies see Handbook pages 550-551.
- For lists of easily confused words, frequently misspelled words, and common homophones see Handbook pages 548-549.

Mechanics

Capitalization Capital letters show the reader the beginning of sentences and the names of specific people, places, or things.

- For a list of specific rules for capitalization see Handbook pages 524-526.

Punctuation Correct punctuation shows readers where to pause and where to stop. It also shows who owns something and the exact words someone has said.

- For help with punctuation see Handbook pages 527-529.

Below is a sample TAAS test page. You will be asked to apply what you have learned about spelling and mechanics.

Here is a sample page from a TAAS test. Read the passage and decide which type of mistake, if any, appears in each underlined section. Choose the best answer. If there is no error, choose "No Mistake."

Sample

West Texas has some amazing mountains. <u>The highest peak in Texas can be found in the Guadalupe Mountains.</u> (1) It is 1,751 feet tall. <u>The three main mountain ranges are the Davis Mountains the Chisos Mountains, and the Guadalupe Mountains.</u> (2) These mountains are home to animals such as jackrabbits, skunks, raccoons, and deer. <u>They are also home to more than 1,000 kinds of Plants.</u> (3)

Check for mistakes in spelling, capitalization, and punctuation.

Use a comma to separate items in a list.

Plants is not a proper noun, so it does not need to be capitalized.

1 ○ Spelling
○ Capitalization
○ Punctuation
○ No mistake

2 ○ Spelling
○ Capitalization
○ Punctuation
○ No mistake

3 ○ Spelling
○ Capitalization
○ Punctuation
○ No mistake

Word Meaning

The student will determine the meaning of words in a variety of written texts.

When we read the English language, we often come across unfamiliar words. There are strategies we can use to figure out the meanings of unfamiliar words so that we can understand what we are reading.

Prefixes and Suffixes Prefixes and suffixes can help us divide words into smaller parts to help us understand word meaning.

- For help with prefix and suffix rules and strategies see Handbook page 543.
- For lists of common prefixes and suffixes see Handbook page 543.

Context Clues Context clues help the reader understand the meanings of unfamiliar words. Sometimes there will be clues in the story that will help you figure out what the unfamiliar word means.

- For help with figuring out what unfamiliar words mean see Handbook pages 556-557.

Special Words Some books have special words that only certain people know. For example, if you were reading a book about plants, there would be special words like *anther, stamen, sepal,* and *stigma* that people familiar with the plants would already know.

TAAS

Below is a sample page from a TAAS test. You will be asked to apply what you have learned about word meanings.

Here is a sample page from a TAAS test. Read the passage. Then read each question that follows the passage. Decide which is the best answer to each question.

Sample

"It's starting to get a little nippy," said Kayla's dad as they climbed up the mountain. "Zip up your jacket so you'll stay warm."

Kayla's family was spending the day hiking in the Chisos Mountains at Big Bend National Park.

Kayla zipped her jacket and looked below at the vast blanket of bluebonnets that stretched for miles across the valley. It was going to be a spectacular day!

Nippy is an antonym for warm. Nippy means cool.

The phrase "stretched for miles" is a context clue for the word vast.

S-1 The word nippy means—

- ○ wet
- ○ chilly
- ○ hot
- ○ sunny

S-2 The word vast means—

- ○ deep
- ○ low place
- ○ invisible
- ○ large area

Practice Test

BE SURE YOU HAVE RECORDED ALL OF YOUR ANSWERS ON THE ANSWER DOCUMENT

DIRECTIONS

Read the passage. Some sections are underlined. The underlined sections may be one of the following:

- **Incomplete sentences**
- **Run-on sentences**
- **Correctly written sentences that should be combined**
- **Correctly written sentences that do not need to be rewritten**

Choose the best way to write each underlined section. If the underlined section needs no change, choose "No mistake."

SAMPLE A

The snow stopped falling everything looked so white. **(SA-1)** It rarely snowed in Harlingen. We couldn't wait to go outside and play. **(SA-2)** We put on our hats, coats, and mittens. We rushed out the door.

SA-1
- ◯ The snow stopped falling. Everything looked so white.
- ◯ The snow stopped falling everything. It looked so white.
- ◯ The snow stopped. Falling looked so white.
- ◯ No mistake

SA-2
- ◯ We couldn't wait. To go outside and play.
- ◯ We couldn't wait to go. Outside and play.
- ◯ Couldn't wait to go outside and play.
- ◯ No mistake

Read the passage. Some parts are underlined. Decide what mistake, if any, needs to be fixed. Choose the correct answer.

SAMPLE B

I got a letter from my aunt. She lives in san Antonio. **(SB-1)**
She told me all about the markit that she goes to every week. **(SB-2)**

SB-1
- ◯ Spelling
- ◯ Capitalization
- ◯ Punctuation
- ◯ No mistake

SB-2
- ◯ Spelling
- ◯ Capitalization
- ◯ Punctuation
- ◯ No mistake

Read the passage and choose the word or words that go in the space.

SAMPLE C

Rivers have many uses. People ______ **(SC-1)** rivers for recreation. Some farmers use rivers to water crops. After treatment, water from some rivers is used for drinking. Rivers also ______ **(SC-2)** us get rid of our waste.

SC-1
- ◯ uses
- ◯ has used
- ◯ was using
- ◯ use

SC-2
- ◯ help
- ◯ were helping
- ◯ helped
- ◯ will help

Live oaks can be found. All over Texas. (1) They drop their leaves, but like pine trees, they are never bare. Live oaks grow about 50 feet tall. Live oaks branch out far. (2) This makes them great trees for climbing! (3) When live oaks are planted on both sides of a road, their branches can grow out over the road and create a beautiful arch.

1
- ◯ Live oaks can be found all over Texas.
- ◯ Live oaks can be. Found all over Texas.
- ◯ Live oaks. They can be found all over Texas.
- ◯ No mistake

2
- ◯ Live oaks grow and branch out 50 feet.
- ◯ Live oaks grow about 50 feet tall. Branches grow out far, too.
- ◯ Live oaks grow about 50 feet tall and branch out far.
- ◯ No mistake

3
- ◯ This makes it. A great tree for climbing.
- ◯ This makes it a great tree. For climbing.
- ◯ This makes the live oak a great tree.
- ◯ No mistake

Go on

Bessie Coleman, the first African-American woman pilot, was a native Texan.

Bessie was determined to learn how to fly. Bessie moved to Chicago to pursue her dream. **(4)** She had a difficult time trying to enroll in an American flight school. Her friend Robert Abbott. Encouraged her to apply to schools in France. **(5)** She boarded a plane for France in 1920. By 1921, Bessie had her pilot's license. She made her first American flight in 1922.

4
- ○ Bessie was determined to learn how to fly so she moved to Chicago to pursue her dream.
- ○ Bessie was determined. Bessie moved to Chicago to pursue her dream.
- ○ Bessie was determined to learn how to fly in Chicago and she wanted to pursue her dream.
- ○ No mistake

5
- ○ Her friend Robert Abbott encouraged her. To apply to schools in France.
- ○ Her friend Robert Abbott encouraged her to apply to schools in France.
- ○ Encouraging her to apply to schools in France, Robert Abbott.
- ○ No mistake

BE SURE YOU HAVE RECORDED ALL OF YOUR ANSWERS ON THE ANSWER DOCUMENT

The ride through Texas seemed to take forever. Cathy and her family were driving from their home in Arkansas to visit her grandparents in Arizona. Her grandparents were having a party for their 50th wedding anniversary. She couldn't wait to get there. (6) She kept wondering why Texas had to be such a huge state. Why couldn't it be more like Delaware? Why couldn't it be more like New Jersey? (7) Then she already would be at her grandparents' house!

6
- ◯ Her grandparents were having a party and she couldn't wait to get there it was there 50th wedding anniversary.
- ◯ Her grandparents were having a party for their 50th wedding anniversary, and she couldn't wait to get there.
- ◯ Having a party for their 50th wedding anniversary she couldn't wait to get there.
- ◯ No mistake

7
- ◯ Why couldn't it be more like Delaware and why couldn't it be more like New Jersey?
- ◯ Why couldn't it be more like Delaware or New Jersey?
- ◯ Why couldn't it be Delaware and New Jersey?
- ◯ No mistake

<u>Jane loves basketball she hopes to play one day for the Lady Longhorns at the University of Texas.</u> **(8)** Jane loves to play basketball as often as she can. <u>She plays on a team at the Y.W.C.A.</u> **(9)** It is good exercise and lots of fun, too. <u>Her team has won five games. Her team has lost two games.</u> **(10)** They are in second place, and there are four games left. She hopes they win the championship.

8
- ◯ Jane loves basketball she hopes to play one day. For the Lady Longhorns at the University of Texas.
- ◯ Jane loves basketball she hopes to play one day for the Lady Longhorns. At the University of Texas.
- ◯ Jane loves basketball. She hopes to play one day for the Lady Longhorns at the University of Texas.
- ◯ No mistake

9
- ◯ She plays. On a team at the Y.W.C.A.
- ◯ She plays on a team. At the Y.W.C.A.
- ◯ At the Y.W.C.A. she plays. On a team.
- ◯ No mistake

10
- ◯ Her team has won five games and her team lost.
- ◯ Her team has won and lost five and two games.
- ◯ Her team has won five games and lost two games.
- ◯ No mistake

BE SURE YOU HAVE RECORDED ALL OF YOUR ANSWERS ON THE ANSWER DOCUMENT

Dear Mrs. Green,

Thank you for visitting (11) and sharing the slides from Big Bend National park (12). Having lived in a small town, I find it hard to imagine that there is a place like Big Bend in Texas (13). I didnt know that there were so many mountains (14). I think it's neat that the park is named for the big bend in the Rio Grande (15)?

11 ○ Spelling
○ Capitalization
○ Punctuation
○ No mistake

12 ○ Spelling
○ Capitalization
○ Punctuation
○ No mistake

13 ○ Spelling
○ Capitalization
○ Punctuation
○ No mistake

14 ○ Spelling
○ Capitalization
○ Punctuation
○ No mistake

15 ○ Spelling
○ Capitalization
○ Punctuation
○ No mistake

Every year Elise and her family go to Padre Island for a week. **(16)** The island is a sand bar that is 100 miles long. It is located along the Texas coast. **(17)** Elise enjoys camping on the island and walking along its beutiful beaches. **(18)** In 1962, Congress acted to pertect this land by making it a **(19)** national seashore. Padre Island means “Father Island.” It was named after Father Nicolas Balli, a spanish priest. **(20)**

16
- ◯ Spelling
- ◯ Capitalization
- ◯ Punctuation
- ◯ No mistake

17
- ◯ Spelling
- ◯ Capitalization
- ◯ Punctuation
- ◯ No mistake

18
- ◯ Spelling
- ◯ Capitalization
- ◯ Punctuation
- ◯ No mistake

19
- ◯ Spelling
- ◯ Capitalization
- ◯ Punctuation
- ◯ No mistake

20
- ◯ Spelling
- ◯ Capitalization
- ◯ Punctuation
- ◯ No mistake

BE SURE YOU HAVE RECORDED ALL OF YOUR ANSWERS ON THE ANSWER DOCUMENT

Jim was always wondering about space. He ______ (21) many nights staring at the sky. Jim ______ (22) studied the stars and found many constellations. He wondered what it would be like to walk on the moon. Would he be scared? ______ (23) didn't think so. The moon seemed like such a ______ (24) place. It might even be more peaceful than Earth!

21 ○ spend
○ will spend
○ is spending
○ spent

22 ○ careful
○ carefuller
○ more carefully
○ carefully

23 ○ Him
○ He
○ His
○ Her

24 ○ peaceful
○ peacefuller
○ peacefullest
○ more peaceful

Mrs. Martin makes the ______ (25) pecan pies. She ______ (26) the pecans off her pecan trees in the backyard. We all help her crack the pecans and get the nuts out of the shells. It's hard work, but it's worth it. Mrs. Martin usually ______ (27) ten pies at once. She gives them to friends. ______ (28) should try one. They're great!

25
- ◯ bestest
- ◯ most best
- ◯ best
- ◯ most bestest

26
- ◯ picks
- ◯ pick
- ◯ will pick
- ◯ are picking

27
- ◯ made
- ◯ makes
- ◯ make
- ◯ are making

28
- ◯ Your
- ◯ Yourself
- ◯ Yours
- ◯ You

BE SURE YOU HAVE RECORDED ALL OF YOUR ANSWERS ON THE ANSWER DOCUMENT

Writing Prompt

Write directions for your teacher telling how to get to your friend's house from your house. Be sure to write about your ideas in detail.

STOP

Watch Out for Fire Ants!

Most Texans have felt the sting of creatures called fire ants. Most of us know to stay away from the mounds of soft soil we see on the ground. These piles are the homes of fire ants.

In the 1930s, red fire ants came to the United States on ships that docked in Alabama. Scientists think they may have been in soil that was on some of these ships. They have been spreading in the U.S. ever since.

Scientists are trying to keep red fire ants from spreading, but it hasn't been easy. They believe that fire ants are here to stay. You can get rid of fire ants temporarily, but after a while they usually return.

1 The word mounds in this story means—

- ◯ hills
- ◯ homes
- ◯ holes
- ◯ dirt

2 The word docked in this story means—

- ◯ sunk in the water
- ◯ broken apart
- ◯ brought near the shore
- ◯ never used

3 The word temporarily in this story means—

- ◯ easily
- ◯ quickly
- ◯ forever
- ◯ for a short time

BE SURE YOU HAVE RECORDED ALL OF YOUR ANSWERS ON THE ANSWER DOCUMENT

We're Late!

Jenny's mom knew how excited Jenny had been about her third-grade school play. It was all about the men and women that helped shape Texas.

Jenny had the part of Clara Driscoll, who was known as the "Savior of the Alamo." Mrs. Garcia helped her daughter rehearse Clara's big speech until she knew it by heart.

Jenny and her mom dashed out the door and into the car. As they drove into the parking lot of the school, they noticed that it was vacant. Not a single car was there.

"Mom, no one is here," cried Jenny. "We missed the entire play." Her eyes welled up with tears.

"We can't be that late," answered Mrs. Garcia. "Let me check something." Mrs. Garcia reached into her purse and pulled out the invitation. After a moment, she turned to Jenny and laughed.

"What is it?" asked Jenny. "I don't think this is funny."

"We're not late, Jenny. In fact, we're early—very early. We're about 24 hours early," said Mrs. Garcia.

Jenny looked at her with a puzzled expression. She didn't understand what her mom meant. Then she smiled. She grabbed the invitation. The open house was scheduled for 6:00 on the 26th. Today was only the 25th!

4 The word <u>rehearse</u> in this story means—

- ◯ save
- ◯ practice
- ◯ write
- ◯ dance

5 The word <u>vacant</u> in this story means—

- ◯ full
- ◯ crowded
- ◯ empty
- ◯ scary

6 The word <u>puzzled</u> in this story means—

- ◯ confused
- ◯ angry
- ◯ lovely
- ◯ excited

BE SURE YOU HAVE RECORDED ALL OF YOUR ANSWERS ON THE ANSWER DOCUMENT

McGRAW-HILL

Language Arts

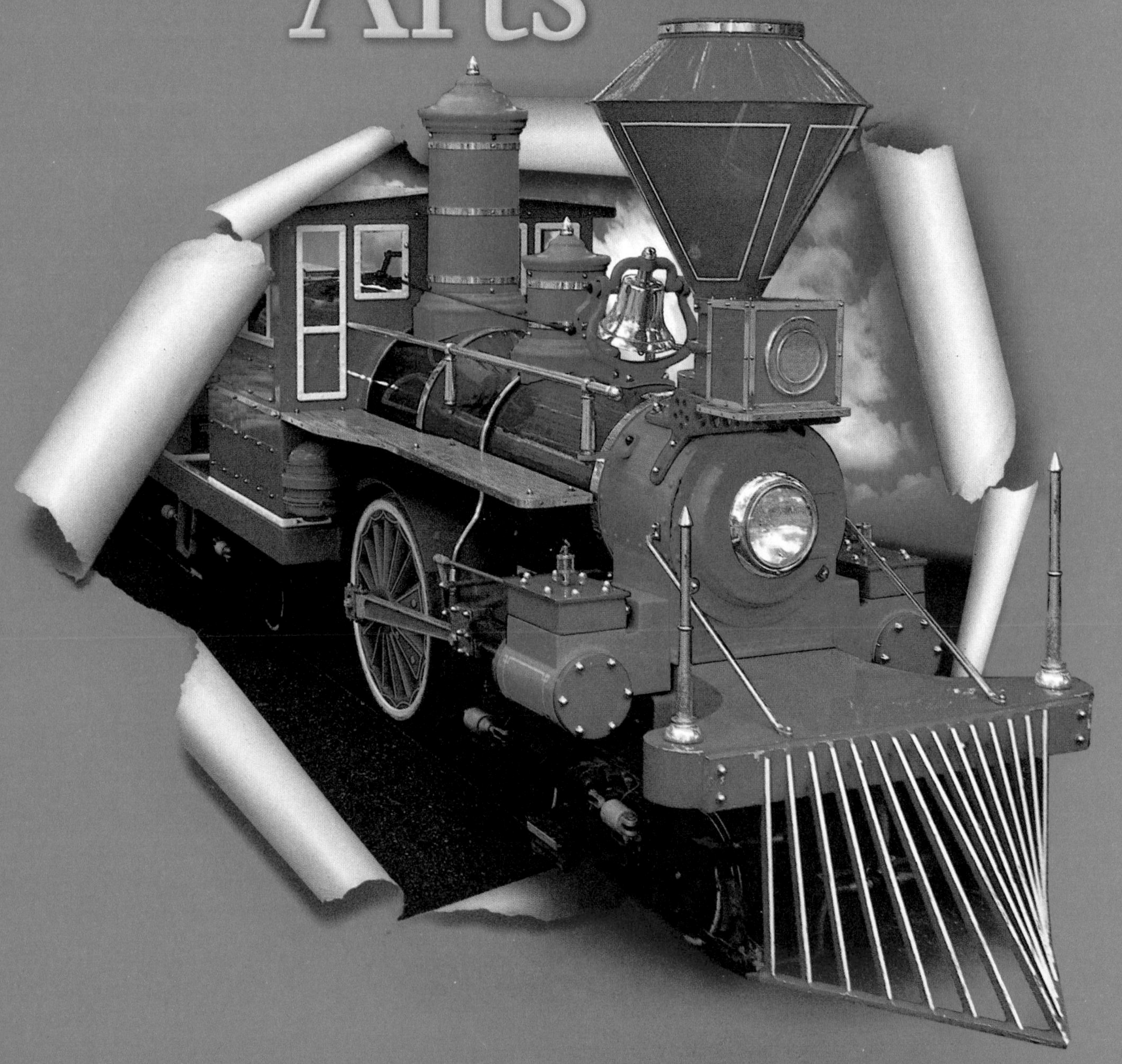

ACKNOWLEDGMENTS

The publisher gratefully acknowledges permission to reprint the following copyrighted material:

"The Amazing Octopus" by David George Gordon. Reprinted by permission of National Geographic *World*.

"Animal Fact/Animal Fable" from *Animal Fact/Animal Fable* by Seymour Simon. Text copyright © 1979 by Seymour Simon. Illustrations copyright © 1979 by Diane de Groat. Reprinted by permission of Crown Publishers, Inc.

"The Bat Boy & His Violin" from *The Bat Boy & His Violin* by Gavin Curtis. Text copyright © 1998 by Gavin Curtis. Illustrations copyright © 1998 E.B. Lewis. Reprinted with the permission of Simon & Schuster Books for Young Readers, an imprint of Simon & Schuster Children's Publishing Division.

"Big Blue Whale" from *Big Blue Whale* by Nicola Davies. Copyright © 1997 by Nicola Davies. Reprinted by permission of Candlewick Press, Inc., Cambridge, MA.

"Charlotte's Web" from *Charlotte's Web* by E.B. White. Text copyright renewed 1980 by E.B. White. Reprinted by permission of HarperTrophy, a division of HarperCollins Publishers.

"Cherokee Summer" from *Cherokee Summer* by Diane Hoyt-Goldsmith. Text copyright © 1993 by Diane Hoyt-Goldsmith. Photographs copyright © 1993 by Lawrence Migdale. Used by permission of Holiday House.

Excerpt adapted from the thesaurus in *Language Arts Today*. Copyright © 1998 McGraw-Hill School Division, a division of the Educational and Professional Publishing Group of The McGraw-Hill Companies, Inc. Reprinted by permission.

Excerpt from the *McGraw-Hill School Dictionary*. Copyright © 1998 McGraw-Hill School Division, a division of the Educational and Professional Publishing Group of The McGraw-Hill Companies, Inc. Reprinted by permission.

"Grandfather's Journey" from *Grandfather's Journey* by Allen Say. Copyright © 1993 by Allen Say. Reprinted with the permission of Houghton Mifflin Company. All rights reserved.

"In My Family" from *In My Family* by Carmen Lomas Garza. Copyright © 1996 by Carmen Lomas Garza. Reprinted with permission of the publisher, Children's Book Press, San Francisco, CA.

"The Merry-Go-Round" by Myra Cohn Livingston from *A Song I Sang to You* by Myra Cohn Livingston. Copyright © 1984, 1969, 1967, 1965, 1959, 1958 by Myra Cohn Livingston. Used by permission of Marian Reiner.

"Protecting the Environment" from *McGraw-Hill Social Studies*. Copyright © 1999 McGraw-Hill School Division, a division of the Educational and Professional Publishing Group of The McGraw-Hill Companies, Inc. Reprinted by permission.

"Spiders at Work" from *Spiders at Work* by Diane Hoyt-Goldsmith. Copyright © 2001 McGraw-Hill School Division, a division of the Educational and Professional Publishing Group of The McGraw-Hill Companies, Inc. Reprinted by permission.

"The Sun, the Wind and the Rain" from *The Sun, the Wind and the Rain* by Lisa Westberg Peters. Text copyright © 1988 by Lisa Westberg Peters. Illustrations copyright © 1988 by Ted Rand. Reprinted by permission of Henry Holt and Company, Inc.

"Whale" from *The Raucous Auk* by Mary Ann Hoberman. Copyright © 1973 by Mary Ann Hoberman. Used by permission of The Viking Press.

(Acknowledgments continued on page 576.)

Contributor

Time Magazine

McGraw-Hill School Division

A Division of The McGraw-Hill Companies

McGraw-Hill School Division
Two Penn Plaza
New York, NY 10121

Printed in the United States of America

ISBN 0-02-244657-5 / 3

2 3 4 5 6 7 8 9 (071/043) 05 04 03 02 01 00

Macmillan / McGraw-Hill Edition

McGRAW-HILL

Language Arts

AUTHORS

Jan E. Hasbrouck

Donna Lubcker

Sharon O'Neal

William H. Teale

Josefina V. Tinajero

Karen D. Wood

Sentences and Personal Narrative

Theme: What's Next?

Grammar  Spiral Review Every Day

Sentences

Writing

Personal Narrative

Review and Assess

UNIT 2 Nouns and Explanatory Writing

Theme: Looking at Nature

Grammar

Spiral Review Every Day

Nouns

Build Skills

Writing

Explanatory Writing

Review and Assess

Verbs and Persuasive Writing

Theme: Just Imagine!

Verbs

Writing

Persuasive Writing

Review and Assess

Verbs and Writing That Compares

Theme: A Closer Look

Grammar

Spiral Review Every Day

Verbs

Writing

Writing That Compares

Review and Assess

Pronouns and Expository Writing

Theme: Think About It

Grammar

Spiral Review Every Day

Pronouns

Build Skills

Writing

Expository Writing

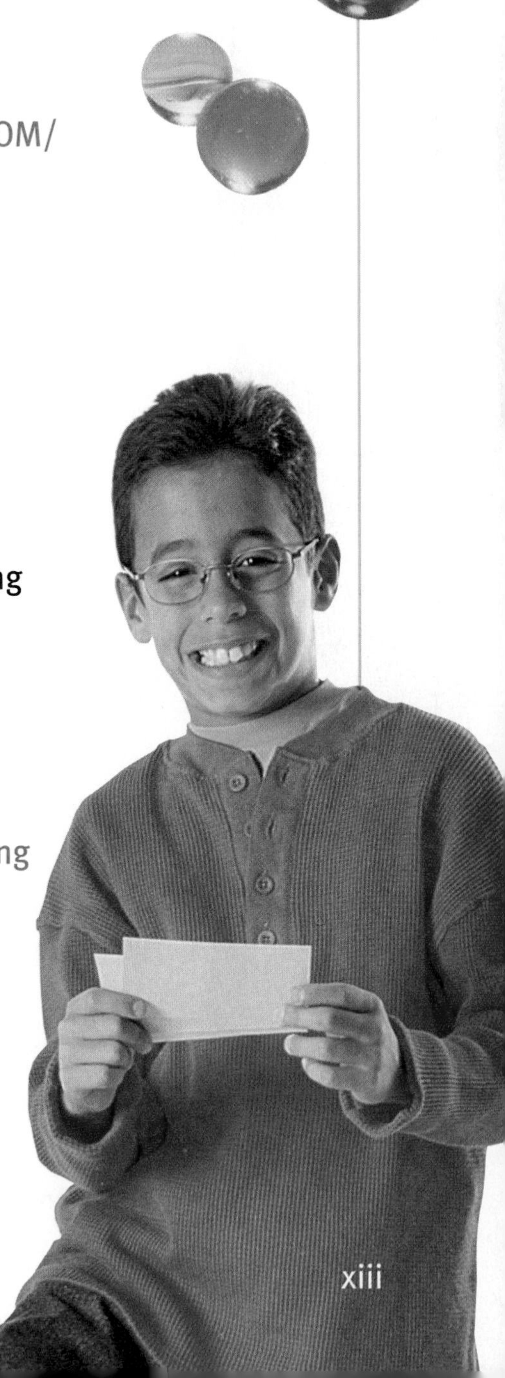

Review and Assess

Adjectives, Adverbs, and Writing a Story

Theme: Seeing All Sides

Grammar  Spiral Review Every Day

Adjectives and Adverbs

Writing

A Story

Review and Assess

Theme
What's Next?

Sentences and Personal Narrative

In this unit you will learn about kinds of sentences. You will also learn how to write a personal narrative. A personal narrative tells a true story about your own life.

Social Studies Link *Diane Hoyt-Goldsmith likes to write about real people and their special experiences. She helped Bridget, a Cherokee Indian girl, tell her own story.*

Summer is a special time for my family. The weather is hot and humid so we go outdoors as much as possible. One of our favorite pastimes is hunting for crawdads. My father and his twin brother used to catch them when they were little boys. Now my dad is an expert.

The best place to look for crawdads is under the rocks near the banks of the creek. If we creep along quietly, we might find one lying out in clear view.

from ***Cherokee Summer*** by Diane Hoyt-Goldsmith

Thinking Like a Writer

Personal Narrative A personal narrative tells a story about the writer's own life. Reread the passage.

- Why do you think Diane Hoyt-Goldsmith wanted to help Bridget share her personal experience?

Sentences The sentences above have subjects—words that tell who or what the sentence is about. Read the passage again.

QUICK WRITE Write the subject of each sentence in the first paragraph of *Cherokee Summer*.

Grammar

Sentences

A **sentence** is a group of words that expresses a complete thought.

Aisha looked out the window.

A **sentence fragment** is a group of words that does not express a complete thought.

Beautiful, sunny day.

Every sentence begins with a capital letter.

Sentences
How is a sentence fragment different from a sentence? Write your answer in your journal.

A sentence names the person or thing you are talking about. It also tells what happened.

Sentences	Sentence fragment
Aisha walked to the beach.	Looked at the ocean
The sun was shining.	Clear blue water

Guided Practice

Name the groups of words that are sentences.

EXAMPLE: Aisha wore a big hat. *sentence*

1. Some suntan lotion.

2. Aisha walked along the shore.

3. A starfish was lying on the sand.

4. Had five long arms.

5. Aisha saw a sand castle.

REVIEW THE RULES

- A sentence tells a complete thought.
- A sentence fragment does not tell a complete thought.
- Begin every sentence with a capital letter.

Grammar

More Practice

A. Write each group of words that is a sentence.

6. Aisha picked up a pink shell.
7. Held the shell to her ear.
8. The roar of the waves.
9. She brought the shell to her mom.
10. The shell reminds Aisha of the beach.
11. In the hot sun.
12. People enjoy the beach.
13. Aisha swims with a friend.
14. A beach towel for Tom.
15. The children fly kites.

Handbook page 502

B. Spiral Review Write the following paragraph. Add words to make each sentence fragment a sentence. Begin each sentence with a capital letter.

16.–20. the sun was going down. Beautiful red sunset. it was time to go home. aisha gathered up her things. walked slowly back to the cottage.

Extra Practice, page 68

Writing Activity A Paragraph

Write sentences about a special day you have had. Make sure your sentences sound natural.

APPLY GRAMMAR: Check to be sure that each sentence expresses a complete thought and begins with a capital letter.

Grammar

Statements and Questions

RULES

A statement is a sentence that tells something.

I saw a butterfly.

A question is a sentence that asks something.

How big is the butterfly?

Use a period to end a statement. Use a question mark to end a question.

Question ⟶ *What color is the butterfly?*

Statement ⟶ *The butterfly is orange and black.*

Sentences

How can you tell the difference between a statement and a question? Write your answer in your journal.

Guided Practice

Name which sentences are statements and which sentences are questions.

EXAMPLE: Butterflies are beautiful. *statement*

1. How did you learn about butterflies?
2. I read a library book about butterflies.
3. Butterflies are wonderful insects.
4. Where do butterflies live?
5. Some butterflies live in North America.

REVIEW THE RULES

- A statement tells something.
- A question asks something.

More Practice

A. For each sentence, write *statement* or *question*.

6. Where do monarch butterflies go in the winter?
7. Most monarch butterflies fly to central Mexico.
8. The butterflies return to the same place each year.
9. How do the butterflies know where to go?
10. No one knows how the butterflies find their way.
11. Monarch butterflies fly south for the winter.
12. How far do monarch butterflies fly?
13. The butterflies fly more than 2,000 miles.
14. Wouldn't the butterflies get very tired on the trip?
15. The wind helps carry the butterflies along.

B. Spiral Review Add words to make each sentence fragment a sentence. Add the correct end mark to each sentence.

16. Some monarch butterflies fly to California
17. Has a big parade
18. Who marches in the butterfly parade
19. Marchers in the parade
20. School children dress up as butterflies

Extra Practice, page 69

Writing Activity A Note

Write a note to a friend about a special event. Use statements and questions in your note.

APPLY GRAMMAR: Circle and check end marks.

Handbook page 502

Grammar

Commands and Exclamations

RULES

A command is a sentence that tells or asks someone to do something.

Take me to the train station.

An exclamation is a sentence that shows strong feeling.

What a wonderful time I had!

Sentences

Write how you know if a sentence is a command or exclamation.

Use a period to end a command. Use an exclamation mark to end an exclamation.

Command ⟶ *Climb aboard the train.*

Exclamation ⟶ *What a great day this is!*

Guided Practice

Name which sentences are commands and which sentences are exclamations.

EXAMPLE: Find a seat. *command*

1. Sit next to me.
2. What a trip this will be!
3. How quickly we're going!
4. Please stay in your seat.
5. Take a look at that view.

REVIEW THE RULES

- A command tells or asks someone to do something.
- An exclamation shows strong feeling.

More Practice

A. Write each sentence. Write *command* if it is a command and *exclamation* if it is an exclamation.

6. Relax and enjoy yourself.

7. Wave to your friends.

8. What a great time I'm having!

9. How long this train is!

10. Look out the window.

11. Wow, this train ride is exciting!

12. Listen to the train whistle.

13. Get off at the next station.

14. How great it feels to ride on a train!

15. Please watch your step.

Handbook page 502

B. Spiral Review **Write the following paragraph. Add words to make each sentence fragment a sentence. End each sentence with the correct end mark.**

16.–20. We will get off at that station? Do you see it. Stay in your seat until the train stops? Fun trip. Hat and coat.

Extra Practice, page 70

Writing Activity A Description

Write a description of something you have enjoyed doing. Use interesting details.

APPLY GRAMMAR: Include a command and an exclamation in your description. Circle each end mark.

Grammar

Sentence Punctuation

RULES

End a statement and a command with a period.

Our class took a whale-watching trip.
Be careful getting on the boat.

End a question with a question mark.

How many whales did you see?

End an exclamation with an exclamation mark.

What a huge whale that is!

Sentences
How can you figure out which end mark to use for a sentence? Write your answer in your journal.

Use a capital letter to begin every sentence. Use the correct end mark for each kind of sentence.

Kind of Sentence	Example	End Mark
Statement	We saw two whales.	.
Command	Take a picture.	.
Question	How big are they?	?
Exclamation	What giants they are!	!

Guided Practice

Tell the kind of sentence. Then name the correct end mark.

EXAMPLE: Where did the whale go?
question; question mark

1. Danny, look over there.
2. Did you see the whale flip its tail?
3. How amazing it is to see a spouting whale!
4. A whale spouts when it blows out its breath.
5. A whale breathes through its blowhole.

REVIEW THE RULES

- A statement and a command end with a period.
- A question ends with a question mark.
- An exclamation ends with an exclamation mark.

Grammar

More Practice

A. Write each sentence. Add the correct end mark.

6. What a lot of whales there are today
7. Why do we see so many whales
8. The whales are going south for the winter
9. Tell me more about whales
10. A blue whale is the largest animal
11. How mighty blue whales look in the ocean
12. What color are humpback whales
13. Humpback whales are black and white
14. Is a dolphin a whale
15. A dolphin is in the whale family

Handbook page 527

B. Spiral Review Write the sentences. Begin and end them correctly. Then write what type of sentence each one is.

16. watch the TV show about whales
17. a humpback whale has no teeth
18. how can a whale eat without teeth
19. some kinds of whales have teeth
20. what big teeth the whales have

Extra Practice, page 71

Writing Activity An Advertisement

Write an ad for a whale-watching trip. Choose just the right words to make your reader want to buy a ticket.
APPLY MECHANICS AND USAGE: Circle and check end marks.

Science Link

Grammar REVIEW

Mixed Review

REVIEW THE RULES

- A sentence expresses a complete thought.
- A sentence fragment does not express a complete thought.
- Every sentence begins with a capital letter.
- A statement tells something. It ends with a period.
- A question asks something. It ends with a question mark.
- A command tells or asks someone to do something. It ends with a period.
- An exclamation shows strong feeling. It ends with an exclamation mark.

QUICK WRITE

Sentences

Write one example of each of the four kinds of sentences.

Practice

A. Write whether each sentence is a statement, question, command, or exclamation.

1. Hal and Rachel want an adventure.
2. What can the children do?
3. What a great idea Rachel has!
4. They can camp out in their yard.
5. Hal, go get your sleeping bag.

B. Write each sentence correctly.

6. dad has a cookout with Hal and Rachel
7. will their dog, Max, camp out too
8. look at all the stars in the sky
9. hal points out the Big Dipper
10. wow, there's a shooting star
11. did you hear a coyote howl
12. a dark shadow sweeps by overhead
13. what a wild place this is
14. are the children scared
15. the children know it is just an owl

C. Challenge Write the following paragraph. Correct each end mark.

16.–20. Something was tapping on the tent? What a fright. What's that sound. Don't be afraid? It's only a tree branch?

Handbook
pages 502, 527

Writing Activity A Book Report

Write a book report about an adventure story you have read and enjoyed. Check the report for spelling and grammar. **APPLY MECHANICS AND USAGE:** Include four kinds of sentences in your report. Check the end marks.

Subjects in Sentences

RULES

Every sentence has two parts. The subject of a sentence tells what or whom the sentence is about.

Alaska has cold, snowy winters.

The subject of a sentence can be one word or more than one word.

Many people enjoy dogsled races.

To express a complete thought, you must name the person, place, or thing you are talking about. You can correct some sentence fragments by adding a subject.

Sentences

How can you decide what the subject of a sentence is? Write your answer in your journal.

Sentence Fragment:
Is a famous racer.

Subject:
Susan Butcher

Susan Butcher is a famous racer.

Guided Practice

Name the subject of each sentence.

EXAMPLE: A dog team pulls a big sled. *A dog team*

1. Alaska has a famous dogsled race.
2. The dogsled race is held in March.
3. The route crosses Alaska.
4. Racers face many dangers along the way.
5. People cheer the racers.

REVIEW THE RULES

- The subject of a sentence names the person, place, or thing the sentence is about.

Grammar

More Practice

A. Write the sentences. Underline each subject.

6. Dogsled drivers are called mushers.
7. The mushers work as hard as their dogs.
8. This day is a big one for Ray and his dogs.
9. Ray McGrath's team has fifteen dogs.
10. Teams run day and night.
11. A strong team can go 70 miles a day.
12. The lead dog guides the others.
13. The race is long and hard.
14. Some teams won't finish the race.
15. The first twenty teams win prizes.

Handbook
page 503

B. Spiral Review **Write the sentences. Add a subject to each sentence fragment. Use correct end marks.**

16. Ray's team is dashing across a frozen lake
17. _____ sees a hole in the ice
18. What will the lead dog do
19. _____ swerves to the side and saves the team
20. _____ crosses the finish line

Extra Practice, page 72

Writing Activity A Journal Entry

Imagine that you watched the finish of a dogsled race. Write a journal entry about what you saw and felt.
APPLY GRAMMAR: Circle the subject of each sentence in your journal entry.

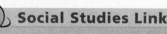

Social Studies Link

Grammar

Predicates in Sentences

RULES

Every sentence has two parts. The predicate of a sentence tells what the subject does or is.

Katie paints beautiful pictures.

Tod is a good actor.

The predicate of a sentence can be one word or more than one word.

Elizabeth sings.

Elizabeth sings a new song.

Sentences

Write how you can tell which words make up the predicate of a sentence.

You can correct some sentence fragments by adding a predicate.

Sentence Fragment:
The children.

Predicate:
do many things.

The children do many things.

Guided Practice

Name the predicate of each sentence.

EXAMPLE: The class needs money for a trip.
needs money for a trip

1. The teacher suggests a bake sale.

2. The children offer other ideas.

3. Kim thinks of a craft sale.

4. Tod writes a play for the class.

5. The play is very funny.

REVIEW THE RULES

- The predicate tells what the subject does or is.

More Practice

A. Write the sentences. Underline each predicate.

6. The play is about a lion family.
7. The lion family lives in Africa.
8. All the children like the play.
9. Katie paints the lion masks.
10. Kim and Sam make the costumes.
11. One lion costume is yellow and brown.
12. The teacher directs the actors.
13. Nancy is the cute lion cub.
14. Luis plays the father lion.
15. The play begins.

Handbook page 504

B. Spiral Review **Write each sentence fragment. Add a subject or predicate to make a complete sentence. Begin each sentence with a capital letter.**

16. ______ raised money for a trip.
17. ______ sold tickets to a show.
18. the children ______.
19. ______ bow at the end of the show.
20. all the people ______.

Extra Practice, page 73

Writing Activity A Letter

Write a letter to a friend about a play or movie you enjoyed. Put in colorful details.

APPLY GRAMMAR: Circle the predicate of each sentence in your letter.

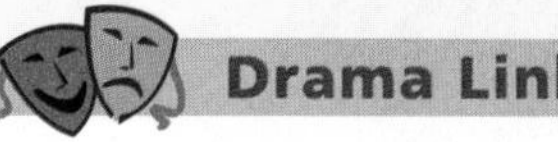

Grammar

Combining Sentences: Compound Sentences

RULES

Two related sentences can be combined with a comma and the word ***and***.

A compound sentence is a sentence that contains two sentences joined by *and*.

A frog lays her eggs in the pond, and the eggs cling together.

Sentences

Write how combining sentences can make your writing more interesting.

Use a comma before *and* when you join two sentences.

Days go by.
The eggs hatch.

Days go by, and the eggs hatch.

Guided Practice

Tell how to combine each pair of sentences.

EXAMPLE: Tadpoles grow fast.
Their shape changes.
Tadpoles grow fast, and their shape changes.

1. A tadpole has a long tail. The tail looks odd.
2. The tadpole's legs start to grow. The tail begins to shrink.
3. The tadpole's gills shrink. It develops lungs.
4. The new legs grow quickly. The tail vanishes.
5. The tadpole is a frog now. Frogs can live on land.

REVIEW THE RULES

- A compound sentence contains two related sentences joined by a comma and the word *and*.

Grammar

More Practice

A. Combine the two sentences. Write the new sentence.

6. Jeff's class visited a pond. They saw a lot of frogs.

7. The class found frog eggs. Jeff put some in a jar.

8. Jeff brought the eggs to school. He put them in a tank.

9. The eggs hatched. Tadpoles swam out.

10. The class fed the tadpoles. The tadpoles grew.

11. The teacher got a camera. The class took some pictures.

12. They looked at the photos. They counted the tadpoles.

13. Jeff counted ten tadpoles. His friend counted more.

14. The children wrote reports. Two boys gave speeches.

15. Jeff read his report. The class asked questions.

Handbook
page 504

B. Spiral Review **Write the sentences. Draw a line between the subject and the predicate.**

16. Jeff's class enjoyed the tadpoles.

17. All the tadpoles grew big.

18. The tank became too small for the tadpoles.

19. The class went back to the pond.

20. The children set the tadpoles free.

Extra Practice, page 74

Writing Activity A Story

Imagine you are in Jeff's class. Write a story about the tadpoles. Describe how you felt when you set them free. **APPLY GRAMMAR:** Use compound sentences in your story. Circle the word that joins the sentences.

Correcting Run-on Sentences

RULES

A run-on sentence joins together two or more sentences that should be written separately.

Abby sat on the wagon seat she waved to the crowd.

You can correct a run-on sentence by separating two complete ideas into two sentences.

Abby sat on the wagon seat. She waved to the crowd.

You can correct a run-on sentence by rewriting it as a compound sentence.

Abby sat on the wagon seat, and she waved to the crowd.

THINK AND WRITE

Sentences

Write how you can tell that a sentence is a run-on sentence.

Guided Practice

Tell how to correct each run-on sentence.

EXAMPLE: Abby's father snapped the reins the oxen moved forward.
Abby's father snapped the reins. The oxen moved forward. or: *Abby's father snapped the reins, and the oxen moved forward.*

1. The people waved they called goodbye.
2. It was spring the weather was warm.
3. It was a long way to California the trip could be dangerous.
4. The oxen were strong the wagons rolled along quickly.
5. The wagons reached a river they rolled right through it.

REVIEW THE RULES

- A run-on sentence contains two or more sentences that should be written separately or rewritten as a compound sentence.

Grammar

More Practice

A. Correct each run-on sentence.

6. Weeks went by the settlers grew tired.
7. One wagon got stuck everyone helped push it.
8. The nights were quiet the travelers slept soundly.
9. Abby saw huge herds of buffalo she saw a wolf.
10. Some days were hot it rained hard on other days.
11. A storm slowed them down they stopped for days.
12. They crossed a desert then they came to mountains.
13. They saw a mountain pass they had arrived at last.
14. California was their new home it was a good place to live.
15. The settlers gave thanks they were happy.

Handbook page 502

B. Spiral Review Write each sentence. Circle the subject and underline the predicate.

16. Abby's family settled in California.
17. California was a good home.
18. Abby's father cleared the land.
19. The crops grew well.
20. Abby made new friends.

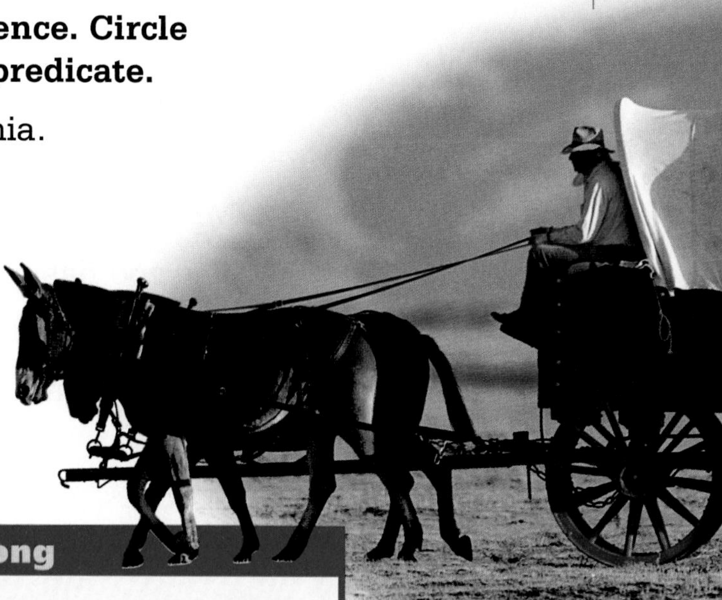

Extra Practice, page 75

Writing Activity A Song

Write a song the settlers might have sung on their way west. Pick words to set the right mood.

APPLY MECHANICS AND USAGE: Fix any run-on sentences.

Music Link

Grammar REVIEW

Mixed Review

REVIEW THE RULES

- The subject of a sentence tells whom or what the sentence is about.
- The predicate of a sentence tells what the subject does or is.
- A compound sentence contains two related sentences joined by a comma and *and.*
- A run-on sentence contains two or more sentences that should be written separately.

Sentences

Write a run-on sentence. Then show one way to fix it.

Practice

A. Write each sentence. Draw a line between the subject and the predicate.

1. The class welcomed some visitors.
2. The visitors talked about their jobs.
3. All the third graders listened carefully.
4. Some children asked questions.
5. Mr. Thompson is a police officer.
6. The policeman brought his police dog.
7. Mrs. Feldman works at the zoo.
8. The zoo has a nursery for baby animals.
9. The teacher thanked each visitor.
10. The students sent thank-you letters.

B. Write each pair of sentences as one sentence. Use a comma before *and*.

11. The third grade went to the zoo. The children saw interesting animals.

12. The children rode a tram. It took them all around the zoo.

13. Raul liked the big ostrich. He grinned at the brightly colored parrots.

14. The elephant was Amy's favorite. She wanted to bring him home.

15. The monkeys chattered. The zoo was noisy.

16. The mother lion slept. Her cubs were quiet.

17. The class went to the petting zoo. The children played with baby animals.

18. Ruthie petted the animals. A calf licked her hand.

19. A baby goat nibbled Chris's sneaker. He laughed.

20. The class loved the zoo. Everyone wants to go back.

Handbook
page 503–504

C. Challenge Write the paragraph. Correct each run-on sentence by making it two separate sentences.

21.–25. Every trip is an adventure for the students they always have an interesting time. They have visited a museum the class has also gone to the zoo. On each trip they learn many new things.

Writing Activity A Postcard

Create a picture postcard of a place you have visited. On one side, draw a picture of the place. On the other side, write about your visit. Be sure to use the "I" point of view.

APPLY GRAMMAR: Include a compound sentence on your postcard. Underline the subject and circle the predicate of each sentence.

Social Studies Link

Common Errors with Fragments and Run-on Sentences

Sometimes a writer makes a mistake and writes a sentence fragment or a run-on sentence. The chart below shows different kinds of errors.

Common Errors	Examples	Corrected Sentences
The sentence has no predicate.	Alicia and her mom.	Alicia and her mom saw the parade.
The sentence has no subject.	Wore red uniforms.	The band wore red uniforms.
Two sentences are joined with no punctuation.	Paco played a flute Lois beat a drum	Paco played a flute. Lois beat a drum.

Sentences

How can you check for sentence fragments in your writing? Write the answer in your journal.

REVIEW THE RULES

FRAGMENTS AND RUN-ON SENTENCES

Every sentence has two parts, a subject and a predicate, and expresses a complete thought.

- A sentence fragment does not express a complete thought.
- You can often correct a sentence fragment by adding a subject or a predicate.
- A run-on sentence contains two or more sentences that should stand alone.
- You can correct a run-on sentence by writing it as two sentences or as a compound sentence.
- Remember, every sentence begins with a capital letter and ends with a punctuation mark.

Practice

A. Read each group of words. Write *F* if it is a fragment. Write *R* if it is a run-on sentence.

1. Washed the car windows.
2. Mom bought a map we traced the route on it.
3. Packed some snacks.
4. Mom and Dad.
5. We started out early the trip was long.

B. Rewrite each run-on sentence. Separate the two complete ideas into two sentences.

6. Dad cooked some fish we ate in the moonlight.
7. Mom rolled out the sleeping bags I crawled into mine.
8. The night was quiet we did not hear a sound.
9. Mom and Dad fell asleep I heard a coyote howl.
10. I closed my eyes soon it was morning.

Handbook
page 502

C. Rewrite each sentence fragment. Add words to make it a complete sentence.

11. Sam and Lisa.
12. Jumped into the water.
13. The water.
14. Swam like a fish.
15. The sun.

Troubleshooter, pages 488–491

Writing Activity Write a Story

Imagine meeting an unusual animal during a camping trip. Write a story about what happened.

APPLY GRAMMAR: Be sure your sentences are complete. Rewrite any sentence fragments. Check for run-on sentences. Separate them into two sentences.

TAAS

Mechanics and Spelling

Directions

Read the passage and decide which type of mistake, if any, appears in each underlined section. Choose the correct answer. If there is no mistake, choose "No mistake."

Does every sentence begin with a capital letter?

Check all underlined sections for spelling.

Is this sentence a statement or a question? Make sure the end mark is correct.

Sample

Last week, I visited my aunt in Chicago. We rode downtown on a train. the train ran on tracks high above the ground. **(1)**

My aunt and I went to the top of the Sears Tower. The Sears Tower is the tallest bilding in the world. **(2)** It has 110 floors! At the top, I could feel the building sway. I was a little nervous. Then I learned that it's supposed to sway. I relaxed and enjoyed the view. The view was great. **(3)**

1
- ○ Spelling
- ○ Capitalization
- ○ Punctuation
- ○ No mistake

2
- ○ Spelling
- ○ Capitalization
- ○ Punctuation
- ○ No mistake

3
- ○ Spelling
- ○ Capitalization
- ○ Punctuation
- ○ No mistake

Test Tip
Remember to read each answer choice before you pick the best one.

Grammar and Usage

TAAS

Directions

Read the passage and choose the word or group of words that belongs in each space.

Sample

Our class went to a science museum. We went into a special area of the museum. It was filled with live butterflies! Many butterflies __(1)__. They sat on our arms, shoulders, and heads. It was very exciting! __(2)__ were beautiful colors. I saw orange ones, yellow ones, and blue ones. Then I saw a colorful butterfly fold its wings. Its wings were brown underneath. The butterfly looked like bark. Sometimes this kind of butterfly rests on a tree trunk __(3)__ then its enemy cannot see it.

You can correct a sentence fragment by adding a predicate.

You can correct a sentence fragment by adding a subject.

You can correct a run-on sentence by writing it as a compound sentence.

1 ○ landed on us
○ everywhere
○ in the air
○ soon

2 ○ Bright and
○ The butterflies
○ Showed
○ It also

3 ○ ,
○ and
○ , and
○ and,

TIME FOR KIDS Writer's Notebook

RESEARCH

RESEARCH

When I want to make sure of the spelling of a word, I use a **dictionary**. The dictionary is divided into words from A to Z. I also use a dictionary to look up meanings of words. Once I know a word's spelling and meaning, I can use it to tell my ideas more clearly.

COMPOSITION SKILLS

WRITING WELL

When I write, first I think of the **main idea** that I want to tell. Then I add **details** that support what I'm saying. The details make my writing more interesting and give information that my readers need to know.

VOCABULARY SKILLS

USING WORDS

Words like <u>begin</u>, <u>finally</u>, and <u>start</u> are **time-order** words. These words help me mark the beginning, middle, and end of a story. And they help the reader to follow my story. What time-order words do you know?

Read Now!

Read the photo essay about a great balloon ride and then decide what is the most important idea that the writer wanted to tell.

TIME FOR KIDS

PHOTO ESSAY

Up, Up and Away

Two men in a balloon travel nonstop around the world.

BREITLING ORBITER 3

Ride of a Lifetime

In 1999, Brian Jones and Bertrand Piccard became the first people to sail around the world in a hot-air balloon. The balloon was named *Orbiter 3*. The two men began their trip in Switzerland. Just 20 days later, it ended in Egypt.

The journey took the men around thunderclouds and across stormy oceans. They even sailed over sandy deserts and snowy mountains. When the pilots finally landed, they had flown 29,056 miles—without stopping.

The men hardly knew each other before the trip. But, said Piccard, "We started as two pilots and ended as two friends."

Jones, left, and Piccard became friends during the long, hard trip.

The balloon touches down in the desert in Egypt.

Flight Path

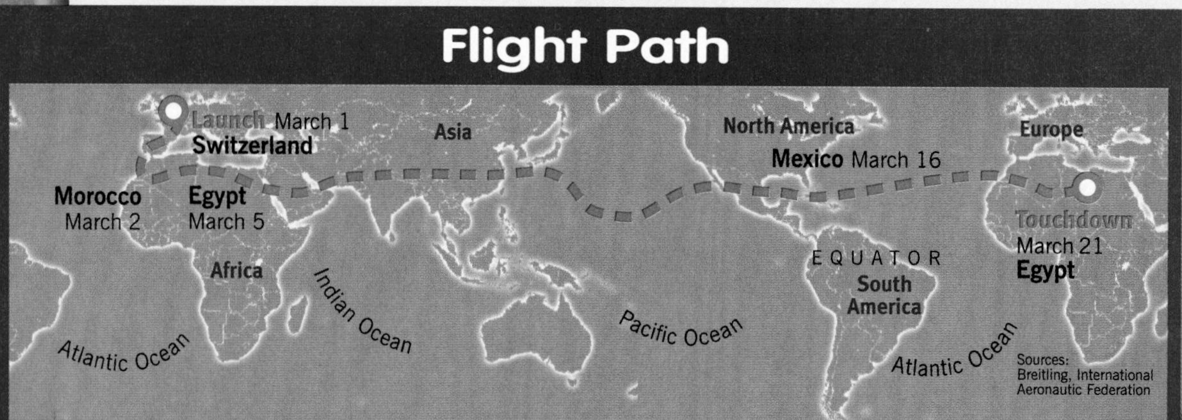

interNET CONNECTION **Go to www.mhschool.com/language-arts for more information on the topic.**

Inside Orbiter 3

A small balloon holds up a tent. It protects the top of the larger balloon.

Inside the balloon is a gas called helium. It makes the balloon float.

Hot air warms the helium and lifts the balloon.

In case of danger, part of the balloon can be torn off. The rest becomes a giant parachute.

The two pilots live in the cabin.

Energy from sunlight helps power the equipment.

How high the balloon sails is controlled by heating air. The air rises into the balloon.

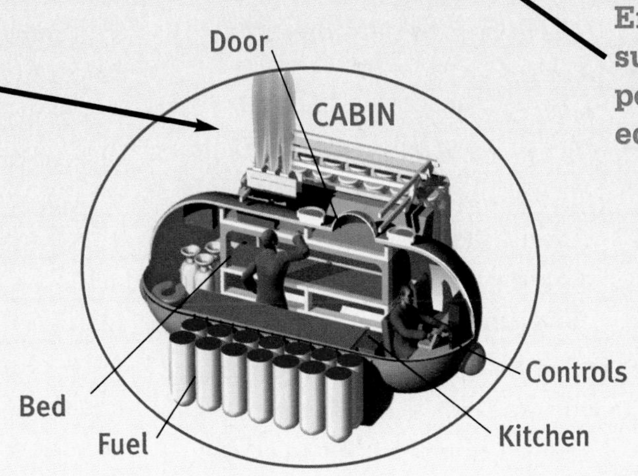

Cover: Fabrice Coffrini/Keystone/AP; this photo Corbis/AFP

Write Now!

The two balloon pilots had a real-life adventure. Think about a real-life adventure you've had and write to tell about it.

Photo: AP

Diagram by Joe Lertola

Dictionary

You use a dictionary to find the meanings of words. A dictionary also shows you how words are spelled and pronounced.

There are two **guide words** at the top of every page. The first guide word is the first word on that page, and the second guide word is the last word on that page.

Entry words are all the words explained in a dictionary. They are listed in alphabetical order.

A **pronunciation key** is usually found at the bottom of every other page in a dictionary. It shows you how to read the pronunciation respelling of the entry word.

Guide words

Entry word

The part of speech tells if a word is a noun, verb, adjective, or adverb.

Example sentence shows how the word is used.

Pronunciation is shown in ( ) and helps you sound out a word.

Definition is the meaning of the word. Each meaning is numbered.

clown ➤ cob

clown A performer who makes people laugh: *A clown tells jokes and performs stunts.* *Noun.*
▲ To act like a clown: *He was clowning around to make his baby brother laugh.* *Verb.*
clown (kloun) *noun, plural* **clowns**; *verb,* **clowned**, **clowning**.

clue Information that helps you answer a question or solve a mystery: *We used the clue to help solve the riddle.*
clue (klü) *noun, plural* **clues**.

coach **1.** A large horse-drawn carriage. A coach is usually closed on all sides. The passengers sit on seats inside. The driver sits outside on a raised seat. **2.** A railroad car for passengers. **3.** A section of low-priced seats on a bus, airplane, or train. **4.** A person who trains athletes or performers. *Noun.*
▲ To teach or train. *Verb.*
coach (kōch) *noun, plural* **coaches**; *verb,* **coached, coaching.**

cob The hard center part of an ear of corn: *The kernels grow on the cob in rows.*
cob (kob) *noun, plural* **cobs**.

PRONUNCIATION KEY:
at; āpe; fär; câre; end; mē; it; īce; pîerce; hot; ōld; sông, fôrk; oil; out; up; ūse; rüle; pu̇ll; tûrn; chin; sing; shop; thin; this; hw in white; zh in treasure. The symbol ə stands for the unstressed vowel sound in about, taken, pencil, lemon, and circus.

A dictionary also tells you how a word can be used in a sentence. This is called the **part of speech**. Look for a word such as *noun, verb, adjective*, or *adverb*. The words are in italics.

Practice

A. Use the dictionary page on page 30 to answer the following questions.

1. What are the guide words?
2. What is the part of speech for the word *clue?*
3. What is the example sentence for *clue?*
4. Which entry word has four meanings or definitions as a noun?
5. What pronunciation is given for the word *cob?*

B. Write how each of the dictionary aids helps you.

6. Entry words
7. Guide words
8. Pronunciation
9. Definition
10. Part of speech

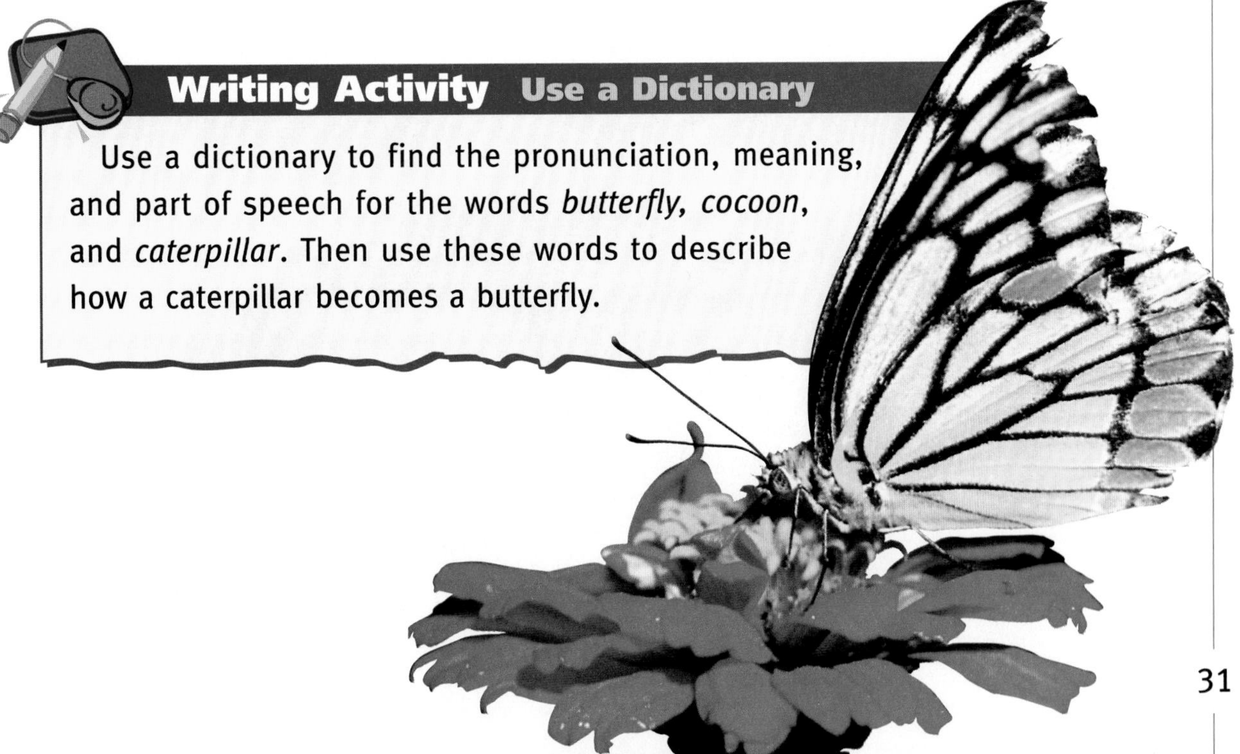

Writing Activity Use a Dictionary

Use a dictionary to find the pronunciation, meaning, and part of speech for the words *butterfly, cocoon*, and *caterpillar*. Then use these words to describe how a caterpillar becomes a butterfly.

Vocabulary: Time-Order Words

DEFINITION

Time-order words tell when things happen and in what order.

first	after	now
next	before	as soon as
then	while	tomorrow
later	this morning	last year
last	yesterday	long ago

Time-Order Words

How can time-order words make your writing clearer? Write your answer in your journal.

Look at the blue words in the paragraph below.

Last week, I made a special birthday card for my friend. First, I folded a piece of paper in half. Then, I drew a picture of my friend and me on the front. Next, I cut out different kinds of letters from magazines to spell "Happy Birthday." I arranged the letters on the inside of the card before I glued them in place. After the glue dried, I signed my name.

Practice

A. Write the sentences and underline the time-order words.

1. Last spring, my family moved to a new town.
2. Before that, we lived with my grandfather.
3. He grew up on a farm in Iowa a long time ago.
4. Now he lives in the town of Oak Prairie.
5. My family visited him there last week.

before	first	next week	while
after	last	yesterday	next

B. Choose a word or words from the box to complete each sentence. Write the complete sentence.

6. Dad and I went to the zoo _____.
7. _____, we went to see the giant panda.
8. _____, we found the monkeys.
9. _____ we saw the monkeys, we visited the tiger.
10. I hope we can go to the zoo again _____.

C. Grammar Link Write these sentences in the correct order. Use the correct end marks.

11. Next, we piled into the car and drove to the beach
12. Can I tell you about my trip while we're eating
13. Later, we packed up our things and came back home
14. First, we packed our car for the trip
15. What huge waves we saw as soon as we got there

Writing Activity A Paragraph

Write about a special trip. Tell how you felt. Use at least three time-order words in your writing.
APPLY GRAMMAR: Make sure each sentence begins and ends correctly.

Composition: Main Idea and Supporting Details

A paragraph should have one main idea, or topic. Often the writer states the main idea in a topic sentence at the beginning of the paragraph. The other sentences in the paragraph tell more about this idea.

GUIDELINES

- **The main idea is what a piece of writing is all about.**
- **In a paragraph, all sentences should work together to tell about, or develop, one main idea.**
- **The main idea is usually stated in a topic sentence.**
- **Supporting details help to develop the main idea.**
- **Use time-order words to connect ideas.**

Main Idea

Why should a writer clearly state the main idea in a piece of writing? Explain how this helps the reader.

Read this paragraph about a personal experience. Notice how the writer states the main idea and tells more about it by adding supporting details.

The topic sentence states the main idea of this paragraph.

A supporting detail tells more about the main idea.

A time-order word connects one idea to another.

I'll never forget the day my family moved to San Antonio. It was a very hot day in July. Before we got to the city, our car broke down. After we got the car fixed, we got lost. When we finally found our house, we were hungry and tired. Luckily, our new neighbors were very friendly. They invited us over for supper. Our very bad day had a very good ending. Now that we are settled, we love it here.

Practice

A. Write each sentence. Write *yes* if it supports the main idea in the box or *no* if it does not.

> *Main Idea: My day at Carson Beach was fun.*

1. The sky was blue, and the sun was shining.
2. My Aunt Lydia lives near Cincinnati.
3. I found a beautiful seashell in the sand.
4. I played in the waves all morning.
5. Next month, I'm going camping at Morton Park.

B. Write a topic sentence for each of the following topics.

6. My First Day of School
7. Trying Something New
8. My Favorite Game
9. The Most Beautiful Place
10. The Best Book I Have Read

C. Grammar Link Write these main idea sentences. Punctuate each one correctly.

11. Will I ever forget my first day at school
12. Today I tried skating for the first time
13. I enjoy playing chess with my dad
14. What a beautiful place Oak Creek Canyon is
15. Have you ever read *Too Many Tamales*

Writing Activity A Paragraph

Write about a special day. Make all your sentences work together to tell about the main idea.

APPLY GRAMMAR: Circle each subject and draw a line under each predicate in your sentences.

TAAS

Better Sentences

Directions

Read the passage. Some parts are underlined. The underlined parts may be one of the following:

- Incomplete sentences
- Run-on sentences
- Correctly written sentences that should be combined

Choose the best way to write each underlined part.

Sentences that run together need to be rewritten correctly.

Is the sentence complete? Check to see if there is a subject as well as a predicate.

Sample

James and Teresa went to the Everglades. <u>They saw many animals some lived in fresh water</u> **(1)**. These included alligators, crocodiles, turtles, and snakes. In the forests, the children saw more things. <u>Many unusual birds, such as the spoonbill</u> **(2)**. James and Teresa enjoyed seeing the different kinds of wildlife.

1
- ○ They saw. Many animals in fresh water.
- ○ They saw animals. Some in fresh water.
- ○ They saw many animals. Some lived in fresh water.

2
- ○ They saw many unusual birds, such as the spoonbill.
- ○ They saw many unusual birds. Such as the spoonbill.
- ○ Many unusual birds, such as the spoonbill they saw.

Test Tip
Read the underlined sections slowly and carefully.

Vocabulary and Comprehension

TAAS

Directions

Read the passage. Then read each question that follows the passage. Choose the best answer to each question.

Sample

Yesterday, I did a trick for my friends. First, I held up two safety pins. I had a pin in each hand. Next, I fastened the pins together. Then I held up the connected pins. The top of one pin was in my right hand. The bottom of the other pin was in my left hand. While I said a special word, I pulled the pins apart. My friends were amazed! Afterward, I showed my friends how to do the trick.

Look for clues around the underlined word to help figure out what it means.

1 How do you think the narrator felt when the trick was over?

- ○ scared
- ○ unhappy
- ○ angry
- ○ pleased

2 In this passage, the word afterward means—

- ○ slowly
- ○ not on time
- ○ after some time
- ○ at the same time

Seeing Like a Writer

Pictures can give you ideas for writing. Imagine that you are in one of these pictures. What would you be doing? How would you feel?

The Blue Pond by Luis Graner Arrufi.

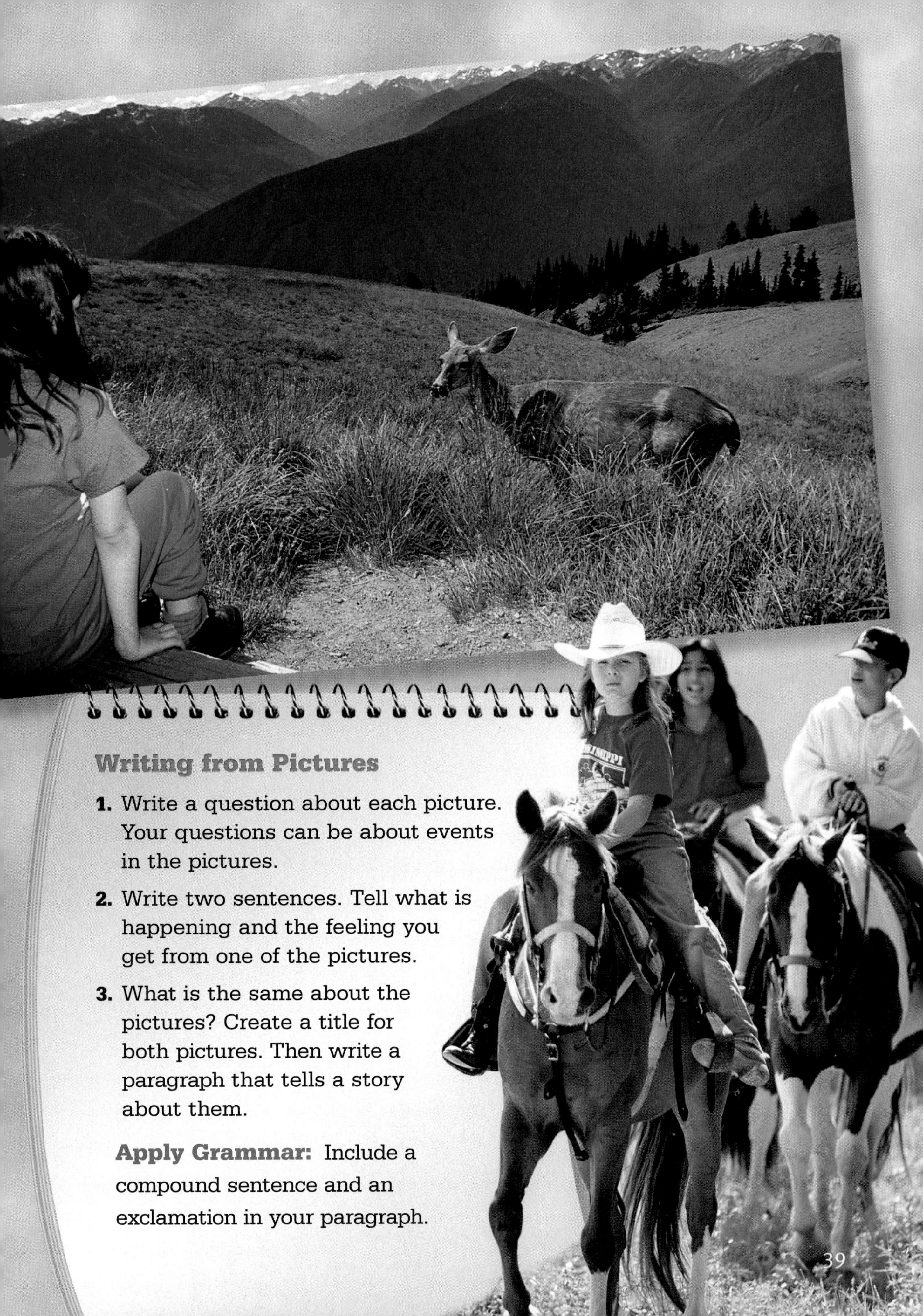

Writing from Pictures

1. Write a question about each picture. Your questions can be about events in the pictures.
2. Write two sentences. Tell what is happening and the feeling you get from one of the pictures.
3. What is the same about the pictures? Create a title for both pictures. Then write a paragraph that tells a story about them.

Apply Grammar: Include a compound sentence and an exclamation in your paragraph.

Personal Narrative

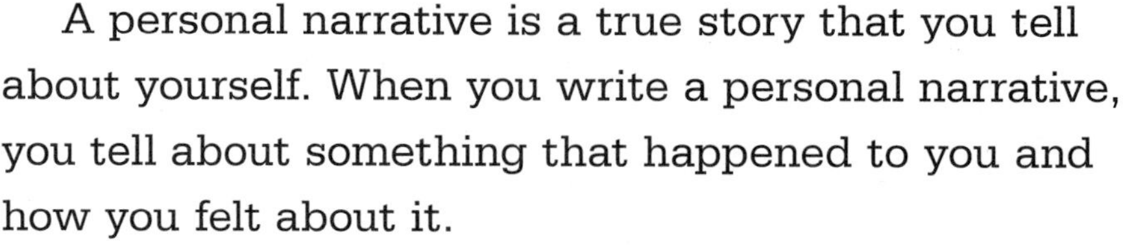

A personal narrative is a true story that you tell about yourself. When you write a personal narrative, you tell about something that happened to you and how you felt about it.

Purpose

Why do you think people write personal narratives? Explain what you think in your journal. Also tell why people like to read them.

Learning from Writers

Read the following examples of personal narrative. What stories do the writers tell? Why do you think they wanted to share their experiences? As you read, notice how each author tells about feelings.

A Man of Two Countries

The last time I saw him, my grandfather said that he longed to see California one more time. He never did.

And when I was nearly grown, I left home and went to see California for myself.

After a time, I came to love the land my grandfather had loved, and I stayed on and on until I had a daughter of my own.

But I also miss the mountains and rivers of my childhood. I miss my old friends. So I return now and then, when I can not still the longing in my heart.

The funny thing is, the moment I am in one country, I am homesick for the other.

— Allen Say, from *Grandfather's Journey*

The Canoe Trip That Never Happened

Last summer, my mom and my aunt suggested we go canoeing on the Green River. I was excited! Before we left, we bought a new tent and life jackets. We studied maps and planned where we should camp each night.

Early one morning, we packed up the car and drove to the Green River. Surprise! The river was brown and full of trash. There had been so much rain, it was flooding. Our careful plans were ruined.

We stayed in motels and visited museums. It was okay, but not as much fun as canoeing. I hope we can try again next year.

— Maryann Kopek

Practice and Apply

Thinking Like a Reader

1. Name three events in Allen Say's narrative in the order they happened.
2. How did Maryann Kopek feel before and after the canoe trip?

Thinking Like a Writer

3. How did the author let you know the order of events in "A Man of Two Countries"?
4. What words did Maryann Kopek use to show how she felt?

5. **Reading Across Texts** Compare the beginning paragraphs of the two personal narratives. Write about how they are alike and different.

Features of Personal Narrative

DEFINITIONS AND **FEATURES**

A personal narrative is writing that tells a true story about your own life. A good personal narrative:

- Tells a story from the writer's **personal experience** using words like *I, my,* and *me.*
- Expresses the writer's **feelings.**
- Has an **interesting beginning, middle,** and **ending.**
- Uses **time-order words** to share events in the order they happened.

▶ A Personal Experience

Reread "A Man of Two Countries" on page 40. Who is the story about?

> So I return now and then, when I can not still the longing in my heart.

The words *I* and *my* let you know that the author is telling about an experience in his own life.

▶ The Writer's Feelings

What words does the author use to tell you about his feelings?

> But I also miss the mountains and rivers of my childhood. I miss my old friends.

When the author says, "I miss my old friends," you can tell he is feeling sad.

▶ An Interesting Beginning, Middle, and Ending

How does Allen Say catch your attention with this beginning?

> The last time I saw him, my grandfather said that he longed to see California one more time.

This beginning may make you wonder why his grandfather's wish was important to the author.

Why is the following sentence a good ending?

> The funny thing is, the moment I am in one country, I am homesick for the other.

▶ Time-Order Words

To help your reader clearly understand what happened, use time-order words and phrases such as *at first, then, last week,* and *finally.*

> After a time, I came to love the land my grandfather had loved...

What time-order phrase did the author use?

Practice and Apply

Create a Features Chart

1. List the features of a good personal narrative.
2. Reread "The Canoe Trip That Never Happened" by Maryann Kopek on page 41.
3. Write one example of each feature in Maryann's writing.
4. Write what you liked about Maryann's personal narrative.

Features	Examples

Prewrite

A personal narrative is a true story about yourself. Writing a personal narrative gives you a chance to tell about your own life.

Purpose and Audience

The purpose for writing a personal narrative is to share how you feel about an experience in your life. It is also to entertain your readers, or audience.

Before you begin to write, think about your audience. Who will be reading your story? How can you help your readers get to know you?

Audience

How will you help your readers know how you feel about a special person? Write your answer.

Choose a Topic

Begin by **brainstorming** a list of people who are special to you. Choose one person to write about. Then **explore ideas** by listing what you remember about being with this person.

I explored my ideas by making a list.
Aunt Jane
Aunt Jane is fun
Lets me try new things
Taught me how to swim
Let me feed baby Alex
Alex spit out the food

PREWRITE

DRAFT

REVISE

PROOFREAD

PUBLISH

Organize • Clustering

Your narrative will have two main parts. First, you will tell about a special person. Then you will tell about something that happened when you were with that person. To plan your narrative, you can use a cluster map. How did this writer organize the ideas from his list?

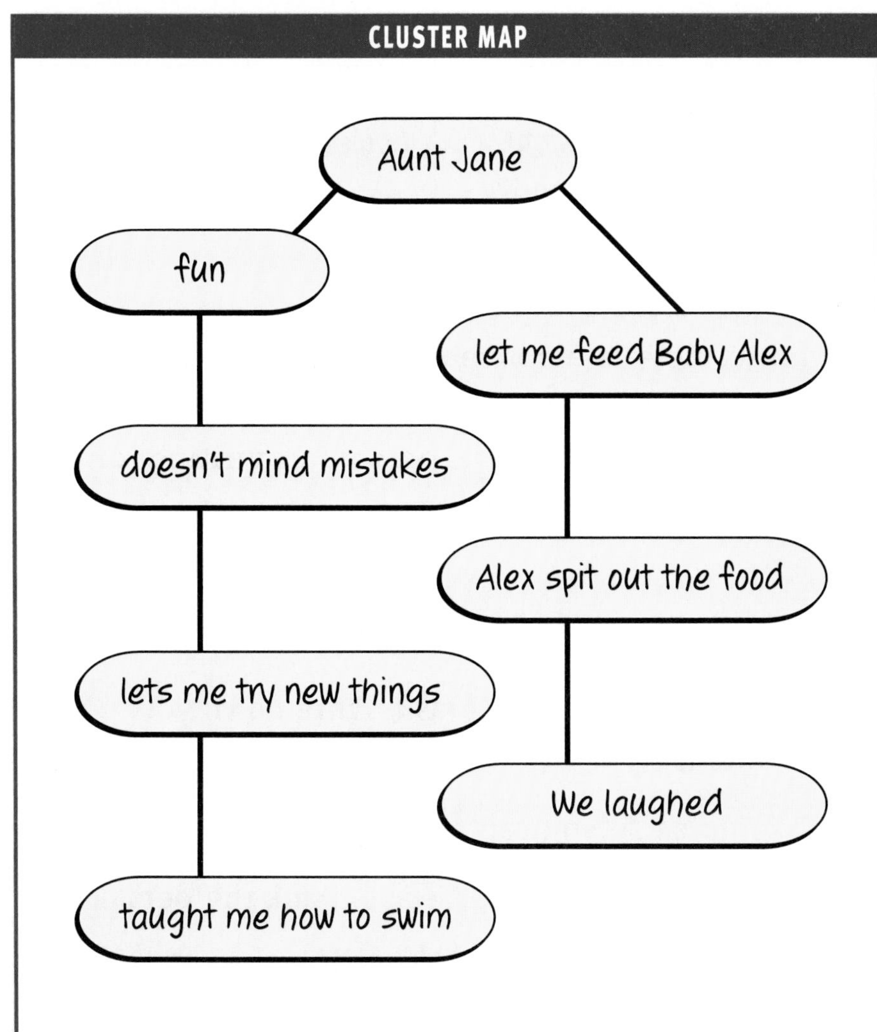

Checklist

Prewriting

- Have you thought about your purpose and audience?
- Have you chosen one person and event to tell about?
- Have you made a list of ideas about the person and the experience?
- Are your ideas organized in a cluster map?
- Do you need to do any research?

Practice and Apply

Plan Your Own Personal Narrative

1. Think about your purpose and audience.

2. Choose a topic.

3. Brainstorm ideas about your topic.

4. Organize your ideas.

Prewrite • Research and Inquiry

▶ Writer's Resources

You may need to get more information for your personal narrative. Make a list of questions. Then decide where you can find the answers.

What Else Do I Need to Know?	Where Can I Find the Information?
What was Alex eating?	E-mail Aunt Jane to find out.
Are there better words to describe what happened?	Look in the dictionary.

▶ Conduct an Interview

An interview is a conversation. One person asks questions and the other person answers. An interview can take place in person, in writing, on the telephone, or by e-mail.

- Know what you want to ask. Write down your questions.
- Take notes so you can remember the answers.
- Be polite and friendly. Always thank the person at the end of an interview.

MAILMAX
new
read
file
print
save
delete
MAILMAX
Aunt Jane, do you remember the first time I tried to feed Alex? What was that orange food in the jar?
Timmy, it was strained squash.

▶ Use a Dictionary

You can find the spelling and meanings of words in a dictionary. Use alphabetical order to find words. Sometimes the dictionary meaning of a word can tell you other ways to say the same thing.

▶ Use Your Research

New information gathered from your research can go into your cluster map. This writer learned two things from his research. How did he change his map?

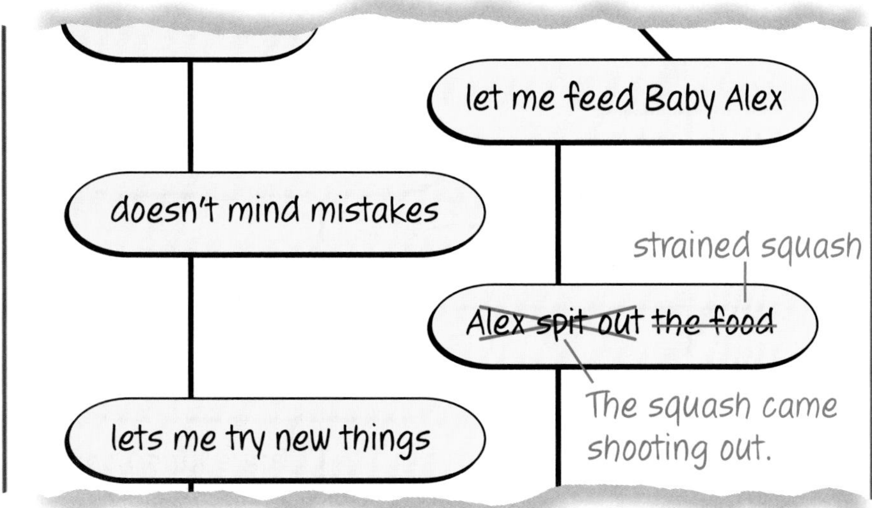

DRAFT

REVISE

PROOFREAD

PUBLISH

Handbook
pages 530, 533

Checklist ✓

Research and Inquiry

- **Did you list your questions?**
- **Did you identify possible resources?**
- **Did you take notes?**

PRACTICE and APPLY

Review Your Plan

1. Look at your cluster map.
2. List questions you have about your topic.
3. Identify the resources you will need to find answers.
4. Add new information you gather to your map.

Writing PROCESS

Draft

Before you begin writing your personal narrative, review the cluster map you made. Think about making a paragraph for each main idea. Include details that support each main idea.

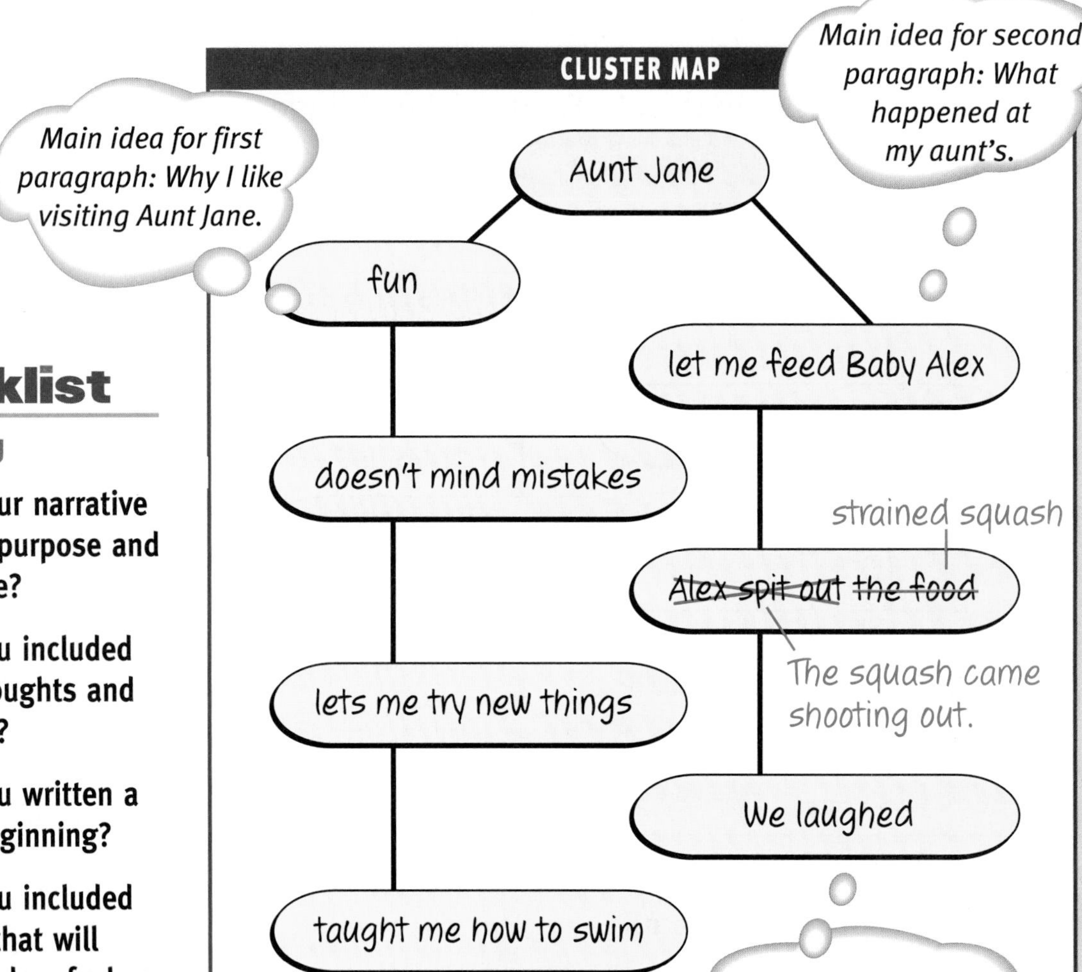
CLUSTER MAP
Main idea for first paragraph: Why I like visiting Aunt Jane.
Main idea for second paragraph: What happened at my aunt's.
Aunt Jane
fun
doesn't mind mistakes
lets me try new things
taught me how to swim
let me feed Baby Alex
strained squash
~~Alex spit out the food~~
The squash came shooting out.
We laughed
This idea can be a good ending.

✓Checklist

Drafting

- Does your narrative fit your purpose and audience?
- Have you included your thoughts and feelings?
- Have you written a good beginning?
- Have you included details that will help readers feel as though they were there?
- Does your narrative have an interesting ending?

Look at how this writer used the ideas in his cluster map to write a first draft. He added details about Aunt Jane in the first paragraph. Then he told about something that happened when he was with her.

DRAFT

This is about my Aunt Jane. Keeps me busy all the time. We have a lot of fun together, even when I make mistakes. She lets me try new things. She even taught me how to swim.

One time a very funny thing happened. Baby Alex was hungry. Aunt Jane asked, "Do you want to try feeding him." So we put Alex into his high chair. We got out a jar of strained squash. I spooned some into Alex's mouth. It came shooting right back out! It got all over me. Alex made a funny face Aunt Jane and I just laughed and laughed.

Main idea of first paragraph

Supporting details tell about the writer's aunt.

Main idea of second paragraph

Supporting details tell what happened.

PRACTICE and APPLY

Draft Your Own Personal Narrative

1. Review your prewriting cluster map.

2. Write about how you felt.

3. Tell about things in the order they happened.

TIP!

TECHNOLOGY

Find out how to change line spacing on your computer. It's a good idea to double space your draft so that you have room to write in changes after you print it out.

Revise

Elaborate

One way to improve your writing is to elaborate. When you elaborate, you add important ideas and details that create a clear picture for the reader. When you revise your personal narrative, you may need to tell more about your feelings.

The writer added a detail that helps the reader know how he feels.

I love to visit
~~This is about~~ my Aunt Jane.

The writer added a description of where the food went to help the reader picture what happened.

my clothes. It was even in my hair.
It got all over ~~me.~~

Word Choice

When you write, it is important to choose just the right words for your topic and audience.

In a personal narrative, you need to find words that will help you tell the events in the order they happened.

First, Then
~~So~~ we put Alex into his high chair. ~~We~~ got out a jar of strained squash.

TIME-ORDER WORDS

first
next
then
later
after
last
before
as soon as
finally
this morning
yesterday
last summer
tomorrow
a long time ago

Better Sentences

As you are revising your draft, read your sentences aloud. How do they sound? Have you used different kinds of sentences? You can change the rhythm of your writing by combining two sentences.

Use *and* to connect two related sentences.

> and
> We got out a jar of strained squash, ^ I spooned some into Alex's mouth.

Handbook
pages 502–504

PRACTICE and APPLY

Revise Your Own Personal Narrative

1. Add details that will make your writing clearer and more interesting.
2. Use words that help the reader know exactly how you felt.
3. Take out information that isn't necessary.
4. **Grammar** Should you combine any sentences?

TECHNOLOGY

Learn how to cut and paste on the computer so that you can easily move sentences and parts of sentences when you revise.

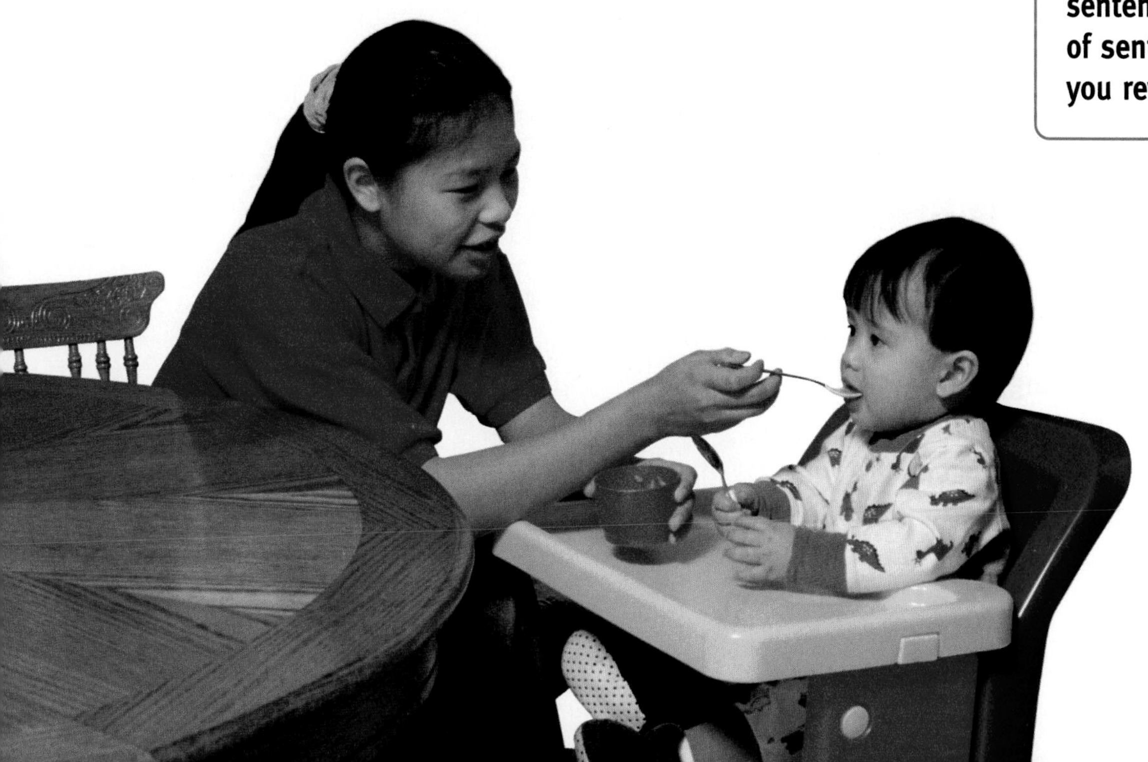

Writing PROCESS

Revise • Peer Conferencing

Read the first draft of your personal narrative aloud to your partner. Your partner may give you some new ideas and suggestions.

How do you feel about Aunt Jane?

This detail belongs in another story.

When did this happen?

This ending makes me smile.

This is about my Aunt Jane. Keeps me busy all the time. We have a lot of fun together, even when I make mistakes. She lets me try new things. She even taught me how to swim.

One time a very funny thing happened. Baby Alex was hungry. Aunt Jane asked, "Do you want to try feeding him." So we put Alex into his high chair. We got out a jar of strained squash. I spooned some into Alex's mouth. It came shooting right back out! It got all over me. Alex made a funny face Aunt Jane and I just laughed and laughed.

Conferencing for the Reader

- Did your partner include features of a personal narrative?
  - personal experience and feelings
  - interesting beginning, middle, and ending
  - time-order words
- Tell your partner what is good about the piece, as well as what could be better.

Think about the comments and suggestions of your partner when you revise your personal narrative. This writer made some changes based on his partner's ideas.

REVISE

My Aunt Jane

I love to visit ~~This is about~~ my Aunt Jane. Keeps me busy all the time. We have a lot of fun together, even when I make mistakes. Best of all, She lets me try new things. ~~She even taught me how to swim.~~

When I visited Aunt Jane last summer, ~~One time~~ a very funny thing happened. Baby Alex was hungry. Aunt Jane asked, "Do you want to try feeding him." First, ~~So~~ we put Alex into his high chair. Then We got out a jar of strained squash, and ~~. I~~ spooned some into Alex's mouth. It came shooting right back out! It got all over ~~me.~~ my clothes. It was even in my hair. Alex made a funny face Aunt Jane and I just laughed and laughed.

PRACTICE and APPLY

Revise Your Own Personal Narrative

1. Read your draft aloud to your partner. Listen to how it sounds.
2. Take notes on your partner's comments.
3. Use the notes from your peer conference to make your draft better.
4. Add a title.

Checklist

Revising

- Does your story suit your purpose and audience?
- Have you described your feelings clearly?
- Did you include enough details? Did you choose words carefully?
- Are the events in time order?
- Do the sentences flow easily when read aloud?
- Did you add a title?

Writing PROCESS

Proofread

After you have revised your narrative, proofread it to find and correct any mistakes in mechanics, grammar and usage, and spelling.

STRATEGIES FOR PROOFREADING

- Reread your revised narrative, each time looking for a different type of mistake. That way you will have a better chance of catching all mistakes.
- Read for correct capitalization.
- Read for correct punctuation.
- Read aloud to check for sentence fragments.
- Check each word carefully to spot spelling mistakes.

TECHNOLOGY

Use the spell checker, but do not expect it to find every error. Read your draft carefully. Make sure that each word is the right word. For example, you may have typed "no" for "on" by mistake.

REVIEW THE RULES

GRAMMAR

- A sentence fragment is a group of words that does not express a complete thought. You can correct a sentence fragment by adding a subject or a predicate.

MECHANICS

- Every sentence begins with a capital letter.
- A statement ends with a period.
- A question ends with a question mark.
- A command ends with a period.
- An exclamation ends with an exclamation mark.

Look at the proofreading corrections made on the draft below. What does the proofreading mark ⊙ mean? Why does the writer use that mark?

PREWRITE
DRAFT
REVISE
PROOFREAD
PUBLISH

PROOFREAD

My Aunt Jane

I love to visit ~~This is about~~ my Aunt Jane. She ~~K~~eeps me busy all the time. We have a lot of fun together, even when I make mistakes. Best of all, ~~S~~she lets me try new things. ~~She even taught me how to swim.~~

When I visited Aunt Jane last summer, ~~One time~~ a very funny thing happened. Baby Alex was hungry. Aunt Jane asked, "Do you want to try feeding him?" ~~So~~

First, we put Alex into his high chair. Then we got out a jar of strained squash, and I spooned some into Alex's mouth. It came shooting right back out! It got all over ~~me~~ my clothes. It was even in my hair. Alex made a funny face. Aunt Jane and I just laughed and laughed.

Checklist

Proofreading

- Did you spell all words correctly?
- Did you begin and end every sentence correctly?
- Is every sentence a complete thought?
- Did you indent the paragraphs?

PROOFREADING MARKS

- ¶ new paragraph
- ^ add
- take out
- ≡ Make a capital letter.
- / Make a small letter.
- (sp) Check the spelling.
- ⊙ Add a period.

PRACTICE and APPLY

Proofread Your Own Personal Narrative

1. Correct spelling mistakes.
2. Include end punctuation for each sentence.
3. Correct sentence fragments.
4. Indent paragraphs.

Publish

Review your personal narrative one more time before you publish. Use this checklist.

✓Self-Check Personal Narrative

- ❑ **Who was my audience? Did I write in a way that will interest and entertain them?**
- ❑ **What was my purpose? Did I share how I felt about my experience?**
- ❑ **Did I begin and end my story in an interesting way?**
- ❑ **Did I use time-order words to tell the order in which things happened?**
- ❑ **Did I write complete sentences? Do they fit together well?**
- ❑ **Did I proofread carefully and correct all mistakes?**

The writer used the checklist to review his narrative. Read "My Aunt Jane" and discuss it with your classmates. Was the piece ready to publish? Why or why not?

My Aunt Jane

by Timmy Chen

I love to visit my Aunt Jane. She keeps me busy all the time. We have a lot of fun together, even when I make mistakes. Best of all, she lets me try new things.

When I visited Aunt Jane last summer, a very funny thing happened. Baby Alex was hungry. Aunt Jane asked, "Do you want to try feeding him?"

First, we put Alex into his high chair. Then we got out a jar of strained squash, and I spooned some into Alex's mouth. It came shooting right back out! It got all over my clothes. It was even in my hair. Alex made a funny face. Aunt Jane and I just laughed and laughed.

Practice and Apply

Publish Your Own Personal Narrative

1. Check your revised draft one more time.
2. Make a neat final copy.
3. Add a cover and some drawings or photos.

TIP!

TECHNOLOGY

Learn how to change the font in your word processing program. For your final copy, choose a font that is easy to read.

LISTENING
SPEAKING
VIEWING
PRESENTING

Present Your Personal Narrative

Before you present your story, you need to plan and practice. There are things you can do to make sure your presentation is a success.

How to Tell Your Story

Strategies for Speaking Remember, you want to entertain your listeners. Try to make them feel as if they are taking part in the experience.

- Make eye contact with your audience so they feel as if you are speaking to them.
- Use a tone of voice that matches the feelings in the story. Speak loudly and clearly so that everyone can hear you.
- Use gestures and facial expressions that match the feelings and actions in the story.

Listening Strategies

- Set a purpose. Are you listening to learn new information or to be entertained?
- Try to picture in your mind what the speaker is describing.
- Don't interrupt. Jot down questions to ask later.
- Keep your eyes on the speaker. Let the speaker know you are paying attention.

Multimedia Ideas

Does your classroom have the technology to project a photograph onto a screen? If so, you might want to project a picture of the person you wrote about as a visual for your oral presentation.

STEP 2

How to Show Your Story

Suggestions for Visuals You can make your presentation clearer and more interesting by adding visuals for your audience to look at as they listen.

- A poster can display your most important ideas.
- Photos or drawings can bring your story to life.
- A diagram or map might help the audience understand exactly where something happened.

Remember to use visuals that are large enough for everyone in the audience to see.

STEP 3

How to Share Your Story

Strategies for Rehearsing The more you practice, the better you will feel when you present your story.

- Ask a friend or family member to listen and make suggestions.
- Practice in front of a mirror.
- Tape-record yourself. Then listen. Practice until you like the way it sounds.

Viewing Strategies

- **Look carefully at the visual displays for information the speaker may not tell you.**
- **Watching the speaker's gestures and facial expressions may help you enjoy the story.**

PRACTICE and APPLY

Present Your Own Personal Narrative

1. Illustrate the story with photographs or drawings.
2. Practice reading your story out loud in front of a mirror.
3. Use a tone of voice that suits your story.
4. Make eye contact with your audience.

Writing Tests

TAAS

A writing test asks you to write one or more paragraphs in response to a prompt. A writing prompt gives you a situation and tells you what kind of writing to do. Look for key words and phrases in the prompt that tell you what you should write about and how you should present your ideas.

Is the purpose of this writing to entertain, inform, or influence the audience?

What words tell what kind of writing this is?

Sometimes the prompt tells who the audience is, but not always.

Prompt

Playing outdoors can be fun during all seasons of the year.

Write a story about a wonderful time you had playing outdoors. Tell what happened and how you felt.

How to Read a Prompt

Purpose Read the prompt again. Look for words that tell you the purpose of the writing. The words "fun" and "a wonderful time" are clues that one purpose will be to entertain.

Audience A prompt may tell you whom to write for. If it does not, think of your teacher as your audience.

Personal Narrative The prompt always tells you what kind of writing you will do. The words "write a story about a wonderful time you had" and "how you felt" tell you that the kind of writing is a personal narrative. In a personal narrative you tell a story about something that happened in your own life.

Test Tip
If you do not understand a prompt, read it again carefully.

How to Write to a Prompt

The following tips can help you take a test with a writing prompt.

Before Writing **Content/Ideas**	• Think about the purpose of your writing. • Remember your audience. • Make a list of events that you want to share.
During Writing **Organization/ Paragraph Structure**	• Begin by writing a good topic sentence. • Use time-order words to tell events in the order they happened in your story. • Write an interesting ending.
After Writing **Grammar/Usage**	• Proofread your writing. • Begin the first word of each sentence with a capital letter. • Use correct end marks. • Spell all words correctly.

Apply What You Learned

Read the prompt on a writing test carefully. Look for words that tell what you should write about. Look for the purpose and audience. Decide how you will organize your ideas.

Prompt

Helping someone can make you feel good.

Write a story telling about a time you helped someone. The person may be a family member, a friend, or a neighbor.

Grammar and Writing Review

pages 2–3

Sentences

A. Write each group of words. Next to each group, write *sentence* or *sentence fragment*.

1. A beautiful summer day.
2. We played happily at the beach.
3. Large waves on the shore.
4. Ate sandwiches for lunch.
5. Two children dug in the sand.

pages 4–5, 6–7

Four Kinds of Sentences

B. Write each sentence. Write *statement*, *question*, *command*, or *exclamation* next to each sentence.

6. My family took a trip to the Painted Desert.
7. Tell me what the desert is like.
8. How beautiful the colors are!
9. The sand is orange, red, and purple.
10. Was it hot in the desert?
11. The desert is very hot in the summer.
12. Winters in the desert are cold.
13. Where is the Painted Desert located?
14. The Painted Desert is in Arizona.
15. We also visited Sunset Crater.
16. What did you bring home from the trip?
17. Look at this arrowhead.
18. What a great find that is!
19. Please let me hold the arrowhead.
20. How amazing this arrowhead seems!

pages 8–9

Mechanics and Usage: Sentence Punctuation

C. Write each sentence. Add capital letters and end marks.

21. the science fair begins tomorrow

22. are you entering the science fair

23. tell me about your science project

24. we made a model of the sun and planets

25. wow, what an interesting project you have

26. how did you put the model together

27. let me show you

28. first, I made clay balls for the nine planets

29. then, I attached them to the sun with wires

30. how proud I would be to win a prize

pages 12–13

Subjects in Sentences

D. Write the sentences. Draw a line under the subject of each sentence.

31. Some people fly in hot-air balloons.

32. A flame heats the air in the balloon.

33. The hot air makes the balloon rise.

34. Air currents move the balloon along.

35. The balloon travels fast and far.

pages 14–15

Predicates in Sentences

E. Write the sentences. Draw a line under the predicate of each sentence.

36. People hold hot-air balloon races.

37. The balloons rise into the air.

38. Balloon pilots find strong air currents.

39. The balloons sail quickly along.

40. The fastest balloon wins.

Unit 1 Review

pages 16–17

Combining Sentences

F. Use *and* to combine each pair of sentences. Write the new compound sentence.

41. Ann set up the fish tank. Gail added the water.

42. The teacher passed out the papers. The students took the test.

43. Pam asked a question. The teacher answered it.

44. The recess bell rang. The students went outside.

45. Stanley drew a picture. Kathy put it up on the wall.

46. The principal visited the class. The students greeted her.

47. Maryann wrote a story. The students acted it out.

48. The students went to the library. Peter found an adventure story.

49. Gym class is on Monday. Art class is on Thursday.

50. Ten students took the bus. Four students walked home.

pages 18–19

Mechanics and Usage: Correcting Run-on Sentences

G. Correct each run-on sentence. Write the two complete ideas as two separate sentences or as a compound sentence.

51. Mike wanted to be a circus clown he went to a school for clowns.

52. Real circus clowns taught the students Mike learned many things.

53. Students learned about face makeup the wigs were in many different colors.

54. Mike was soon walking on stilts all the students learned crazy jokes.

55. Clown school was a lot of fun Mike got a job with the circus.

Unit 1 Review

pages 32–33

Vocabulary: Time-Order Words

H. Write the sentences in the correct order. Use the time-order words in the sentences as a guide.

56. Last, I won a prize at the ring-toss game.

57. One afternoon, we went to a fair.

58. After we ate, I tried some games.

59. Then, we visited the food booths.

60. First, we bought tickets.

pages 34–35

Composition: Main Idea and Supporting Details

I. Write a sentence that states a main idea for each of the topics. Then write three supporting details for each idea.

61. A Trip to Remember

62. My Favorite Place

63. An Amazing Adventure

64. The First Day of School

65. Winning the Prize

pages 54–55

Proofreading a Personal Narrative

J. 66.–75. Write the following paragraph correctly. Correct the punctuation, grammar, and spelling mistakes. Use capital letters correctly. There are 10 mistakes.

My first day at summer camp was both skary and happy? It was scary because it was my first time away from home by myself it was happy becuase everyone at camp was so nice. After we unpacked, we gathered in the main lodge Each camper told her naime and something about herself then we held hands in a circle and sang the camp song. what fun it was!

Project File

PROJECT 1 A Poem

A poem paints a picture or expresses a feeling with words. Poets choose words for their sounds as well as their meanings.

Whale
by Mary Ann Hoberman

A whale is stout about the middle,
He is stout about the ends,
& so is all his family
& so are all his friends.

He's pleased that he's enormous,
He's happy he weighs tons,
& so are all his daughters
& so are all his sons.

He eats when he is hungry
Each kind of food he wants,
& so do all his uncles
& so do all his aunts.

Rhyme *Some poems have rhyme, which means words that end with the same sounds.*

Rhythm *A poem may have a rhythm, which means a set beat, or sound pattern, when lines are read aloud.*

Repetition *A poet may repeat words or phrases to add rhythm or to stress an idea.*

Form *Poems can take different forms. This poem has groups of lines called stanzas.*

Write a poem Think of a favorite person, place, idea, or animal. What makes it so special?

Share your thoughts and feelings about the subject you chose in a poem. Decide how to write your poem. What describing words might you use? Will you use words that rhyme? What words might you repeat to create rhythm?

PROJECT 2

A Journal Entry

Jones and Piccard's nonstop journey around the world in a hot-air balloon made history. Learn more about what it is like to fly in a hot-air balloon. Then imagine that you are a balloon pilot making a historic trip.

Balloon Adventures Write a journal entry describing the best part of the adventure. Be sure to include your feelings about this event and to choose words that are vivid and interesting.

Extra Practice

Sentences

A. Write the group of words in each pair that is a sentence.

1. The lighthouse is tall. The tall lighthouse.
2. Mia sees the open door. An open door.
3. No light inside. Mia enters the dark building.
4. Mia climbs the stairs. Up the narrow stairs.
5. A long climb. The stairs are steep.
6. Mia grips the railing. Holds on tightly.
7. At the top. Mia gets to the very top.
8. Mia looks out the window. Across the water.
9. The sailboats. Mia sees colorful sailboats.
10. Mia is excited. Sees wonderful things.

B. Write *sentence* if the group of words is a sentence. Write *not a sentence* if the group of words is not a sentence.

11. Fred drove to the bus station.
12. Parked the car.
13. Asked for directions.
14. Fred followed the directions.
15. Fred found his ticket.
16. The bus station was crowded.
17. Fred wanted a book.
18. Went to a gift shop.
19. Bought a book.
20. Fred will get on the bus soon.

Statements and Questions

A. Write each sentence. Write *statement* next to each sentence that tells something. Write *question* next to each sentence that asks something.

1. What grade are you in?
2. I am in third grade.
3. How many boys are in your class?
4. How many girls are in your class?
5. We have a new teacher.
6. Which subject do you like best?
7. I like science.
8. My favorite subject is math.
9. We study music and art in our school.
10. Is Mr. Wilkes the art teacher?

B. Write each sentence. Write *statement* if it is a statement and *question* if it is a question. Add the correct end mark.

11. The class will visit the new museum
12. The Air and Space Museum is in the city
13. When do the children leave on the trip
14. The bus comes at ten o'clock
15. What things will they see in the museum
16. The museum has airplanes from long ago
17. An old plane sits on the floor
18. Can people climb inside the plane
19. Will the guide talk about space travel
20. The children will see a movie about space

Grammar

Extra Practice

Commands and Exclamations

A. Write each sentence. Write *command* next to each sentence that gives an order. Write *exclamation* next to each sentence that shows strong feeling.

1. Look at the rainbow.
2. What a wonderful surprise you will see!
3. Count the different colors in the rainbow.
4. How beautiful the rainbow looks!
5. Make a wish for something special.
6. Watch the rainbow disappear.
7. What a great time we had!
8. Try to learn more about rainbows.
9. Please find a book on rainbows in the library.
10. How many books on rainbows there are!

B. Write each sentence. Write *command* if it is a command and *exclamation* if it is an exclamation. Add the correct end mark.

11. What a great bike that is
12. How nice that color is
13. Take care of your new bike
14. Don't leave your bike outside
15. Wear your helmet when you ride your bike
16. Ask your mom if you can go for a ride
17. Take a ride with me
18. What a great day this is for riding a bike
19. How fast your bike goes
20. Help me fix my bike, please

Sentence Punctuation

A. Write whether each sentence is a *statement*, *question*, *command*, or *exclamation*. Then write the name of the correct end mark for each sentence.

1. Do you want to play ball?
2. What a great idea that is!
3. I'll get my ball and my glove.
4. Bring your new bat, Ashley.
5. Wear your team shirts.
6. The sun is very bright today.
7. Please wear your caps.
8. Take water with you.
9. When will the game begin?
10. How pretty the park looks today!

B. Write each sentence. Begin and end the sentences correctly.

11. ray visited the Alamo
12. have you been to the Alamo
13. the Alamo is in Texas
14. did Davy Crockett fight at the Alamo
15. the Alamo was once a mission
16. what a place the Alamo is
17. what is the famous saying about the Alamo
18. santa Anna was a Mexican general
19. did Santa Anna fight against the Texans
20. find out more about the Alamo

Extra Practice

Subjects in Sentences

A. Write each sentence. Write *subject* next to the sentences in which the subject is underlined.

1. Goldfish live in ponds.
2. Some people keep goldfish in aquariums.
3. People in China breed goldfish.
4. The fantail is a kind of goldfish.
5. Some goldfish have long tails.
6. People buy goldfish for pets.
7. A pet fish needs care.
8. Fish need fresh water and food.
9. The water should be warm.
10. The fishbowl should be clean.

B. Write the sentences. Draw a line under the subject of each sentence.

11. Mexico City is the capital of Mexico.
12. My grandparents live in Mexico City.
13. Many roads lead to Mexico City.
14. The parks are beautiful.
15. Alameda Park has many poplar trees.
16. People shop in outdoor markets.
17. Most newspapers are printed in Spanish.
18. Some newspapers are printed in English.
19. Heavy rains can cause floods.
20. The nights are cool.

Predicates in Sentences

A. Write each sentence. Write *predicate* next to the sentences in which the predicate is underlined.

1. <u>The weather</u> changed quickly.
2. Dark clouds <u>formed in the sky</u>.
3. The strong wind <u>broke tree branches</u>.
4. <u>Lightning</u> streaked across the sky.
5. Thunder <u>broke the silence</u>.
6. Heavy rain <u>poured down on the town</u>.
7. <u>People</u> ran for shelter.
8. <u>Cars</u> splashed water and mud.
9. Umbrellas <u>bent in the wind</u>.
10. <u>The storm</u> lasted a long time.

B. Write each sentence. Draw a line under each predicate.

11. The boat bounced across the water.
12. Waves rocked the boat.
13. The captain turned the wheel.
14. The sailors held the wet ropes.
15. Passengers clung to the rails of the boat.
16. Everyone watched the water.
17. A whale swam next to the boat.
18. Dolphins jumped into the air.

19. Passengers screamed with delight.
20. Water splashed everywhere.

Grammar

Extra Practice

Combining Sentences

A. Write each sentence. If it is a compound sentence, circle the word that joins the two sentences. If it is not a compound sentence, write *not compound*.

1. The sky is blue, and the clouds are gone.
2. The sun is bright, and the air is warm.
3. There is very little rain, and the ground is dry.
4. Animals dig many holes in the sand.
5. A lizard has a long tail.
6. The children get off the bus, and the teachers meet them.
7. A roadrunner races by, and Maria takes its picture.
8. Linda finds a big cactus, and Vic guesses its age.
9. Desert flowers are colorful.
10. You will not be bored in the desert.

B. Combine each pair of sentences. Write the new compound sentence.

11. The ocean is beautiful. Many people like to visit it.
12. Levi walks along the shore. He feels the sand squishing under his toes.
13. The tide rushes in. The waves are rough.
14. The wind blows the sand. It piles up in dunes.
15. The tide is low. The children can walk for miles.
16. We collect seashells. Some people build sandcastles.
17. Seaweed is an ocean plant. Some sea animals eat it.
18. Dolphins live in the ocean. You can see them playing.
19. Crabs dig in the sand. Shrimp swim in the sea.
20. Lee smells the salty air. She listens to the waves.

Correcting Run-on Sentences

A. Write each run-on sentence as two sentences.

1. Sara looked at Brutus he was muddy and wet.
2. Sara filled the tub she wanted to wash her pet.
3. Sara added soap she put the dog in the tub.
4. The dog was covered with bubbles he looked silly.
5. Brutus shook off the bubbles he got Sara all wet.
6. Sara laughed she looked like a marshmallow.
7. Sara washed Brutus carefully she took him out of the tub.
8. Brutus shook himself dry he rolled in the grass.
9. Sara told Brutus to stop he was rolling into the mud.
10. Sara filled the tub again Brutus needed another bath.

B. Correct each run-on sentence. Write the complete ideas in two separate sentences or rewrite the sentence as a compound sentence.

11. José ate his lunch then he ran outside.
12. José wanted to play ball his friends were at the ballpark.
13. José grabbed his baseball mitt he got on his bike.
14. José rode his bike fast it was getting dark.
15. Storm clouds rolled across the sky José rode faster.
16. José got to the park the rain began to fall.
17. The baseball teams waited soon the rain stopped.
18. José's team was losing by one run the team needed a hit.
19. José got his turn at bat he was nervous.
20. José had two strikes he wanted his team to win.

Theme Looking at Nature

UNIT 2

Nouns and Explanatory Writing

In this unit you will learn about kinds of nouns. You will also learn how to write an explanation of how to make or do something step by step.

Science Link *The earth made a real mountain. A girl named Elizabeth made a sand mountain. Read to see what steps are involved in making each mountain.*

This is the story of two mountains. The earth made one. Elizabeth in her yellow sun hat made the other.

The earth made its mountain millions of years ago. It began as a pool underground, first fiery hot and soft, then cold and rock-hard.

Elizabeth made hers on the beach today with bucketsful of wet sand.

Eons passed. The earth cracked and shifted until the rock of its mountain slowly rose.

Elizabeth quickly piled her sand high. She patted it smooth all the way around.

from ***The Sun, the Wind and the Rain*** by Lisa Westberg Peters

Thinking Like a Writer

Explanatory Writing Explanatory writing gives directions or explains how to do something. Reread the passage.

- What are the steps for making a real mountain and a sand mountain?

Nouns The author uses nouns—words that name people, places, or things. Read the passage again.

QUICK WRITE List the nouns in the passage under these categories: Person, Place, Thing.

Grammar

Nouns

RULES

A noun is a word that names a person, place, or thing.

The family visited the city by bus.

Look at each group of nouns. Think of other words you could add to each group.

Person	Place	Thing
girl	woods	flower
teacher	beach	clothes
brother	park	table

Nouns

In your journal, write how you can tell if a word is a noun.

Guided Practice

Name the words in each sentence that are nouns.

EXAMPLE: The mother went to the library.
mother, library

1. Two girls went to the museum.
2. The rooms were full of paintings.
3. Statues stood in the garden.
4. The father rode in a taxi.
5. The driver drove along the streets.

REVIEW THE RULES

- A noun names a person, place, or thing.

More Practice

A. Write the sentences. Draw a line under each noun.

6. The family had a picnic in the park.

7. A squirrel begged for some peanuts.

8. The brothers rowed a boat on the lake.

9. The two sisters flew kites.

10. Their mother threw crumbs to the ducks.

11. Two boys rode bikes.

12. The children waved to the bikers.

13. Joggers ran along a path.

14. Flowers bloomed under the trees.

15. Bees buzzed around the food.

Handbook
page 505

B. Spiral Review Write the sentences. Use a noun in each blank. Circle each subject. Draw a line under each predicate.

16. The _____ went to the circus.

17. Twelve _____ came out of one car.

18. A _____ danced on a thin rope.

19. _____ jumped through hoops.

20. The _____ enjoyed the show.

Extra Practice, page 148

Writing Activity An Article

Write an article about your favorite place. Pick just the right words to help the reader picture this place. **APPLY GRAMMAR:** Draw a line under each noun in your article.

Social Studies Link

Grammar

Singular and Plural Nouns

RULES

A singular noun names one person, place, or thing.

A plural noun names more than one person, place, or thing.

Add *-s* to form the plural of most singular nouns.

gardens *birds* *farmers*

Add *-es* to form the plural of singular nouns that end in *s, sh, ch,* or *x*.

buses *dishes* *benches* *foxes*

Nouns

How can you decide whether a word is a singular noun or a plural noun? Write your answer in your journal.

Most plural nouns end in *-s* or *-es*.

friend + *s* = *friends*

wish + *es* = *wishes*

Guided Practice

Tell the plural of each singular noun.

EXAMPLE: class *classes*

1. chicken

2. glass

3. box

4. apple

5. horse

6. breeze

7. friend

8. wish

9. beach

10. space

REVIEW THE RULES

- Add *-s* or *-es* to form the plural of most singular nouns.

Grammar

More Practice

A. Write the sentences. Write the plural of each underlined noun.

11. Carrie and Gina watch many bird.
12. Two nests are in some bush.
13. The mother robins perch on branch.
14. The girls do not disturb the chick.
15. Gina takes pictures of the young robin.
16. Carrie sees a robin carry bug to the nest.
17. The little birds make loud chirp.
18. The baby birds open their mouth wide.
19. Their mother feeds them their lunch.
20. The two girls prefer sandwich.

Handbook page 505

B. Spiral Review **Write the sentences. Add capital letters and end marks where needed. Use the correct noun in ( ).**

21. what do (robin, robins) and bluejays eat
22. some birds eat small (animal, animals)
23. an (owl, owls) can catch a mouse
24. hummingbirds sip nectar from (flower, flowers)
25. wow, those birds have a sweet (treat, treats)

Extra Practice, page 149

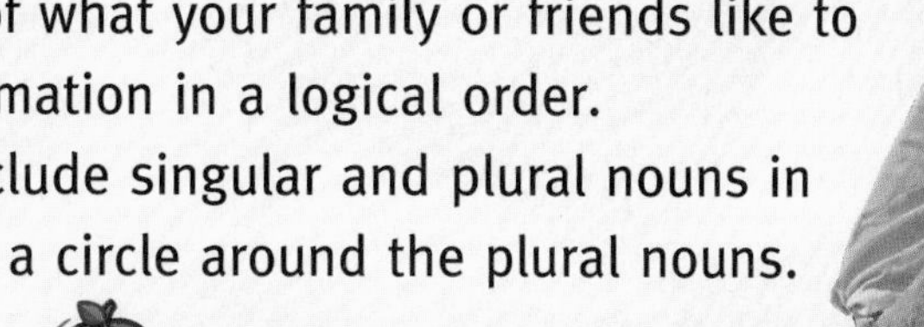

Writing Activity A Description

Write a description of what your family or friends like to eat. Arrange your information in a logical order.

APPLY GRAMMAR: Include singular and plural nouns in your description. Draw a circle around the plural nouns.

Health Link

Grammar

Plural Nouns with *-ies*

RULES

To form the plural of nouns ending in a consonant and *y*, change the *y* to *i* and add *-es*.

We write in our diaries.

Nouns that end in a consonant and *y* have a special way of forming the plural.

lady ⟶ *ladi* + *es* ⟶ *ladies*

Nouns

Write how you know when to change *y* to *i* and add the letters *-es* to form a plural noun.

Guided Practice

Tell the plural of each noun.

EXAMPLE: butterfly *butterflies*

1. cherry
2. puppy
3. lily
4. story
5. daisy
6. party
7. bakery
8. baby
9. penny
10. family

REVIEW THE RULES

- To form the plural of a noun that ends in a consonant and *y*, change the *y* to *i* and add *-es*.

Grammar

Handbook page 505

More Practice

A. Write the sentences. Write the plural form of each noun in ( ).

11. We all have different (hobby).

12. Amy reads adventure (story).

13. Ed studies bees and (butterfly).

14. You collect old (penny).

15. We raise lots of (bunny).

16. Mr. Chan grows giant (lily).

17. Mrs. Jones picks (berry) and makes jam.

18. Grandma knits hats for (baby).

19. Sue makes necklaces out of (daisy).

20. Rob raises (guppy) and other fish.

B. Spiral Review **Write the sentences. Draw one line under singular nouns. Add correct end marks.**

21. Two students made an airplane

22. They used wood, paper, and plastic

23. Did they use glue or nails

24. The boys made the plane fly

25. Their friends watched the sky

Extra Practice, page 150

Writing Activity A Journal Entry

Write a journal entry about a hobby you have or would like to have. Tell why that hobby interests you.

APPLY GRAMMAR: Include plural nouns in your journal entry. Draw a line under each plural noun.

Grammar

More Plural Nouns

RULES

Some nouns have special plural forms.

Two children watched three mice play.

A few nouns have the same singular and plural forms.

We saw four deer and two moose.

Nouns with special plural forms do not end in *-s* or *-es*.

Singular	Plural	Singular	Plural
man	men	sheep	sheep
woman	women	deer	deer
child	children	moose	moose
tooth	teeth	foot	feet
mouse	mice	goose	geese

Nouns

How can you tell when a noun has a special plural form? Write your answer in your journal.

Guided Practice

Tell the plural of each noun in ( ).

EXAMPLE: The (child) were on a camping trip.
children

1. Two (woman) planned the camping trip.
2. Everyone saw two (moose) in the lake.
3. One big moose had huge (tooth).
4. Several (deer) raced across a field.
5. A flock of (goose) flew overhead.

REVIEW THE RULES

- Some nouns form their plurals in a special way.
- Some nouns do not change to form the plural.

Handbook page 505

More Practice

A. Write the sentences. Complete each sentence with the correct plural form of the noun in ( ).

6. The children saw several wild (sheep).

7. The trip leaders pointed out a herd of (deer).

8. Several (goose) swam in a pond.

9. Two (man) were fishing in a stream.

10. They were as quiet as (mouse).

11. Two (deer) watched from the woods.

12. Some (child) wanted to fish, too.

13. Marc wanted to see some (moose).

14. Two (woman) said it was time to leave.

15. One child had sore (foot) from walking so far.

B. Spiral Review Use *and* to join each pair of sentences. Write the new sentence. Circle each noun.

16. The children picked berries. The men caught some fish.

17. The women built a fire. The men cooked the fish.

18. One woman told funny stories. The campers laughed.

19. The night was dark. An owl hooted.

20. The campers were tired. The children slept well.

Extra Practice, page 151

Writing Activity A Short Story

Write a story about a trip or other special event. Include your feelings about your subject.

APPLY GRAMMAR: Use nouns with special plural forms in your story. Circle each of these nouns.

Grammar

Common and Proper Nouns

RULES

A common noun names any person, place, or thing.

The boy lives in a city.

A proper noun names a special person, place, or thing and begins with a capital letter.

Juan lives in Miami.

Proper nouns are capitalized. Common nouns are not.

Common Nouns	Proper Nouns
girl	Ellen
street	Main Street
holiday	Thanksgiving

Nouns

Write how you can decide if a word is a common noun or a proper noun.

Guided Practice

Tell which words are common nouns and which are proper nouns.

EXAMPLE: ocean *common noun*

1. city
2. Santa Fe
3. Monday
4. mountain
5. state
6. North Carolina
7. Ms. Shapiro
8. teacher
9. August
10. book

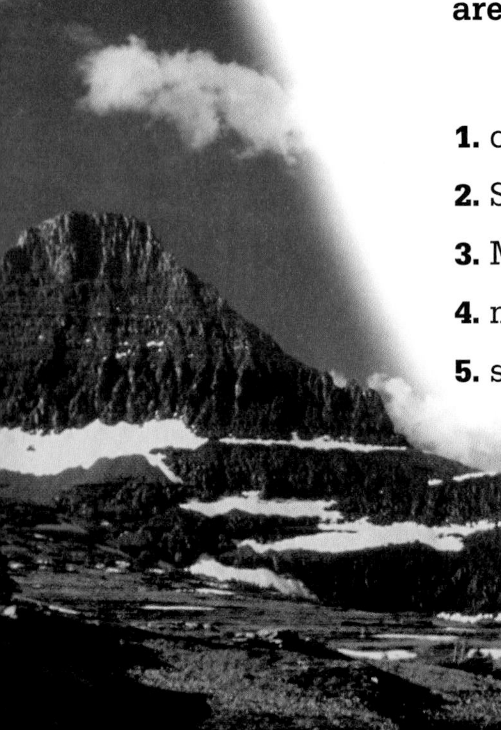

REVIEW THE RULES

- A common noun names any person, place, or thing.
- A proper noun names a special person, place, or thing and begins with a capital letter.

Grammar

More Practice

A. Write the underlined nouns. Write *common* or *proper* next to each.

11. Sam Griffin lives in New Mexico.

12. His neighbors have a son named Miguel.

13. Miguel's nickname is Mike.

14. Mike and Sam are best friends.

15. The boys go to Alta Vista Elementary School.

16. Both students write for the school newsletter.

17. The newsletter is called The Alta Vistan.

18. The writers hold a meeting every Tuesday.

19. Sam wrote an article about coyotes.

20. Mike wrote about a show at the Children's Museum.

Handbook page 506

B. Spiral Review Write the paragraph correctly. Write each complete idea as a separate sentence. Use correct end marks. Circle each plural noun.

21.–30. Many animals live in the mountains you can see coyotes and rabbits. Hawks soar in the sky. The woods are full of deer you may see wild sheep.

Extra Practice, page 152

Writing Activity Directions

Write directions to your house from your school. Arrange the directions so that they can be followed easily.

APPLY GRAMMAR: Use common and proper nouns in your directions. Circle each proper noun.

Grammar

Capitalization

RULES

Capitalize each important word of a proper noun.

The name of a day, month, or holiday begins with a capital letter.

Monday *September* *Fourth of July*

All important words in the titles of books begin with a capital letter.

Spiders at Work

Nouns

In your journal, write how you can tell which nouns should begin with a capital letter.

Begin the first word and all the important words of a proper noun or a book title with capital letters.

*Mary Jane read a book called **The Sun, the Wind and the Rain.***

Guided Practice

Tell how to write the underlined words correctly.

EXAMPLE: Tammy got the book on friday. *Friday*

1. Tomorrow is thanksgiving.
2. We read a new book on monday.
3. The girl wants to read *winter in the arctic* next.
4. That will be a good book to read in december.
5. My friend jeff is reading *the clever wolf*.

REVIEW THE RULES

- **Capitalize** important words of a **proper noun**, the **title of a book**, and the name of a **day, month,** or **holiday**.

Handbook
pages 525–526

More Practice

A. Write the sentences. Write the words in ( ) correctly.

6. The class is reading a book called (aesop's fables).
7. The author lived long ago in (greece).
8. In (november) the class will start a new book.
9. The book tells a story about (thanksgiving).
10. The book's title is (the first thanksgiving).
11. The author of the book is (toby marner).
12. The story takes place in the town of (plymouth).
13. Plymouth is a town in (massachusetts).
14. The holiday was started by the (pilgrims).
15. Next, we will read about (martin luther king).

B. Spiral Review Write the sentences. Add a subject or end mark. Circle nouns with special plural forms.

16. _____ is reading about the Pilgrims.
17. What foods did they eat
18. The men hunted deer in the woods
19. The _____ grew corn.
20. What a feast they had at Thanksgiving

Extra Practice, page 153

Writing Activity A News Report

Write a news report about a parade you saw. Use words to describe the parade that will keep your readers interested.
APPLY MECHANICS AND USAGE: Include proper nouns in your report and circle the capital letter in each one.

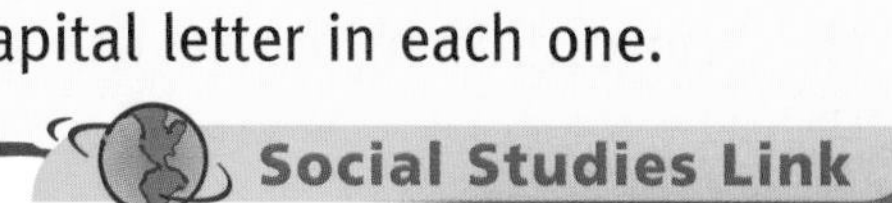

Grammar REVIEW

Mixed Review

REVIEW THE RULES

- A noun names a person, place, or thing.
- A singular noun names one person, place, or thing.
- A plural noun names more than one person, place, or thing.
- Add *-s* or *-es* to form the plural of most singular nouns.
- Form the plural of nouns ending in a consonant and *y* by changing *y* to *i* and adding *-es*.
- Some nouns have special plural forms, and a few nouns have the same singular and plural form.
- A common noun names any person, place, or thing.
- A proper noun names a special person, place, or thing, and begins with a capital letter.

Nouns
Write a sentence about your school or family. Use common, proper, and plural nouns.

Practice

A. Write the sentences. Write each underlined singular noun as a plural noun.

1. We take the child to the farm.
2. Ana sees the small pony in a field.
3. Chuck picks the ripe, red strawberry.
4. Keri picks fruit from the blueberry bush.
5. Tomas helps feed the horse.
6. Some girls watch the pretty butterfly.
7. A boy shouts when he sees the red fox run away.
8. Luke eats the red cherry.
9. The baby goat made the children laugh.
10. The children write about the visit in their diary.

B. Write the sentences. Write the words in ( ) correctly.

11. In (april), many people plant their gardens.

12. Ken works in his garden every (saturday).

13. Ken follows directions in a book titled (city gardens).

14. Many flowers bloom in (may).

15. By (july), the garden is full of plants.

16. Ken's garden is the best garden in (chicago).

17. People walking down (river street) admire it.

18. By (october), the pumpkins are ripe.

19. Ken wants pumpkin pie on (thanksgiving).

20. Thanksgiving is a (november) holiday.

Handbook pages 505–506, 525–526

C. Challenge Write the paragraph. Correct mistakes in plural nouns or proper nouns.

21.–25. Ariel lives in Savoy, massachusetts. She got a surprise on the fourth of july. Some deers made a mess of her garden. They nipped off plants with their strong tooths. Ariel saw the prints of their foots in the soil.

Writing Activity A Book Jacket

Create a jacket for a gardening book. Use an interesting title for the front cover and describe the book on the inside flap. Include important details about the topic.

APPLY GRAMMAR: Use plural and proper nouns in your description. Circle each proper noun.

Art Link

Grammar

Singular Possessive Nouns

RULES

A **possessive noun** is a noun that shows who or what owns or has something.

*The **boy's** camera is new.*
*I liked **Cindy's** pictures.*

Add an **apostrophe** (') and an *s* to a singular noun to make it possessive.

lion + 's = lion's *mother + 's = mother's*

Nouns

In your journal, write how you can make a singular noun show ownership.

Guided Practice

Tell the possessive form of each singular noun.

EXAMPLE: bear *bear's*

1. school
2. Juan
3. girl
4. father
5. Carla
6. wolf
7. teacher
8. friend
9. Mr. Roth
10. team

REVIEW THE RULES

- A possessive noun shows who or what owns something.
- Add an apostrophe (') and an *s* to form the possessive of a singular noun.

More Practice

A. Write the possessive form of each noun in ( ).

11. Today is our (class) field trip.

12. We walk through the (zoo) gates.

13. The (zebra) stripes are black and white.

14. The (gorilla) swing is a huge tire.

15. The (lioness) cubs are playful.

16. Keith is startled by the (tiger) roar.

17. The (elephant) ears are floppy.

18. Everyone laughs at the (monkey) tricks.

19. The (seal) food is small fish.

20. The (zookeeper) day is very busy.

Handbook page 506

B. Spiral Review **Write each sentence. Capitalize each proper noun. Add the correct end mark.**

21. Did you read the book in september

22. The book shows animals in the bronx zoo

23. We told luis about the book

24. Anna read the book on monday

25. Who read the book on tuesday

Extra Practice, page 154

Writing Activity A Paragraph

Write a paragraph about a group trip you took. Make sure your paragraph shows your personal voice.

APPLY GRAMMAR: Use possessive nouns and circle them.

Social Studies Link

Grammar

Plural Possessive Nouns

RULES

Add an apostrophe (') to make most plural nouns possessive.

The farmers' fields are large.

Add an apostrophe (') and an *s* to form the possessive of plural nouns that do not end in *s*.

The children's garden is pretty.

Check the spelling of a plural noun to decide whether to add (') or ('s) to make the noun possessive.

girls + ' = girls'
women + 's = women's

Nouns

How can you decide when a word is a plural possessive noun? Write your answer in your journal.

Guided Practice

Tell whether each word is a singular possessive noun or a plural possessive noun.

EXAMPLE: insect's *singular*

1. farmers'
2. bees'
3. hive's
4. women's
5. Stan's
6. child's
7. Megan's
8. parents'
9. boys'
10. geese's

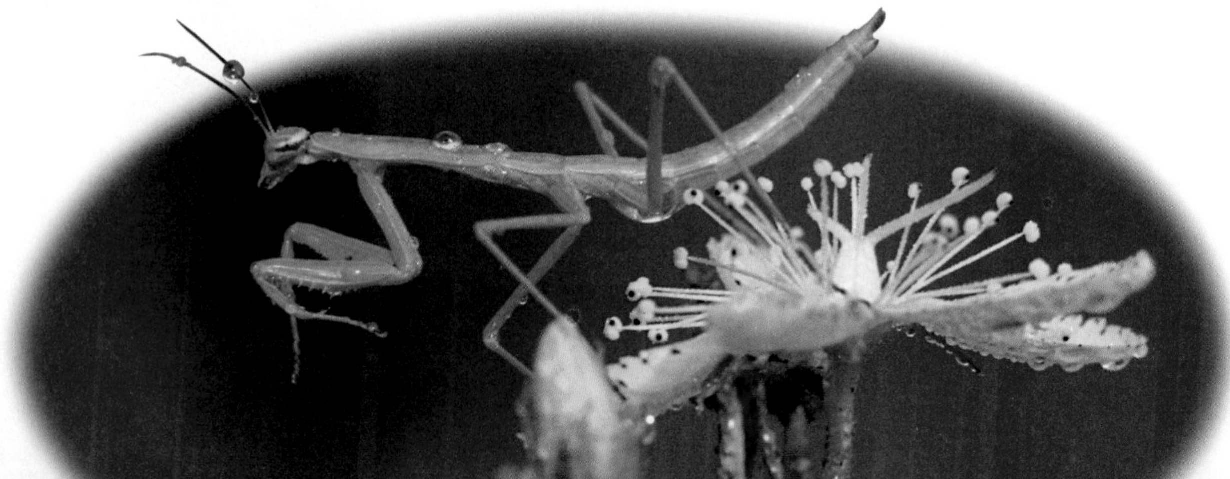

REVIEW THE RULES

- Add an apostrophe (') to form the possessive of most plural nouns.
- Add an apostrophe (') and an *s* to form the possessive of plural nouns that do not end in *s*.

Grammar

More Practice

A. Write the possessive form of the plural noun in ( ).

11. Some insects are (people) friends.

12. Many people love the (bees) honey.

13. Bees sip the (flowers) sweet nectar.

14. Ladybugs are (gardeners) helpers.

15. The (ladybugs) job is eating harmful bugs.

16. The small (beetles) color is often red or yellow.

17. Do you know a (children) song about ladybugs?

18. The praying (mantises) work is helpful, too.

19. The big (insects) strong jaws catch harmful bugs.

20. Some insects eat the (farmers) crops.

Handbook page 506

B. Spiral Review Write each sentence. Draw a line under the subject. Circle each plural noun.

21. Silk comes from the cocoons of silk moths.

22. The silk moths have caterpillars called silkworms.

23. The silkworms produce fine silk threads to make cocoons.

24. Workers unwind the cocoons into threads.

25. Machines weave the silk threads into cloth.

Extra Practice, page 155

Writing Activity A Description

Write a description of an insect. Use colorful words.

APPLY GRAMMAR: Circle plural possessive nouns you use.

Science Link

Grammar

Combining Sentences: Nouns

RULES

You can combine two sentences by joining two nouns.

Use *and* or *or* to join the two nouns. Leave out the words that repeat.

Crows are black birds. Ravens are black birds.
Crows and ravens are black birds.

Sometimes you can join nouns that are subjects.

Joan saw the crows.
Al saw the crows.
→ *Joan and Al saw the crows.*

Sometimes you can join nouns in the predicate.

Birds eat grain.
Birds eat insects.
→ *Birds eat grain or insects.*

Nouns

How can combining sentences make your writing more interesting? Write your answer in your journal.

Guided Practice

Tell how you can combine each pair of sentences.

EXAMPLE: A crow's nest is lined with grass. A crow's nest is lined with feathers.
A crow's nest is lined with grass and feathers.

1. Chuck read about birds. Ria read about birds.
2. Chuck studies owls. Chuck studies hawks.
3. Owls eat small animals. Hawks eat small animals.
4. Ria likes herons. Ria likes cranes.
5. Herons live in Texas. Cranes live in Texas.

REVIEW THE RULES

- Two sentences can be combined by joining two nouns with *and*.

Grammar

More Practice

A. Combine each pair of sentences. Use the word *and* to join two nouns. Write the new sentence.

6. Herons eat fish. Herons eat frogs.
7. Cranes fly south. Robins fly south.
8. Falcons are in danger. Storks are in danger.
9. Passenger pigeons have died out. Dodos have died out.
10. Children save birds. Adults save birds.
11. Ostriches cannot fly. Emus cannot fly.
12. Penguins swim underwater. Loons swim underwater.
13. Birds nest in trees. Birds nest in bushes.
14. Crabs have hard shells. Clams have hard shells.
15. I tell stories about crows. I tell stories about cranes.

Handbook page 507

B. Spiral Review Use *and* to join each pair of sentences. Write the new sentence. Circle possessive nouns.

16. Aesop's stories are famous. People enjoy them.
17. The fables' animals talked. They acted like people.
18. A fox wanted a crow's food. He tricked the crow.
19. The ant's food was stored. It had enough for the winter.
20. The hare's speed did not help. It lost the race.

Extra Practice, page 156

Writing Activity An Ad

Write an ad for a group that wants to save birds. Make sure your ideas keep the reader's attention.

APPLY GRAMMAR: Include sentences in which you have joined two nouns with *and*.

Science Link

Grammar

Abbreviations

RULES

An abbreviation is a shortened form of a word.

Doctor Brown *Dr. Brown*

An abbreviation begins with a capital letter and ends with a period.

You can abbreviate titles before a name.

Mrs. Ruth Shapiro *Mr. John Hudson*
Ms. Martin *Dr. Ana Gomez*

You can abbreviate days of the week.

Sun. Mon. Tues. Wed. Thurs. Fri. Sat.

You can abbreviate some months.

Jan. Feb. Mar. Apr. Aug. Sept. Oct. Nov. Dec.

THINK AND WRITE

Nouns

How can you decide which words to abbreviate? Write your answer in your journal.

Guided Practice

Name what each abbreviation stands for.

EXAMPLE: Apr. *April*

1. Dr.
2. Sat.
3. Mar.
4. Tues.
5. Dec.
6. Jan.
7. Oct.
8. Mon.
9. Mr.
10. Thurs.

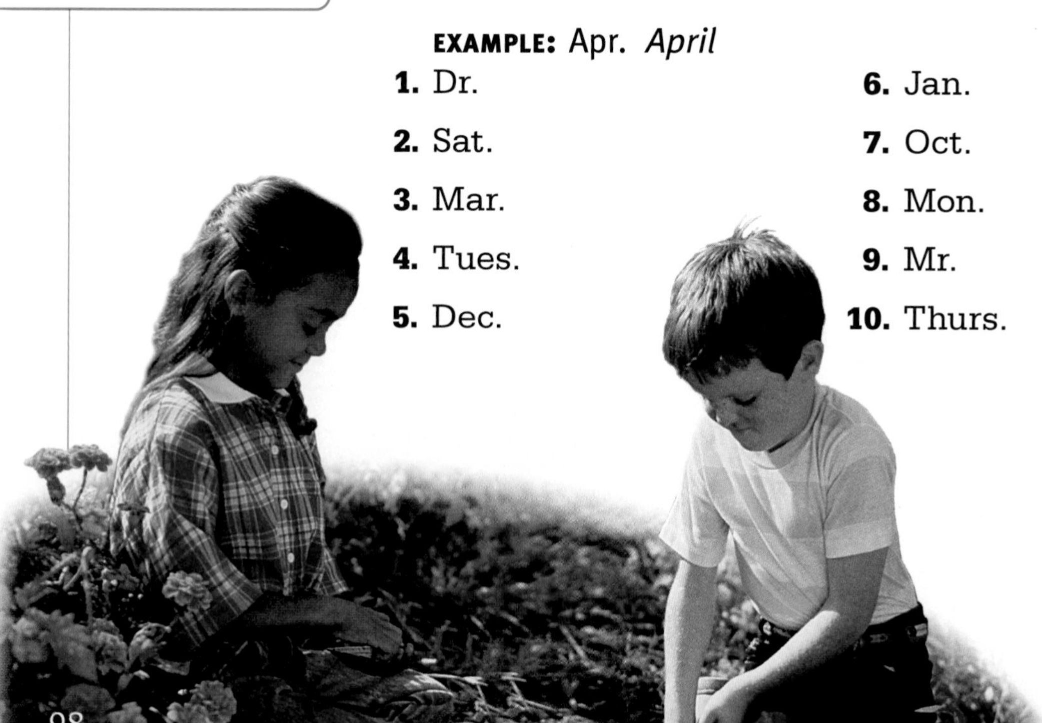

REVIEW THE RULES

- An abbreviation is the shortened form of a word.
- Abbreviations begin with a capital letter and end with a period.

More Practice

A. Write each abbreviation correctly.

11. aug
12. Sun
13. mrs
14. oct.
15. Mr
16. thurs
17. Mar
18. dr
19. apr
20. fri

page 522–523

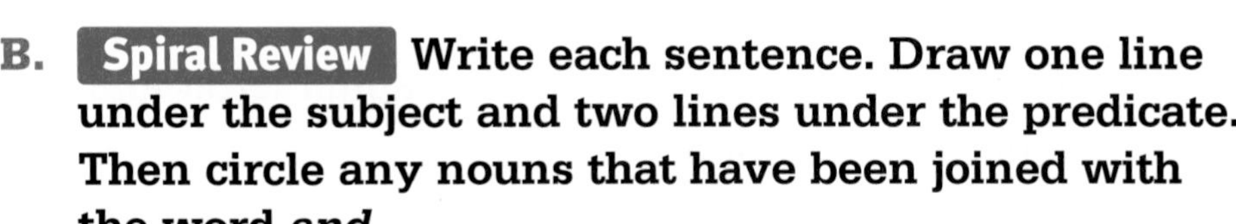

B. Spiral Review Write each sentence. Draw one line under the subject and two lines under the predicate. Then circle any nouns that have been joined with the word *and*.

21. Flowers and trees begin as seeds.
22. Plants need water and sunlight to grow.
23. Insects and animals eat plants.
24. Squirrels eat seeds and nuts.
25. Hummingbirds and bees like flowers.

Extra Practice, page 157

Writing Activity A Letter

Write a letter to the editor of the school newspaper or a local newspaper about a topic that interests you. Make sure your ideas are arranged in a logical order.

APPLY MECHANICS AND USAGE: Use abbreviations in the heading and date in your letter. Draw a line under each abbreviation.

Mixed Review

REVIEW THE RULES

- A possessive noun shows who or what owns something.
- Add an apostrophe (') and an *s* to a singular noun to make it possessive.
- Add an apostrophe to make most plural nouns possessive.
- Add an apostrophe and an *s* to form the possessive of plural nouns that do not end in *s*.
- Two sentences can be combined by joining two nouns with *and*.
- An abbreviation is a shortened form of a word.
- An abbreviation begins with a capital letter and ends with a period.

Nouns

Write a sentence about a new pet and its owner. Use a possessive noun.

Practice

A. Write each sentence. Use the possessive form of the singular or plural noun in ( ).

1. Our (school) pet show is today.
2. Look at all the (children) pets.
3. Two (boys) dogs have fancy collars.
4. My (parrot) cage is decorated with ribbons.
5. I like the spotted (mice) colors.
6. Some (students) pets are unusual.
7. (Carmen) lizard has a long, green tail.
8. There is a castle in (Lucy) fish tank.
9. The (hamsters) wheel is noisy!
10. It is the (judges) job to decide on the winners.

B. Combine each pair of sentences. Use the word *and* to join two nouns.

11. Sandy had pet gerbils. Matt had pet gerbils.

12. Gerbils are cute. Hamsters are cute.

13. The dogs were noisy. The cats were noisy.

14. Charles likes lovebirds. Charles likes parakeets.

15. Parakeets can talk. Parrots can talk.

16. The judges looked at fish. The judges looked at mice.

17. Mr. Rose judged the pet show. Ms. Lewis judged the pet show.

18. The cats were brushed. The kittens were brushed.

19. Two cats won blue ribbons. Two poodles won blue ribbons.

20. The children had fun at the show. The teachers had fun at the show.

Handbook
pages 506–507, 522–523

C. Challenge Write the following paragraph. Correct mistakes in abbreviations and possessive nouns.

21.–25. The school's pet show was held on oct. 2. Many teachers's children brought their pets. The judge's name was mrs Wong. Mr Reynolds helped hand out the prizes. Next apr. we will have another pet show.

Writing Activity A Review

Write a review of a school event. Use vivid words to describe the event.

APPLY GRAMMAR: Include possessive nouns in your review.

Common Errors with Plurals and Possessives

Writers often make mistakes when writing plural nouns and possessive nouns.

Common Errors	Examples	Corrected Sentences
Using an apostrophe in a plural noun	The girl's walk slowly.	The girls walk slowly.
Leaving out an apostrophe in a possessive noun	The girls nose is red.	The girl's nose is red.
Putting an apostrophe in the wrong place in a possessive noun	The childrens' mother was waiting.	The children's mother was waiting.

Nouns

In your journal, explain the difference between plural nouns and possessive nouns.

REVIEW THE RULES

PLURALS AND POSSESSIVES

A plural noun names more than one person, place, or thing. A possessive noun shows who or what owns or has something.

- To form the possessive of a singular noun, add an apostrophe and *s* (*'s*).
- To form the possessive of a plural noun that ends in *-s,* add an apostrophe (').
- To form the possessive of a plural noun that does not end in *-s,* add an apostrophe and *s* (*'s*).
- Remember Most plural nouns are formed by adding *-s* or *-es*.

Practice

A. Read each sentence. Write whether the underlined word is *plural* or *possessive*.

1. The lot is filled with <u>cars</u>.
2. The <u>child's</u> parents watch the game.
3. Their <u>friends</u> come to cheer the team.
4. Five <u>runners</u> race down the track.
5. The judge holds up the <u>winner's</u> hand.

B. Write each sentence. Use the possessive form of each noun in ( ).

6. Stan parked his (parents) car in the lot.
7. He saw his (friend) red cap in the crowd.
8. He walked by some (women) bikes.
9. Stan heard the (children) voices at the baseball game.
10. The (umpire) call was very loud.

C. Write each sentence. Fix the incorrect word in ( ).

11. We saw many (artists) booths at the fair.
12. My two (neighbors') had a rag-doll display.
13. Some (womens) paintings hung in a booth.
14. All the (weavers') showed their rugs.
15. One (girls) greeting cards were for sale.

Troubleshooter pages 492–493

Handbook
pages 505–507

Writing Activity Write About a Fair

Think about what you might see at a fair. Write a paragraph that tells what the fair has on display.
APPLY GRAMMAR: Check the way you write plural nouns and possessive nouns in your paragraph. Make corrections if necessary.

Test Power

TAAS

Mechanics and Spelling

Directions

Read the passage and decide which type of mistake, if any, appears in each underlined section. Choose the correct answer. If there is no mistake, choose "No mistake."

How do you form the plural of most nouns? Check all underlined sections for spelling.

Is there a proper noun here? Remember, all proper nouns begin with a capital letter.

Look for a possessive noun. Does it need an apostrophe?

Sample

Arizona has many different landforms. <u>It has deserts, mountains, and canyons</u> (1). One of the state's deserts is the Sonoran Desert. Lizards and snakes live in the dry desert climate. <u>The mountains of arizona</u> (2), on the other hand, are covered with forests. Animals such as mountain lions, elk, and bighorn sheep live in the mountains. <u>Arizonas Grand Canyon</u> (3) is famous. The walls of the canyon are almost a mile high. Visitors are amazed by its enormous size and beautiful colors.

1
- ○ Spelling
- ○ Capitalization
- ○ Punctuation
- ○ No mistake

2
- ○ Spelling
- ○ Capitalization
- ○ Punctuation
- ○ No mistake

3
- ○ Spelling
- ○ Capitalization
- ○ Punctuation
- ○ No mistake

Test Tip
Take your time and do your work carefully.

Grammar and Usage

Directions

Read the passage and choose the word or group of words that belongs in each space.

Sample

Some very unusual fish live in the deepest part of the ocean. One of the strangest __(1)__ is the viperfish. The viperfish is a very long fish. It has a big head and a big mouth full of several long __(2)__. Sticking out of a fin on the back of the viperfish is a long spine. The tip of this spine glows in the dark ocean water.

The gulper is another strange fish that lives in the deep ocean. It has a body like an eel. A __(3)__ mouth is huge. Its jaws are about one-third the size of its body.

Check to see if the sentence needs a singular or plural noun.

Some nouns have special plural forms.

Add an apostrophe and an s to a singular noun to make it possessive.

1 ○ creature
○ creatures
○ Creature
○ Creatures

2 ○ tooths
○ toothes
○ teeth
○ teeths

3 ○ gulper's
○ gulpers'
○ gulpers
○ gulpers's

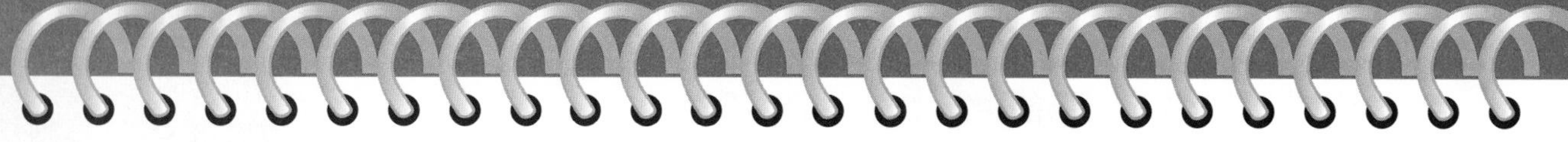

TIME FOR KIDS Writer's Notebook

RESEARCH

RESEARCH

Whenever I want to find a book in the library media center, I use the **card catalog**. Each book is listed in three ways, by author, by subject, and by title, and everything is arranged in ABC order. Sometimes card catalogs are on computers, but other times they're on real cards.

COMPOSITION SKILLS

WRITING WELL

Good writers need to make sure that their stories follow a **logical order**. I put myself in my readers' shoes. I ask myself: "If I were reading this, would I know what this story is about?"

VOCABULARY SKILLS

USING WORDS

Words like artwork and workshop are **compound words**. They are made from two separate words. When I write, I use them to explain a specific idea. What compound words do I know?

Read Now!

As you read the photo essay that follows, jot down two subjects you could research using the library card catalog.

TIME FOR KIDS

PHOTO ESSAY

From TRASH to TREASURE

This helicopter was made from flip-flop sandals. Rubber bands send it flying.

Turning GARBAGE into ART

Mexican bottle-cap furniture.

For hundreds of years, people have been turning their trash into artwork and toys. They twist wire into a tiny bike. Or they shape metal into a boat that floats. More than 800 of these "trash" treasures made up a museum show.

Kids and grown-ups could go to a workshop to make their own art from tin cans or old yogurt containers.

The show proved that recycling means more than tossing out trash. It reminded kids and grown-ups that you don't need a high-tech toy to have fun. "You don't have to have a big expensive toy in order to keep yourself entertained," said Charlene Cerny. She worked on the show. And that's not a lot of garbage!

This squiggly sculpture is made from recycled material.

interNET CONNECTION **Go to www.mhschool.com/language-arts for more information on the topic.**

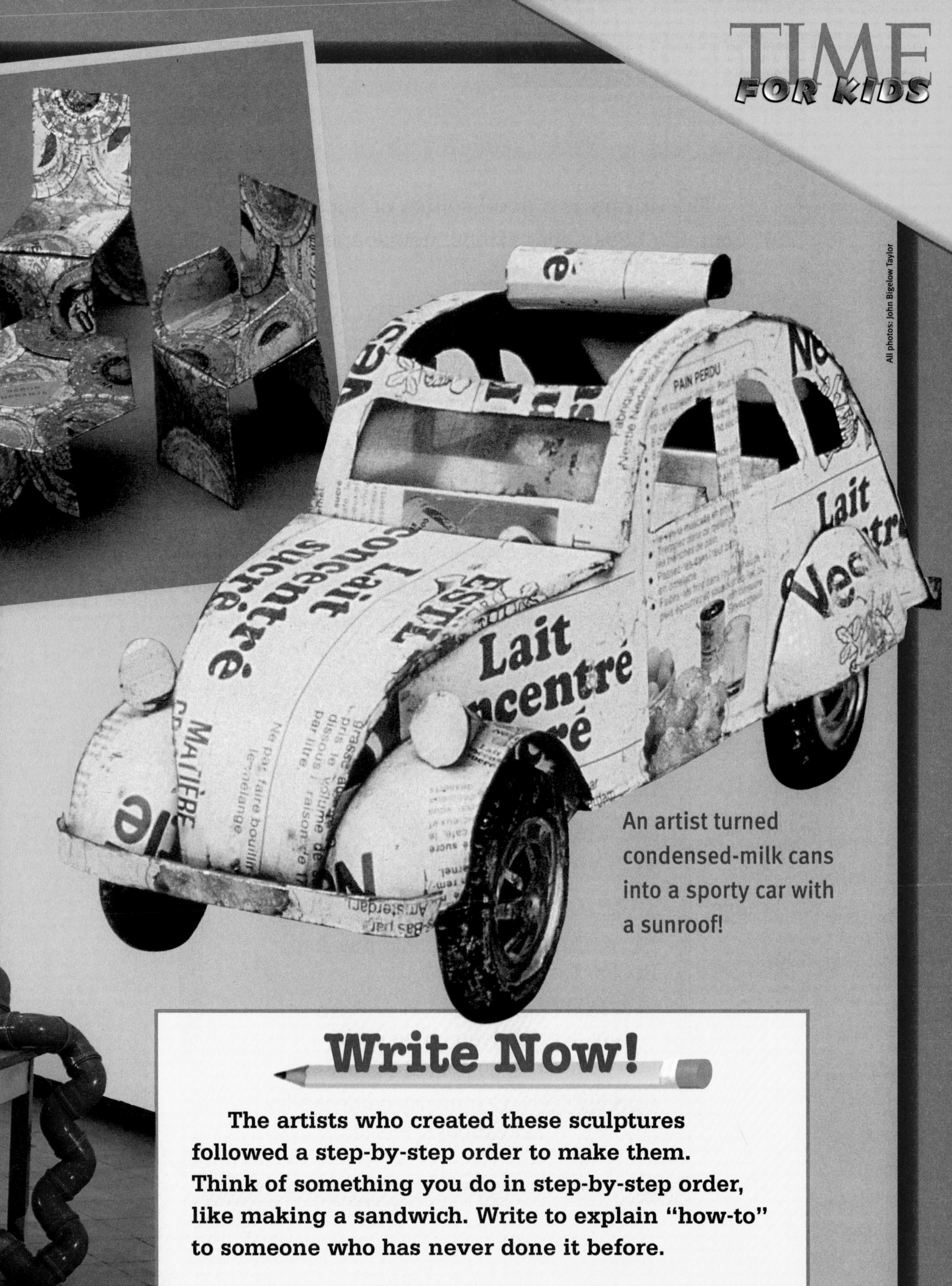

All photos: John Bigelow Taylor

An artist turned condensed-milk cans into a sporty car with a sunroof!

Write Now!

The artists who created these sculptures followed a step-by-step order to make them. Think of something you do in step-by-step order, like making a sandwich. Write to explain "how-to" to someone who has never done it before.

Library Resources

The **library** is a good source of information. The library contains books, magazines, newspapers, videos, CDs, and other materials.

To locate information in a library, you can use the **Library Card Catalog** or **PAC (Public Access Catalog)**. In some libraries, the information is listed on index cards. In most public libraries, the catalog, or PAC, is on the computer.

The card catalog is a list of all the books and other materials that are available in the library. Items are listed three ways: by title, author, and subject.

The card catalog contains a **title card** and an **author card** for every book in the library. Each nonfiction book also has a **subject card**. The cards are arranged in alphabetical order.

The computer catalog in your library may have an item that looks like this.

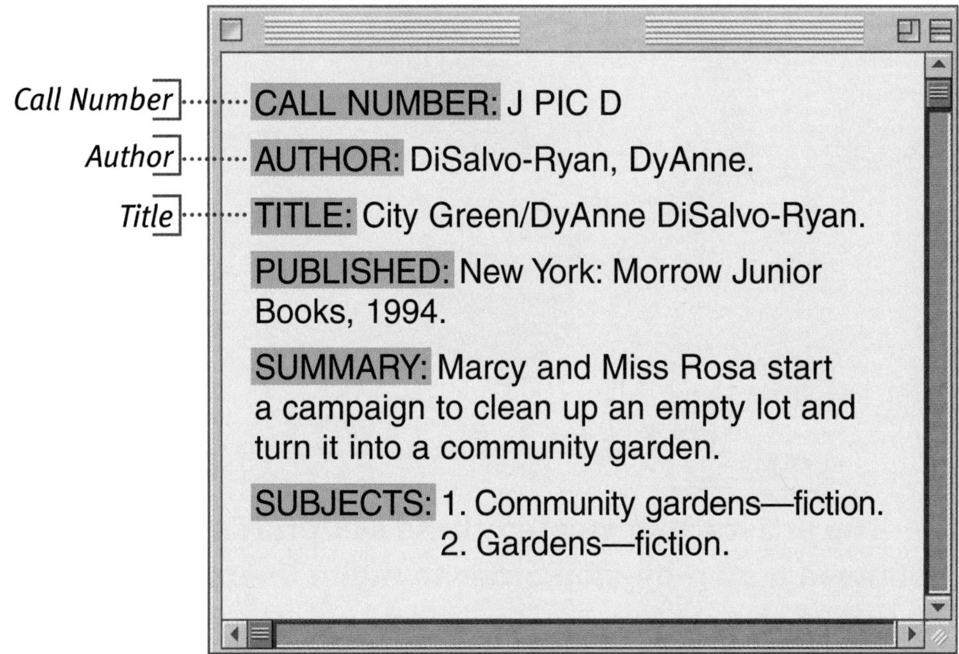

Call Number
Author
Title
CALL NUMBER: J PIC D
AUTHOR: DiSalvo-Ryan, DyAnne.
TITLE: City Green/DyAnne DiSalvo-Ryan.
PUBLISHED: New York: Morrow Junior Books, 1994.
SUMMARY: Marcy and Miss Rosa start a campaign to clean up an empty lot and turn it into a community garden.
SUBJECTS: 1. Community gardens—fiction.
2. Gardens—fiction.

Every book in the library has a **call number**. This number identifies what category of book it is and can help you locate the book on the shelves.

Practice

A. Write what cards in the card catalog you would use to find the following information.

1. Books about how circuses got started
2. A book about flags written by Walter Morris
3. A list of books by Louisa May Alcott
4. A book called *Charlie and the Chocolate Factory*
5. Books about jungle animals

B. Write how each of these aids helps you find information in the library.

6. Card Catalog
7. Title Card
8. Author Card
9. Subject Card
10. Call Number

Go to: www.mhschool.com/language-arts

for more information on using library resources.

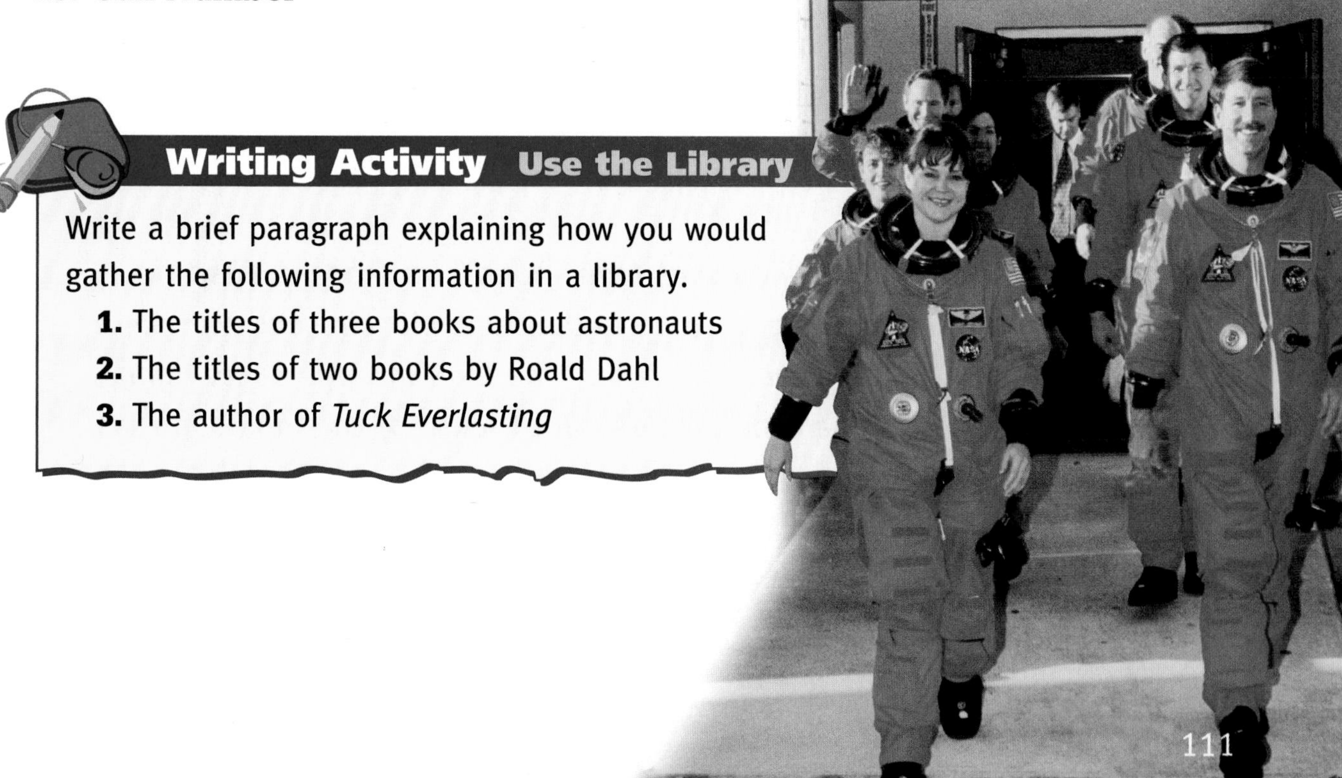

Writing Activity Use the Library

Write a brief paragraph explaining how you would gather the following information in a library.

1. The titles of three books about astronauts
2. The titles of two books by Roald Dahl
3. The author of *Tuck Everlasting*

Vocabulary: Compound Words

DEFINITION

A compound word is a word made from two or more words joined together.

after + noon = afternoon   some + time = sometime

sunlight = light from the sun

bluebird = bird that is blue

birdhouse = house for a bird

notebook = book for notes

seashell = shell from the sea

bathtub = tub for a bath

paintbrush = brush for paint

snowball = ball made of snow

handmade = made by hand

sailboat = boat with a sail

Compound Words

How can you tell the difference between compound words and other words? Write your answer in your journal.

Look at the blue words in the paragraph below. They are compound words.

Pine cones make good bird feeders. First, tie ribbon or string to the cone. Mix birdseed with pieces of bread. Then stuff the food into the cone. Hang the cone outside out of reach of cats and squirrels.

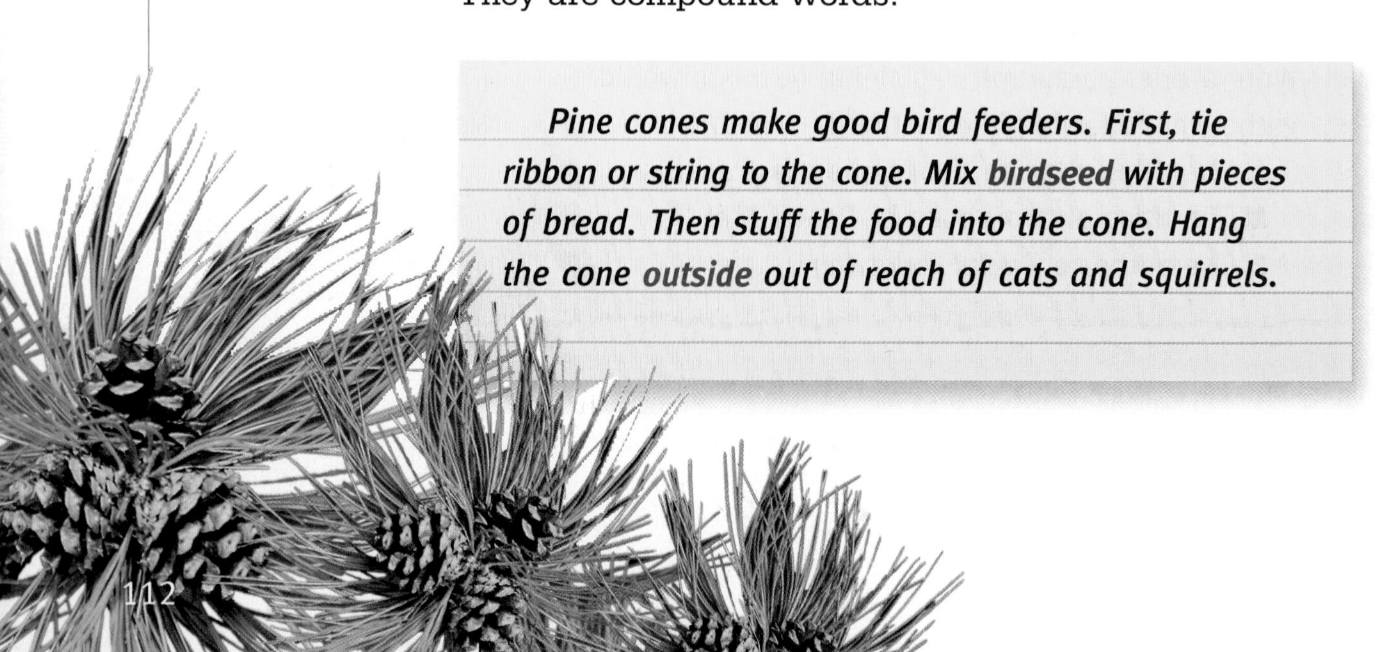

Practice

A. Write the sentences. Circle each compound word.

1. Kate has a bird feeder in her backyard.
2. Kate fills the feeder with sunflower seeds.
3. The bluebirds are very beautiful.
4. Kate takes snapshots of the birds.
5. The girl keeps the pictures in a scrapbook.

A: row	rain	out
high	pan	sun

B: rise	cakes	way
doors	boat	storm

B. Write each sentence. Add a compound word made by joining a word from Box A with a word from Box B.

6. The family camped _____.
7. Kate watched the _____ each morning.
8. Kate and her dad made _____ every day.
9. The family went on the lake in a _____.
10. A sudden _____ soaked them.

C. Grammar Link **Write the sentences. Draw a line between the two words that make up each compound word. Write each proper noun correctly.**

11. We went to the seashore in august.
12. I found some seashells for fred.
13. Seaweed washed up on bailey beach.
14. Tall sailboats dotted casco bay.
15. Next weekend, I will sail on saturday.

Writing Activity A Journal Entry

Write a journal entry about a time you spent outdoors. Tell what you did. Use two compound words.
APPLY GRAMMAR: Use possessive nouns correctly.

Composition: Organization

To help the reader follow ideas, events, or instructions, a writer presents ideas and details in an order that makes sense.

GUIDELINES

- **Begin with a topic sentence that states the main idea.**
- **When you explain how to do something, organize the details in the order in which the instructions need to be carried out.**
- **Write exact, step-by-step details.**

THINK AND WRITE

Organization

How can you organize step-by-step details to make your instructions easy to understand? Write your answer.

Read these instructions. Notice how the writer organizes ideas.

A topic sentence tells what the paragraph is about.

Details tell exactly what to do and are given in step-by-step order.

Time-order words show the order of the steps.

You can make a scope to spy on underwater life. First, cut the top and bottom off a large milk carton. Next, cover the bottom and sides with thick, clear plastic. Hold the plastic to the carton with a rubber band. Then tape the plastic to the inside of the open end. After you put your scope together, take it to a pond or stream. Hold the plastic-covered end in the water. Then look down into the scope. Finally, watch the underwater action!

Practice

A. Write the paragraph. Draw a line under the topic sentence. Circle each time-order word.

1.–5. Make a dog's face from a square of paper. First, fold the square in half to make a triangle. Second, fold the triangle in half to make a smaller triangle. Then hold the triangle so that the longest side is at the top. Next, fold down the right corner and the left corner to form the ears. Last, fold the bottom center point all the way back and draw a face on the dog.

B. Write the sentences. Organize them in an order that makes sense.

6. An ocean in a bottle is fun and interesting.

7. Last, twist on the bottle cap and rock the bottle.

8. Next, use food color to make the water blue.

9. First, fill a clear bottle halfway with water.

10. Then fill the bottle to the top with cooking oil.

C. Grammar Link **Write the sentences in paragraph form. Fill in time-order words where needed. Draw a line under each noun.**

11. You can grow a plant at home.

12. ______, fill a small container with soil.

13. ______, plant a few seeds in the container.

14. ______, sprinkle the seeds with water.

15. ______, place the watered seeds in a sunny window.

Writing Activity A Friendly Letter

Write a letter to a friend explaining something. Organize your ideas in a way that makes sense.

APPLY GRAMMAR: Check to be sure you have used the correct forms of possessive and plural nouns. Circle any irregular plural nouns.

TAAS

Better Sentences

Directions

Read the passage. Some parts are underlined.
The underlined parts may be one of the following:

- **Incomplete sentences**
- **Run-on sentences**
- **Correctly written sentences that should be combined**

Choose the best way to write each underlined part.

A complete sentence has both a subject and a predicate.

Look for sentences with the same words that can be combined to make one sentence.

Sample

Here's how to make a wind vane. First, an arrow out of cardboard. **(1)** Next, attach a straw to one side of the arrow. Then push a pin through the straw. You can also push a needle through a straw. **(2)** Finally, push the point of the pin into the eraser of a pencil. Test your wind vane outdoors on a windy day.

1 ○ First, an arrow and cardboard.
○ First an arrow, then cardboard.
○ First, cut an arrow out of cardboard.

2 ○ Then push through the straw.
○ Then push a pin or needle through the straw.
○ Then push a pin and through the straw.

Test Tip
Read the passage slowly and carefully.

Vocabulary and Comprehension

TAAS

Directions

Read the passage. Then read each question that follows the passage. Choose the best answer to each question.

Sample

Yesterday, I saw something in the field by my house. I didn't see it right away. Its color matched the grass. Then it moved. Although it had wings, it didn't fly. It did a lot of jumping. I thought it was a <u>grasshopper</u>. Its body was about three inches long. It had big eyes on the sides of its head. I looked it up in my bug book. It was a grasshopper.

Look for smaller words that have been combined to make the compound word.

1 What does the word <u>grasshopper</u> mean in this passage?

- ○ a plant that looks like grass
- ○ an insect that hops in the grass
- ○ a hopping dance
- ○ a color

2 What conclusion can you draw about a grasshopper, based on the facts presented?

- ○ It can fly.
- ○ It eats a lot.
- ○ It is easy to see.
- ○ It is green.

Seeing Like a Writer

What tasks are being done in the pictures? Think about how you would explain these tasks. What details would you include? How would you organize the details?

El Picapedrero by Diego Rivera.

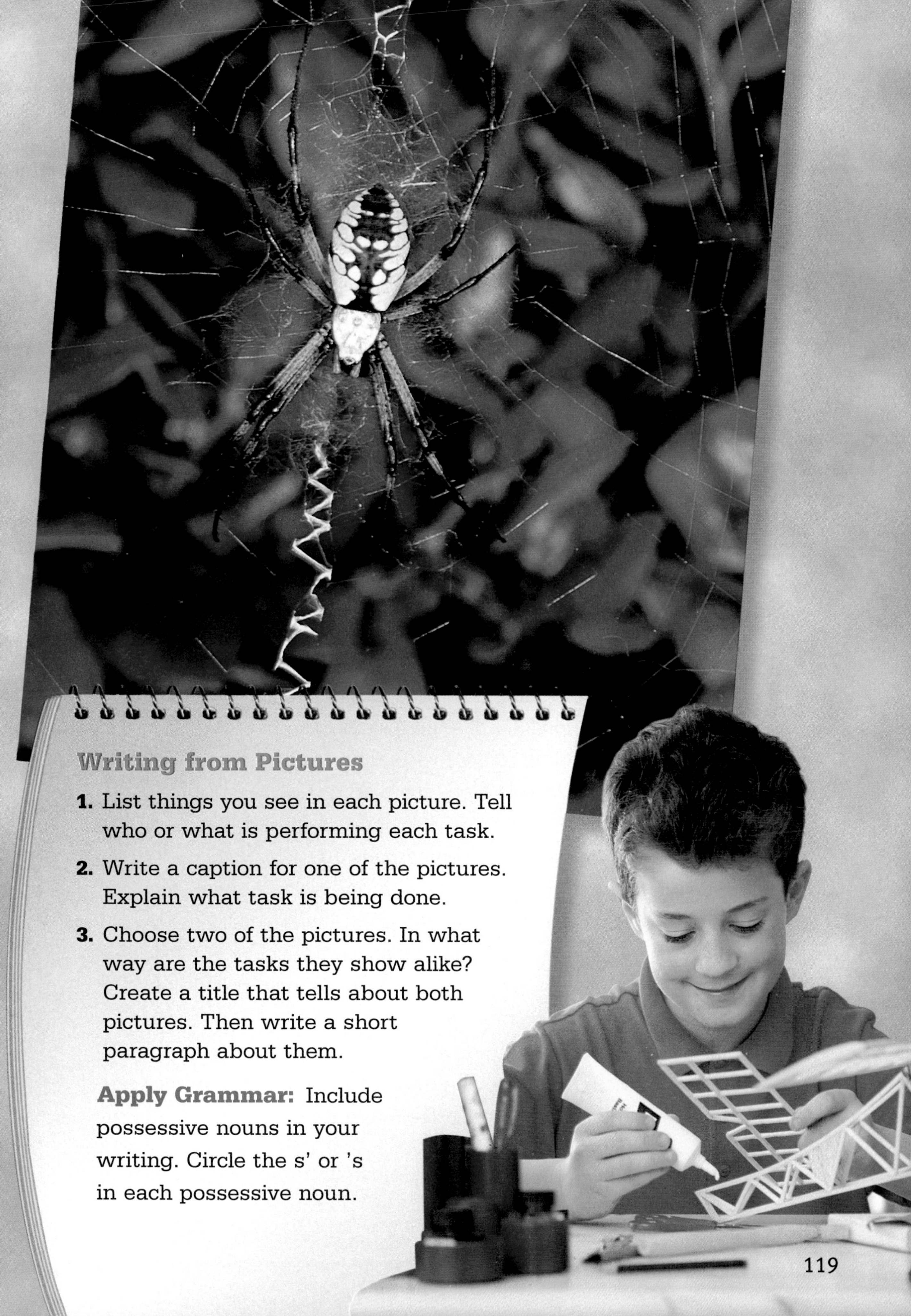

Writing from Pictures

1. List things you see in each picture. Tell who or what is performing each task.
2. Write a caption for one of the pictures. Explain what task is being done.
3. Choose two of the pictures. In what way are the tasks they show alike? Create a title that tells about both pictures. Then write a short paragraph about them.

Apply Grammar: Include possessive nouns in your writing. Circle the s' or 's in each possessive noun.

Explanatory Writing

Have you ever told someone how to do or make something? Explanatory writing explains how to do something step by step.

THINK AND WRITE

Purpose

Why do you think people write and read instructions? Write your answer in your journal.

Learning from Writers

Read the following examples of explanatory writing. What do the writers explain? How did they organize their writing? As you read, look for exact details and words that help the reader understand the order of the steps.

Nature's Web Maker

The garden spider is one of nature's best builders. Let's look at how it makes its web between two plants.

First, the spider makes a bridge line by spinning out a long silk thread. Air currents blow one end of this thread to another plant where it sticks. The spider travels along the bridge line it has made. It drops another line down to a plant below and travels down it. Then it comes back up with another silk thread to make a triangle. The spider keeps spinning. Back and forth, up and down, the spider goes. The web now looks something like the spokes of a wheel. Then the spider lays the trap—a long thread of sticky silk that spirals around the spokes until it reaches the center of the wheel. When the spider gets a victim, it can race down the spokes because they are dry, not sticky, and capture its prey.

—Diane Hoyt-Goldsmith, from *Spiders at Work*

How to Plan a Family Picnic

You can have a good family picnic if you follow some simple steps. First, pick the perfect spot. This might be a park or a lake. Second, make sure that everyone will like the food on the menu. It would be awful to spend all that time cooking and find out that your cousins hate chicken! Third, give everyone a little job to do. If Uncle Harry is minding the little kids, they won't stick their fingers in the pies. Fourth, serve the food before everyone gets too hungry. Finally, make sure everyone at the picnic helps clean up. Follow these rules, and your family will have a lot of fun.

— Miguel Santos

Practice and Apply

Thinking Like a Reader

1. In "Nature's Web Maker," how does the spider begin its web?
2. How many steps are explained in "How to Plan a Family Picnic"? Name them.

Thinking Like a Writer

3. In "Nature's Web Maker," what details are used to make the first step clear?
4. How did the author of "How to Plan a Family Picnic" make the order of the steps clear?

5. **Reading Across Texts** Compare how the instructions in the two samples are organized. Tell what is the same and what is different.

Features of Explanatory Writing

DEFINITIONS AND FEATURES

Explanatory writing gives directions or explains how to do something. Good explanatory writing:

- Tells **how to** complete a specific task.
- Presents **step-by-step instructions.**
- Gives **clear details** that are easy to follow.
- Uses **time-order** or **space-order words** to make instructions clear.

How To

Reread "Nature's Web Maker" by Diane Hoyt-Goldsmith on page 120. What specific task does the author explain?

> The garden spider is one of nature's best builders. Let's look at how it makes its web between two plants.

The first two sentences tell what the writing will explain.

Step-by-Step Instructions

When you write instructions, the steps need to be in the order they are carried out.

> First, the spider makes a bridge line by spinning out a long silk thread. Air currents blow one end of this thread to another plant where it sticks.

What time-order word helps make the steps easier to follow?

▶ Clear Details

Exact details help your readers understand each step. The sentence below describes how the web looks.

> The web now looks something like the spokes of a wheel.

Can you picture in your mind exactly how the web looks?

▶ Space-Order Words

Sometimes it is just as important to show *where* something takes place as *when* it takes place. To help your readers clearly understand directions, use space-order words, such as *up*, *across*, *between*, *in front of*, and *under*.

> The spider travels along the bridge line it has made. It drops another line down to a plant below and travels down it.

What space-order words did the author use?

Practice and Apply

Create a Features Chart

1. List the features of good explanatory writing.
2. Reread "How to Plan a Family Picnic" by Miguel Santos on page 121.
3. Write one example of each feature in Miguel's writing.
4. Write the feature of Miguel's writing that was most helpful to you in following the instructions.

Features	Examples

Prewrite

Explanatory writing gives directions or explains how to do or make something. Writing how-to instructions gives you a chance to share what you know how to do.

Purpose and Audience

The purpose of writing instructions is to explain how to complete a task step by step.

Think about your audience before you begin to write. Who will be following your directions? How can you make them easy to understand?

Audience

How can you help your readers follow the directions? Write your answer.

Choose a Topic

Begin by **brainstorming** a list of things you know how to do well. Choose a topic your readers might be interested in.

After choosing your topic, **explore ideas** by listing the steps to follow. Think about the order of each step.

I explored my ideas by listing the steps.

<u>A Cake for Birds</u>

Get foods birds like.

Mix them together.

Press them into a cake.

Chill the cake.

Put it outside.

Organize • Sequence

When you explain how to do something, you write the steps in a certain order, or sequence. To plan your instructions, you can use a sequence chart. Start with a sentence that helps your audience understand your purpose. List in order the steps you need to follow. What idea has this writer added to his chart?

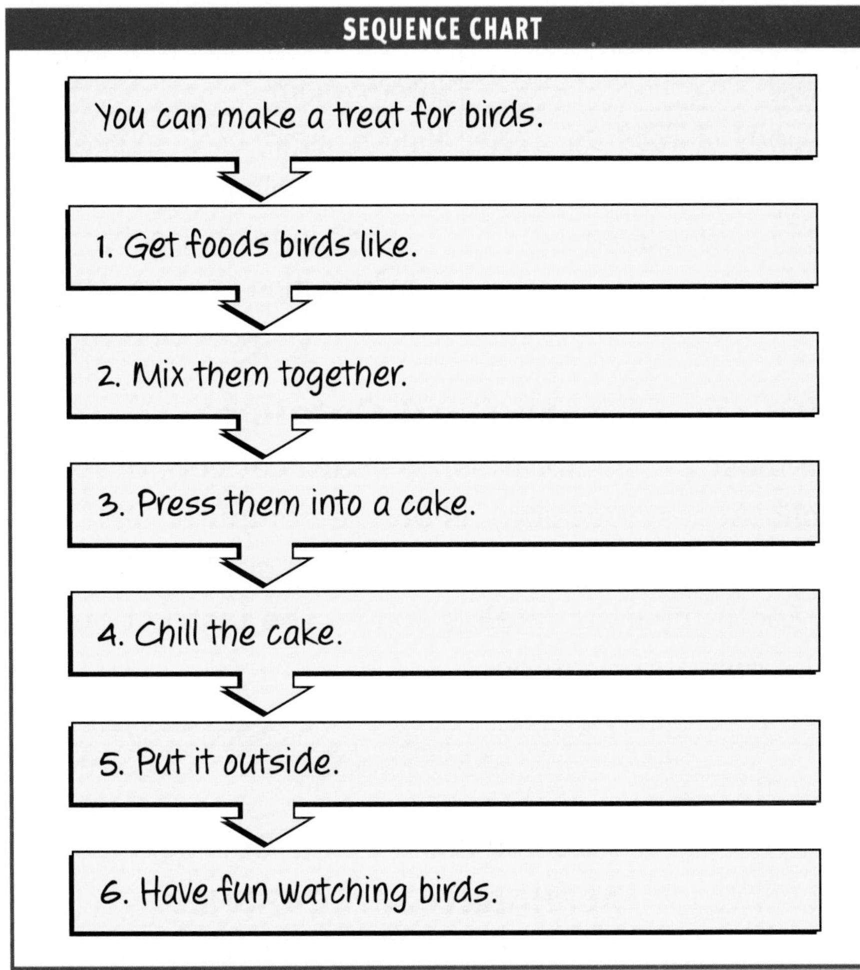

SEQUENCE CHART
You can make a treat for birds.
1. Get foods birds like.
2. Mix them together.
3. Press them into a cake.
4. Chill the cake.
5. Put it outside.
6. Have fun watching birds.

Checklist

Prewriting

- Have you thought about your purpose and audience?
- Have you chosen a topic and explored ideas about it?
- Are your ideas organized in a chart?
- Did you begin by stating your purpose?
- Have you checked the order of the steps?
- Do you need to do any research?

Practice and Apply

Plan Your Own Instructions

1. Brainstorm ideas for a topic.
2. Think about your purpose and audience.
3. Choose a topic.
4. Organize the details in step-by-step order.

Writing PROCESS

Prewrite • Research and Inquiry

▶ Writer's Resources

You may need to do some research to get more information for your instructions. First, make a list of your questions. Then decide what resources you need in order to answer your questions.

What Else Do I Need to Know?	Where Can I Find the Information?
What kinds of food do birds like?	Find a library book on birds.
Where should you put the cake?	Use the table of contents or the index to locate information.

▶ Use the Library Card Catalog

In most public libraries, the card catalog, or PAC (Public Access Catalog), is on the computer. All books are listed by author, title, and subject. To use the electronic card catalog, follow the instructions on the computer screen.

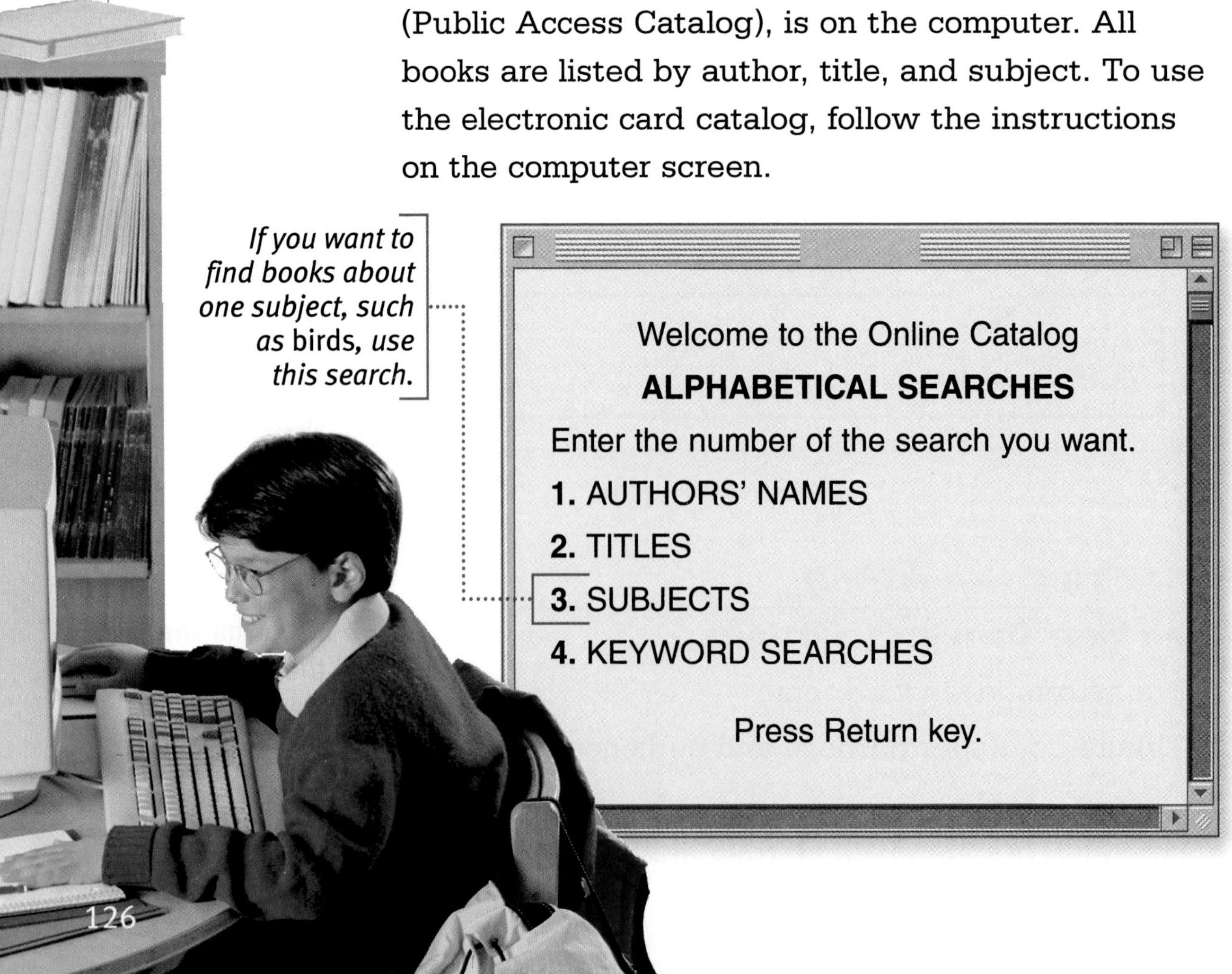

If you want to find books about one subject, such as birds, *use this search.*
Welcome to the Online Catalog
ALPHABETICAL SEARCHES
Enter the number of the search you want.
1. AUTHORS' NAMES
2. TITLES
3. SUBJECTS
4. KEYWORD SEARCHES
Press Return key.

▶ Use Parts of a Book

The table of contents appears at the front of a book. It lists the titles and beginning page numbers of all the sections of the book. An index appears at the back of a book. It lists all the important topics in alphabetical order. The index and the table of contents can help you find information quickly.

▶ Use Your Research

You can add the new information gathered from your research to your sequence chart. The writer learned some important things from his research. How did he change his chart?

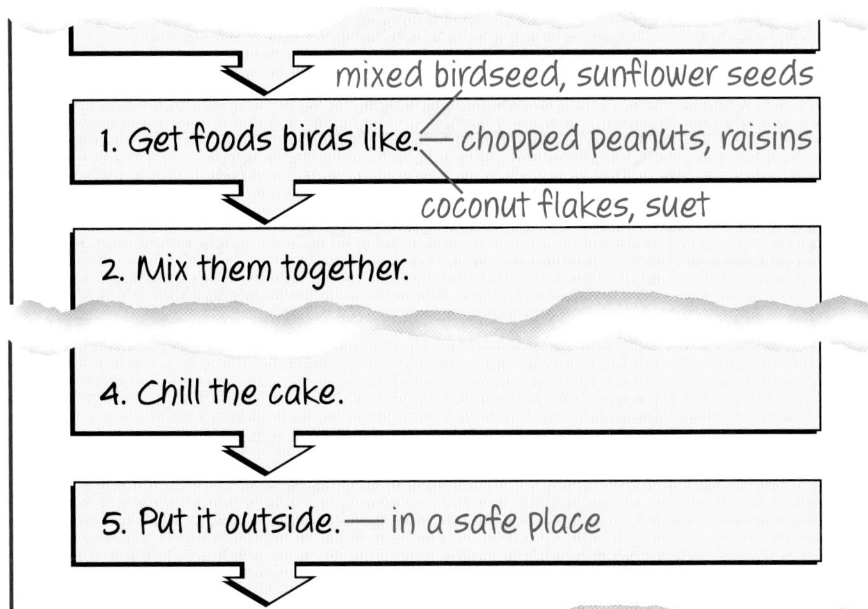

mixed birdseed, sunflower seeds
1. Get foods birds like.— chopped peanuts, raisins
coconut flakes, suet
2. Mix them together.
4. Chill the cake.
5. Put it outside.— in a safe place

Handbook
pages 532–534

Research and Inquiry

- Did you list your questions?
- Did you identify possible resources?
- Did you take notes?

PRACTICE and APPLY

Review Your Plan

1. Look at your prewriting chart.
2. List questions you have about your topic.
3. Identify the resources that will help you find answers to your questions.
4. Add new information you gather to your chart.

Writing PROCESS

Draft

Before you begin writing your instructions, review the chart you made. Which steps are related? Think about putting related steps in the same paragraph. Include details that describe the steps and support the main idea of each paragraph.

SEQUENCE CHART
You can make a treat for birds
Main idea for first paragraph: What you can make and what you need
1. Get foods birds like.
mixed birdseed, sunflower seeds
chopped peanuts, raisins
coconut flakes, suet
2. Mix them together.
3. Press them into a cake.
Main idea for second paragraph: Order of steps telling how to make the cake
4. Chill the cake.
5. Put it outside. — in a safe place
6. Have fun watching birds.
This idea can be a good ending.

Checklist

Drafting

- Does your how-to writing fit your purpose and audience?
- Have you told how to complete a task?
- Have you presented step-by-step directions?
- Did you include details that are easy to follow?

PREWRITE
DRAFT
REVISE
PROOFREAD
PUBLISH

Look at how this writer used the ideas in his chart to write a first draft. He began with a topic sentence that stated the main idea. In the first paragraph, he added details about the foods birds like. In the second paragraph, he wrote the directions in step-by-step order.

DRAFT

You can make a treat to feed birds. First, gather foods that birds like. You can use mixed birdseed. You can use sunflower seeds. Add some chopped peanuts, raisins, or coconut flakes. You also need some suet to hold the foods together.

Put all the ingredients in a bowl and mix them together Press down hard to form a cake. Chill the cake. When the suet cake is firm, remove it from the bowl. Put the birds treet outside where they can reach it safely. Finally, have fun watching the birds enjoy their treat!

Main idea of first paragraph

Details tell what you will need.

Directions are given in step-by-step order.

Last sentence is a good ending.

TECHNOLOGY

Give your document a name that you will remember. You may wish to include the word *draft* in the name.

PRACTICE and APPLY

Draft Your Own Instructions

1. Review your prewriting chart.
2. Explain how to do or make something.
3. Write directions in step-by-step order.

Revise

Elaborate

When you elaborate, you add ideas and details that make your writing clearer and more interesting. When you revise your instructions, you may wish to add words that explain the meaning of unfamiliar words.

By adding these details, the writer makes the opening sentence livelier.

> special hungry
> You can make a ^ treat to feed ^ birds.

The writer added words that tell the reader the meaning of the word *suet*.

> Add some chopped peanuts, raisins, or coconut flakes. You also need some suet ^, or hard fat, to hold the foods together.

SPACE-ORDER WORDS

top
above
over
middle
halfway
between
bottom
down
below
under
inside
outside
beside

Word Choice

When you are writing, it is important to choose just the right words for your topic and purpose.

In how-to writing, you need to use words that show the order of the steps to follow. You also need to choose words that describe where things go.

> Next,
> ^ Put all the ingredients in a bowl and mix them together. Press down hard to form a cake ^ in the bottom of the bowl.

Better Sentences

As you revise your draft, check your sentences to make sure they go together well. Read the sentences aloud. Are they all short? Do they repeat words and sound choppy? If so, you may want to combine two short sentences into one longer sentence.

Sometimes you can combine sentences by joining two nouns.

> You can use mixed birdseed. ~~You can use~~ and sunflower seeds.

PREWRITE
DRAFT
REVISE
PROOFREAD
PUBLISH

Handbook
page 507

PRACTICE and APPLY

Revise Your Own Instructions

1. Take out information that is not necessary.
2. Add details that will make your writing clearer and more interesting.
3. Add time-order or space-order words.
4. **Grammar** Can you combine any short sentences?

TECHNOLOGY

When you begin revising your draft, you can rename your work using the SAVE AS feature so that you can cut and paste from the original work if you change your mind.

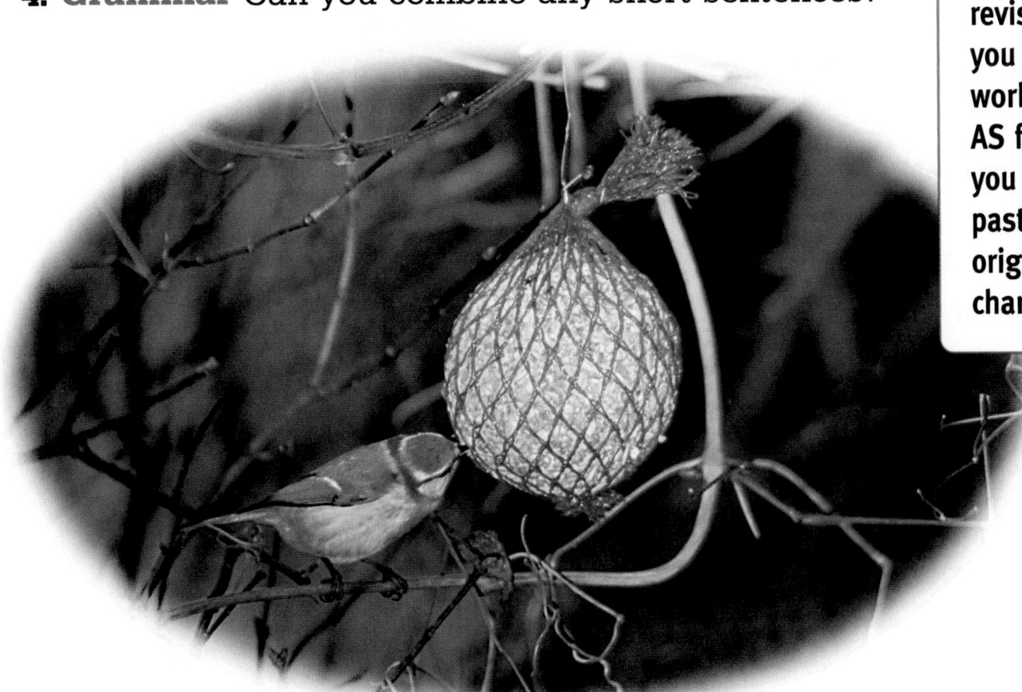

Writing PROCESS

Revise • Peer Conferencing

Share your first draft with a partner. Your partner may have some helpful suggestions.

This sounds like fun to do!

How do you chill the cake?

Where would a safe place be?

Good ending!

You can make a treat to feed birds. First, gather foods that birds like. You can use mixed birdseed. You can use sunflower seeds. Add some chopped peanuts, raisins, or coconut flakes. You also need some suet to hold the foods together.

Put all the ingredients in a bowl and mix them together Press down hard to form a cake. Chill the cake. When the suet cake is firm, remove it from the bowl. Put the birds treet outside where they can reach it safely. Finally, have fun watching the birds enjoy their treat!

Conferencing for the Reader

- Does your partner's piece have the features of explanatory writing?
  - tells how to do or make something
  - step-by-step instructions
  - clear details
  - time-order or space-order words
- Be sure to tell your partner what you liked about the piece, as well as ways to improve it.

As you revise your instructions, think about your partner's comments and suggestions. This writer made some changes based on his partner's ideas.

REVISE

How to make a cake for Birds

You can make a special treat to feed hungry birds. First, gather foods that birds like. You can use mixed birdseed ~~. You can use~~ and sunflower seeds. Add some chopped peanuts, raisins, or coconut flakes. You also need some suet, or hard fat, to hold the foods together. Next, put all the ingredients in a bowl and mix them together Press down hard to form a cake in the bottom of the bowl. Chill the cake in the refrigerator. When the suet cake is firm, remove it from the bowl. Put the birds treet outside where they can reach it safely. A good place is on top of a pole. Finally, have fun watching the birds enjoy their treat!

Practice and Apply

Revise Your Own Instructions

1. Share your draft with a partner and write down your partner's helpful suggestions.
2. Use information from your peer conference to improve your draft.
3. Read your draft aloud and listen to how it sounds.
4. Think of a good title.

Checklist

Revising

- Do your instructions suit your purpose and audience?
- Did you write the instructions in step-by-step order? Did you describe each step in detail?
- Have you included time-order and space-order words?
- Do you like how your sentences sound?
- Did you add a good title?

Proofread

After you have revised your how-to writing, you will need to proofread it to find and correct any mistakes in mechanics, grammar and usage, and spelling.

STRATEGIES FOR PROOFREADING

- Reread your revised instructions. Each time, look for a different type of mistake. **That way, you'll have a better chance of catching all the mistakes.**
- Read the title for correct capitalization of important words.
- Check the ending of each possessive noun.
- Reread for missing end marks.
- Check each word carefully for spelling mistakes.

Spelling

When a one-syllable word ends in one vowel followed by one consonant, double the consonant before adding an ending that begins with a vowel. *(chop + ed = chopped)*

REVIEW THE RULES

GRAMMAR

- To form possessive nouns: **Add an apostrophe (') and an *s* to a singular noun and to plural nouns that do not end in *s*. Add an apostrophe to most plural nouns that end in *s*.**
- **You can combine two sentences by joining nouns with the word *and*. Leave out the words that repeat.**

MECHANICS

- **Each important word in a** proper noun **and a** book title **begins with a capital letter.**
- **An** abbreviation **begins with a capital letter and ends with a period.**

Look at the proofreading corrections made on the draft below. What does the proofreading mark ≡ mean? Why does the writer use this mark?

PROOFREAD

How to make a cake for Birds

You can make a special treat to feed hungry birds. First, gather foods that birds like. You can use mixed birdseed and ~~You can use~~ sunflower seeds. Add some chopped peanuts, raisins, or coconut flakes. You also need some suet, or hard fat, to hold the foods together.

Next, Put all the ingredients in a bowl and mix them together. Press down hard to form a cake in the bottom of the bowl. Chill the cake in the refrigerator.

When the suet cake is firm, remove it from the bowl. Put the bird's, treat ~~treet~~ outside where they can reach it safely. A good place is on top of a pole. Finally, have fun watching the birds enjoy their treat!

PREWRITE

DRAFT

REVISE

PROOFREAD

PUBLISH

Checklist ✓

Proofreading

- Do you use capital letters correctly?
- Did you add the correct ending to possessive nouns?
- Did you indent each paragraph?
- Did you spell all the words correctly?

PROOFREADING MARKS

- ¶ new paragraph
- ^ add
- ~~~ take out
- ≡ Make a capital letter.
- / Make a small letter.
- (sp) Check the spelling.
- ⊙ Add a period.

PRACTICE and APPLY

Proofread Your Own Instructions

1. Correct any mistakes in capitalization.
2. Fix incorrect endings of possessive nouns.
3. Correct spelling mistakes.
4. Indent each paragraph.

Publish

Before you publish, review your instructions one more time. A checklist like the one below can help you.

Self-Check Explanatory Writing

- ☐ **What was my purpose? Did I state it in a topic sentence at the beginning?**
- ☐ **Who was my audience? Did I use clear details that will help everyone follow my instructions?**
- ☐ **Did I write the instructions in a step-by-step order?**
- ☐ **Did I use time-order or space-order words to help the audience understand what to do?**
- ☐ **Did I use different types of sentences? Do they fit together well?**
- ☐ **Did I proofread carefully and correct any mistakes?**

The writer used the checklist to review his instructions. Read "How to Make a Cake for Birds" and discuss the published piece. Do you think it was ready to publish? Why do you think so?

How to Make a Cake for Birds

by Jeff Moore

You can make a special treat to feed hungry birds. First, gather foods that birds like. You can use mixed birdseed and sunflower seeds. Add some chopped peanuts, raisins, or coconut flakes. You also need some suet, or hard fat, to hold the foods together.

Next, put all the ingredients in a bowl and mix them together. Press down hard to form a cake in the bottom of the bowl. Chill the cake in the refrigerator.

When the suet cake is firm, remove it from the bowl. Put the birds' treat outside where they can reach it safely. A good place is on top of a pole. Finally, have fun watching the birds enjoy their treat!

Handwriting

If you are not writing on a computer, use your neatest handwriting when you publish. Write on one side of the paper only and leave wide margins on all sides.

PRACTICE and APPLY

Publish Your Own Instructions

1. Give your revised draft one final check.
2. Copy your draft neatly.
3. Add some drawings or photos.

LISTENING
SPEAKING
VIEWING
PRESENTING

Present Your Explanatory Writing

To present your instructions successfully, you need to plan and practice. There are things you can do to give a good presentation.

STEP 1

How to Give Your Instructions

Strategies for Speaking Remember that your purpose is to explain how to do or make something. Try to help your listeners understand your directions.

- On note cards, write your instructions in step-by-step order.
- Look directly at your audience.
- Speak slowly and clearly, and loudly enough so that everyone can hear.

Listening Strategies

- **Set a purpose. Are you listening to find out how to do something or for enjoyment?**
- **Try to picture in your mind the steps the speaker is describing.**
- **Listen quietly and politely. Let the speaker know you are interested in what she or he is saying.**
- **Hold your questions until the speaker is finished.**

Multimedia Ideas

Do you have access to video equipment? You may want to have someone videotape you as you carry out the directions. You can talk about each step as you do it.

STEP 2

How to Show Your Instructions

Suggestions for Visuals Visuals can add interest and make your presentation clearer.

- A large poster can show the most important steps in your instructions.
- A drawing or diagram can help your audience understand how to make something.
- You can show a videotape or still photos of someone following the steps in your instructions.

Be sure to write clear labels or captions for your visuals.

STEP 3

How to Share Your Instructions

Strategies for Rehearsing The more you practice, the more comfortable you will feel when you present your instructions to an audience.

- Make your presentation to a friend or family member and ask for suggestions.
- Tape-record yourself. Then listen and think about ways to improve the way you sound.
- Rehearse in front of a mirror.

Viewing Strategies

- **Watch the speaker's gestures.**
- **Look carefully at any visual displays. Visuals may show details that the speaker does not tell you.**
- **Read all the labels and captions on the visuals.**

Practice and Apply

Present Your Own Instructions

1. Write step-by-step directions on note cards.
2. Choose or create photos, drawings, or diagrams to help your audience understand your directions.
3. Practice presenting your instructions out loud in front of a mirror.

TAAS

Writing Tests

On a writing test, you are asked to write one or more paragraphs in response to a prompt. Remember to read the prompt carefully. Look for key words and phrases that describe the topic and explain how you should present your ideas.

Who will be the audience for the writing?

What is the purpose? Is it supposed to entertain, influence, or inform ?

Look for words that tell what kind of writing this is.

Prompt

Think of a science project you did in school.

Write a paragraph <u>for your teacher</u> <u>explaining how</u> you did the project. Be sure to include details about <u>what you did and how you did it</u>.

How to Read a Prompt

Purpose Read the prompt again and look for key words that tell you the purpose of the writing. In this prompt, the words "explaining how" tell you that the purpose is to inform.

Audience Sometimes a prompt will tell you whom to write for. This prompt tells you that your audience is your teacher.

Explanatory Writing The words "what you did and how you did it" tell you that this is explanatory writing. When you do explanatory writing, you explain how to do something. Explanatory writing gives step-by-step instructions and clear details that are easy to follow.

Test Tip
Read the prompt carefully before you begin to write.

How to Write to a Prompt

Here are some tips to remember when you are given a writing prompt.

Before Writing **Content/Ideas**	• Know the purpose of your writing. • Keep your audience in mind. • Make notes about the steps you want to include.
During Writing **Organization/ Paragraph Structure**	• Write a good topic sentence. • In explanatory writing, put the steps in an order that is easy to follow. • Use time-order or space-order words to make instructions clear.
After Writing **Grammar/Usage**	• Proofread your writing. • Check for correct capitalization. • Check punctuation. • Correct any misspelled words. • Be sure you used the correct forms of singular and plural nouns.

Apply What You Learned

Always look for purpose and audience in a prompt. Figure out the kind of writing. Think about how you will organize your ideas.

Prompt

A friend of yours has never taken a book out of the library.

Write directions telling your friend how to take out a book. Explain all the steps. Give details that are clear.

Unit 2 Review

Grammar and Writing Review

pages 78–79

Nouns

A. Write each sentence. Draw a line under the nouns.

1. The boy watched the fish.
2. A gray shark swam in the sea.
3. An eel wriggled like a snake.
4. Small fish gathered in a school.
5. One fish had yellow stripes.

pages 80–83

Singular and Plural Nouns

B. Write each sentence. Use the plural of the noun in ( ).

6. Lucy and Tim found some berry (bush).
7. Tim began picking (berry).
8. Tim's (finger) were stained purple.
9. Tim's (lip) were purple, too!
10. Lucy and Tim brought the fruit to their (family).

pages 84–85

Irregular Plural Nouns

C. Write each sentence. Use the plural of the noun in ( ).

11. Three (woman) hiked in the woods.
12. The group saw two shy (deer).
13. A flock of (goose) swam in a lake.
14. Two (moose) were feeding nearby.
15. One moose pulled up plants with its strong (tooth).
16. The moose had long legs and small (foot).
17. Some (man) were fishing in a boat.
18. The hikers passed a group of (child).
19. The boys and girls were as quiet as (mouse).
20. Everyone was watching two mountain (sheep).

pages 86–87

Common and Proper Nouns

D. Write each sentence. Draw one line under common nouns. Draw two lines under proper nouns.

21. Maria went on a trip in September.

22. The family visited the White House.

23. The children saw the Washington Monument.

24. Next Monday was Labor Day.

25. Maria would go back to school on Wednesday.

pages 88–89

Mechanics and Usage: Capitalization

E. Write each sentence. Write each noun in ( ) correctly.

26. Next (monday) is a holiday.

27. The holiday is called (presidents' day).

28. This holiday comes every (february).

29. We read about the holiday in (the big book of holidays).

30. The day honors (president lincoln) and other presidents.

pages 92–93

Singular Possessive Nouns

F. Write each sentence. Use the possessive form of the singular noun in ( ).

31. Did you ever think about an (animal) tail?

32. The (tail) shape is important.

33. A (beaver) flat tail helps the beaver steer when it swims.

34. A (monkey) long, thin tail can cling to a branch.

35. A (horse) bushy tail brushes off flies.

36. A (kangaroo) broad tail helps it balance.

37. A (fish) flat tail moves it through the water.

38. A baby elephant holds onto its (mother) thin tail.

39. What is your (dog) tail good for?

40. The tail shows your (pet) feelings.

Unit 2 Review

pages 94–95

Plural Possessive Nouns

G. Write each sentence. Use the possessive form of the plural noun in ( ).

41. The (hikers) boots are sturdy.

42. The (children) backpacks are light.

43. The (guides) names are Matt and Terry.

44. A girl takes pictures of some (birds) nests.

45. Two (women) cameras are out of film.

46. The hikers pass some (farmers) fields.

47. The (cows) tails swish back and forth.

48. The (sheep) wool looks soft.

49. The (wildflowers) colors are beautiful.

50. Two (boys) feet are sore from hiking.

pages 96–97

Combining Sentences: Nouns

H. Combine each pair of sentences. Use the word *and* to join two nouns. Write the new sentences.

51. Joan worked in the garden. Nick worked in the garden.

52. Joan planted tomatoes. Joan planted squash.

53. Nick watered the beans. Nick watered the peas.

54. Karen wanted to help. Roberto wanted to help.

55. The girls enjoyed the work. The boys enjoyed the work.

pages 98–99

Mechanics and Usage: Abbreviations

I. Write each abbreviation correctly.

56. Dr Michael Swanson

57. aug.

58. Thurs

59. Mrs Lauren Chen

60. sept

61. Feb

62. ms Cynthia Page

63. mr Hector Martinez

64. apr.

65. sat

Unit 2 Review

pages 112–113

Vocabulary: Compound Words

J. **Write each sentence. Underline the compound word.**

66. We walked along in the bright sunlight.

67. Waves were breaking on the seashore.

68. I saw a sailboat in the distance.

69. We left only footprints in the sand.

70. My friend picked up pretty seashells.

pages 114–115

Composition: Organization

K. **Write these sentences in the correct order.**

71. Next, shape the clay and sticks into a rounded mound.

72. First, get several toothpicks or twigs.

73. You can make a beaver lodge.

74. Last, dig out a room at the bottom.

75. Then mix the toothpicks or twigs with clay.

pages 134–135

Proofreading Explanatory Writing

L. **76–85. Write the following paragraph correctly. Correct the punctuation, grammar, and spelling mistakes. Use capital letters correctly. There are 10 mistakes.**

How a Robin builds a nest

A mother robin builds a nest for her eggs She makes the frame with twiggs and weed stalks. Standing in the middle of the nest, the robbin forms the side's. Next, she shapes the nest into a cup. Then the bird lines the nest wit mud and grass Last of all, she adds a soft, dry lining. The mother robins nest is finished in 6 to 20 day.

Project File

PROJECT 1 A Friendly Letter

A friendly letter is a letter to a person you know. A friendly letter has six parts. Think about why each part is needed.

You will need to know the form for a letter when you write your persuasive letter in the next unit.

3310 Vine Street
Minneapolis, MN 55408
October 17, 20__

Dear Kevin,

Our class has been learning about butterflies and moths. Did you know that butterflies and moths start out as caterpillars?

One interesting kind of caterpillar is called an inchworm. That doesn't mean an inchworm is an inch long. That's not how the inchworm got its name! Inchworms got their name by the way they move. An inchworm has a long, skinny body. It has two sets of sucker feet at the ends. First, the inchworm folds its body in half. Next, it inches its front end forward. Then it folds itself in half again. It keeps going that way. The inchworm looks like it's measuring things!

Can you guess two other names for the inchworm? They're looper and measuring worm!

Your friend,
Rafe

Heading *Gives the address of the person writing the letter.*

Date *Tells when the letter was written.*

Greeting *Usually starts with* Dear *and includes the name of the person the letter is written to.*

Body *Is the main part of the letter.*

Closing *Tells that the letter is about to end.*

Signature *Is the name of the person writing the letter.*

For more information, see Handbook page 553.

Write a friendly letter You can help a friend who doesn't understand a science or nature topic, such as how a caterpillar becomes a butterfly. First, think of a topic you can explain to your friend.

Be sure to present your ideas in an order that makes sense. Include enough details to help your friend understand what you are explaining.

TIME FOR KIDS PHOTO ESSAY

PROJECT 2

A How-To Article

Making art objects and toys is a fun way to recycle trash. What happens to the bottles, cans, and plastic that go into a recycling bin? Find out more about recycling. Then think about how to explain one part of the process.

Recycled Products Write a how-to article about how to prepare materials for recycling or how recycled materials are turned into new products. Choose photos from magazines or draw pictures to illustrate your article.

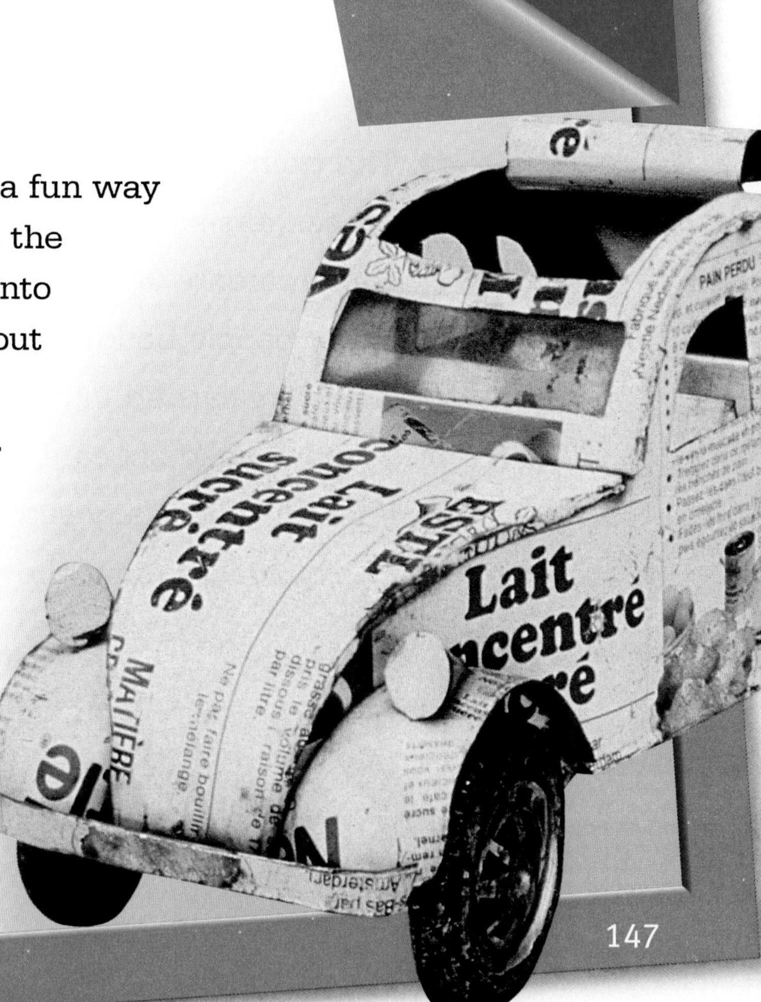

Extra Practice

Nouns

A. Write each sentence. Write which of the underlined words are nouns.

1. Six friends went to the fair.
2. The fairgrounds were packed with people.
3. People could buy food, hats, and flags.
4. Pat rode the pony.
5. Brian played several games.
6. Chris found the horses in the barn.
7. Jen ran to pet the rabbits.
8. Sue liked the sheep.
9. Parents and children watched the geese.
10. Families had fun at the fair.

B. Write the sentences. Draw a circle around each noun.

11. The train rolled down the track.
12. The conductor blew the whistle.
13. The train stopped at the station.
14. Passengers stepped onto the platform.
15. Grandparents waved to grandchildren.
16. Other people bought tickets.
17. Travelers carried luggage.
18. The train had six cars and an engine.
19. Each car had many seats.
20. The conductor shut the doors.

Singular and Plural Nouns

A. Write each noun. Write *singular* or *plural* next to each noun.

1. books
2. box
3. dishes
4. glasses
5. truck
6. chairs
7. bike
8. skates
9. lunch
10. sandwiches

B. Write the sentences. Write the plural of each underlined noun.

11. Our family went to some sandy beach.
12. Seth packed three large lunch.
13. I put two towel in the bag.
14. Bill forgot the key to the car.
15. Dad put sunscreen on our shoulder.
16. The lifeguard watched the swimmer.

17. The wave were gentle.

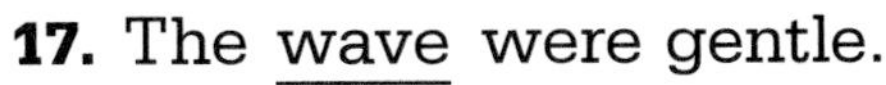

18. Beth built castle in the sand.
19. Jenny flew her kite.
20. I read my book.

Grammar

Extra Practice

Plural Nouns with *-ies*

A. Write the sentences. Underline the plural noun in each sentence.

1. Most cities have more than one library.
2. The ladies walk to the new library.
3. It has two copies of a favorite book.
4. The mysteries are on the top shelf.
5. Many libraries have a computer.
6. I search for short stories.
7. Anna returns a book about bunnies.
8. Joe reads about puppies.
9. Leah finds two old diaries.
10. Families can share a book.

B. Write the sentences. Write the plural form of each noun in ( ).

11. The (sky) were clear.
12. There were (butterfly) floating in the air.
13. A ladybug landed on the (daisy).
14. Joe wanted to pick (berry).
15. He took his (puppy) with him.
16. They chased the (bunny).
17. The (blueberry) grew on bushes.
18. Where do (cranberry) grow?
19. The trees were full of (cherry).
20. We shared the fruit with several (family).

More Plural Nouns

A. Write the sentences. Underline the plural noun in each sentence.

1. The pond was full of geese.
2. The children ran in the grass.
3. There were several sheep grazing near the pond.
4. Two men were fishing.
5. Dina put her feet in the water.
6. The cold water made her teeth chatter.
7. Women were jogging around the pond.
8. Three moose were sleeping near the pond.
9. I saw some mice in the tall grass.
10. Dan saw two deer near the pond.

B. Write the sentences. Write the plural form of each underlined noun.

11. The child went to the zoo.
12. They saw deer with large antlers.
13. Some of them saw sheep in the barn.
14. They saw some mouse inside a wagon.
15. The man helped pull the wagon.
16. The woman rode in the wagon.
17. Wild goose flew over us.
18. The birds have webbed foot.
19. A horse showed its big tooth.
20. We saw moose and elephants.

Grammar

Extra Practice

Common and Proper Nouns

A. Write each noun. Write *common* or *proper* next to each one.

1. Longfellow Elementary School
2. school
3. September
4. blackboard
5. computer
6. Mr. Matthews
7. teacher
8. Friday
9. recess
10. Labor Day

B. Write each sentence. Draw one line under each common noun. Draw two lines under each proper noun.

11. Pam and Sam Franks are twins.
12. Samantha is shorter than her sister.
13. Their cousins own Plainview Ranch.
14. Mr. Franks, their father, owns a farm.
15. Mrs. Franks is a teacher at their school.
16. The girls raise pigs.
17. Sam won a prize at the Miller County Fair.
18. The name of her pig is Petunia.
19. Petunia won a blue ribbon in the contest.
20. The family enjoyed the fair on Saturday.

Capitalization

A. Write each proper noun correctly.

1. tuesday

2. memorial day

3. rio grande

4. chicago

5. july

6. abraham lincoln

7. walt disney

8. december

9. thursday

10. san diego zoo

B. Write each sentence. Write the proper nouns correctly.

11. Today is flag day.

12. We read a book called *our first flag*.

13. On wednesday, we will read another book.

14. Ms. davis wrote the book.

15. It is called *state flags*.

16. Did you know betsy ross made the first flag?

17. The flag of the united states has stars and stripes.

18. We celebrate this holiday in june.

19. I read the book *salute to flags* to our class.

20. We will have no school on friday.

Extra Practice

Singular Possessive Nouns

A. Write each singular noun. Write the possessive form of each noun next to it.

1. beaver
2. cat
3. cow
4. bird

5. rabbit
6. dog
7. whale
8. butterfly
9. spider
10. porcupine

B. Write each sentence. Use the possessive form of the noun in ( ).

11. (Rosa) family has a pet dog.
12. The (dog) name is Trouble.
13. (Trouble) name fits him.
14. The dog chewed (Mom) slipper.
15. He stole (Dad) favorite shirt.
16. The (trainer) name is Max.
17. (Max) name is short for Maxine.
18. Trouble is (Maxine) favorite dog.
19. Trouble likes to chase the (family) cat, Lipton.
20. The (cat) favorite hiding place is under my bed.

Plural Possessive Nouns

A. Write the words. Write whether each word is a singular possessive noun or a plural possessive noun.

1. students'
2. boys'
3. lion's
4. bear's
5. bees'
6. groundhog's
7. children's
8. skunks'
9. snakes'
10. Roy's

B. Write each sentence. Use the correct possessive form of the plural noun in ( ).

11. The (players) uniforms are blue.
12. The (referees) shirts are black and white.
13. Two (months) practice has made the players good.
14. Mike read the (coaches) notes.
15. We saw the (managers) names on the notes.
16. Rajah learned about the (catchers) jobs on the field.
17. He visited the (owners) offices.
18. The (trainers) suggestions were good.
19. The (fans) cheers were loud.
20. The (women) team won by one run.

Grammar

Extra Practice

Combining Sentences: Nouns

A. Write each pair of sentences. Circle the two nouns that you can join with *and* to combine the sentences. Underline the words that repeat.

1. Whales are mammals. Humans are mammals.
2. Do whales have spouts? Do dolphins have spouts?
3. Abdul likes whales. Abdul likes sharks.
4. Sean likes sharks. Sean likes porpoises.
5. Whales live in the ocean. Porpoises live in the ocean.
6. Are whales dying out? Are porpoises dying out?
7. Abdul lived in the city. Sean lived in the city.
8. Sean likes science. Sean likes reading.
9. Sean reads about fish. Sean reads about mammals.
10. The boys are swimmers. The boys are divers.

B. Combine each pair of sentences. Use the word *and* to join two nouns. Write the new sentence.

11. Mia likes animals. Mia likes sports.
12. She has lived in Florida. She has lived in California.
13. Carlos liked the ocean. Mia liked the ocean.
14. Sara watched the seals. Sara watched the seahorses.
15. The seals were playful. The dolphins were playful.
16. Children waved to ships. Parents waved to ships.
17. The girls collected shells. The boys collected shells.
18. The sisters caught crabs. The sisters caught fish.
19. Jamal sailed today. Jim sailed today.
20. Carlos went swimming. Mia went swimming.

Abbreviations

A. Write the abbreviations. Then write what each abbreviation stands for.

1. Sun.
2. Sept.
3. Mr.
4. Thurs.
5. Nov.
6. Sat.
7. Dr.
8. Wed.
9. Aug.
10. Oct.

B. Write each abbreviation correctly.

11. dr.
12. mon
13. mrs
14. Dec
15. tues.
16. gov
17. Apr
18. jan
19. fri
20. feb

UNIT 3

Verbs and Persuasive Writing

In this unit you will learn about verbs. You will also learn about persuasive writing. Persuasive writing tries to make people think or act in a certain way.

Social Studies Link *A hotel in Sweden offers its guests an unusual place to stay. Read to see how the author gives persuasive reasons for visiting the Ice Hotel.*

At one hotel in Sweden, the cold doesn't have to sneak in. Guests *know* it will nip at their toes, fingers, and noses. Welcome to the Ice Hotel! The building and some of the furniture are made of ice and snow.

Why would anyone spend money to stay in a hotel like this? Kerstin Nilsson, who works there, says people love the beauty of the place. "It is pure winter—white and fresh snow." And she says there are "beautiful northern lights in the sky." It is also very quiet.

"A Very Cool Place to Visit" from ***Time for Kids***

Thinking Like a Writer

Persuasive Writing Persuasive writing tries to make people think or act in a certain way. Reread the passage.

- What are the author's most persuasive or convincing reasons for visiting the Ice Hotel?

Verbs The author uses some action verbs—words that show action. Read the passage again.

QUICK WRITE Find two action verbs in the passage. Then write sentences using each verb.

Grammar

Action Verbs

RULES

An **action verb** is a word that shows action.

*Gina **dances** on stage.*

Some action verbs tell about actions that are hard to see.

*Gina **planned** the talent show.*

In a sentence, the action verb tells what the subject of the sentence does.

Two children sing a song.

subject *verb*

THINK AND WRITE

Verbs

In your journal, write how you know if a word is an action verb.

Guided Practice

Name the action verb in each sentence.

EXAMPLE: Bess plays the guitar. *plays*

1. Maya and Kathy tell jokes.
2. Kevin plans his magic tricks.
3. Three boys make some puppets.
4. Rafael writes the advertisements.
5. Cara and Herb arrange the chairs.

Grammar

REVIEW THE RULES

- An action verb is a word that shows action.

More Practice

A. Write each sentence. Draw a line under the action verb.

6. The talent show begins in ten minutes.
7. Kevin wears a black suit.
8. Maya stretches her arms and legs.
9. Bess loses her music sheets.
10. All the performers wait backstage.
11. The show starts on time.
12. Tom greets the audience.
13. The curtain rises above the stage.
14. Many people fill the theater.
15. Everyone expects a good show.

Handbook page 508

B. Spiral Review Write the sentences. Add a noun to complete each sentence. Underline each proper noun. Add a capital letter where needed.

16. Many _____ attend the talent show at Kennedy School.
17. the _____ laugh when Tim tells jokes.
18. Some _____ perform well on stage.
19. the _____ clap at the end of the show.
20. our next _____ is in March.

Extra Practice, page 226

Writing Activity An Advertisement

Write an ad for a school talent show. Use words that will make people want to come.

APPLY GRAMMAR: Include action verbs in your ad. Draw a line under the action verbs that you use.

Grammar

Present-Tense Verbs

RULES

The tense of a verb tells when the action takes place.

A verb in the present tense tells what happens now.

Anna finds a box of costumes.

Follow these rules when you use present-tense verbs with singular subjects.

Add *-s* to most verbs.	Anna finds several hats.
Add *-es* to verbs that end in *sh, ch, ss, zz,* or *x*.	Anna reaches for a sea captain's hat.
Change *y* to *i* and add *-es* to verbs that end with a consonant and *y*.	Anna tries on the hat.

THINK AND WRITE

Verbs

Write how you know when to add *-es* to a verb.

Guided Practice

Name the correct present-tense form of the verb in ( ). Spell the word correctly.

EXAMPLE: Anna (carry) the hat downstairs. *carries*

1. Anna (tell) Josh about the box of costumes.
2. Josh (hurry) toward the box.
3. Willy the cat (watch) Josh.
4. Sally (give) us the costumes.
5. Anna (push) her foot into a boot.

REVIEW THE RULES

- Add *-s* or *-es* to most present-tense verbs with singular subjects.
- Change *y* to *i* and add *-es* to verbs that end with a consonant and *y*.

Handbook
page 509

More Practice

A. Write each sentence. Use the present-tense verb form.

6. The room (buzz) with excitement.

7. Sally (wrap) a long shawl around herself.

8. Anna (dress) as a sea captain.

9. Josh (look) through some old photographs.

10. A photo (show) Dad in cowboy clothing.

11. Dad (carry) a small calf.

12. Dad (wear) a cowboy hat.

13. Dad's hat (match) his outfit.

14. Josh (try) on a cowboy hat.

15. Sally (fix) her costume.

B. Spiral Review Write each sentence. Circle possessive nouns. Underline each singular subject.

16. Karen wears a crown and a cape.

17. Josh fixes the hat's band.

18. The colorful cape matches Karen's dress.

19. Dad's old hats look as good as new.

20. The children's costumes please the cat.

Extra Practice, page 227

Writing Activity A Bumper Sticker

Write a bumper sticker to persuade people to "try on" different hats. Keep your message short and to the point. **APPLY GRAMMAR:** Use present-tense verbs in your message.

Grammar

Subject-Verb Agreement

RULES

A present-tense verb must agree with its subject. Do not add *-s* or *-es* to a present-tense verb when the subject is plural.

Three friends plan a tree house.

Do not add *-s* or *-es* to a present-tense verb when the subject is *I* or *you*.

You make good suggestions.

I write our ideas on paper.

Verbs

How do you know whether or not to add *-s* or *-es* to a present-tense verb? Write the answer in your journal.

Guided Practice

Tell the correct present-tense form of the verb in ( ).

EXAMPLE: A big tree (grow) in my backyard. *grows*

1. Three friends (want) a tree house in that tree.
2. You (draw) a picture of our tree house.
3. I (like) your picture.
4. My parents (look) at our plan.
5. Dad (buy) lumber for the tree house.

REVIEW THE RULES

- A *present-tense verb* must agree with its subject.
- Do not add *-s* or *-es* to a present-tense verb when the subject is plural or *I* or *you*.

Grammar

More Practice

A. Write each sentence. Use the present-tense verb form.

6. Dad (saw) some boards in half.

7. Mom (get) a box of nails.

8. Mom and Dad (nail) boards together.

9. The children (help) when they can.

10. Our friends (watch) carefully.

11. You (put) a small table in the tree house.

12. Matt and I (make) a bench.

13. I (paint) the door red.

14. Matt (create) a flag for the tree house.

15. Our tree house (look) like your picture.

Handbook
page 511

B. Spiral Review Write each sentence. Circle the action verb. Draw a line under plural nouns. Add end marks.

16. We invite friends to a party

17. Who writes the invitations

18. Jeff brings two big pizzas

19. Chris carries a basket of berries

20. Two children give us a welcome mat

Extra Practice, page 228

Writing Activity A Description

Write a description of a tree house. Include details that help your readers picture the tree house.

APPLY GRAMMAR: Use action verbs in the present tense. Underline each present-tense action verb that you use.

Grammar

Letter Punctuation

RULES

The greeting of a letter begins with a capital letter and ends with a comma.

The closing of a letter begins with a capital letter and ends with a comma.

The comma after the greeting separates it from the body of the letter. The comma after the closing separates it from the signature.

Dear Emma, ⟵ Greeting

Thank you for the wonderful gift. ⟵ Body
I hope to see you soon.

Love, ⟵ Closing

Grandpa ⟵ Signature

THINK AND WRITE

Letter Punctuation

How do you know where to place a comma at the beginning and end of a letter? Write your answer in your journal.

Guided Practice

Name the correct item in each pair.

EXAMPLE: a. dear Madeline, b. Dear Madeline,
Correct item: b

1. a. Dear, Michael b. Dear Michael,

2. a. Sincerely, b. Sincerely

3. a. Yours Truly, b. Yours truly,

4. a. Dear Pedro, b. dear Pedro,

5. a. Your friend b. Your friend,

REVIEW THE RULES

- The greeting and the closing of a letter begin with a capital letter and end with a comma.

Grammar

More Practice

A. Write each item correctly.

6. Dear Mr. Trent

7. your friend
Stan

8. dear Aunt Helen

9. love
Daniel

10. sincerely yours
Grace

11. Dear julia

12. yours truly
Paul

13. dear carlos

14. love
Grandma

15. sincerely
ben

Handbook
pages 524, 528

B. Spiral Review **Write the letter. Add capital letters, commas, and end marks where needed.**

16.–20. Dear grandpa,

I will visit you in july. When will you visit our home in texas

Love
Dara

Extra Practice, page 229

Writing Activity A Poster

Create a poster about using capital letters and commas in the opening and closing of a letter. Arrange your information so it is clear.

APPLY GRAMMAR: Use action verbs in your poster. Circle the action verbs you use.

Art Link

Grammar REVIEW

Mixed Review

REVIEW THE RULES

An action verb shows action.

Add *-s* or *-es* to most present-tense verbs if the subject is singular. If a verb ends with a consonant and *y*, change the *y* to *i* and add *-es*.

If the subject of a sentence is plural or is *I* or *you*, do not add *-s* or *-es* to the verb in the present tense.

The greeting and the closing of a letter begin with a capital letter and end with a comma.

QUICK WRITE

Verbs

Write five sentences about chores you do at home. Use an action verb in each sentence.

Practice

A. Write each sentence. Use the correct present-tense form of the verb in ( ).

1. Mother (work) late on Fridays.
2. The children (make) dinner.
3. Jack (vote) for pizza.
4. The two girls (like) chili better.
5. Lili (measure) the beans.
6. Jan (fix) a salad.
7. I (put) the dishes on the table.
8. Lili (finish) the chili.
9. Jan and Lili (wash) the dishes after dinner.
10. Jack (dry) the dishes carefully.

B. Write each line of the letter. Add commas and capital letters to the greeting and closing. Circle the action verbs in the sentences.

11. dear Uncle Cal

12. You gave us a great idea.

13. Now we surprise Mom on Friday nights.

14. Mom works hard all week.

15. We cook dinner for her.

16. We serve dinner at six o'clock.

17. She loves our surprises.

18. We plan a new meal each week.

19. Sometimes we print out a menu.

20. love
Jack

Handbook
pages 508–509, 511, 524, 528

C. Challenge Write this letter. Correct mistakes in the spelling of present-tense verbs. Also add commas and capital letters where needed.

21.–25. Dear Jack

This cookbook containes good recipes. One recipe mixs up quickly and easily. I tries new recipes often.

love,

Uncle Cal

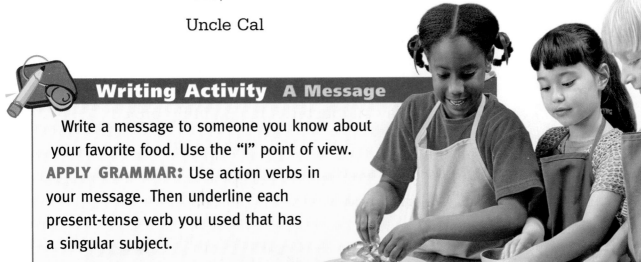

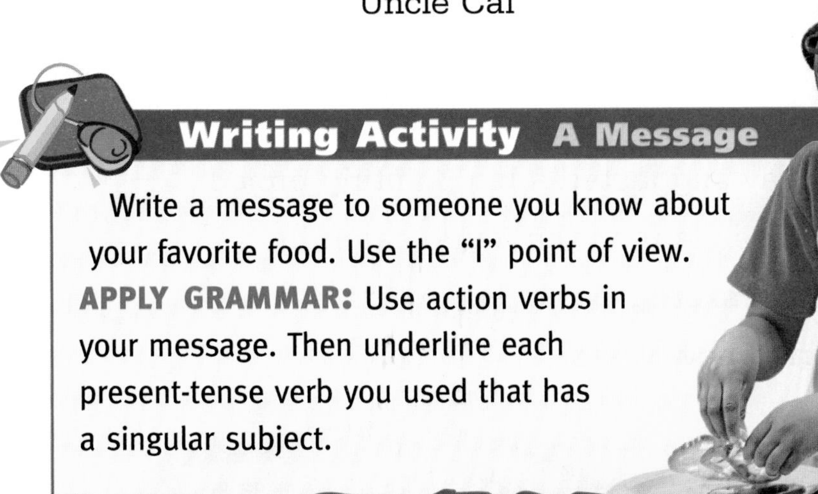

Writing Activity A Message

Write a message to someone you know about your favorite food. Use the "I" point of view. **APPLY GRAMMAR:** Use action verbs in your message. Then underline each present-tense verb you used that has a singular subject.

Grammar

Past-Tense Verbs

RULES

A past-tense verb tells about an action that has already happened. Add *-ed* to most verbs to form the past tense.

Last week we painted a mural.

Change the spelling of some verbs when adding the *-ed* ending.

Change the y to i before adding *-ed* if the verb ends with a consonant and y.	cry → cried marry → married
Drop the e and add *-ed* to verbs that end with e.	dance → danced like → liked
Double the consonant and add *-ed* to verbs that end with one vowel and one consonant.	wag → wagged grin → grinned

Verbs

In your journal, write how you know when to use the past tense.

Guided Practice

Name the past-tense verb in each sentence.

EXAMPLE: It snowed every day last week. *snowed*

1. We stayed inside for recess.
2. Ms. Gray suggested a big painting project.
3. The class planned the mural carefully.
4. We each sketched the design first.
5. We tried new ideas.

REVIEW THE RULES

- A verb in the past tense tells about a past action.
- Add *-ed* to most verbs to form the past tense.

Grammar

More Practice

A. Write each sentence. Use the past tense of the verb in ( ).

6. Mel and Tami (carry) a big roll of paper.

7. We (unroll) the paper on the floor.

8. The mural paper (stretch) across the room.

9. Christy and Ron (gather) all the paints.

10. We (grab) all the paintbrushes.

11. We (place) the paints on the table.

12. Sue (bump) into the table.

13. The paint (spill) on the floor.

14. Sue (cry) out.

15. We (clean) up all the paint.

Handbook
page 510

B. Spiral Review Write the sentences. Write *common nouns* next to each sentence with only common nouns. Underline each predicate. Circle each present-tense verb.

16. The children finished the mural.

17. The class displays the mural on a wall.

18. The students enjoy their work.

19. Sally painted a funny clown.

20. Rico draws a picture of the beach.

Extra Practice, page 230

Writing Activity Journal Entry

Write a journal entry about something that happened in school. Tell the events in the order in which they happened. **APPLY GRAMMAR:** Use past-tense verbs in your writing.

Grammar

Future-Tense Verbs

RULES

A future-tense verb tells about an action that is going to happen. Use the special verb *will* to write about the future.

Tomorrow we will start our camping trip.
I will listen to the weather forecast.

Verbs can show actions that happen now or in the past. They can also show actions that will happen in the future.

Verbs
In your journal, write how you can tell if a verb is in the future tense.

Guided Practice

Name the verb in each sentence. Then tell whether the verb is in the present, the past, or the future tense.

EXAMPLE: She will tell us about the weather.
will tell—future

1. Most people want information about the weather.
2. We need weather information for decisions.
3. Many people will listen to today's forecast.
4. You packed your raincoat in your backpack.
5. Farmers will cut their hay before the rain.

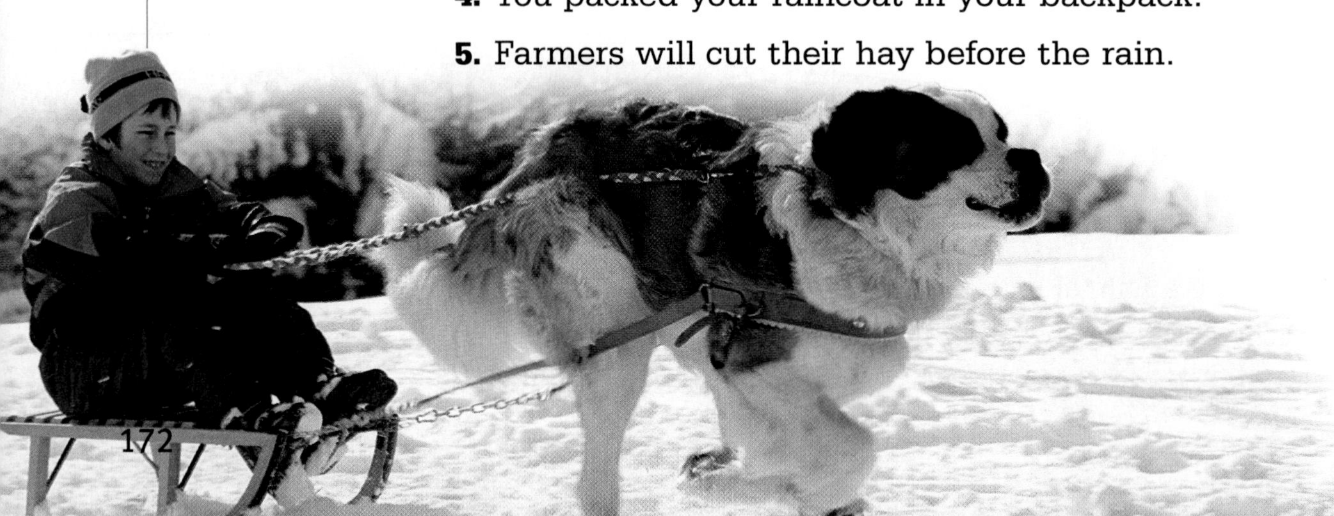

REVIEW THE RULES

- A verb in the future tense tells about a future action.
- Use *will* with verbs in the future tense.

More Practice

A. Write each sentence. Write the verb in the future tense.

6. Scientists predict the weather.
7. These scientists gather a lot of information.
8. Weather facts come from many instruments.
9. Instruments report the weather on Earth.
10. Satellites observe weather from space.
11. The news reporter shows us a weather map.
12. It snows in the Rocky Mountains.
13. It rains in the Midwest.
14. Storms develop along the East Coast.
15. The West Coast enjoys good weather.

Handbook page 510

B. Spiral Review Write each sentence. Circle each noun. Change each past-tense verb to the future tense.

16. Jim watched the news on television.
17. The sun shines in the morning.
18. The good weather lasted for days.
19. Mom and Dad hiked to the lake.
20. Rain falls on our tent.

Extra Practice, page 231

Writing Activity Weather Forecast

Write a weather forecast for tomorrow. Give the forecast for morning, noon, and night in an order that makes sense. **APPLY GRAMMAR:** Use the future tense to tell about tomorrow's weather. Underline all future-tense verbs.

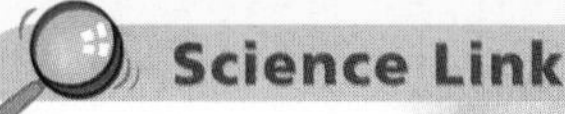

Science Link

Grammar

Combining Sentences: Verbs

RULES

You can join two sentences with the same subject by combining the predicates.

Billy watches birds.

Billy feeds birds.

Billy watches and feeds birds.

Use the word *and* to combine the predicates.

Grandpa designs birdhouses.

Grandpa builds birdhouses.

Grandpa designs and builds birdhouses.

Verbs

How can combining two predicates improve the flow of your sentences? Write the answer in your journal.

Guided Practice

Tell how to combine each pair of sentences.

EXAMPLE: Billy draws a design.
Billy colors a design.
Combine predicates: Billy draws and colors a design.

1. Grandpa measures the wood. Grandpa cuts the wood.

2. Grandpa draws a pattern. Grandpa traces a pattern.

3. Grandpa glues the sides. Grandpa nails the sides.

4. Billy places the roof carefully. Billy attaches the roof carefully.

5. Billy sands the birdhouse. Billy paints the birdhouse.

REVIEW THE RULES

- You can combine two sentences with the same subject by joining the predicates.

More Practice

A. Use *and* to combine the predicates of each pair of sentences. Write the new sentence.

6. Billy writes a sign. Billy paints a sign.
7. Billy mixes some birdseed. Billy measures some birdseed.
8. Grandpa gets the ladder. Grandpa climbs the ladder.
9. Grandpa hangs the birdhouse. Grandpa straightens the birdhouse.
10. Billy smiles. Billy claps.
11. A bird finds the seed. A bird eats the seed.
12. The bird sees the house. The bird likes the house.
13. The bird lays three eggs. The bird cares for three eggs.
14. Three baby birds hatch. Three baby birds fly.
15. Billy thanks Grandpa. Billy hugs Grandpa.

page 513

B. Spiral Review Write each sentence. Underline verbs and possessive nouns. Correct each abbreviation.

16. Billy showed the birdhouse to his neighbors.
17. Mr Adams likes the boy's birdhouse.
18. Mrs Clark wanted a birdhouse, too.
19. Mr Jones asked Billy for directions.
20. Billy hurries to Grandpa's house.

Extra Practice, page 232

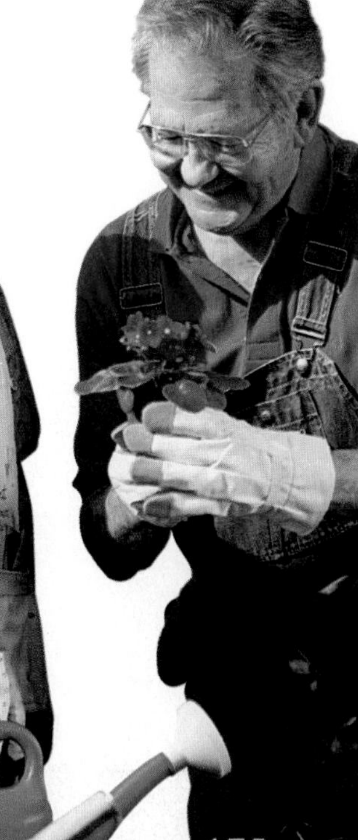

Writing Activity A Thank-You Letter

Write a letter to thank someone for something nice he or she did for you or helped you do. Say what you really feel. **APPLY GRAMMAR:** Combine sentences that have the same subject. Underline the word that joins the predicates.

Grammar

Commas in Dates and Places

RULES

Use a comma between the names of a city or town and a state.

Dallas, Texas

Use a comma between the day and the year in a date.

July 17, 1999

Use commas when writing place names and dates.

(city) (state)	(day) (year)
Louisville, Kentucky	*March 10, 2001*

THINK AND WRITE

Commas

Write how you know when to use a comma in a date or a place name.

Guided Practice

Tell where to place a comma in each item.

EXAMPLE: July 4 1776 — *July 4, 1776*
Ames Iowa — *Ames, Iowa*

1. February 17 1914
2. Denver Colorado
3. October 3 2000
4. St. Louis Missouri
5. Jersey City New Jersey
6. Los Angeles California
7. January 1 2020
8. Atlanta Georgia
9. November 10 1900
10. Boston Massachusetts

REVIEW THE RULES

- Use commas to separate items in dates and place names.

More Practice

A. Write the sentences. Add a comma where needed.

11. Kylie's vacation starts on July 1 2001.

12. The Page family will visit Laramie Wyoming.

13. Mr. Page was born in Laramie on May 10 1966.

14. Mrs. Page comes from Portland Oregon.

15. Kylie was born in Twin Falls Idaho.

16. Kylie's birthday is on August 8 1990.

17. The Pages live in Rapid City South Dakota.

18. The family moved from Salt Lake City Utah.

19. Kylie's grandparents live in Tampa Florida.

20. Kylie visited her grandparents on March 10 1998.

B. Spiral Review Write the sentences. Add capital letters and end marks where needed. Circle future-tense verbs.

21. Peter will sail the pacific ocean

22. Ben wants to visit austin, texas

23. Will you leave for chicago in august

24. city bridges is an interesting book

25. Come to the white house with me

Extra Practice, page 233

Grammar

Handbook page 528

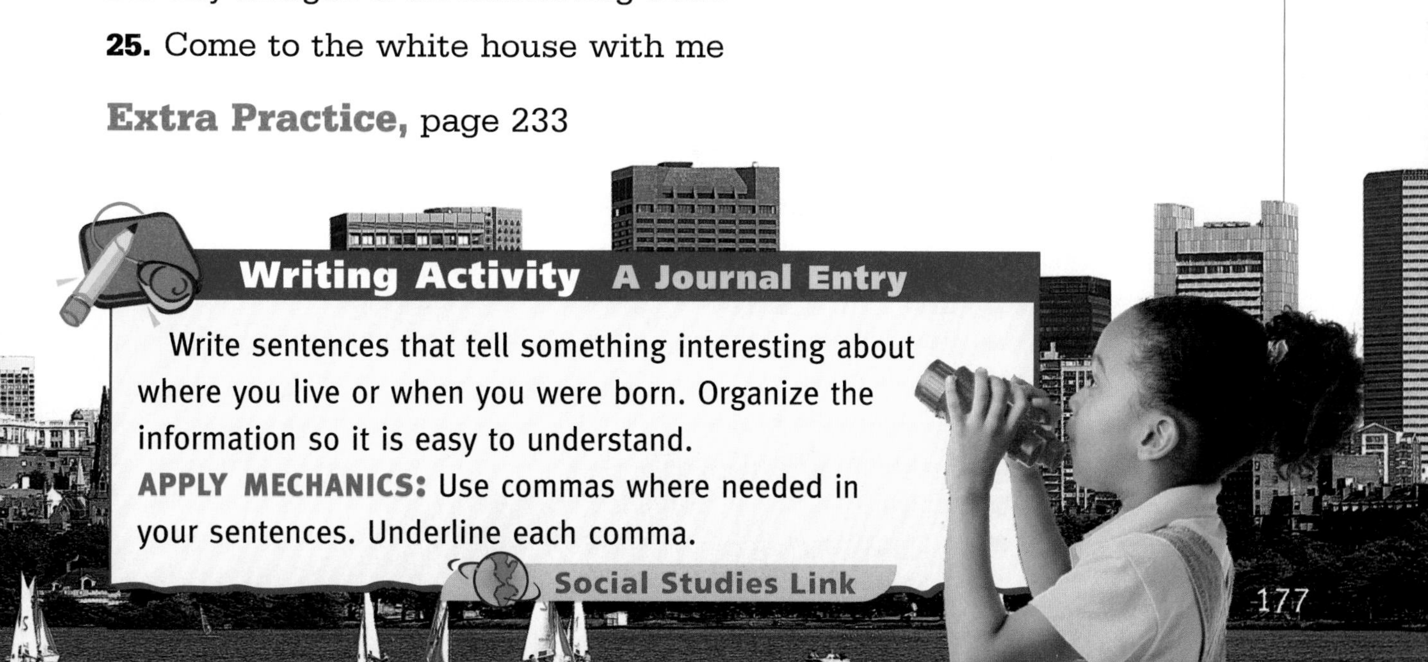

Writing Activity A Journal Entry

Write sentences that tell something interesting about where you live or when you were born. Organize the information so it is easy to understand.

APPLY MECHANICS: Use commas where needed in your sentences. Underline each comma.

Social Studies Link

Grammar REVIEW

Mixed Review

REVIEW THE RULES

- Add *-ed* to most verbs to show an action that happened in the past.
- Use *will* with action verbs to tell about something that is going to happen in the future.
- Use *and* to join the predicates of two sentences with the same subject.
- Use a *comma* to separate the day and the year in a date and the city and the state in a place name.

Verbs

Write three sentences about a trip to the doctor. Use a past-tense verb, a present-tense verb, and a future-tense verb.

Practice

A. Write each sentence. Use the verb in the tense shown in ( ).

1. Ned (trip, past tense) over a rock.
2. Mr. Farrin (carry, past tense) Ned to the car.
3. Ned (go, future tense) to the doctor.
4. The doctor (look, past tense) at Ned's foot.
5. Ned (sprain, past tense) his ankle.
6. The doctor (wrap, past tense) the ankle well.
7. Ned (listen, past tense) to the doctor.
8. He (thank, past tense) the doctor for her help.
9. Ned (use, future tense) crutches for a few weeks.
10. The ankle (heal, future tense) soon.

B. Write each pair of sentences as one sentence. Use *and* to combine the predicates.

11. People come. People see the doctor.

12. Patients read. Patients wait quietly.

13. The nurse opens the door. The nurse says hello.

14. Dr. Lee listens. Dr. Lee talks to patients.

15. The doctor thinks. The doctor makes notes.

16. Meg has a headache. Meg feels sick.

17. Paul steps on the scale. Paul is weighed.

18. Sheri's arm is red. Sheri's arm itches.

19. I look at an eye chart. I read the letters.

20. We say good-bye. We close the door.

C. Challenge **Write the following paragraph. Correct each verb-tense mistake. Add a comma where needed. Combine the two underlined sentences.**

21.–25. Yesterday, Ned will visit the doctor. His office is in Canton Ohio. Dr. Smith looks at Ned's foot. <u>Dr. Smith smiled. Dr. Smith said, "It looks fine."</u> Tomorrow, Ned played soccer again.

Grammar REVIEW

Handbook
pages 509–510, 513, 528

Writing Activity A Caption

Draw a picture of a doctor's office. Then write a caption for your picture that includes details of interest to the reader.
APPLY GRAMMAR: Write the month, date, and year you drew your picture.

Social Studies Link

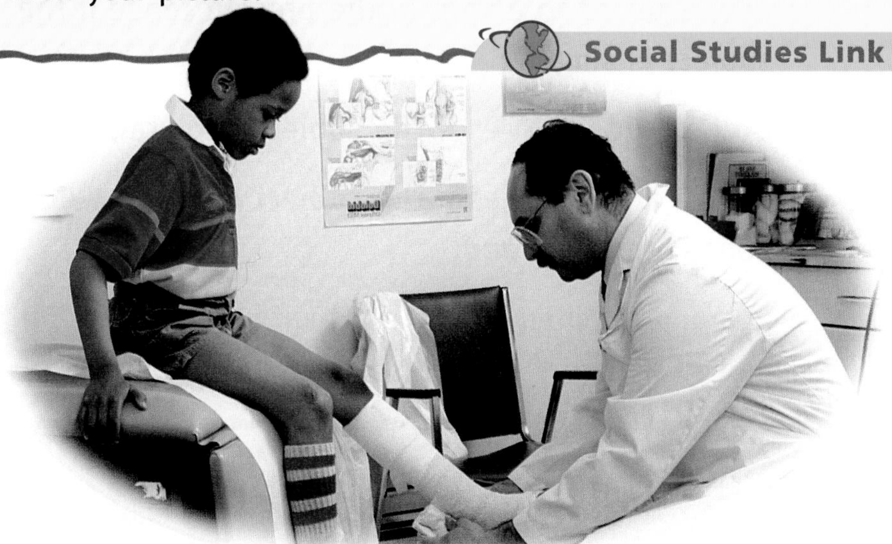

Common Errors with Subject-Verb Agreement

Sometimes a writer forgets to make subjects and verbs agree. Present-tense verbs must always agree with their subjects. The chart below shows some common subject-verb errors.

Common Errors	Examples	Corrected Sentences
Using a plural verb with a singular subject	Pat throw the ball hard.	Pat throws the ball hard.
Using a singular verb with a plural subject	The boys watches the game.	The boys watch the game.
Using a singular verb when the subject has two nouns joined by and	Bill and Jane wants to play.	Bill and Jane want to play.

Verbs

How do you know whether to add *-s* to a verb in a sentence? Write the answer in your journal.

REVIEW THE RULES

SUBJECT-VERB AGREEMENT

- In every sentence, the subject and the verb must agree.
- Add *-s* or *-es* to a verb in the present tense if the subject is singular.
- Do not add *-s* or *-es* if the subject is plural.
- Do not add *-s* or *-es* if the subject contains two nouns joined by *and*.
- Remember When a verb ends with a consonant and *y*, change *y* to *i* and add *-es*.

Practice

A. Read each sentence. Write *yes* if the subject and verb agree. Write *no* if they do not agree.

1. The children meet at the community center.
2. Paul and Ray make paper hats.
3. Maria dance on the wooden stage.
4. One girl sings a song for the group.
5. Mr. Gomez clap for us.

B. Write each sentence. Choose the verb in ( ) that agrees with the subject.

6. The children (go, goes) into the game room.
7. Sumi and Van (find, finds) a game of checkers.
8. Van (try, tries) to win the first game.
9. Kathleen (get, gets) a ball and two paddles.
10. She and Tony (play, plays) two games of table tennis.

C. Write each sentence correctly. Make the incorrect verb in ( ) agree with the subject.

11. Adam and Josh (carries) the dishes to the sink.
12. Rose (wash) the plates and cups.
13. Paco (dry) them with a soft towel.
14. Ana and I (sets) pretty place mats on the table.
15. Vic (arrange) the flowers in a vase.

Troubleshooter, pages 494–495

Handbook
page 511

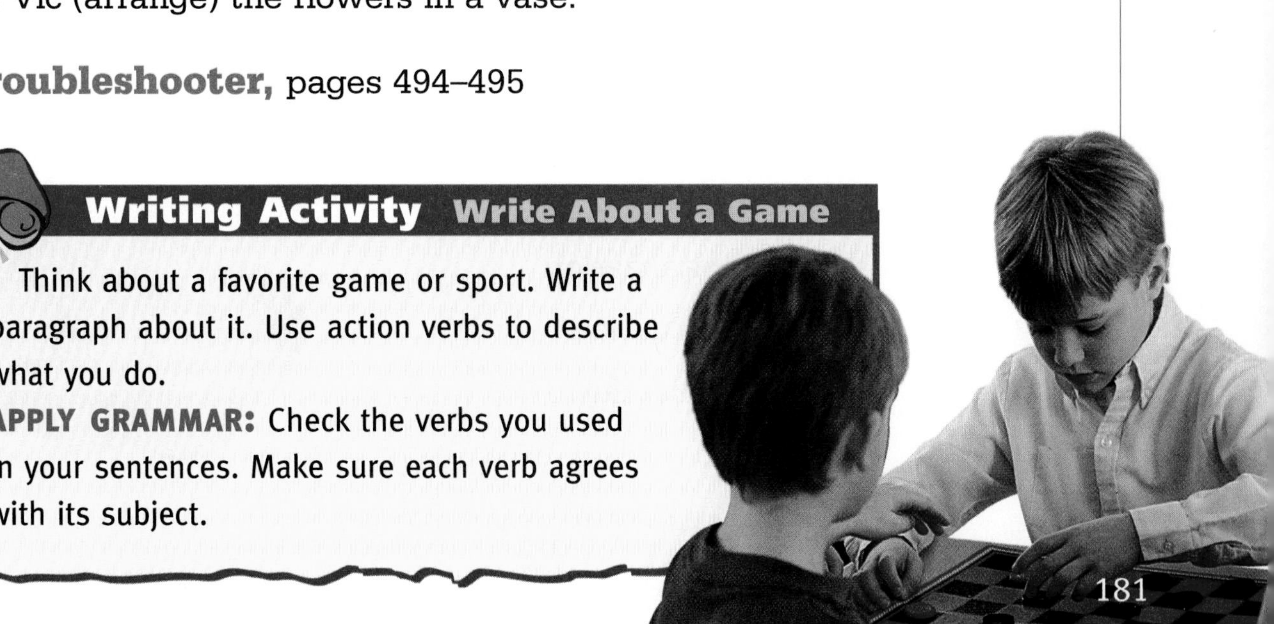

Writing Activity Write About a Game

Think about a favorite game or sport. Write a paragraph about it. Use action verbs to describe what you do.

APPLY GRAMMAR: Check the verbs you used in your sentences. Make sure each verb agrees with its subject.

Mechanics and Spelling

TAAS

Directions

Read the passage and decide which type of mistake, if any, appears in each underlined section. Choose the correct answer. If there is no mistake, choose "No mistake."

Is there a proper noun? Check to see if it begins with a capital letter.

Are there names of a town and a state? Check to see if a comma is needed between them.

Is the past-tense verb spelled correctly? Make sure the e *is dropped before adding* -ed.

Sample

Nori likes to make greeting cards for her friends and family. She just made a birthday card for her uncle. Nori lives in new york. Her uncle (1) lives far away in Forest Ohio (2). Nori decided to put a forest on the front of the card. She drew ten trees on green paper. Then she cut out each tree and pasteed it on the card (3). She drew a small picture of her uncle by one tree. Nori wrote a birthday poem on the inside of the card.

1
- ○ Spelling
- ○ Capitalization
- ○ Punctuation
- ○ No mistake

2
- ○ Spelling
- ○ Capitalization
- ○ Punctuation
- ○ No mistake

3
- ○ Spelling
- ○ Capitalization
- ○ Punctuation
- ○ No mistake

Test Tip
Read the test carefully before choosing each answer.

Grammar and Usage

TAAS

Directions

Read the passage and choose the word or group of words that belongs in each space.

Sample

After Nori made her uncle a birthday card, she wrote the following letter.

Dear Uncle Ted,

I hope you have a very happy birthday. Do you like this card I made for you? I __(1)__ it's fun to make cards. Next month, I __(2)__ a card for Aunt Pat. I know she __(3)__ horses. She can expect a card from me decorated with beautiful horses.

Love,

Nori

When the subject is I, *you do not add* s *or* es *to a present-tense verb.*

Remember, the special verb will *is used to tell about the future.*

Be sure that a present-tense verb agrees with its subject.

1 ○ think
○ thinks
○ thinking
○ will think

2 ○ makes
○ made
○ making
○ will make

3 ○ like
○ likes
○ liking
○ is like

TIME FOR KIDS Writer's Notebook

RESEARCH

I like to know as much about a subject as I can before I write a story. I read and take **notes**. Written notes help me remember the main ideas of what I read. It helps organize my ideas, too!

WRITING WELL

Sometimes the hardest part of writing a story is figuring out how it should end. A good **ending** will sum up the story. It will remind the reader of my main idea. I hope it will give the reader something to think about, too.

USING WORDS

Adding a syllable before a word can change its meaning. For example, adding the letters "un" to "usual" changes the meaning. That syllable is called a **prefix**. Prefixes help me say exactly what I want to say. What words do you know that have prefixes?

Read Now!

As you read the photo essay, take notes about the three projects so you can tell someone who hasn't read the essay about them.

TIME FOR KIDS

PHOTO ESSAY

SUPER KID

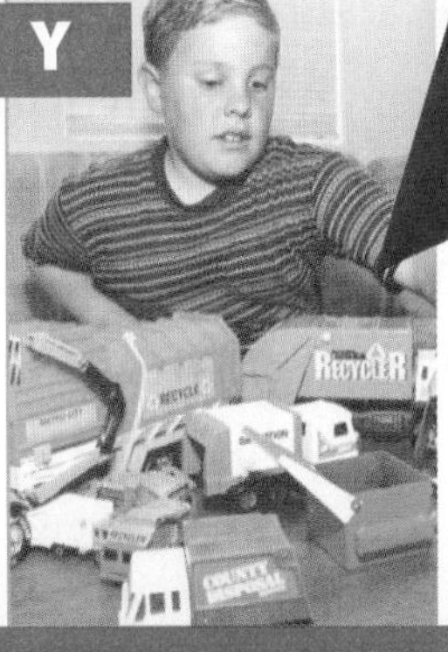

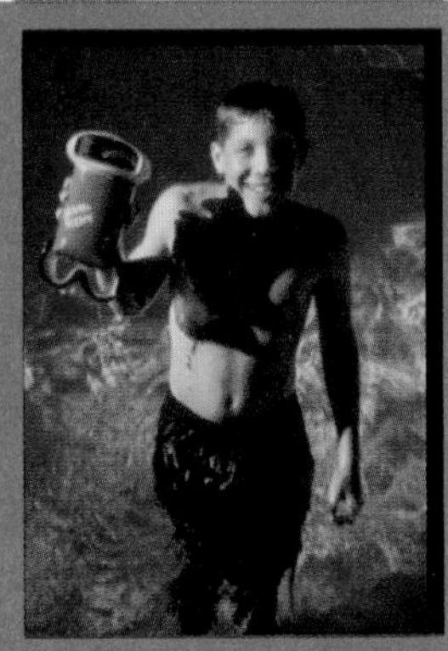

Kid Heroes!

Kids Are Doing It!

Here's a look at some super U.S. kids. Some are helping out the environment. Some are making others feel good. And one is coming up with some great new inventions. It just goes to prove: You can do anything if you set your mind to it!

Brian Diggs/AP

Malik Waleed, 6, had one of his poems shown in the train station.

Poetry Express

Subway riders in Washington, DC, are stopping to read incredible poems written by kids. The poems are at 10 train stops in the busy city.

What are the poems about? Snow falling, the coming of a new year, love, fear, and peace.

The kids had mixed feelings about letting people read their private thoughts. "I would feel glad that someone read my poem," one girl said. "But I would feel sad if they missed their train."

interNET CONNECTION Go to www.mhschool.com/language-arts for more information on the topic.

Splashy Ideas

You might say Richie Stachowski makes a big splash in the toy business. He invents water toys!

Richie, who lives in California, said, "I wanted to bring things that you can do on land into the water." One big idea is Richie's Water Talkies. It lets kids talk underwater.

Richie is "chief inventing officer" of his company. Will Richie's ideas ever dry up? "I know what kids like," he says. "I'll always invent things."

Make Your Garden Grow

Melissa Zinder goes to Nuckols Farm School in Richmond, Virginia. Melissa and some classmates decided to help make their school grounds more beautiful. That's why they planted 275 tulip and daffodil bulbs.

Melissa says the hard work of planting was worth it. She loved seeing the bulbs' first green leaves poke through the dirt. Anyone can help the planet, she says. "You just have to put your mind to it."

Photo in circle: Lori Cross/Nuckols Farm Elementary School

Write Now!

Is there something you'd like to invent or a problem you'd like to solve? Write to tell people how important your project is and persuade them to get involved.

Note-taking and Summarizing

When you read a newspaper, magazine, or encyclopedia article for information, you need to remember the facts. You can take notes about the main idea and the important details.

Here is an article about an octopus and the notes that one student wrote. When you take notes, you can write single words, groups of words, or sentences.

Octopuses Do What Comes Naturally

How brainy are octopuses? Experiments show that octopuses are able to learn and solve problems, which may be signs of intelligence.

"Octopuses are smart enough to solve simple puzzles after a few tries," explains Roland Anderson, a marine biologist at the Seattle Aquarium in Washington State. "For example, I've seen an octopus squeeze through a tiny hole in its tank at the aquarium to catch a live crab. If the crab is small, the octopus will bring the whole animal back to its den and eat it. However, if the crab is too big to fit through the hole, the octopus will kill it, take it apart, and then pass the body through the hole, bit by bit."

Notes

Does an octopus use its brain?

Study done by scientist at Seattle Aquarium

Octopus squeezed small crab into hole
and ate it

Problem: larger crab too big for hole

Octopus broke crab in pieces

Dropped pieces into hole

You can use your notes to write a summary. A **summary** briefly states the main idea and the important details. A summary uses complete sentences.

Summary

Does an octopus use its brain to solve problems? A scientist used crabs of different sizes to see what a hungry octopus would do. The octopus grabbed a small crab, squeezed into a hole, and ate it. The octopus broke a larger crab into pieces to solve the problem of getting it into the hole.

Practice

A. Read each note below about the article on page 188. Write *main idea* if a note states the main idea. Write *important detail* for all other notes.

1. Seattle Aquarium
2. live crabs: one large, one small
3. octopus solved simple problem
4. large crab too big for hole
5. dropped pieces into hole

B. Write the answer to each question.

6. What information should you look for when taking notes?
7. When you take notes, what form can they be in?
8. What can you use your notes to write?
9. How is a summary different from an article?
10. Do you need to write complete sentences when you take notes or when you write a summary?

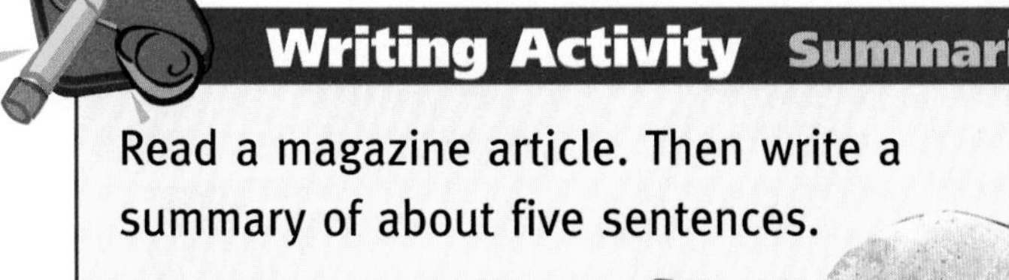

Writing Activity Summarizing

Read a magazine article. Then write a summary of about five sentences.

Vocabulary: Prefixes

DEFINITION

A prefix is a word part that is added to the beginning of a word. It changes the meaning of the base word.

dis- + like = dislike
re- + read = reread
un- + cut = uncut

Prefix	Meaning	Example
dis-	not, the opposite of	**disappear**
re-	again, back	**rebuild**
un-	not, the opposite of	**untie**

THINK AND WRITE

Prefixes
How can you decide if a word begins with a prefix? Write your answer in your journal.

Look at the blue words in the paragraph below.

Visit your town library. Look for favorite stories to borrow and reread. Don't leave the new books and magazines unopened. Find movies and music, too. The library has something for everyone.

Practice

A. Write each sentence. Circle the word that has a prefix.

1. Ken reread a book about mice.
2. Gina dislikes reading about bats.
3. I love bats and disagree with Gina.
4. This book tells about unusual plants.
5. Ken replaced the plant book on the shelf.

B. Write each sentence. Choose a prefix and a base word from the box to make the missing word.

Prefixes:	*dis-*	*re-*	*un-*		
Base Words:	*able*	*appeared*	*read*	*lock*	*opened*

6. Alec _____ a story about an island.
7. Peg is _____ to find a new mystery book.
8. Carla _____ the book about soccer.
9. One book tells how to _____ secret codes.
10. Paul _____ behind the tall piles of books.

C. Grammar Link **Use the meaning of the prefix to explain the meaning of the verb in each sentence.**

11. We would never disobey the library's rules.
12. Anna reentered the music room.
13. The librarian unwrapped the new books.
14. New books quickly disappear from the shelves.
15. We will return our books next week.

Writing Activity A Letter

Write a letter to someone about why you like to go to the library. In your letter, use two words with prefixes. **APPLY GRAMMAR:** Include a compound predicate.

Composition: Leads and Endings

Writers use a strong beginning, or lead, to get the reader's attention. They use a good ending to help readers feel that the piece of writing is complete.

GUIDELINES

- The **lead** is the opening of a piece of writing and should grab the reader's attention.
- The lead may give the main idea.
- The **ending** is the last part of a piece of writing and should help readers feel the writing is complete.
- The ending may draw a conclusion, restate the main idea, or sum up what the writer said.

THINK AND WRITE

Leads and Endings

Why is a strong lead and a good ending important to a piece of writing? Write your answer.

Read this letter. Notice how the writer begins and ends the invitation.

A good lead draws the reader in.

A good ending helps the reader feel the writing is complete.

Dear Aunt Betty,

Have you ever been to Seal Point? Please spend August 4 with us. We'll have a picnic at Seal Point. We can watch the seals and fly kites. If it rains, we'll go to the new science museum. Please come. We'd like to help you celebrate your birthday.

Love,

Liz

Practice

A. Write the sentences. Write *lead* or *ending* to identify each sentence.

1. Here's what will happen at the Art Fair.
2. Let me tell you about my funny day.
3. That trip was the best we've ever had.
4. Have you ever made your own pizza?
5. In closing, I hope you can come on July 17.
6. I'm glad *that* day is over.
7. Visit Seal Point Park! Here's why.
8. The kitten was in her bed all the time.
9. Finally, I saw a moose.
10. See the city from a helicopter.

B. Write a lead for each topic.

11. Learning to Ride a Horse
12. Announcing a School Play
13. A New Baby in the Family
14. The Day the Puppy Got Loose
15. Selling a Bicycle

C. 16.–20. Grammar Link **Write an ending for each topic listed above. Use the past tense for at least two sentences. Use the future tense for two sentences.**

Writing Activity An Advertisement

Write an ad for an everyday item, such as shampoo, a yo-yo, or sneakers. Get the reader's attention with a strong lead and a good ending.

APPLY GRAMMAR: Use action verbs in your ad, and underline them.

Better Sentences

Directions

Read the passage. Some parts are underlined. The underlined parts may be one of the following:

- **Incomplete sentences**
- **Run-on sentences**
- **Correctly written sentences that should be combined**

Choose the best way to write each underlined part.

Look out for run-on sentences that need to be separated.

Remember, sometimes sentences that have the same words can be combined.

Sample

My hobby is making animals out of small rocks. I have a rock zoo I am always looking for rocks. **(1)** Some of my rocks are flat and smooth. Others are round and rough.

All of my rock animals have names. There's a raccoon named Rocky. There's a panda named Pebbles. **(2)** Having a rock zoo is a lot of fun.

1
- ○ I have a rock zoo. Looking for rocks.
- ○ I have a rock zoo. I am always looking for rocks.
- ○ I am always look for my rock zoo.

2
- ○ There's a raccoon and a panda. Named Rocky and Pebbles.
- ○ A raccoon named Rocky, and there's a panda named Pebbles.
- ○ There's a raccoon named Rocky and a panda named Pebbles.

Vocabulary and Comprehension

TAAS

Directions

Read the passage. Then read each question that follows the passage. Choose the best answer to each question.

Sample

There was a park in our town with old playground equipment. A group of people in the town wanted to repaint the equipment. The mayor of the town said OK.

One morning, the people met at the playground. A few people brought cans of paint. Others brought brushes. Everyone got to work. At the end of the day, the playground was beautiful! The slide was bright yellow with red spots. The seesaw was green with pink stripes. All of the benches were light blue.

Look for word parts that you know.

1 The word repaint in this passage means to—

- ○ build again
- ○ paint again
- ○ not paint
- ○ paint the back of

2 Which word from the passage describes an opinion about the playground?

- ○ stripes
- ○ blue
- ○ yellow
- ○ beautiful

Test Tip
Read the questions before you begin a test to find out what they cover.

Seeing Like a Writer

Look at the pictures. What could you write about each one? Imagine you are in one of the pictures. What do you think about what is happening? What do you want?

Traffic Conditions by Norman Rockwell.

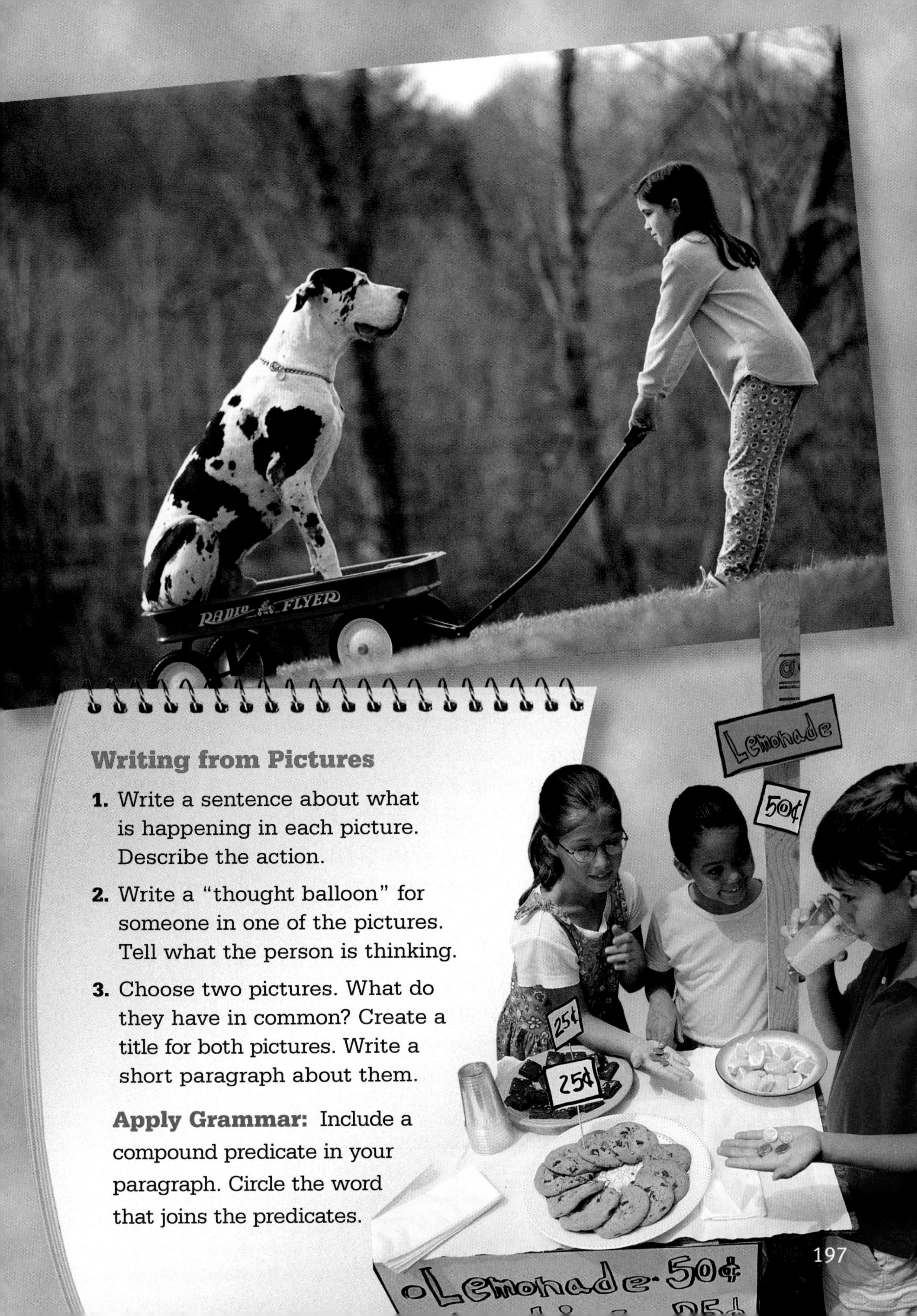

Writing from Pictures

1. Write a sentence about what is happening in each picture. Describe the action.
2. Write a "thought balloon" for someone in one of the pictures. Tell what the person is thinking.
3. Choose two pictures. What do they have in common? Create a title for both pictures. Write a short paragraph about them.

Apply Grammar: Include a compound predicate in your paragraph. Circle the word that joins the predicates.

Persuasive Writing

Have you ever felt so strongly about something that you wrote a letter to share your opinion? That's persuasive writing. Persuasive writing tries to make readers think or act in a certain way.

Purpose

Why do people write to persuade? Explain why sharing your opinions with others is important.

Learning from Writers

Read the following examples of persuasive writing. What does each writer want the reader to think or do? Think about how the writer tries to make the reader agree with his or her point of view.

Protecting the Environment

"Save the Whales." "Give a hoot...Don't pollute!" Protecting the environment and its resources is important and takes work. Just putting a bumper sticker on a car is not enough. Every day you can help protect the environment. Every time you use a bottle, can, or piece of paper, you can save it for recycling.

There are other ways you can help protect the environment. A few years ago some eight-year-old girls in California wanted to help their community fight air pollution. They knew that plants and trees improve the air. So they decided to plant trees and other plants around their community. Today their community is a more beautiful place to live.

You, your classmates, and everyone in your community are important resources. You can help protect our natural resources for years to come.

— from a social studies textbook

501 Paloma Road
San Diego, California 92129
September 4, 20_ _

Dear Mr. Scully,

I think Leo should win the award for the best pet-care report. He presented a wonderful report that made sense. The report explained what to do and why it was important. Leo even brought in his pet turtle Charlie to show us what he meant. Please give the award to Leo. Thank you.

Sincerely,
Amber Hawk

Practice and Apply

Thinking Like a Reader

1. What does the writer of "Protecting the Environment" want readers to do?
2. Why does Amber believe that Leo should win the award?

Thinking Like a Writer

3. How are the writer's feelings stated in "Protecting the Environment"?
4. Why does Amber use facts to support her opinion?

5. **Reading Across Texts** Compare the two examples. How are they alike and how are they different in the way they try to persuade their readers?

Features of Persuasive Writing

DEFINITIONS AND FEATURES

Persuasive writing tries to make people think or act a certain way. Good persuasive writing:

- Clearly **states an opinion** about the topic.
- Supports the main idea with **convincing reasons and facts.**
- Organizes reasons in an **order that makes sense.**
- Uses **opinion words.**

▶ States an Opinion

Reread "Protecting the Environment" on page 198. How does the writer feel about the environment? What opinion does the writer have?

> Protecting the environment and its resources is important and takes work.

The word *important* tells you that the writer feels strongly about protecting the environment. The writer's opinion is stated clearly.

▶ Convincing Reasons and Facts

Convincing reasons and facts help persuade the reader. How does this suggestion persuade you that you can help protect the environment?

> Every time you use a bottle, can, or piece of paper, you can save it for recycling.

The suggestion shows how everyone can do simple things every day to help the environment.

▶ Order That Makes Sense

To help readers understand your ideas, put your supporting facts and reasons in an order that makes sense. After suggesting everyday things we can do, this writer introduced other ideas.

> There are other ways you can help protect the environment. A few years ago some eight-year-old girls in California wanted to help their community fight air pollution.

The writer gave readers everyday ideas before telling about a bigger project—planting trees and plants. Why did it make sense to "start small"?

▶ Opinion Words

Words such as *I think* and *I believe* signal the writer's opinion. *You can, must, need,* and *should* are opinion words writers use to persuade people to act.

> Every day you can help protect the environment.

What opinion words did the writer use?

PRACTICE and APPLY

Create a Features Chart

1. List the features of persuasive writing.
2. Reread Amber Hawk's letter to Mr. Scully on page 199.
3. Write one example of each feature in Amber's writing.
4. Does Amber convince you? Explain why or why not.

Features	Examples

Writing PROCESS

Prewrite

Persuasive writing presents your opinion about something. Writing a persuasive letter gives you a chance to share your opinion with someone else.

Purpose and Audience

The purpose of persuasive writing is to explain what you think in a way that will persuade your reader to think or act in a certain way.

As you plan your persuasive letter, think about the reader. Whom are you trying to persuade? You need strong facts and reasons to get people to act.

Audience

How will you persuade the reader to believe your idea is a good one? Write your answer.

Choose a Topic

Start by **brainstorming** a list of possible topics. Think of topics you have strong opinions about. From your list, choose a topic that you really believe in.

Once you choose a topic, **explore ideas** about it by listing reasons that support you opinions.

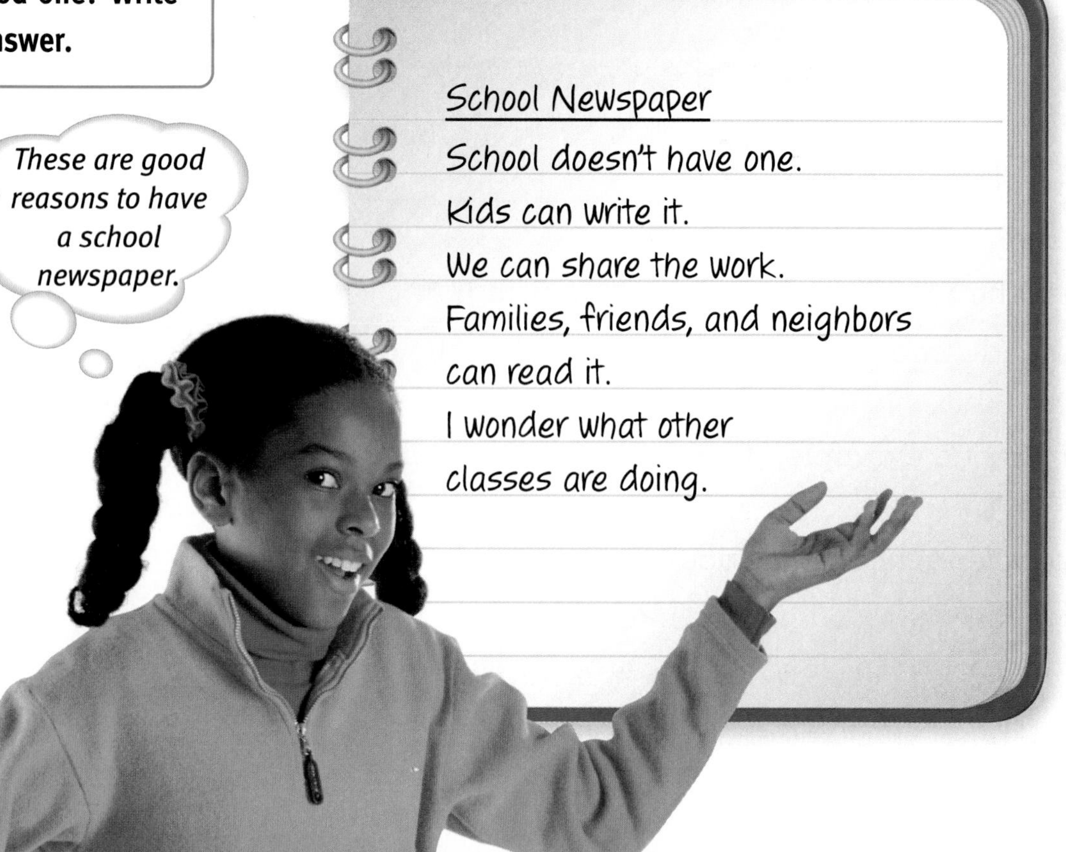

These are good reasons to have a school newspaper.
School Newspaper
School doesn't have one.
Kids can write it.
We can share the work.
Families, friends, and neighbors can read it.
I wonder what other classes are doing.

Organize • Facts and Opinions

Opinions in a persuasive letter should be supported by facts and reasons. These ideas must be presented in an order that makes sense. A fact-and-opinion chart can help you organize your ideas. Look at how this writer organized her ideas as opinions and supporting reasons.

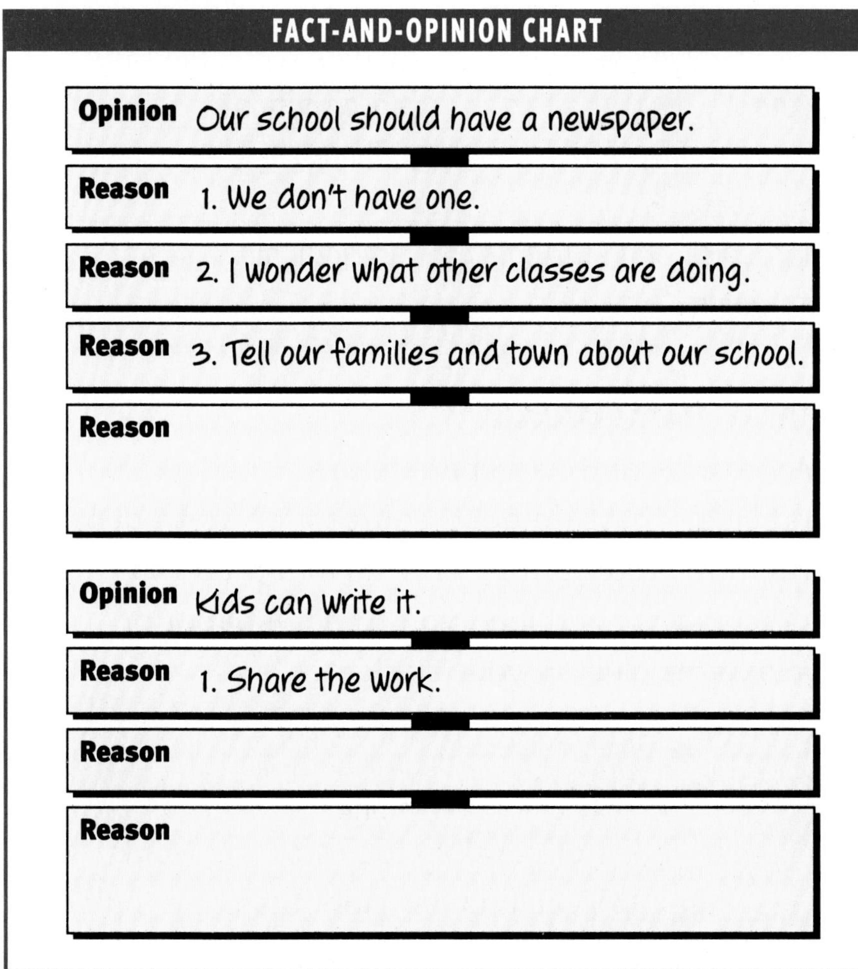

FACT-AND-OPINION CHART
Opinion Our school should have a newspaper.
Reason 1. We don't have one.
Reason 2. I wonder what other classes are doing.
Reason 3. Tell our families and town about our school.
Reason
Opinion Kids can write it.
Reason 1. Share the work.
Reason
Reason

PRACTICE and APPLY

Plan Your Own Persuasive Letter

1. Think about your purpose and audience.
2. Brainstorm a list of topics.
3. Choose a topic and explore ideas about it.
4. Organize the facts and opinions.

Checklist ✓

Prewriting

- Did you list subjects you feel strongly about?
- Did you think about your purpose and the reader?
- Did you choose a topic?
- Did you use facts and reasons to support your opinions?
- Do you need to do any research?

Prewrite • Research and Inquiry

Writer's Resources

You may need to do research to get facts or ideas for your persuasive letter. First, make a list of questions. Then decide where you might find the answers.

What Else Do I Need to Know?	Where Can I Find the Information?
Who should write a school newspaper?	Library
What topics can students write about?	Periodicals

Read Periodicals

Magazines and newspapers are called periodicals. They are good sources for up-to-date information. Your library may have a guide to periodicals that will lead you to newspaper or magazine articles on your subject.

STRATEGIES FOR USING PERIODICALS

- Prepare a list of possible topics or key words. You may need to search under more than one topic to find helpful articles.
- Ask the librarian to help you with your search.
- Take notes or make photocopies of pages with important information.

PREWRITE
DRAFT
REVISE
PROOFREAD
PUBLISH

▶ Use Other Library Resources

Library resources can include books, magazines, CD-ROMs, videotapes, and other media. The reference librarian can show you how to find information on your topic in the card or computer catalog.

▶ Use Your Research

Information you find in your research can go in your chart. From her research, this writer learned that students can run a school newspaper. What other ideas did she discover?

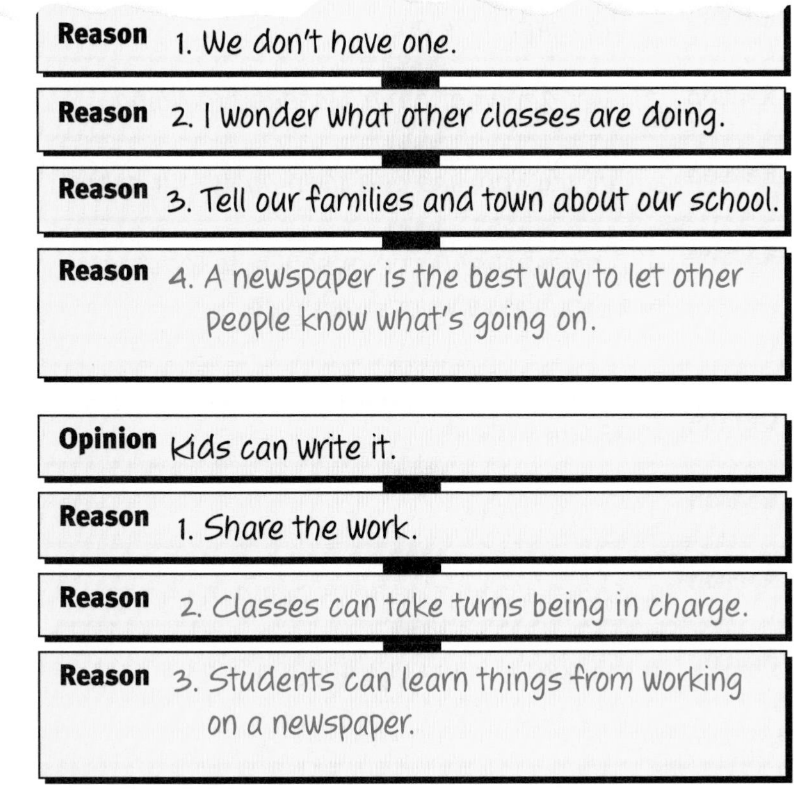

Reason 1. We don't have one.
Reason 2. I wonder what other classes are doing.
Reason 3. Tell our families and town about our school.
Reason 4. A newspaper is the best way to let other people know what's going on.
Opinion Kids can write it.
Reason 1. Share the work.
Reason 2. Classes can take turns being in charge.
Reason 3. Students can learn things from working on a newspaper.

Handbook
pages 531–535

Checklist ✓

Research and Inquiry

- **Did you list your questions?**
- **Did you identify your resources?**
- **Did you make notes?**

PRACTICE and APPLY

Review Your Plan

1. Look back at your prewriting chart.

2. List your questions.

3. Find out where you could look for answers.

4. Add new information you find to your chart.

Writing PROCESS

Draft

Look at your chart before you begin to write your persuasive letter. Think about writing a paragraph for each opinion. Use your listed facts and reasons to support the opinion. Present your ideas in an order that makes sense.

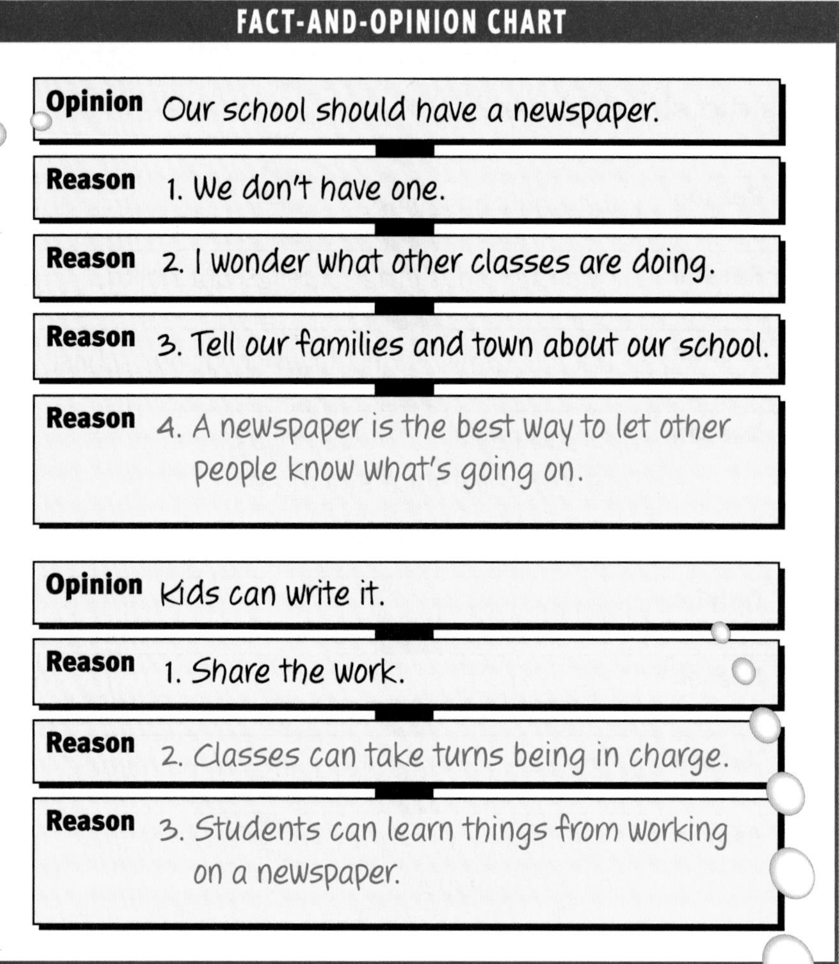
FACT-AND-OPINION CHART
Opinion Our school should have a newspaper.
Reason 1. We don't have one.
Reason 2. I wonder what other classes are doing.
Reason 3. Tell our families and town about our school.
Reason 4. A newspaper is the best way to let other people know what's going on.
Opinion Kids can write it.
Reason 1. Share the work.
Reason 2. Classes can take turns being in charge.
Reason 3. Students can learn things from working on a newspaper.

This main idea is a good lead for the first paragraph.

Main idea for the second paragraph: Students can create the paper.

Checklist

Drafting

- Does your letter fit your purpose and audience?
- Did you clearly state your opinions?
- Did you support your opinions with convincing reasons and facts?
- Are your opinions presented in an order that makes sense?

Look at how this writer turned ideas from the chart into paragraphs. First she stated her idea for a school newspaper. Then, she added supporting reasons.

DRAFT

September 14 20__

Dear Principal lin

The Brooksville School need a school newspaper We don't have one. a newspaper will help us learn about each other. I wonder what other classes are doing. I want to read about everything. To tell our families and Town.

A school newspaper can help students. They can do things together. Students can write. They can publish the newspaper Clases can take turns being in charge. A newspaper is important.

Sincerely,

Alisha Beal

Main idea: The school needs a school newspaper.

These reasons explain why the writer thinks the school should have a newspaper.

These details tell how students can create the newspaper.

TECHNOLOGY

Find out how to change the space between lines on the computer. If you use double space for your draft, you'll have room to make changes.

Practice and Apply

Draft Your Own Persuasive Letter

1. Look again at your prewriting chart.

2. Clearly state your opinions.

3. Support your opinions with facts and reasons.

Writing PROCESS

Revise

Elaborate

You can improve your writing by elaborating. When you elaborate, you add important details. As you revise your persuasive letter, you may need to add facts or reasons to support your opinions.

This writer added details to make her reasons for wanting a newspaper clearer.

> I wonder what other classes are doing.
> their projects and trips.
> I want to read about ~~everything.~~

Here the writer explained how working on a newspaper could help students.

> will teach us how to work
> A school newspaper ~~can help students. They~~
> ~~can do things~~ together.

Word Choice

When you write, choose words that will help make your opinion clear.

In a persuasive letter, opinion words attract the reader's attention. They help focus the reader on your ideas and show the reader that you believe in your ideas.

> We ought to know
> ~~I wonder~~ what other classes are doing.

OPINION WORDS

- I believe
- I think
- would be better
- should
- know
- must
- need
- ought
- require
- want
- agree

PREWRITE
DRAFT
REVISE
PROOFREAD
PUBLISH

Better Sentences

When you revise, look at your sentences. Listen to them as you read your letter aloud. Do your sentences fit together? Have you included different kinds of sentences?

Sometimes you can combine two sentences with the same subject by joining the two predicates.

> Students can write ~~. They can~~ the articles and publish the newspaper.

PRACTICE and APPLY

Revise Your Own Persuasive Letter

1. Add details or reasons to support your opinions.
2. Listen to your opening statement. Does it clearly state your opinion?
3. Add opinion words to persuade your readers.
4. **Grammar** Are there some sentences that you should combine?

TIP!

TECHNOLOGY

Use the header feature to put your name, class, and date at the top of every page.

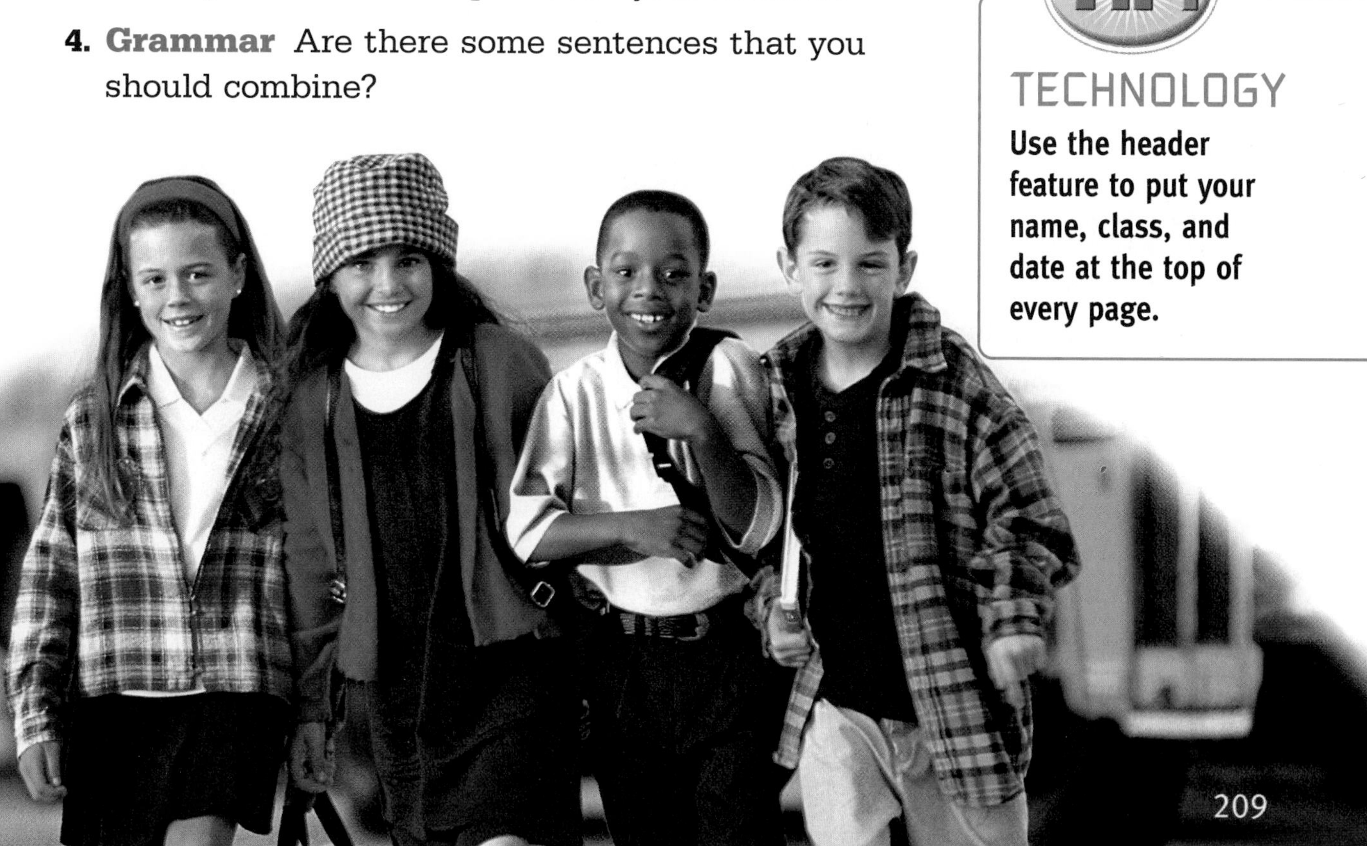

Revise • Peer Conferencing

Trade your first draft with a partner. Read each other's writing. Then ask each other for ideas.

September 14 20__

Dear Principal lin

The Brooksville School need a school newspaper We don't have one. a newspaper will help us learn about each other. I wonder what other classes are doing. I want to read about everything. To tell our families and Town.

A school newspaper can help students. They can do things together. Students can write. They can publish the newspaper Clases can take turns being in charge. A newspaper is important.

Sincerely,

Alisha Beal

A school newspaper is a great idea!

You don't need this sentence.

What do you want Mr. Lin to do?

Conferencing for the Reader

- Did your partner include these features of a persuasive letter?
  - clear statement of opinion
  - supporting reasons and facts given in an order that makes sense
  - opinion words
- Make suggestions. Also tell your partner what you like about the letter.

Revise your letter using your partner's comments and suggestions. How did this writer do it?

REVISE

September 14 20__

Dear Principal lin

The Brooksville School need a school newspaper ~~We don't have one~~. a newspaper will help us learn about each other. We ought to know ~~I wonder~~ what other classes are doing, such as their projects and trips. We need ~~I want to read about everything~~. To tell our families and Town about our school.

A school newspaper will teach us how to work ~~can help students. They can do things~~ together. We ~~Students~~ can write the articles and ~~They can~~ publish the newspaper ourselves. Clases can take turns being in charge. Please let us start our school newspaper. ~~A newspaper is important~~.

Sincerely,

Alisha Beal

Practice and Apply

Revise Your Own Persuasive Letter

1. Read your letter aloud to your partner.
2. Use your notes from the peer conference to make your draft better.
3. Make your opening statement strong.

PREWRITE | DRAFT | REVISE | PROOFREAD | PUBLISH

Checklist

Revising

- Does your letter fit your purpose and audience?
- Do your sentences fit together well?
- Are your opinions supported by facts?
- Have you used opinion words to help persuade your audience?
- Is your opening statement strong?

Proofread

You need to proofread your revised letter. Correct mistakes in mechanics, grammar and usage, and spelling.

STRATEGIES FOR PROOFREADING

- Reread your letter several times. **Look for a different kind of error each time.**
- Look for errors in capitalization and punctuation.
- Make sure each verb agrees with its subject. **Reread aloud and change verbs that don't sound right.**
- Use a dictionary or computer spell checker for spelling mistakes.

TIP!

TECHNOLOGY

Print a copy of your letter. It's easier to check mistakes on paper than on the computer screen.

REVIEW THE RULES

GRAMMAR

- A verb must agree with the time of the action. A present-tense verb tells what is happening now. A past-tense verb tells about a past action. A future-tense verb tells about an action that is going to happen.

MECHANICS

- Use a comma between the name of a city or town and the state.
- Use a comma between the day and the year in a date.
- Capitalize the first word of the greeting and the closing in a letter.
- Use a comma after the greeting and the closing in a letter.

Look at the proofreading corrections made on the draft. What does the proofreading mark / mean?

PROOFREAD

September 14 20__

Dear Principal lin,

The Brooksville School need a school newspaper. We don't have one. a newspaper will help us learn We ought to know about each other. I wonder what other classes are doing, such as their projects and trips. We need I want to read about everything. To tell our families and Town about our school.

A school newspaper will teach us how to work can help students. They can do things together. We Students can write the articles and They can publish the newspaper. Classes Clases can take turns being in charge. Please let us start our school newspaper. A newspaper is important.

Sincerely,

Alisha Beal

PREWRITE

DRAFT

REVISE

PROOFREAD

PUBLISH

Checklist

Proofreading

- Did you use commas correctly?
- Does each verb agree with its subject?
- Did you indent each paragraph?
- Did you capitalize all proper nouns?
- Did you spell all words correctly?

PROOFREADING MARKS

- ¶ new paragraph
- ^ add
- take out
- ≡ Make a capital letter.
- / Make a small letter.
- (sp) Check spelling.
- ⊙ Add a period.

Practice and Apply

Proofread Your Own Persuasive Letter

1. Check verb tenses and capitalization.
2. Use commas in the greeting, closing, and date.
3. Correct spelling mistakes.

Writing PROCESS

Publish

Look at your persuasive letter one more time before you publish it. A list like the one below can help you check your writing.

Self-Check Persuasive Letter

- ❑ What is my purpose? Will the reader understand my ideas?
- ❑ Did I explain my ideas so that the reader will agree with them?
- ❑ Did I use opinion words to make my position clear?
- ❑ Did I support my opinions with reasons and facts?
- ❑ Are my verbs in the tenses I want?
- ❑ Do my sentences fit together well?
- ❑ Are my ideas presented in an order that makes sense?
- ❑ Did I proofread and correct all mistakes?

This writer used the checklist to look over her writing. Think about her ideas as you read the letter. Do you think the letter is ready to be published? Why or why not?

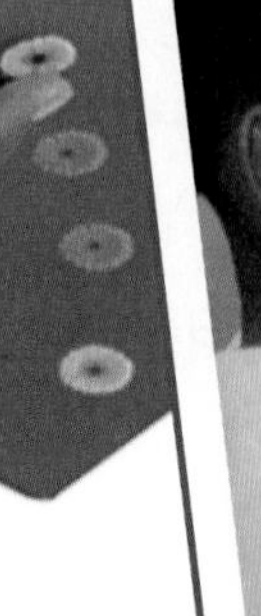

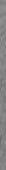

PREWRITE
DRAFT
REVISE
PROOFREAD
PUBLISH

September 14, 20_ _

Dear Principal Lin,

The Brooksville School needs a school newspaper. A newspaper will help us learn about each other. We ought to know what other classes are doing, such as their projects and trips. We need to tell our families and town about our school.

A school newspaper will teach us how to work together. We can write the articles and publish the newspaper ourselves. Classes can take turns being in charge. Please let us start our school newspaper.

Sincerely,
Alisha Beal

PRACTICE and APPLY

Publish Your Own Persuasive Writing

1. Check your revised draft one more time.
2. Make a neat final copy.
3. Add drawings or photographs.

TIP!

TECHNOLOGY

Does your school have a web site? You might want to publish your letter at the web site for other classes to read.

LISTENING
SPEAKING
VIEWING
PRESENTING

Present Your Persuasive Writing

To present your letter as a speech, you need to plan and practice. This will help make your presentation successful.

STEP 1

How to Present Your Persuasive Speech

Strategies for Speaking Remember that your purpose is to get the audience to agree with you. Show them that your idea really is great.

- Write each main idea and important details on a note card.
- Speak clearly. Emphasize key words.
- Pause briefly after talking about important points. Give the audience time to think about what you've said.

Listening Strategies

- Listen carefully for words that tell you the speaker's opinion or point of view.
- Listen to decide if the speaker's ideas make sense.
- Make notes and ask questions after the speech.

Multimedia Ideas

Make a tape of cheers that support your topic. Play the tape before you begin speaking to help interest the audience.

STEP 2

How to Show Your Speech

Suggestions for Visuals Help persuade your audience by adding visuals or handing out samples.

- Make a banner that clearly states your topic.
- Make samples of an item related to your topic to hand out afterward.
- Show pictures or diagrams about your topic to help interest the audience.

Brookville News

STEP 3

How to Share Your Speech

Strategies for Rehearsing The more you practice, the more comfortable you'll feel giving your speech.

- Practice with a friend or a family member. Practice the hard parts again.
- Ask your practice audience for suggestions.
- Show that you believe in your idea.

Viewing Strategies

- Look at the visuals carefully. Read all the labels.
- Think about how visuals can help to persuade you.
- Decide if the visuals support the speaker's opinions.

PRACTICE and APPLY

Rehearse Your Own Persuasive Speech

1. Write your main ideas on note cards.
2. Create a banner or handouts to help "sell" your idea.
3. Practice your speech. Practice again.
4. Look at the audience as you speak.

TAAS

Writing Tests

On a writing test, you will be asked to write something in response to a prompt. Remember to read the prompt carefully. Look for key words and phrases that tell you what to write about and how to present your ideas.

This prompt tells who the audience is.

This word tells you what kind of writing this is.

Look for words that are clues to the purpose of this writing.

Prompt

Your school is going to have a school newspaper. It needs a name. Think of a name for the newspaper. Write a letter to <u>your principal</u> telling your idea for a name. Give your <u>opinion</u> about why your name for the newspaper is a good one. Try to <u>make your principal choose your name.</u>

How to Read a Prompt

Purpose Find key words in the prompt to help you figure out the purpose of the writing. The words "make your principal choose your name" tell you that the purpose will be to influence your audience.

Audience This prompt tells you whom to write for. The words "your principal" tell who your audience will be.

Persuasive Writing The word "opinion" tells what kind of writing you should do. When you write your opinion about a subject, it is persuasive writing. Persuasive writing tries to make people think or act in a certain way.

Test Tip
Take your time and do your work carefully.

How to Write to a Prompt

Here are some tips to remember when you are given a writing prompt.

Before Writing **Content/Ideas**	• Figure out the purpose of your writing. • Be sure you know your audience. • Decide how you feel about a topic. Write down reasons that support your feelings.
During Writing **Organization/ Paragraph Structure**	• Start with a good topic sentence. • Organize your reasons in an order that makes sense. • Use opinion words.
After Writing **Grammar/Usage**	• Always proofread your writing. • Use correct punctuation and capitalization. • Spell all words correctly. • Be sure you used correct verb forms.

Apply What You Learned

First, read the prompt on a writing test to find out your writing purpose and topic. Then decide how you will organize your ideas.

Prompt

Your teacher has decided to take your class on a field trip.

Write a letter to your teacher telling about where you want to go. Try to make your teacher choose your place. Give your opinion on why it is the best place. Explain your reasons.

Unit 3 Review

Grammar and Writing Review

pages 160–161

Action Verbs

A. Write the sentences. Circle each action verb.

1. My brother builds model cars.
2. I play the piano every day.
3. My mom plants a garden.
4. Dad paints pictures with watercolors.
5. My sister writes a story.

pages 162–163

Present-Tense Verbs

B. Write each sentence. Use the correct present-tense form of the verb in ( ).

6. Ana (watch) Karla paint pictures.
7. Ana (wish) she could paint, too.
8. Karla (try) to paint a picture of a cat.
9. Ana (copy) Karla's brush strokes.
10. Ana's painting (look) just like Karla's.

pages 164–165

Subject–Verb Agreement

C. Write each sentence. Use the correct verb in ( ).

11. Our class (like, likes) birds.
12. We (make, makes) bird feeders.
13. One group (mix, mixes) peanut butter and seeds.
14. Another group (put, puts) the food in a mesh bag.
15. One bird (fly, flies) around the bird feeder.
16. Some birds (perch, perches) on the bag.
17. A blue jay (peck, pecks) at the food.
18. The class (watch, watches) the birds.
19. Some children (paint, paints) bird pictures.
20. All the students (enjoy, enjoys) the birds.

Unit 3 Review

pages 166–167

Mechanics and Usage: Letter Punctuation

D. Write the greetings and closings of these letters correctly.

21. dear Mom

22. yours truly
Anita

23. Dear mr. Able

24. sincerely
brandon

25. love
aunt lucy

pages 170–171

Past-Tense Verbs

E. Write each sentence. Use the past tense of the verb in ( ).

26. Rita's grandmother once (dance) in a ballet company.

27. She (show) Rita one of her ballerina outfits.

28. Rita (try) on the ballerina costume.

29. The girl (decide) to take ballet lessons.

30. Rita's grandmother (hug) her.

pages 172–173

Future-Tense Verbs

F. Write each sentence. Change the verb in ( ) to the future tense.

31. We (write) reports about our favorite sports.

32. Elaine (reads) an article about ice hockey.

33. Bobby (shows) us pictures of baseball players.

34. Anita (tells) us about a basketball team.

35. The teacher (videotapes) our presentations.

36. A panel of sports writers (speaks) to the class.

37. The writers (answer) questions about local teams.

38. We (ask) questions about the new football field.

39. We (play) sports in our school.

40. Each team (appears) in the school newspaper.

Unit 3 Review

pages 174–175

Combining Sentences: Verbs

G. Combine each pair of sentences. Use *and* to join the two predicates. Write the new sentence.

41. The beach is warm. The beach is sunny.

42. Harry builds a small sand castle. Harry decorates a small sand castle.

43. Marilyn sees Harry. Marilyn helps Harry.

44. The water touches the sand castle. The water covers the sand castle.

45. Harry sees a sea gull. Harry hears a sea gull.

46. Marilyn finds shells. Marilyn gathers shells.

47. The children play. The children wade.

48. Harry finds a tide pool. Harry examines a tide pool.

49. A fish jumps. A fish dives.

50. The children plan a big new sand castle. The children build a big new sand castle.

pages 176–177

Mechanics and Usage: Commas in Dates and Places

H. Write each group of words. Add a comma where needed.

51. February 2 2001

52. Nome Alaska

53. Austin Texas

54. Charleston South Carolina

55. May 31 1949

pages 190–191

Vocabulary: Prefixes

I. Write each sentence. Circle the word that has a prefix. Then write the prefix and the meaning of the word.

56. Peter wrote a story about a bear that disappeared.

57. Peter rewrote the story several times.

58. The story about a bear was unusual.

59. Peter was uncertain how to end his story.

60. The missing bear suddenly reappeared.

pages 192–193

Composition: Leads and Endings

J. Write each sentence. Then write if it is a lead or ending.

61. The day began like any hot day in July.

62. Fortunately, that was the last time we saw the crocodile.

63. Have you ever wondered how Babe Ruth hit so many home runs?

64. The song was over when the singer sat down.

65. I guess that's why my baby brother is so smart.

pages 212–213

Proofreading a Letter

K. 66–75. Write the following letter correctly. Correct the punctuation, grammar, and spelling mistakes. Use capital letters correctly. There are 10 mistakes.

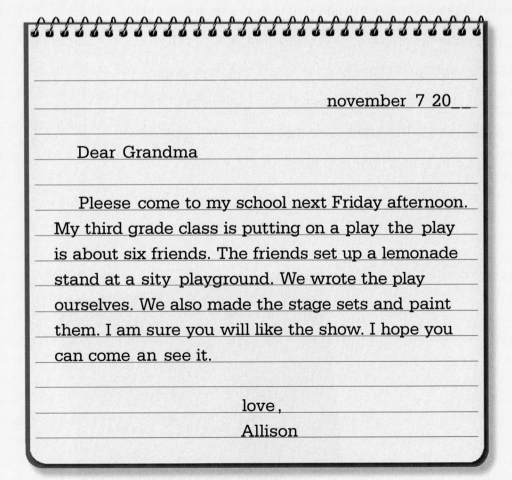

november 7 20__

Dear Grandma

Pleese come to my school next Friday afternoon. My third grade class is putting on a play the play is about six friends. The friends set up a lemonade stand at a sity playground. We wrote the play ourselves. We also made the stage sets and paint them. I am sure you will like the show. I hope you can come an see it.

love,
Allison

Project File

PROJECT 1 A Book Review

A book review tells what a book is about. It tells what you think about the book. Read the following book review.

The Mysterious Tadpole
by Steven Kellogg

Title tells the title of the book.

Author's Name tells who wrote the book.

What would you do if you had a pet tadpole that grew larger than a whale? That's what Alphonse had to figure out in this funny book.

Begin the review with something that will grab the reader's attention.

One of Alphonse's problems is that he lives in the city. When his tadpole grows too big for his parents' apartment, he needs a place where the tadpole can swim.

Alphonse asks the librarian, Miss Seevers, to help him solve his problem. One thing that helps is that Alphonse trains his tadpole to fetch things in water.

Tell where the story takes place, who the characters are, and what happens but not how it ends.

I liked this book because it is a funny story. The pictures that the artist drew also made me laugh. If you like a funny book, this is a good book for you.

End the review by telling why you like or dislike the book.

Share a book with a friend

Think of a book you really like that a friend might enjoy. List the important things you remember about the book.

Then write a review that will encourage your friend to read the book. Be sure to include the title, the author's name, where the story takes place, who the main characters are, one thing that happens in the book, and why you like it.

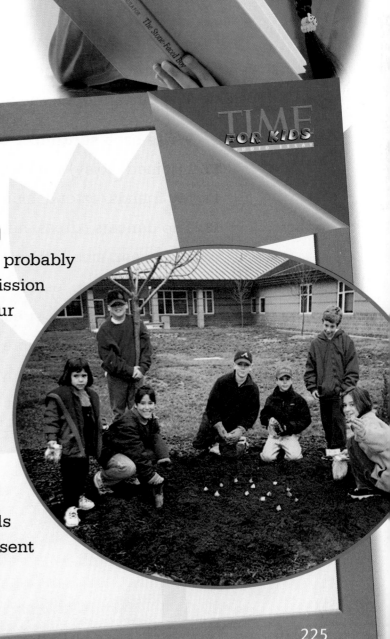

TIME FOR KIDS

PROJECT 2

A Persuasive Speech

The kid heroes you read about probably had to be persuasive to get permission for their projects. Look around your school or community for project ideas. Choose one problem you would like to solve.

Community Heroes Write a persuasive speech to convince your principal, the mayor, or another person to let you carry out the project. Prepare visual aids to go with your speech. Then present your speech to the class.

Grammar

Extra Practice

Action Verbs

A. Write each sentence. Underline the action verb.

1. Lucia writes a play.
2. Terrell designs the scenery.
3. His friends make props.
4. Ms. Garza sews the costumes.
5. Kaitlyn creates a program.
6. The crowd enters the hall.
7. The actors wait behind the curtain.
8. The people look toward the stage.
9. Mr. Jones plays the piano.
10. The curtain opens at the sound of music.

B. Write each sentence. Use the correct word in ( ).

11. I (joined, noisy) a dance club.
12. My friends (attend, music) dance class every week.
13. The dancers (dress, new) in black tights.
14. We (wear, small) taps on our shoes.
15. Dancers (listen, ears) carefully to the music.
16. I (imagine, idea) a special day.
17. We (dance, song) before a big audience.
18. Everyone (cheers, happy) our performance.
19. I (bow, grateful) in front of the happy crowd.
20. I (awake, surprise) from my dream!

Present-Tense Verbs

A. Write each sentence. Choose the correct verb in ( ).

1. Armando (play, plays) his flute every day.
2. His friend Vera (like, likes) his music.
3. The teacher (listen, listens) to Armando's music.
4. She (write, writes) a letter to a famous flute player.
5. The musician (reply, replies) to the letter.
6. Mr. Shen (visit, visits) the school.
7. The student (meet, meets) the flute player.
8. He (explain, explains) the parts of the flute to Armando.
9. He (teach, teaches) Armando a new piece of music.
10. The principal (invite, invites) Mr. Shen to perform for the school.

B. Write each sentence. Use the correct present-tense form of the verb in ( ). Spell the verb correctly.

11. The musician (carry) his flute to the gym.
12. Vera (rush) to get a front seat.
13. Mr. Shen (hold) the instrument gently.
14. He (press) the keys to play the music.
15. The song (sound) lovely.
16. The teacher (enjoy) the concert.
17. Bruce (hope) to be a singer.
18. He (take) singing lessons every week.
19. The teacher (say) Bruce sings well.
20. Bruce (practice) singing with Armando.

Extra Practice

Subject-Verb Agreement

A. **Write the verb in each sentence. If the sentence has a singular subject, write *singular* next to the verb. If the sentence has a plural subject, write *plural*.**

1. I notice many birds in our backyard.
2. The birds need food.
3. I build a bird feeder.
4. Ramon and Keisha help me.
5. My friends use pine cones.
6. My neighbors gather many cones.
7. Ramon brings peanut butter.
8. Keisha gets plastic spoons.
9. We spread peanut butter on the pine cones.
10. My brother hangs the pine cones on a tree.

B. **Write each sentence. Write the correct present-tense form of the verb in ( ).**

11. The birds (love, loves) our peanut butter cones.
12. Ramon, Keisha, and I (make, makes) another bird feeder.
13. I (string, strings) cranberries on a long thread.
14. You (tie, ties) the string of cranberries to another tree.
15. A rabbit (notice, notices) the red cranberries.
16. The animal (reach, reaches) up.
17. The rabbit (chew, chews) the berries on the string!
18. Ramon (climb, climbs) up the tree.
19. He (wrap, wraps) the string of cranberries around a branch.
20. The birds (peck, pecks) at the berries on the tree branch.

Letter Punctuation

A. Choose the correct item in each pair. Write the letter for your answer.

1. a. dear Mr. Murphy, b. Dear Mr. Murphy,

2. a. Dear, Cameron b. Dear Cameron,

3. a. sincerely Yours, Dan b. Sincerely yours, Dan

4. a. Your friend, Teri b. Your, friend Teri

5. a. Dear Skyler, b. dear Skyler,

6. a. Love Renee, b. Love, Renee

7. a. Dear, Grandma Kim, b. Dear Grandma Kim,

8. a. Love, Uncle Ralph b. love, Uncle Ralph

9. a. yours truly, Tomas b. Yours truly, Tomas

10. a. Sincerely, Julie b. Sincerely, Julie,

B. Write each item correctly.

11. dear Mrs. Colby

12. Your Cousin Marion

13. most, sincerely Adam

14. Love Aunt JoAnn

15. dear Edmund

16. yours Truly Hayley

17. Dear, Tad

18. very Truly, yours Brooke

19. dear, Mr. Willey

20. love Uncle Stuart

Extra Practice

Past-Tense Verbs

A. Write each sentence. Underline the past-tense verb.

1. It looked like a snowy day.
2. Dad cooked eggs for breakfast.
3. Kenji liked the whole wheat toast.
4. I sipped fresh apple juice.
5. We carried our dishes to the sink.
6. Snowflakes drifted slowly to the ground.
7. Kenji grabbed his snow pants and mittens.
8. I gathered my gloves and scarf.
9. Mom opened the front door.
10. Cold air roared into the warm kitchen.

B. Write each sentence. Use the past tense of the verb in ( ).

11. We (walk) toward the backyard.
12. Kenji (roll) two snowballs.
13. I (stack) the small snowball on top of the big one.
14. The children (dry) their hands.
15. I (fetch) two twigs for the snowman's arms.
16. Kenji (use) a carrot for the snowman's nose.
17. The snowman (smile) with its crooked mouth.
18. The snowman still (need) a scarf.
19. I (plop) a hat on the snowman's head.
20. We (wave) good-bye to our friend.

Future-Tense Verbs

A. Write each sentence. Write whether each underlined verb is in the *past*, *present*, or *future* tense.

1. Years ago, people <u>traveled</u> by horse and buggy.
2. They <u>admired</u> the countryside.
3. Horses still <u>pull</u> buggies.
4. Today, people <u>drive</u> cars instead of buggies.
5. A creative person <u>designed</u> a horseless buggy.
6. People <u>enjoyed</u> a new way of traveling.
7. In the future, we <u>will travel</u> in new ways.
8. Someone <u>will invent</u> a faster way to travel.
9. Someday, maybe people <u>will live</u> in outer space.
10. I <u>want</u> a spaceship of my own.

B. Write each sentence. Write the verb in the future tense.

11. Our class hosts a science fair.
12. Students display their projects.
13. I enter my spaceship design in the contest.
14. Some projects show designs for the home.
15. Tina invents a new egg cooker.
16. Sheila creates a robot.
17. Mrs. Francis picks the winning entry.
18. The winner receives a ribbon.
19. We celebrate by having a party.
20. The class plans projects for next year's fair.

Extra Practice

Combining Sentences: Verbs

A. Write each sentence. Underline the predicate. Circle the word that joins two verbs.

1. Sarah likes and shows pets.
2. She plans and arranges a pet parade.
3. Mel washes and combs his dog.
4. Jody brushes and fluffs her cat's fur.
5. Sarah leads and directs the parade.
6. Some pets show off and do tricks.
7. Valerie's parrot talks and squawks loudly.
8. Jody's cat meows and prances.
9. Mel's dog jumps and spins.
10. The crowd claps and cheers for the funny pets.

B. Combine each pair of sentences. Use *and* to join the two predicates. Write the new sentence.

11. Mom plans a camping trip. Mom arranges a camping trip.
12. Dad buys the food. Dad packs the food.
13. Ana finds the camping gear. Ana sorts the camping gear.
14. Luis chooses some outdoor clothes. Luis packs some outdoor clothes.
15. Mom chops some firewood. Mom stacks some firewood.
16. Mom builds a campfire. Mom lights a campfire.
17. Dad washes some vegetables. Dad cooks some vegetables.
18. Everyone sings after dinner. Everyone plays after dinner.
19. The children toast marshmallows. The children eat marshmallows.
20. The family sleeps under the stars. The family dreams under the stars.

Commas in Dates and Places

A. Choose the correct item in each pair. Write the letter for your answer.

1.	a. July 25, 1996	b. July, 25 1996
2.	a. Aurora, Illinois	b. Aurora Illinois,
3.	a. April 8 1993	b. April 8, 1993
4.	a. St., Louis Missouri	b. St. Louis, Missouri
5.	a. Nome Alaska	b. Nome, Alaska
6.	a. June 18, 1966	b. June 18, 19,66
7.	a. January 9, 1954	b. January, 9, 1954
8.	a. Seattle, Washington	b. Seattle Washington
9.	a. August, 11, 2001	b. August 11, 2001
10.	a. Flint Michigan	b. Flint, Michigan

B. Write the sentences. Add commas where they are needed.

11. Lindsey lives in Landview Pennsylvania.

12. She moved there on February 12 1998.

13. Before that, she lived in New York New York.

14. I visited her on August 2 2000.

15. I met her on her birthday in Orlando Florida.

16. I returned home on August 9 2000.

17. Lindsey was born on August 6 1990.

18. My mother was born in Tampa Bay Florida.

19. My favorite city to visit is Toronto Ontario.

20. I went there on December 31 2000.

Grammar

Cumulative Review

Unit 1 Sentences

A. Write each group of words. Write *sentence* if the group of words is a sentence. Write *not a sentence* if the group is not a sentence.

1. Sophia's first day at school.
2. The teacher introduced Sophia.
3. Sophia said hello to everyone.
4. Went to the playground.
5. Sophia met two new friends.

B. Write each sentence correctly. Write *statement*, *question*, *command*, or *exclamation* next to each.

6. we will go to Florida
7. what fun you will have there
8. do you like to fly
9. look at the view below
10. will we land soon

C. Write each sentence. Draw one line under the subject and two lines under the predicate.

11. The zookeeper visited our class.
12. Nikki talked about wild animals.
13. Tigers hunt at night.
14. Monkeys swing in trees.
15. Polar bears like cold weather.

D. Use *and* to combine each pair of sentences.

16. The children visited the zoo. The zookeeper greeted them.
17. The lions sat on the rocks. We saw them eat lunch.
18. The seals swam fast. Everyone clapped.
19. The monkeys swung in the trees. We watched them.
20. The zoo is a great place. The children had fun.

Cumulative Review

E. Correct each run-on sentence. Write the two complete ideas as two separate sentences.

21. Clara Barton was a teacher she lived in New Jersey.

22. She became a nurse a war had started.

23. She nursed the soldiers many men were hurt.

24. She started the American Red Cross many people joined it.

25. You can visit her home it is in Maryland.

Unit 2 Nouns

A. Write each sentence. Draw one line under each singular noun. Draw two lines under each plural noun. Write the plural form of each singular noun.

26. My family enjoyed the rides at the fair.

27. A woman was selling handmade quilts.

28. A man gently clipped a sheep with clippers.

29. We saw a goose and some ducks.

30. One child won a stuffed bunny with floppy ears.

B. Write the sentences. Write the correct abbreviation of each underlined word. Begin every proper noun with a capital letter.

31. On january 4, we will go to england.

32. On saturday, we will visit the city of london.

33. Every monday, the guards parade there.

34. Look at all the people at the british museum.

35. Will mister johnson meet us there?

36. On tuesday january 12, we will take the train to scotland.

37. We will stay in the city of edinburgh.

38. I would like to visit edinburgh castle.

39. Mister gregory will be our guide.

40. We will fly home on sunday.

Grammar

Cumulative Review

C. Write the possessive form of each noun.

41. Ramon

42. parents

43. wolf

44. neighbors

45. women

46. butterflies

47. fox

48. sheep

49. bus

50. boys

D. Use *and* to combine the subjects of each pair of sentences. Write the new sentence.

51. Whales swim in the sea. Dolphins swim in the sea.

52. Rocks wash up on the beach. Shells wash up on the beach.

53. Seashells are fun to collect. Pebbles are fun to collect.

54. Gulls fly overhead. Terns fly overhead.

55. Clams are in the wet sand. Mussels are in the wet sand.

Unit 3 Verbs

A. Write the verb in each sentence. Write *past*, *present*, or *future* next to each verb.

56. Mom drives us to soccer practice.

57. Mr. Russo will help us win the game.

58. Vic and I practiced yesterday.

59. We play on the third-grade team.

60. We will play the fourth-grade team.

Cumulative Review

B. Write each sentence. Use the correct verb in ( ).

61. The farmers in Iowa (grow, grows) corn.

62. Ben (works, work) on a large farm.

63. They (plant, plants) the corn in April.

64. Ben (harvests, harvest) it in late summer.

65. Ben (uses, use) modern machinery on his job.

C. Write each item correctly. Add a comma where it is needed.

66. dear Aunt Barbara

67. sincerely Angela

68. Sacramento california

69. May 3 2000

70. Chicago Illinois

D. Use *and* to combine the predicates of each pair of sentences. Write the new sentence.

71. Uncle Luis lights the fire. He broils the hamburgers.

72. Ana peels the apples. Ana puts them on a plate.

73. Gina boils the potatoes. She sets them aside to cool.

74. Dan slices tomatoes. Dan peels a cucumber.

75. Raquel makes the punch. She adds the ice cubes.

Verbs and Writing That Compares

UNIT 4

In this unit you will learn about different kinds of verbs. You will also learn about comparative writing. Writing that compares looks at things and tells how they are alike and how they are different.

Science Link *As a child, Carmen Lomas Garza became interested in horned toads. Read to find out what she compares them to and what similarities and differences she describes.*

When we were kids, my mother and grandmother would get mad at us for playing in the hot sun in the middle of the day. They'd say we were just like the horned toads at high noon, playing outside without a care.

I was fascinated by the horned toads. They're shaped like frogs, but they're not frogs. They're lizards. They have horns all over their bodies to protect them from bigger animals that want to eat them.

from ***In My Family*** by Carmen Lomas Garza

Thinking Like a Writer

Writing That Compares Writing that compares shows how topics are alike and how they are different. Reread the passage.

- How are horned toads like frogs? How are they different?

Linking Verbs The author used different forms of the linking verb *be*. Read the paragraphs again.

QUICK WRITE Write the different forms of the verb *be* that are found in each paragraph.

Grammar

Main and Helping Verbs

RULES

Sometimes a verb may be more than one word.

has cleaned   *is sweeping*

The **main verb** tells what the subject does or is.

Linda has cleaned her room.

The **helping verb** helps the main verb show an action.

Linda has cleaned her room.

Verbs

When would you use a helping verb? Write the answer in your journal.

Verbs Often Used as Helping Verbs

have	*am*	*was*
has	*is*	*were*
had	*are*	*will*

Guided Practice

Tell which word in each sentence is the main verb and which is the helping verb.

EXAMPLE: Dad has asked for a mop.
main verb: asked; helping verb: has

1. My sister was taking out the trash.
2. My brother had washed the dishes.
3. Mom and Amy will scrub the stairs.
4. Paulo is dusting the top shelf.
5. Dad has vacuumed the rug.

REVIEW THE RULES

- The **main verb** tells what the subject does or is.
- The **helping verb** helps the main verb show an action.

Grammar

More Practice

A. Write each sentence. Underline each main verb. Circle each helping verb.

6. We are cleaning our house.
7. Carol is washing the floor.
8. We are dusting the bookcase.
9. Toby is working hard.
10. He has scrubbed the floor.
11. Juan and Carlos have polished the furniture.
12. I am washing the windows.
13. Mom will rake the leaves.
14. Dad will mow the grass.
15. I have watered the garden.

Handbook page 512

B. Spiral Review Write the sentences. Use the future tense. Circle helping verbs. Capitalize proper nouns.

16. We (plan) a neighborhood cleanup.
17. juan and ricky (pick) up litter.
18. carol (donates) some trash bags.
19. I (ask) dad for help.
20. He (provides) a trash can.

Extra Practice, page 310

Writing Activity A Paragraph

Write a paragraph about a project that you have worked on. Describe the work in an order that makes sense.
APPLY GRAMMAR: Circle the helping verbs in your writing.

Grammar

Using Helping Verbs

RULES

Use the helping verbs *has, have,* and *had* to help main verbs show an action in the past. Both the main verb and the helping verb must agree with the subject of the sentence.

Rule	Example
Use *has* with a singular subject and *he, she,* or *it.*	*Pam has visited the bakery.* *She has talked to the baker.*
Use *have* with a plural subject and with *I, you, we,* or *they.*	*The children have talked about food.* *I have asked questions.*
Use *had* with a singular or plural subject.	*The baker had baked bread.* *The bakers had baked bread.*

THINK AND WRITE

Verbs

When would you use the helping verbs *has, have,* and *had?* Write the answer in your journal.

Guided Practice

Tell which is the correct helping verb in ( ).

EXAMPLE: I (have, has) ordered food. *have*

1. The baker (have, has) baked white bread.
2. You (have, has) listed the kinds of bread.
3. The children (have, has) tasted the bagels.
4. Daryl (have, has) finished all the bread.
5. We (had, has) enjoyed the party.

REVIEW THE RULES

- Use the helping verbs *has, have,* and *had* to help main verbs show an action in the past. Both the main verb and the helping verb must agree with the subject.

Grammar

More Practice

A. Write each sentence. Choose the correct helping verb.

6. The chef (had, have) created a new soup.

7. We (have, has) watched the chef cook.

8. One helper (have, has) washed the vegetables.

9. He (have, had) peeled the vegetables, too.

10. Two cooks (has, have) followed the chef's directions.

11. They (have, has) chopped the meat.

12. The chef (have, has) picked the spices.

13. One man (had, have) added salt.

14. I (have, has) tasted the soup.

15. You (has, had) written the recipe.

Handbook page 512

B. Spiral Review Write each sentence. Use the correct verb in ( ). Use the past tense of the underlined verb.

16. Tony and Tina (has, have) <u>bake</u> a birthday cake.

17. Tony (have, has) <u>measure</u> the flour.

18. Tina (have, has) <u>add</u> two eggs.

19. They (has, have) <u>mix</u> everything together.

20. The children (has, have) <u>frost</u> the cake.

Extra Practice, page 311

Writing Activity A Description

Write a description of a party. Choose words that help your readers feel like they are at the party.

APPLY GRAMMAR: Include the helping verbs *has, have,* or *had* in your writing. Circle these helping verbs.

Grammar

Linking Verbs

RULES

A linking verb does not show action. It connects the subject to a noun or an adjective in the predicate. The verb *be* is a common linking verb.

The day is sunny.

An action verb tells what the subject does.

We joined a nature walk.

Verbs

When would you use a linking verb? Write your answer in your journal.

The verb *be* tells what the subject is or is like. It has special forms in the present tense.

We are cool. I am happy. Terry is our guide.

The verb *be* has special forms in the past tense.

We were cool. I was happy. Terry was our guide.

Guided Practice

Name the verb in each sentence. Tell if the word is a linking verb or an action verb.

EXAMPLE: The forest was dark. *was, linking verb*

1. That tree is an elm.
2. I walked on the path.
3. Rolf was the first to see a mushroom.
4. These ferns are beautiful.
5. The children listened to bird sounds.

Grammar

REVIEW THE RULES

- The linking verb *be* does not show action.

More Practice

A. Write each sentence. Draw a line under each verb. Write *linking verb* or *action verb* to describe each verb.

6. This nature walk is a real treat.

7. We stay with our guide.

8. I am a nature lover.

9. Birds were high in the trees.

10. Terry points out plants and animals.

11. Our long walk was interesting.

12. Some plants are new to me.

13. The fir trees were so tall.

14. It was a great hike.

15. Our guide taught us many things.

Handbook page 508

B. Spiral Review Write the sentences. Circle each plural subject. Draw one line under each present-tense verb. Draw two lines under each helping verb.

16. Yellowstone National Park is in Wyoming.

17. This park also spreads into Idaho and Montana.

18. Many people have visited the park.

19. Visitors were walking throughout the park.

20. Hikers have climbed the mountains.

Extra Practice, page 312

Writing Activity A News Report

Write a news report about a popular park. Make your writing sound like a newspaper report.

APPLY GRAMMAR: Use action and linking verbs in your report. Circle each linking verb.

Social Studies Link

Grammar

Using Linking Verbs

RULES

Use the linking verbs *is, am,* and *was* when the subject of the sentence is singular.

> *I am a good swimmer.*
> *Gerry is a fine athlete.*
> *The teacher was new in our school.*

Use *are* and *were* with a plural subject and *you.*

> *They are friends.*
> *We were early.*
> *You were not late.*

Verbs

Write how you can tell the difference between the present-tense and the past-tense forms of *be*.

The verb *be* must agree with the subject in both the present and past tenses.

Subject	Present Tense	Past Tense
singular noun and *he, she, it*	*is*	*was*
I	*am*	*was*
plural noun and *we, you, they*	*are*	*were*

Guided Practice

Tell which form of the verb *be* is correct.

EXAMPLE: Hal (was, were) my swim teacher. *was*

1. Yesterday (is, was) my first time in the pool.
2. I (was, were) afraid of the water.
3. We (is, were) eager students.
4. Now I (am, is) not afraid anymore.
5. They (is, are) good swimmers.

REVIEW THE RULES

- Use *is, am,* and *was* with singular subjects.
- Use *are* and *were* with plural subjects and ***you***.

Grammar

More Practice

A. Write each sentence. Use the correct verb in ( ).

6. Last year we (were, was) swimming buddies.
7. I (were, was) just a beginner last year.
8. This summer we (are, is) partners again.
9. Today I (is, am) ready for my lesson.
10. Our new teacher (is, are) Ms. Gates.
11. Ms. Gates (is, was) also our health teacher.
12. Gerry and I (is, are) helpers today.
13. Gerry (is, was) great on the diving board.
14. Yesterday we (was, were) contestants in a swim race.
15. The teacher said that Gerry (was, were) the winner.

Handbook page 508

B. Spiral Review **Write each sentence. Use the past or future tense as shown in ( ). Add commas where needed.**

16. (past) We start our trip in Austin Texas.
17. (past) My family stop in Atlanta Georgia.
18. (past) We arrive in Maine on July 14 2000.
19. (past) We are in Bangor Maine, for a week.
20. (future) I save money for the next trip in 2002.

Extra Practice, page 313

Writing Activity A Diary Entry

Write in a diary about the first day you learned something new. Share your feelings with your reader.

APPLY GRAMMAR: Use linking verbs in your writing. Circle the linking verbs.

Commas in a Series

RULES

Use commas to separate three or more words in a series.

Do not use a comma after the last word in a series.

Mom, Dad, and Ed told us about baseball.

Commas help make the meaning of a sentence clear.

Ed Mary Lou and I went to the baseball game.

Ed, Mary Lou, and I went to the baseball game.

Commas

Write how commas help make the meaning of a sentence clear.

Guided Practice

Tell where a comma is needed in each sentence.

EXAMPLE: Sally has a hat glove and bat.
after hat *and after* glove

1. The coach is working with Gary Mike and Lee.
2. Tanya showed us how to touch first second and third base.
3. Catching throwing and running are important skills.
4. The ball can hit the grass the dirt or the wall.
5. Baseball players can hit catch and throw the ball.

REVIEW THE RULES

- Use commas to separate words in a series.

More Practice

A. Write each sentence. Add commas where needed.

6. We learned about strikeouts errors and stolen bases.
7. I played catcher pitcher and shortstop.
8. Gary ran through the infield outfield and base paths.
9. Each team will try to steal tag and slide into bases.
10. Vera David and Curt are learning to bunt.
11. Kevin leaned reached and caught the ball.
12. Sam had a strikeout a home run and a single.
13. Wendy hit a long straight and powerful home run.
14. Larry ate a hot dog popcorn and peanuts.
15. We cheered clapped and chanted for our team.

Handbook page 528

B. Spiral Review Write each sentence with the present-tense form of *be*. Underline each proper noun.

16. Coach Green (be) proud of the Mudville Bears.
17. Roger (be) a great pitcher.
18. Sally (be) the captain of our team.
19. We (be) the best team in Mudville.
20. You (be) the best fans.

Extra Practice, page 314

Writing Activity A Character Sketch

Write a sketch about a favorite baseball player or another sports star. Use details that capture the readers' attention and make them want to meet the person.

APPLY MECHANICS AND USAGE: Use words in a series in your sketch. Circle the commas.

Social Studies Link

Grammar REVIEW

Mixed Review

REVIEW THE RULES

- The main verb tells what the subject is or does. The helping verb helps the main verb show an action.
- Use the helping verbs *has, have,* and *had* to help main verbs show an action in the past.
- The linking verb *be* does not show action.
- Use *is, am,* and *was* with singular subjects.
- Use *are* and *were* with plural subjects and *you.*
- Use commas to separate three or more words in a series.

QUICK WRITE

Verbs

Write five sentences about a family. Use action verbs and linking verbs.

Practice

A. Write the sentences. Underline each linking verb. Circle each action verb.

1. The whole family is here.
2. The twins are the youngest children.
3. Grandpa is our oldest relative.
4. Our family is very large.
5. Cousins traveled here from many places.
6. Uncle Steven's kids were here first.
7. I am the fourth child in my family.
8. All the cousins played games.
9. Aunt Holly drove her car from Alaska.
10. A friend snapped photos of all of us.

B. Write each sentence. Draw one line under the main verb. Circle the helping verb.

11. Grandma is talking about her childhood.

12. Aunt Kate was showing us pictures.

13. We have asked everyone to listen.

14. I have learned about my family.

15. Donna was drawing the family tree.

16. Donna has listed all our names.

17. Grandma has saved birth records from Mexico.

18. I am looking at old photos.

19. Jim had created a film about the family.

20. Pat is interviewing Grandpa.

C. Challenge Write the following paragraph in the present tense. Write the correct form of each verb. Use commas where needed.

21.–25. I were happy. My cousins José, Rosa and Joshua were here. My brother was late. Some aunts have coming from Texas.

Handbook pages 508, 512, 528

Writing Activity A Message

Write a message for a family member. Include interesting details to capture your reader's attention.

APPLY GRAMMAR: In your message use some main and helping verbs.

Grammar

Irregular Verbs

RULES

An irregular verb has a special spelling to show that an action happened in the past.

present tense: *The Browns go on vacation.*
past tense: *The Browns went on vacation.*

Some irregular verbs have a special spelling when used with *have*, *has*, or *had*.

The Browns have gone on vacation.
The Browns had gone on vacation.

Verbs

How can you decide if a verb is irregular? Write your answer in your journal.

Present	Past	Past with have, has, or had
come	came	come
do	did	done
say	said	said
go	went	gone
run	ran	run
see	saw	seen

Guided Practice

Tell the correct past form of each present-tense verb in ( ).

EXAMPLE: Karen (see) the highway first. *saw*

1. I (go) to Arizona with my family.
2. My friend Karen (come) with us.
3. Our vacation had (begin).
4. We (see) the Grand Canyon.
5. I have (see) an amazing sight!

Grammar

REVIEW THE RULES

- **Irregular verbs** have a special spelling for the past tense and when used with *have*, *has*, or *had*.

More Practice

A. Write each sentence. Use the past tense of the verb.

6. We (go) into the Grand Canyon.
7. A guide (come) to lead us down a trail.
8. We (see) colorful canyon walls.
9. Suddenly, an animal (run) by.
10. The guide (say) the animal was a wild burro.
11. Then we (see) someone riding a mule.
12. We (go) by lots of desert plants.
13. Soon we (come) to a large river.
14. Dad (say) it was the Colorado River.
15. I (run) to dip my feet into the cool water.

Handbook page 514

B. Spiral Review Write each sentence. Circle each past form of a verb. Name the proper nouns.

16. The Colorado River flows through the Grand Canyon.
17. Some people have rafted down the Colorado River.
18. The park has offered mule trips.
19. Many visitors have hiked in the Grand Canyon.
20. Hikers see many sights in this Arizona park.

Extra Practice, page 315

Writing Activity An Invitation

Invite friends to see your vacation pictures. Give clear, organized information about time and place.

APPLY GRAMMAR: In your invitation, use as many irregular verb forms as you can. Circle each irregular verb form you use.

Grammar

More Irregular Verbs

RULES

An irregular verb has a special spelling to show that an action happened in the past.

The parade began on time.

Verbs

Write how you can tell which special spelling to use for an irregular verb.

Present	Past	Past with have, has, or had
begin	*began*	*begun*
eat	*ate*	*eaten*
give	*gave*	*given*
grow	*grew*	*grown*
sing	*sang*	*sung*
bring	*brought*	*brought*

Guided Practice

Tell the past form of each present-tense verb in ( ).

EXAMPLE: This country (grow) over the years. *grew*

1. Dad (begin) to tell us about the Fourth of July.
2. He (give) us information about the holiday.
3. Dad (bring) out books about the Fourth of July.
4. The family has (begin) to read the books.
5. This morning we (sing) "America the Beautiful."

Grammar

REVIEW THE RULES

- Irregular verbs have a special spelling to show an action has happened in the past.

More Practice

A. Write each sentence. Change each present-tense verb in ( ) to the past tense.

6. The band concert (begin) at noon.
7. We (bring) chairs to sit on.
8. Jordan had (give) me the program.
9. We (sing) along with the music.
10. Jenny had (bring) some snacks.
11. She (give) us peanuts and popcorn.
12. Soon we had (eat) all the food.
13. The sky had (grow) very dark.
14. The fireworks show (begin) on time.
15. The show has (give) us a thrill.

Handbook
page 514

B. Spiral Review **Write each sentence. Change each present-tense verb in ( ) to the past tense. Add commas where needed. Circle any common nouns.**

16. This morning the parade (come) down Main Street.
17. Two children (run) by with red white and blue balloons.
18. I (see) floats bands and horses.
19. Len (say) he liked the marching band.
20. The parade has (go) by.

Extra Practice, page 316

Writing Activity A Postcard

Write a postcard to a friend. Tell what you did on the Fourth of July. Make sure you organize your sentences.
APPLY GRAMMAR: Use irregular verbs in your card.

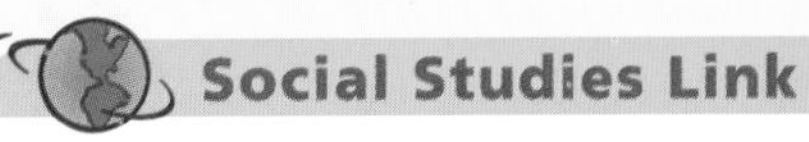
Social Studies Link

Grammar

Contractions with *Not*

RULES

A contraction is a shortened form of two words.

An apostrophe (') shows where one or more letters have been left out.

isn't = *is not*   *haven't* = *have not*

Usually a verb does not change its spelling in a contraction with *not*.

Contractions with not

has not	*hasn't*	cannot	*can't*
have not	*haven't*	do not	*don't*
had not	*hadn't*	does not	*doesn't*
is not	*isn't*	did not	*didn't*
are not	*aren't*	were not	*weren't*
was not	*wasn't*	will not	*won't*

The word *won't* is a special contraction. The spelling of the verb *will* changes.

will not ⟶ *won't*

THINK AND WRITE

Contractions

How can you decide where to place an apostrophe (') in a contraction? Write your answer in your journal.

Guided Practice

Tell which words make up each contraction.

EXAMPLE: The letter wasn't on time. *was not*

1. This letter isn't what I expected.
2. The letter doesn't make any sense.
3. We haven't read the letter.
4. I can't tell what the words say.
5. I won't answer the letter.

REVIEW THE RULES

- A contraction is a shortened form of two words.
- An apostrophe (') shows where letters are missing.

More Practice

A. Write the sentences. Write the words that make up each contraction.

6. The letter didn't come in the mail.
7. We weren't home when the letter arrived.
8. The letter can't be from my pen pal.
9. We aren't sure who wrote the letter.
10. The letter wasn't signed.
11. I don't understand the writing.
12. I won't let that stop me.
13. It isn't an impossible task.
14. The letter doesn't mention my name.
15. I haven't found a return address.

B. Spiral Review Write each sentence. Use the correct form of the verb. Use a contraction for underlined words.

16. Alex (begin) to read the letter.
17. Alex has (use) his code book.
18. The coded messages <u>were not</u> hard to read.
19. Alex <u>did not</u> read very fast.
20. It <u>was not</u> long before we read the letter, too.

Extra Practice, page 317

Writing Activity A Letter

Write a letter to someone you would like to have as a pen pal. Choose words that will help your reader get to know you.

APPLY GRAMMAR: Use contractions in your letter.

Grammar

Handbook
page 512

Grammar

Combining Sentences: Verbs

RULES

Two sentences with the same subject can be combined. Use the word *and* to join the predicates.

Jason watched the stars.
Jason read about the sun.
Jason watched the stars and read about the sun.

By combining sentences, you can make your writing flow more smoothly.

Separate
Jason sketches rockets.

Jason builds model spaceships.

Combined
Jason sketches rockets and builds model spaceships.

Verbs
Write how combined sentences can sometimes improve your writing.

Guided Practice

Tell how to combine each pair of sentences.

EXAMPLE: The stars glowed. The stars sparkled.
Join the predicates: The stars glowed and sparkled.

1. Mr. Lee built spaceships. Mr. Lee needed a helper.
2. Terry took the job. Terry worked hard.
3. Mr. Lee took out several tools. Mr. Lee showed them to Terry.
4. Terry watched Mr. Lee. Terry carefully followed his suggestions.
5. Mr. Lee liked Terry. Mr. Lee thanked him for his help.

REVIEW THE RULES

- You can combine sentences with the same subjects. Use the word *and* to join the predicates.

More Practice

A. Write each pair of sentences as a combined sentence.

6. The spaceship sat on the ground. The spaceship would not start.

7. Terry invented a new starter. Terry showed it to Mr. Lee.

8. Mr. Lee saw the starter. Mr. Lee was surprised.

9. Terry entered the spaceship. Terry took his seat.

10. Mr. Lee fastened his seatbelt. Mr. Lee smiled.

11. Terry put in a new starter. Terry flicked a switch.

12. The spaceship roared. The spaceship rumbled.

13. The ship left the ground. The ship soared upward.

14. Terry guided the spacecraft. Terry landed it safely.

15. Mr. Lee cheered. Mr. Lee shook Terry's hand.

Handbook page 513

B. Spiral Review **Write the sentences. Combine each pair by joining nouns, predicates, or both sentences.**

16. Mr. Smith pointed out Mars. Mr. Smith pointed out Venus.

17. The spaceship lands. The two passengers get off.

18. Reporters arrive. Terry talks to them.

19. Reporters take pictures. Reporters interview Mr. Smith.

20. Stars are in space. Planets are in space.

Extra Practice, page 318

Writing Activity A Summary

Think of what you would take on a trip. List and count the total items. Write a summary of your preparations.
APPLY GRAMMAR: In your summary, combine some sentences with the same subjects. Circle the word *and*.

Math Link

Grammar

Apostrophes

RULES

Use an apostrophe (') with nouns to show possession.

Add *'s* to singular nouns or plural nouns that do not end in *s*.

Rico's report   Tammy's speech   children's stories

Add an apostrophe to plural nouns ending in *s*.

teachers' desks   *students' writing*

Use an apostrophe in a contraction to show where letters are missing.

don't   *can't*   *isn't*

Apostrophes

How is an apostrophe useful? Write your answer in your journal.

Apostrophes are used in *possessive nouns* and *contractions*.

possessive ⟶ *woman's hat*
contraction ⟶ *haven't*

Guided Practice

Name the word in each sentence that uses an apostrophe. Tell if each word shows possession or is a contraction.

EXAMPLE: Leo's story is about the moon.
Leo's, possession

1. Our teacher's lesson was fun.
2. We listened to Ashley's speech.
3. The speech didn't last long.
4. My report isn't ready.
5. We haven't read the other reports.

REVIEW THE RULES

- Use an apostrophe (') with nouns to show possession.
- Use an apostrophe in a contraction to show where letters are missing.

Grammar

More Practice

A. Write the sentences. Underline each word that has an apostrophe. Write *possession* or *contraction* to show how the apostrophe is used.

6. I haven't forgotten my speech.

7. The students' reports are very interesting.

8. Alice's report is due today.

9. Alice can't find her report about volcanoes.

10. Did you like the children's speeches?

11. One report was about people's homes.

12. There isn't a better topic.

13. I won't forget what I learned.

14. I couldn't choose the best report.

15. All my classmates' reports were great.

Handbook pages 506, 512, 529

B. Spiral Review **Write the paragraph. Correct each apostrophe mistake.**

16.–20. All the student's reports were about transportation. Andys report was about airplane travel. His report wasnt very long. Andy didnt mind reading his report to the class. The teachers comments were great!

Extra Practice, page 319

Writing Activity A Letter

Write a letter responding to an invitation to travel.
APPLY MECHANICS AND GRAMMAR: Use contractions and possessives in your writing. Circle apostrophes.

Grammar REVIEW

Mixed Review

REVIEW THE RULES

Irregular verbs have a special spelling for the past tense and when used with *have*, *has*, or *had*.

Some verbs join with *not* to form contractions. An **apostrophe** shows where one or more letters have been left out.

To **combine two sentences** with the same subject, use the word *and* to join the predicates.

Use an apostrophe with nouns to show possession. Add *'s* to singular nouns or plural nouns that do not end in *s*.

Verbs

Write five sentences about playing outdoors in the winter. Use irregular verbs, possessive nouns, and contractions.

Practice

A. Write each sentence. Use the correct past form of the verb in ( ).

1. It has (grow) very cold.
2. We have (bring) out our warm clothes.
3. What (do) the weatherman say about snow?
4. Children (run) to get their sleds.
5. We (go) down the hill.
6. Dan has (give) me his gloves.
7. More snow (begin) to fall.
8. We (see) a huge snowman.
9. Julie (come) inside to warm up.
10. We (sing) songs by the fireplace.

Grammar
REVIEW

More Practice

B. Write each pair of sentences as a combined sentence.

11. The wind blows hard. The wind howls.

12. The children skate on the pond. The children slide down the hill.

13. One skater spins out of control. One skater falls.

14. We play in the snow. We build a snow fort.

15. We scoop up the snow. We make a big fort.

16. We strap on our skis. We ski down the hill.

17. Susan gets very cold. Susan shivers.

18. We dress warmly. We drink hot chocolate.

19. The sun shines. The sun melts some snow.

20. We leave for the day. We go home.

Handbook
pages 512–514; 529

C. Challenge Write the following paragraph. Use an apostrophe where needed. Combine the two sentences with the same subject.

21.–25. Gina isnt here. She was supposed to bring Pollys sled. Gina cant carry the sled alone. Dad helps Gina. Dad carries the sled. He doesnt mind helping Gina.

Writing Activity A Poem

Write a poem about a special day you spent with family or friends. Choose your words carefully to show your feelings.

APPLY GRAMMAR: Use some irregular verbs and contractions with *not* in your poem.

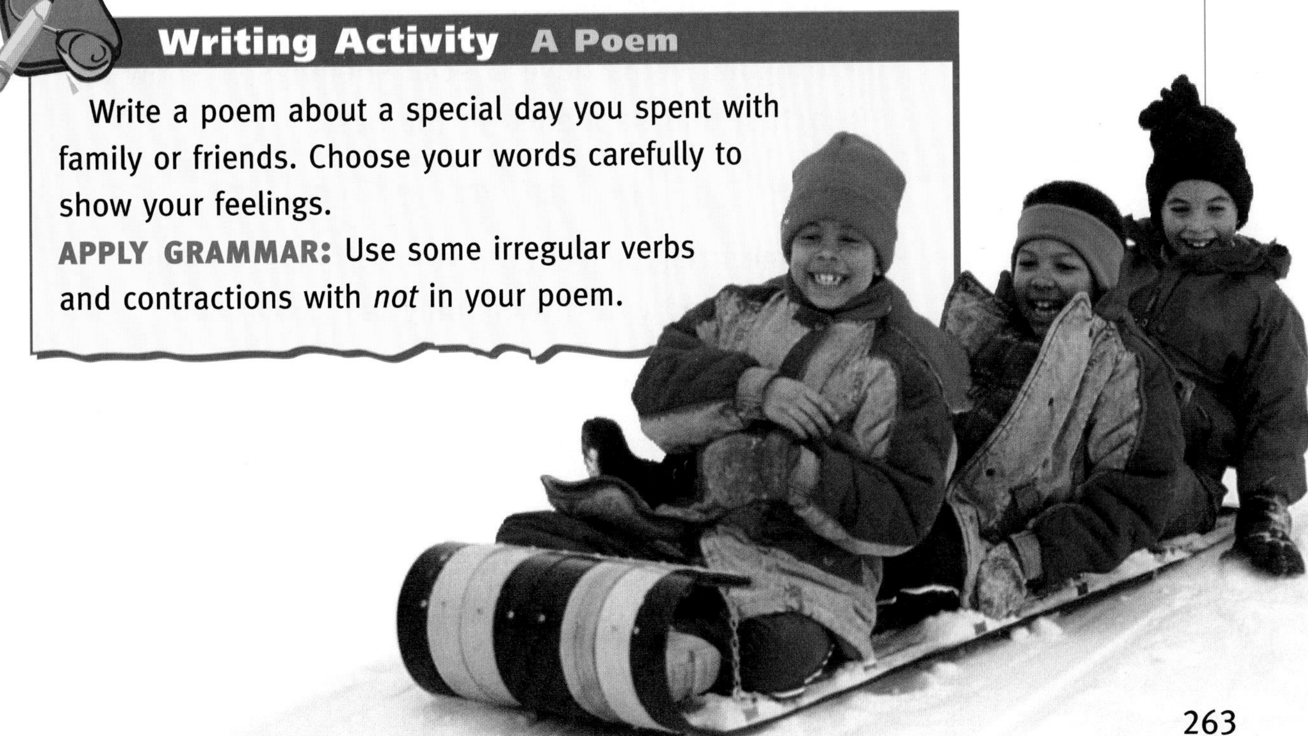

Grammar
COMMON ERRORS

Common Errors with Past-Tense Verbs

Most verbs in the past tense end in *-ed*. However, some verbs have special spellings to show the past tense. It is important to learn which verbs are irregular.

Common Errors	Examples	Corrected Sentences
Forming the past tense of irregular verbs incorrectly	Matt runned to the park.	Matt ran to the park.
Using the wrong irregular verb form for the past tense	I done my homework early.	I did my homework early.
Using the wrong irregular verb form for the past with have	I have saw that movie already.	I have seen that movie already.

Verbs

How do you know when a verb does not add *-ed* to show past tense? Write the answer in your journal.

REVIEW THE RULES

PAST-TENSE VERBS

- **Irregular verbs** have special spellings to show an action that happened in the past.

  sing ⟶ *past tense = sang*

- Some irregular verbs have a different spelling when used with the helping verb *have*.

  sing ⟶ *past with* have *= have sung*

- **Remember** Add *-ed* to most verbs to show past tense.

Practice

A. Write each sentence. Draw a line under the irregular verb.

1. I saw my grandparents in the distance.
2. My grandparents have come to our field day.
3. My grandmother brought me some granola.
4. I have eaten a banana.
5. My grandfather gave me a bottle of water.

B. Write each sentence. Use the correct past form of the verb in ( ).

6. I (eat) my snack before the race.
7. I (go) to the starting line.
8. My grandparents (say), "Good luck."
9. The races had (begin) on time.
10. The runners (run) to the finish line.

C. Write each sentence. Replace the incorrect verb in ( ) with the correct verb.

11. I (seen) many runners pass by.
12. I (runned) faster and faster.
13. I had (went) around the track twice.
14. I (goed) across the finish line.
15. I have (did) my best.

Troubleshooter, pages 496–497

Handbook
page 514

Writing Activity Write a Letter

Write about something you did that made you proud. Try to include at least three irregular verbs in your letter. **APPLY GRAMMAR:** Be sure to use the correct form of the verbs in your letter. Use a dictionary if necessary.

Mechanics and Spelling

TAAS

Directions

Read the passage and decide which type of mistake, if any, appears in each underlined section. Choose the correct answer. If there is no mistake, choose "No mistake."

Are there words in a series? Check to see if commas are needed between them.

Look for a contraction. Check if an apostrophe is needed to show where letters are missing.

Check the spelling of irregular verbs when used with the helping verb have.

Sample

Robert just learned a new word game. Nell showed him how to play the game. The idea of the game is to make words. Players use cubes with letters on them to spell the words. The cubes are red white and yellow **(1)**. Each color is worth a certain number of points. The game ends when a player cant **(2)** spell a word. Robert loves the game. He has taught his friend Pedro **(3)** how to play it.

1 ○ Spelling
○ Capitalization
○ Punctuation
○ No mistake

2 ○ Spelling
○ Capitalization
○ Punctuation
○ No mistake

3 ○ Spelling
○ Capitalization
○ Punctuation
○ No mistake

Test Tip
Remember to read each answer choice before choosing the best one.

Grammar and Usage

Directions

Read the passage and choose the word or group of words that belongs in each space.

Sample

My dad and I look at the stars. We wait for a night with a black sky and no clouds. Sometimes we look through a telescope. My dad knows a lot about stars and planets. He __(1)__ them.

Some of the stars form pictures. It __(2)__ easy to find the Big Dipper. Many of the star pictures are animals. I __(3)__ the names of most of the animals. I am writing a list of the star groups I have seen.

Be sure to match the pronoun he *with the right form of the helping verb.*

Remember to use the right form of the linking verb with the pronoun it.

Be sure to match the pronoun I *with the right form of the helping verb.*

1
- ○ study
- ○ are studying
- ○ has studied
- ○ have studied

2
- ○ will
- ○ are
- ○ am
- ○ is

3
- ○ have learned
- ○ has learned
- ○ am learned
- ○ is learned

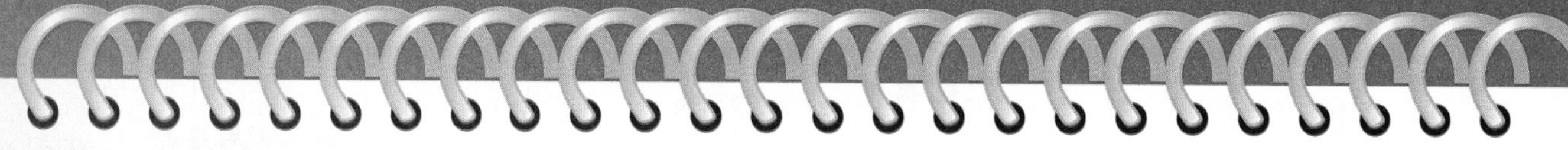

TIME FOR KIDS Writer's Notebook

RESEARCH

RESEARCH

When I write about numbers, I use a **graph** or **chart** to get my point across. Graphs usually make it easier for readers to understand numbers, too.

COMPOSITION SKILLS

WRITING WELL

"The cloud-covered volcano roared to life. Its snow-covered top melted under red-hot ash." I like to use **descriptions** in my writing to help readers "see" what I am saying. It helps make my story come alive. How would you describe an erupting volcano?

VOCABULARY SKILLS

USING WORDS

I can add certain letters to the end of a word to change its meaning, like soft and softly. Those letters are called a **suffix**. Using words with suffixes helps me express my ideas clearly.

Read Now!

As you read the photo essay about volcanoes, write down two words you can change by adding a suffix.

TIME FOR KIDS

PHOTO ESSAY

VOLCANOES

New tools are helping to predict when they'll blow.

Kilauea volcano in Hawaii has been erupting almost without stop since 1983.

KABOOM!

Volcanoes are bubbling around the world. In fact, at least 550 active volcanoes circle the globe. These volcanoes put the lives of 500 million people in possible danger.

The good news is that scientists can help keep people safe from volcanoes. They are using satellites and machines to track them. The machines tell scientists if a volcano is going to blow its top before it does.

The only way to protect humans is to get them safely out of the volcano's way. Volcano expert Richard Fiske says, "You can't stop volcanoes. All we can do is learn to get along with them."

The photographers in this truck ran from the 1991 eruption of Mount Pinatubo in the Philippines.

interNET CONNECTION Go to www.mhschool.com/language-arts for more information on the topic.

Danger Spots

Many of the world's volcanoes are in an area called the Ring of Fire. The Ring of Fire surrounds the Pacific Ocean.

MT. PINATUBO

This volcano erupted in 1991. The eruption was so powerful that it did some damage to the environment.

MT. RAINIER

This inactive volcano rises 14,410 feet above sea level.

RING OF FIRE

Kamchatka chain

Aleutian chain

Mt. Rainier

Mt. Saint Helens

Mt. Pinatubo

Indonesian chain

Mt. Vesuvius

MT. SAINT HELENS

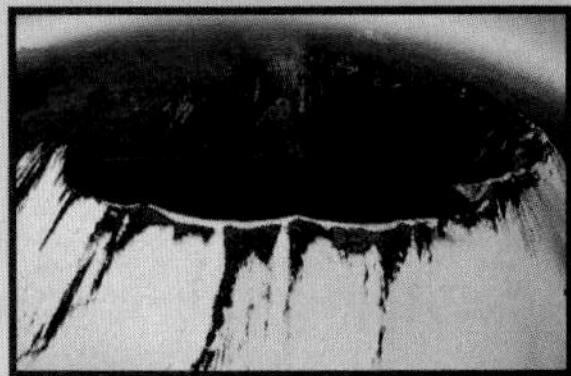

Mt. Saint Helens has erupted several times since 1980. The eruptions blasted away part of the volcano.

MT. VESUVIUS

Mt. Vesuvius has erupted many times. Two towns were destroyed when it erupted in A.D. 79.

Write Now!

Using the map and the photos, write to compare volcanoes around the world. How are they similar? How are they different?

Cover: Darodents/Pacific Stock
This page clockwise from upper left: David Harlow/USGS; Tom Bean/DRK Photo; Roger Ressmeyer/Corbis; Steve Raymer/National Geographic Society

Graphs

A **graph** is a diagram that shows the relationship between two or more things. You can use a graph to compare the information it shows.

Three kinds of graphs are bar graphs, circle graphs, and line graphs. Each graph has a title that shows what the graph is about. The labels tell what kind of information the graph contains.

Study the graphs. What can you learn from each?

A **bar graph** uses bars to show and compare information. Along one side, there is a list of numbers that help you make comparisons.

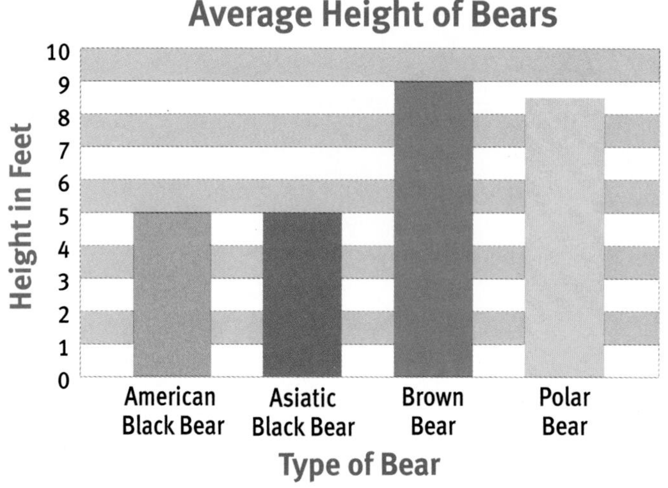

A **circle graph** compares parts of a whole. On a circle graph, find the information by noting the size of each part.

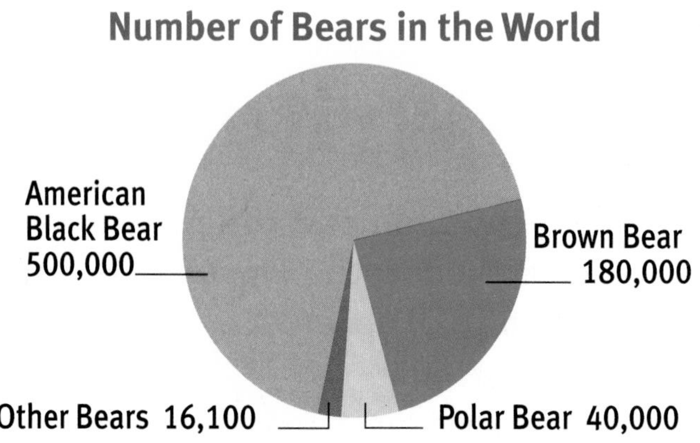

A **line graph** usually shows changes over a period of time. Find the information at each point along the line.

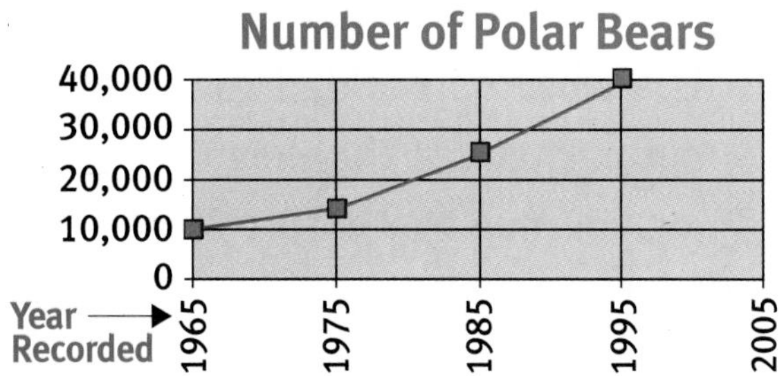

Practice

A. Look at the three graphs. On which graph would you find the following information?

1. The number of brown bears in the world.
2. The tallest bear.
3. The average size of a polar bear.
4. The number of polar bears in 1995.
5. The second largest number of bears in the world.

B. Write each sentence. If the information is shown on one of the graphs, write *yes*. If not, write *no*.

6. Polar bears eat more than brown bears.
7. Brown bears are the largest bears.
8. There are fewer polar bears than brown bears.
9. There were only 5,000 polar bears in 1995.
10. There are more black bears than brown bears.

Writing Activity Use a Graph

Write five questions that can be answered by using the information shown on the graphs on these two pages. Use the questions to play a question and answer game with a partner.

Vocabulary: Suffixes

DEFINITION

A suffix is a word part added to the end of a base word. A suffix changes the meaning of the base word. Sometimes you need to drop a final *e* or change a final *y* to *i* when adding a suffix.

manage + -er = manager   easy + -ly = easily

Suffix	Meaning	Example
-er, -or	one who _____	sailor
-less	without	careless
-able	able to be	readable
-ly	in a _____ way	suddenly
-ful	full of	hopeful

Suffixes

How can using words with suffixes help you create more interesting sentences? Write your answer.

Look at the blue words in the paragraph below.

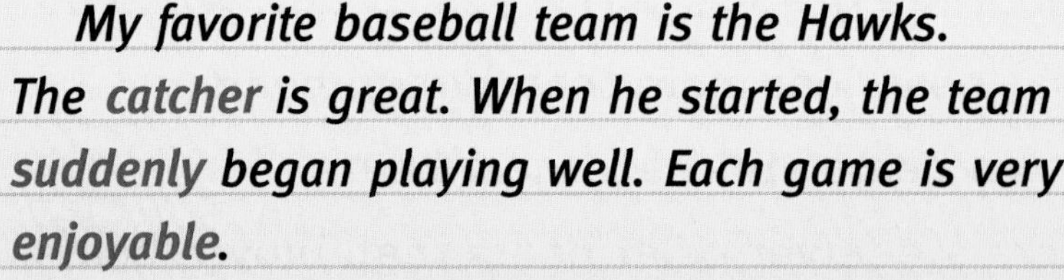
My favorite baseball team is the Hawks. The catcher is great. When he started, the team suddenly began playing well. Each game is very enjoyable.

Practice

A. Write each sentence. Circle the word with a suffix.

1. After two innings, the baseball game was scoreless.
2. The next player at bat for the Hawks was Pete.
3. Pete hit the ball hard and quickly ran to first base.
4. Then Sammy, always dependable, hit a home run.
5. Joyful fans cheered and whistled as he crossed home plate.

B. Write each sentence. Add a word made from a suffix and a base word in the box.

Suffixes: -ly -er -or -less -ful

Base Word: announce easy fault success visit

6. The ______ introduced both teams.
7. Yesterday, the ______ were the Coyotes.
8. The Hawks played a ______ game.
9. My favorite team won ______.
10. The team is having a ______ season.

C. Grammar Link **Write each sentence. Add a word made by adding a suffix to the underlined main verb. Circle the helping verb.**

11. Harry will report the game. He is a TV______.
12. Mark is pitching today. He is the best ______.
13. I have always liked Mark. He is a ______ person.
14. I have collected baseball cards for years. I am a______.
15. I will value my cards of Hawks. They are ______ to me.

Writing Activity A Paragraph

Write a short paragraph about your favorite sport. Include two words that have suffixes in your paragraph.

APPLY GRAMMAR: Use past-tense verbs and circle them.

Composition: Writing Descriptions

A writer uses description to paint a clear and colorful picture for the reader.

GUIDELINES

- A description can be about persons, places, or things.
- Each paragraph of a description has a main-idea sentence that tells what the paragraph is about.
- Use sensory details to describe how things look, sound, smell, taste, and feel.
- Use likenesses and differences to order details in writing that compares.

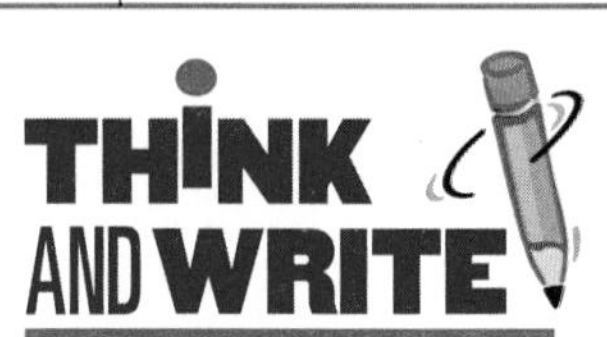

Writing Descriptions

How can a writer paint a picture with words? Write a brief explanation.

Read the following paragraphs. Notice how the writer uses sensory words to describe how butterflies and moths are alike.

A main-idea sentence for the first paragraph

Sensory words paint a picture for the reader.

Details describing differences are in another paragraph.

There are several ways that butterflies and moths are alike. Both are insects, and most have four wings. They both have colored scales over their delicate wings. Butterflies, like moths, live in all parts of North America. Some live in wet climates. Others live in dry places. Each likes to sip sweet nectar from flowers.

Butterflies and moths are different in many ways. Butterflies fly in the day, while moths fly at night. Unlike butterflies, moths like bright lights.

Practice

A. Write the sentences. Draw a line under the sensory word in each sentence that describes how something looks, sounds, smells, tastes, or feels.

1. Yesterday the sky was blue.
2. My aunt and I went to a beach with soft sand.
3. We heard noisy children playing in the water.
4. There was a fishy smell in the air.
5. We were thirsty and enjoyed a drink of sour lemonade.

B. Add a sensory detail to complete each sentence. Write the complete sentence.

6. My aunt and I ate _____ sandwiches.
7. We went to a park with _____ flowers.
8. Some musicians played _____ music.
9. We sat on the _____ grass and listened.
10. My aunt and I rode home in a _____ taxi.

C. Grammar Link **Write each sentence. Use the correct verb in ( ). Add a sensory detail.**

11. The city's traffic (has, have) often sounded _____.
12. The city's rivers (was, were) looking _____.
13. Most of the streets (is, are) looking _____.
14. In the park, the air (has, have) always smelled _____.
15. The park's grass (has, have) felt _____.

Writing Activity A Paragraph

Write a paragraph that describes a city or country scene. Use a main-idea sentence and sensory details.

APPLY GRAMMAR: In your paragraph, use the present-tense or past-tense forms of the verbs *be*, *have*, and *do*. Circle the helping and linking verbs.

TAAS

Better Sentences

Directions

Read the passage. Some parts are underlined. The underlined parts may be one of the following:

- **Incomplete sentences**
- **Run-on sentences**
- **Correctly written sentences that should be combined.**

Choose the best way to write each underlined part.

Check to see if sentences can be combined.

Correct a fragment by adding a subject or predicate.

Sample

I watched a program about parrots. It was an interesting program. (1) Did you know there are many kinds of parrots? My favorite is the parakeet. It has blue feathers. Others green and bright red feathers. (2) Most parrots have long pointed tails. All parrots can make sounds; some can even talk.

1 ○ I watched a TV program about parrots was interesting.

○ I watched an interesting program about parrots.

○ The TV program about parrots? It was interesting.

2 ○ Others are green and bright red feathers.

○ Other parrots green and bright red feathers.

○ Others have green and bright red feathers.

Test Tip
Pay careful attention to the details as you read the passage.

Test Power

TAAS

Vocabulary and Comprehension

Directions

Read the passage. Then read each question that follows the passage. Decide which is the best answer to each question.

Sample

I read a book about parrots. Now I know more about these birds. Not all parrots have pointed tails. One kind has a square tail. I was surprised to learn that one kind of parrot comes out only at night. This <u>nocturnal</u> bird is the owl parrot.

Most parrots eat nuts, seeds, and fruits. All parrots lay white eggs, but they lay them in different places. Some parrots lay eggs on the ground. Others lay eggs in cracks between rocks.

Look for clues near the underlined word to help you figure out what it means.

1 The word <u>nocturnal</u> in this passage means—

○ a fast bird

○ like an owl

○ able to fly

○ active at night

2 In what ways are parrots alike?

○ All fly at night.

○ All lay eggs between rocks

○ All lay white eggs.

○ All have square tails.

Test Tip
What do you think the test will ask about the underlined word?

Seeing Like a Writer

Look at the pictures carefully. What things in each picture could you write about? How are the things alike and how are they different?

Exotic Birds by John J. Audubon.

Writing from Pictures

1. Write a sentence about something in each picture. Tell what the thing is.
2. List words that describe how two things in one picture are alike or different.
3. Choose two pictures that you think are connected in some way. Write a short paragraph that explains the connection you see. Give your paragraph a title.

Apply Grammar: Use linking verbs and a contraction with *not* in your paragraph. Circle the apostrophe in the contraction.

Writing That Compares

Sometimes a writer will describe two things by explaining how they are alike and how they are different. This is called writing that compares.

THINK AND WRITE

Purpose

How does describing things by comparing them help readers? Write your answer in your journal.

Learning from Writers

Read the following examples of writing that compares. What are the writers describing? As you read, notice how the writers use facts and details to tell how things are alike and how they are different.

Bigger Than a Dinosaur

The blue whale is the biggest creature that has ever lived on Earth! Female blue whales are a little bigger than the males. Blue whales can grow to 100 feet long and weigh 150 tons—that's heavier than 25 elephants or 115 giraffes.

Reach out and touch the blue whale's skin. It's springy and smooth like a hard-boiled egg, and it's as slippery as wet soap.

Look into its eye. It's as big as a teacup and as dark as the deep sea. Just behind the eye is a hole as small as the end of a pencil. The hole is one of the blue whale's ears—sticking-out ears would get in the way when the whale is swimming.

The blue whale lives all of its long life in the sea. But it is a mammal like us, and it breathes air, not water. From time to time, it has to come to the surface to breathe through the blowholes on top of its head.

—Nicola Davies, from *Big Blue Whale*

Uranus

Uranus is very different from Earth. The planet Earth has one moon, but the planet Uranus has at least 15 moons. Another way Uranus is different is that it has several rings.

Both Uranus and Earth are part of the same solar system, but they move differently. Earth spins like a top. Earth takes one day to rotate once. It takes Earth one year to go around the sun. Uranus, however, rolls on its side like a ball. Unlike Earth, it takes Uranus about 17 hours to rotate once and about 84 years to go around the sun.

Uranus was the first planet to be discovered by a telescope. It has a light-blue color. From space, Earth also looks blue.

— Michael Franklin

Practice and Apply

Thinking Like a Reader

1. What two facts about the size of a blue whale did you learn from "Bigger Than a Dinosaur"?
2. Name one way Earth and Uranus are alike and one way they are different.

Thinking Like a Writer

3. How did Nicola Davies help you better understand a blue whale's size?
4. How did the writer of "Uranus" organize facts to show how the planets are alike and different?

5. **Reading Across Texts** What words do the writers use to help them compare and contrast two things?

Features of Writing That Compares

DEFINITIONS AND **FEATURES**

Writing that compares looks at two things and describes how they are alike and how they are different. Successful writing that compares:

- Explains **how two things are alike.**
- Explains **how two things are different.**
- Organizes details in **an order that makes sense.**
- Uses **compare and contrast words.**

How Two Things Are Alike

Reread "Bigger Than a Dinosaur" on page 282. What does the author compare a whale's skin to?

> Reach out and touch the blue whale's skin. It's springy and smooth like a hard-boiled egg...

The author compares the whale's skin to a hard-boiled egg. She explains that these two things are alike because both are springy and smooth.

How Two Things Are Different

The sentence below tells how female blue whales and male blue whales are different. Why do you think the author included this detail?

> Female blue whales are a little bigger than the males.

This fact helps the reader understand that the size of blue whales varies. The reader may also find the information interesting and surprising.

▶ An Order That Makes Sense

Presenting details in an order that makes sense helps keep comparisons clear. In the sentences below, the author describes a whale's eye and then a whale's ear.

> Look into its eye. It's as big as a teacup and as dark as the deep sea. Just behind the eye is a hole as small as the end of a pencil. The hole is one of the blue whale's ears....

Why does the order of these details make sense?

▶ Compare and Contrast Words

To help your readers understand how the ideas in your writing are related, you need to use words that will help them compare and contrast two things.

> It's springy and smooth like a hard-boiled egg, and it's as slippery as wet soap.

What words did the author use to compare a whale's skin to a hard-boiled egg and to wet soap?

Practice and Apply

Create a Features Chart

1. List the features of writing that compares.
2. Reread "Uranus" by Michael Franklin on page 283.
3. Write one example of each feature in Michael's writing.
4. Write what you liked about Michael's writing.

Features	Examples

Prewrite

Writing that compares tells how things are alike and how they are different. This kind of writing gives you a chance to write about related ideas.

Purpose and Audience

The purpose of writing that compares is to describe two things. Think about your audience before you begin to write. How will you present your ideas to them?

Choose a Topic

Think about what you would like to compare. If you decide to compare animals, **brainstorm** pairs of animals in one group that are alike in some ways. Choose two animals. Then **explore ideas** for your topic by listing the things you know about the animals.

Audience

How will you help your audience understand how the subjects you compare are alike and how they are different? Write your answer.

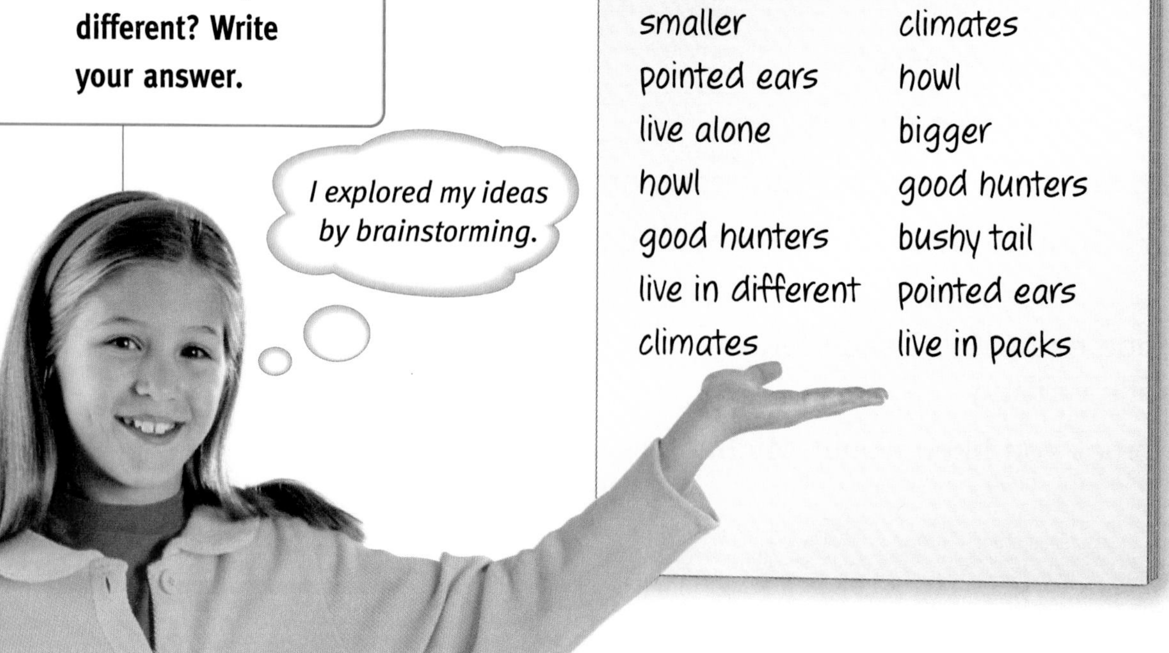

I explored my ideas by brainstorming.
Coyotes
bushy tail
smaller
pointed ears
live alone
howl
good hunters
live in different climates
Wolves
live in different climates
howl
bigger
good hunters
bushy tail
pointed ears
live in packs

Organize • Sort

When you compare two things, you need to sort the details into two groups. One group of details tells how the two things are alike, and the other group of details tells how they are different. You can use a Venn diagram to organize the details. How did this writer organize the details from her list?

VENN DIAGRAM

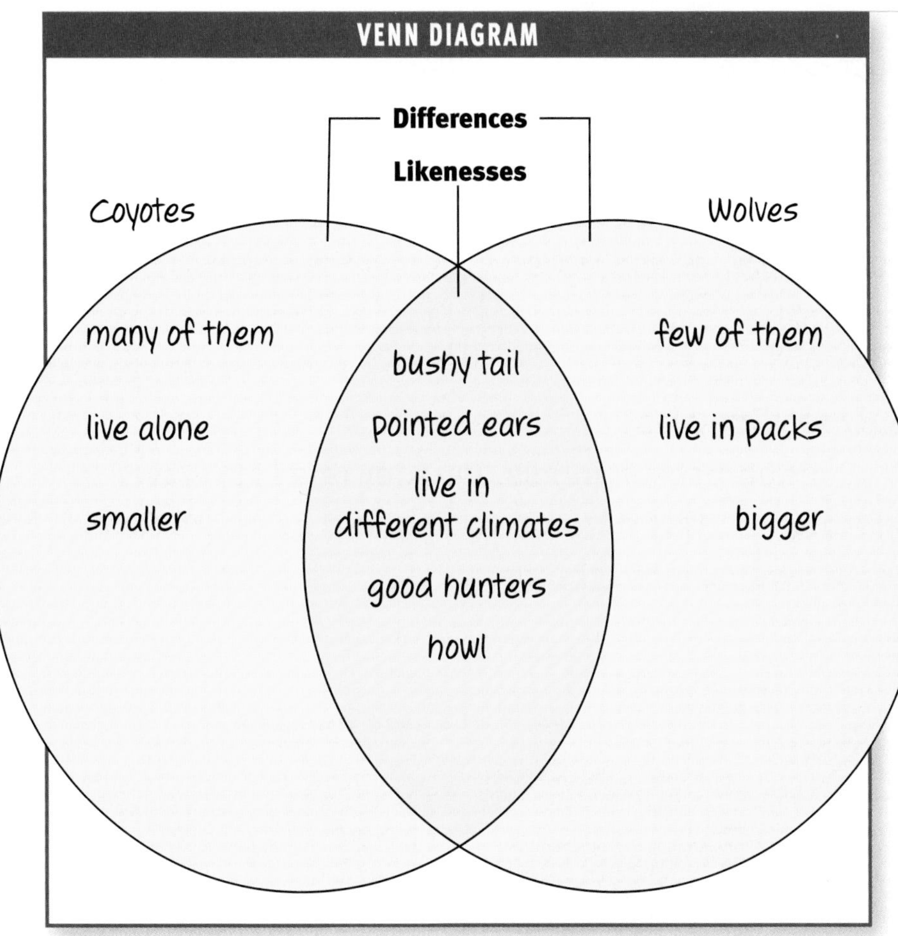

Checklist

Prewriting

- **Have you thought about your purpose and audience?**
- **Have you chosen two things to compare and explored ideas about them?**
- **Did you organize details in an order that makes sense?**
- **Do you need to do any research?**

PRACTICE and APPLY

Plan Your Own Writing That Compares

1. Think about your purpose and audience.
2. Brainstorm ideas for a topic.
3. Choose a topic and explore ideas.
4. Organize your ideas.

Writing PROCESS

Prewrite • Research and Inquiry

▶ Writer's Resources

You may need to do some research to gather information for your writing that compares. Make a list of questions. Then decide what resources you need to find the answers.

What Else Do I Need to Know?	Where Can I Find the Information?
Can coyotes run faster than wolves?	Look at graphs showing speeds of animals.
What do coyotes and wolves eat?	Search the Internet.

▶ Use Graphs

A graph uses symbols, bars, or lines to show information. Use a graph to find and compare facts about two or more things.

This part of the bar graph lists the names of the things being compared.

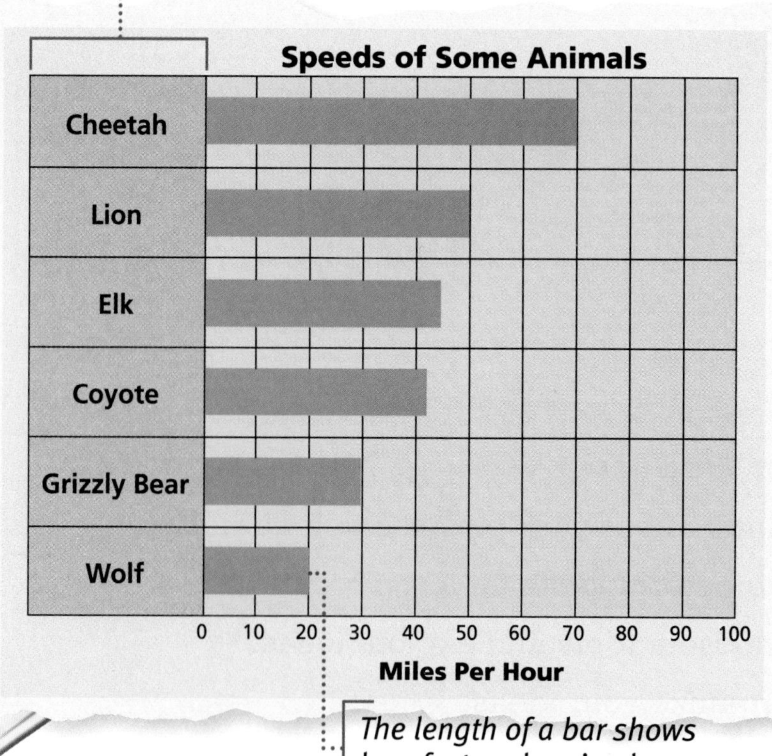

The length of a bar shows how fast each animal can run.

▶ Search Online

A computer that is connected to the Internet can help you research your topic. Follow instructions to connect to the Internet. Then do a "keyword search" by typing in the name of your subject. The first list you see can point you toward more specific sites on the World Wide Web. Keep clicking on "Go" until you find the information you need for your writing.

Use Your Research

Add the new information from your research to your Venn diagram. What new facts did this writer learn from her research?

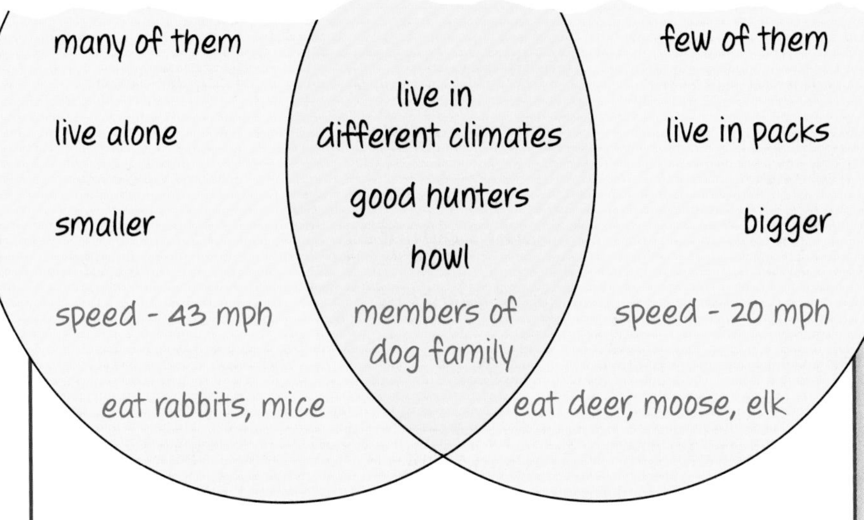

PREWRITE
DRAFT
REVISE
PROOFREAD
PUBLISH

Handbook
pages 536–537

Checklist

Research and Inquiry

- **Did you write down questions?**
- **Did you decide what resources to use?**
- **Did you take notes?**

PRACTICE and APPLY

Review Your Plan

1. Look at your prewriting diagram.
2. List questions you have about your topic.
3. Identify the resources you will need to find answers.
4. Add new information you gather to your diagram.

Writing PROCESS

Draft

Before you begin your writing that compares, review the Venn diagram you made. Think about making a paragraph for likenesses and a paragraph for differences. Include details that support each main idea.

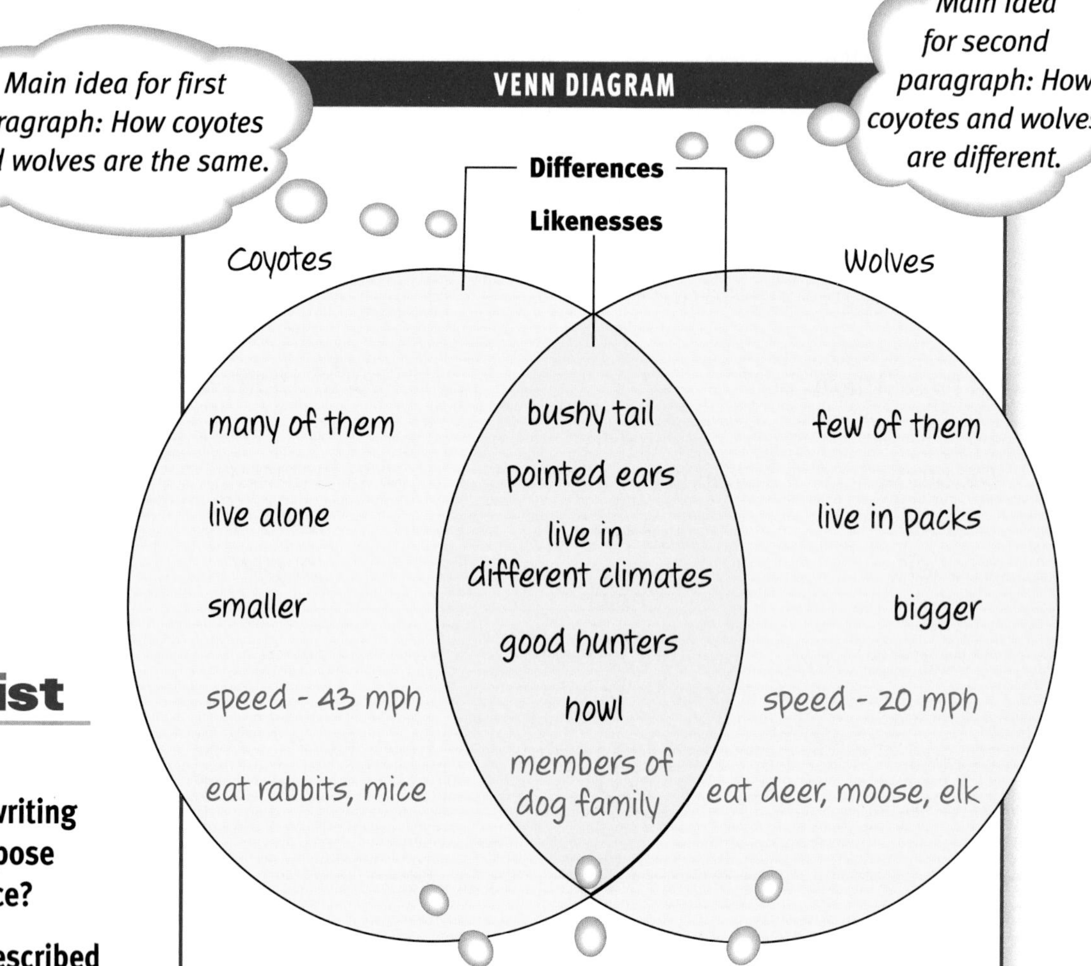

Details describe the animals.

Checklist

Drafting

- Does your writing fit your purpose and audience?
- Have you described how two things are alike?
- Have you described how two things are different?
- Have you organized your ideas in an order that makes sense?

Look at how this writer used the information in her diagram to write a first draft. She used details from the middle of the diagram in the first paragraph. She put details from the rest of the diagram in the second paragraph.

PREWRITE
DRAFT
REVISE
PROOFREAD
PUBLISH

DRAFT

Coyotes and wolfs are the same in many ways. Coyotes are like wolves because both are wild members of the dog family. Both have pointed ears and a bushy tail. Both can live in different climates, and both are good hunters. Both howl at night.

Coyotes and wolves are different. Coyotes is smaller and faster than wolves. Wolves live in packs, but most coyotes live alone. These animals also eat different food. Wolves eat deer moose or elk. Coyotes eat rabbits and mice. Coyotes can run 43 miles per hour, and wolves can run 20 miles per hour.

Main idea of first paragraph

Supporting details tell ways coyotes and wolves are alike.

Main idea of second paragraph

Supporting details tell ways coyotes and wolves are different.

PRACTICE and APPLY

Draft Your Own Writing That Compares

1. Review your prewriting diagram.
2. Write paragraphs that describe how two things are alike and how they are different.
3. Give details in an order that makes sense.

TECHNOLOGY

If you need to change the order of details, you can use the cut and paste feature to move words and sentences.

Revise

Elaborate

As you work on your draft, you can elaborate. When you elaborate, you add details that help make your writing clearer. When you revise your writing that compares, you may need to add details to help your reader understand the information about the animals.

The writer added words to explain what a pack is.

family groups called
Wolves live in ^ packs, but most coyotes live alone.

The writer added words to make it clear that the animals that wolves eat are large.

large animals, like
Wolves eat ^ deer moose or elk.

Word Choice

Good writers think about their topic and audience when they choose words to use.

In writing that compares, you need to find words that will help you compare and contrast two things.

In one way,
^ Coyotes are like wolves because both are wild members of the dog family. Both ^ have pointed ears and a bushy tail.
(also inserted after "Both")

COMPARE/ CONTRAST WORDS

alike
same
like
another
also
too
different
and
but
yet
however
although
in one way
in another way
in other ways

PREWRITE
DRAFT
REVISE
PROOFREAD
PUBLISH

Better Paragraphs

Read your paragraphs aloud. Listen to how they sound. Are the paragraphs connected? Do you have a strong closing paragraph?

You may want to add a connecting phrase to help readers move smoothly from one paragraph to the next.

> In other ways,
> ^ Coyotes and wolves are different.

The writer changed this detail to an imaginative closing paragraph.

> In some places, you can hear both animals at
> ^ ~~Both howl at night~~.
> night, howling at the moon.

TECHNOLOGY

Learn how to use the thesaurus on a computer to replace repeated or general words with more exact or interesting choices.

PRACTICE and APPLY

Revise Your Own Writing That Compares

1. Add details to help the reader picture what you are describing.
2. Use compare and contrast words.
3. Add words or phrases to connect your paragraphs.
4. Include an interesting closing paragraph.
5. **Grammar** Have you used the correct forms of linking verbs?

Writing PROCESS

Revise • Peer Conferencing

Share your writing with a partner. Read your first draft aloud and ask your partner for ideas and suggestions.

Coyotes and wolfs are the same in many ways. Coyotes are like wolves because both are wild members of the dog family. Both have pointed ears and a bushy tail. Both can live in different climates, and both are good hunters. Both howl at night.

Coyotes and wolves are different. Coyotes is smaller and faster than wolves. Wolves live in packs, but most coyotes live alone. These animals also eat different food. Wolves eat deer moose or elk. Coyotes eat rabbits and mice. Coyotes can run 43 miles per hour, and wolves can run 20 miles per hour.

I like these details. They help me picture the animals.

Can you add a compare and contrast word?

These details don't make sense here. You need a better ending.

Conferencing for the Reader

- Did your partner include features of writing that compares? Did he or she
  - explain how two things are alike and different?
  - use details in an order that makes sense?
  - use compare and contrast words?
- Tell your partner what is good about the writing as well as what could be better.

When you revise your writing, think about your partner's ideas. This writer made some changes based on her partner's suggestions.

REVISE

Coyotes and Wolves

Coyotes and wolfs are the same in many ways. In one way, Coyotes are like wolves because both are wild members of the dog family. Both also have pointed ears and a bushy tail. Both can live in different climates, and both are good hunters. ~~Both howl at night.~~

In other ways, Coyotes and wolves are different. Coyotes is smaller and faster than wolves. Wolves live in family groups called packs, but most coyotes live alone. These animals also eat different food. Wolves eat large animals, like deer moose or elk. Coyotes, however, eat rabbits and mice. Coyotes can run 43 miles per hour, and wolves can run 20 miles per hour.

In some places, you can hear both animals at night, howling at the moon

Practice and Apply

Revise Your Own Writing That Compares

1. Listen to your draft as you read it aloud to a partner.
2. Write down ideas that your partner suggests.
3. Use the suggestions you like to revise your draft.
4. Add a title.

Checklist

Revising

- Is your writing right for your purpose and audience?
- Do you need to describe anything in more detail?
- Did you use compare and contrast words?
- Did you write your ideas in an order that makes sense?
- Do your sentences and paragraphs blend together for smooth reading?
- Did you add a good title?

Writing PROCESS

Proofread

Proofread your revised writing to find and correct any mistakes in mechanics, grammar and usage, and spelling.

STRATEGIES FOR PROOFREADING

- Reread your revised draft. Each time, look for a different type of mistake.
- Check for correct spelling. Use a dictionary.
- Check for correct punctuation. Make sure that each sentence has the correct end mark.
- Check that you used capital letters correctly.
- Check for correct forms of linking verbs. Read aloud to make sure subjects and verbs agree.

TIP!

Spelling

To make plurals of words that end with one *f* or *fe*, you usually change the *f* to *v* and add *-es* or *-s*. (wolf = wolves)

REVIEW THE RULES

GRAMMAR

- Use the correct form of the linking verb *be*. Use the present-tense form *is* with a singular noun, and *are* with a plural noun. Use the past-tense form *was* with a singular noun, and *were* with a plural noun.

MECHANICS

- Use commas to separate three or more words in a series.
- An apostrophe (') takes the place of letters left out of a contraction.
- An apostrophe is used with nouns to show possession.

Look at the proofreading corrections made on the draft below. What does the mark ⌒ mean? Why does the writer use this mark?

PROOFREAD

Coyotes and Wolves

Coyotes and wolves are the same in many ways. In one way, coyotes are like wolves because both are wild members of the dog family. Both also have pointed ears and a bushy tail. Both can live in different climates, and both are good hunters. ~~Both howl at night.~~

In other ways, coyotes and wolves are different. Coyotes are smaller and faster than wolves. Wolves live in family groups called packs, but most coyotes live alone. Coyotes can run 43 miles per hour, and wolves can run 20 miles per hour. These animals also eat different food. Wolves eat large animals, like deer, moose, or elk. Coyotes, however, eat rabbits and mice.

In some places, you can hear both animals at night, howling at the moon.

PRACTICE and APPLY

Proofread Your Own Writing That Compares

1. Check forms of the linking verb *be*.
2. Add missing punctuation marks.
3. Correct spelling mistakes and indent paragraphs.

Checklist

Proofreading

- Did you correct any incorrect forms of the verb *be*?
- Did you end each sentence correctly?
- Did you use an apostrophe to show letters left out of a contraction?
- Did you spell all words correctly?
- Did you indent each paragraph?

PROOFREADING MARKS

- ¶ new paragraph
- ^ add
- ⌒ take out
- ≡ Make a capital letter.
- / Make a small letter.
- (sp) Check spelling.
- ⊙ Add a period.

Writing PROCESS

Publish

Look over your writing one more time before you publish it. Use the checklist below.

Self-Check Writing That Compares

- ❑ Did I clearly explain how two things are alike and different?
- ❑ Did I use compare and contrast words?
- ❑ Did I tell things that will inform and interest my audience?
- ❑ Did I organize details in a way that makes sense?
- ❑ Did I use connecting phrases to make my paragraphs flow smoothly?
- ❑ Did I write a strong closing paragraph?
- ❑ Did I use correct forms of verbs?
- ❑ Did I proofread and correct any mistakes?

Before publishing "Coyotes and Wolves," the writer used the checklist to review her writing. Read her writing with a partner and talk about it. Do you think the checklist helped her? What makes you think so?

Coyotes and Wolves

by Emily Wilson

Coyotes and wolves are the same in many ways. In one way, coyotes are like wolves because both are wild members of the dog family. Both also have pointed ears and a bushy tail. Both can live in different climates, and both are good hunters.

In other ways, coyotes and wolves are different. Coyotes are smaller and faster than wolves. Coyotes can run 43 miles per hour, and wolves can run 20 miles per hour. Wolves live in family groups called packs, but most coyotes live alone. These animals also eat different food. Wolves eat large animals, like deer, moose, or elk. Coyotes, however, eat rabbits and mice.

In some places, you can hear both animals at night, howling at the moon.

Practice and Apply

Publish Your Own Writing That Compares

1. Check your revised draft one more time.
2. Make a neat final copy.
3. Add a cover and graphs or pictures.

TIP!

Handwriting

Leave a margin on each side of the paper as you write your final copy. Look ahead to the end of each line to see if a word will fit. Do not try to fit a word into a space that is too small.

LISTENING

SPEAKING

VIEWING

PRESENTING

Present Your Writing That Compares

You need to plan how you will present your writing. There are things you can do to help you make a good presentation.

STEP 1

How to Present a Speech

Strategies for Speaking Remember that your purpose is to inform your listeners. Try to get their attention and keep it.

- Before you begin your speech, you might ask a question.
- To help you remember important information, write details on note cards.
- Look at different listeners as you are speaking.

Listening Strategies

- Set a purpose. Listen for new information.
- Pay attention to the order of details and try to picture what the speaker is describing.
- Write down questions to ask at the end of the presentation.

Multimedia Ideas

Did you talk about sounds in your speech? Does your school have an audiotape player? If so, you may want to play a tape of the sounds at the end of your speech. Look for tapes in a library.

STEP 2

How to Show Your Ideas

Suggestions for Visuals Visuals can let your audience see what you are describing.

- Photos or drawings can colorfully show different features.
- A graph can show facts for the audience to compare.
- A map can show where things are.

Remember to use visuals that clearly show the things you talk about in your speech.

STEP 3

How to Share Your Speech

Strategies for Rehearsing The more you practice, the more relaxed you will be when you give your speech.

- Rehearse your speech with a partner.
- Practice speaking loudly, clearly, and with expression.
- Try out different gestures that you might use.

TIP!

Viewing Strategies

- **Look carefully at the visuals and read all the labels or captions.**
- **Watch the speaker point out visuals and show that you are paying attention.**
- **Jot down questions you have about a visual.**

PRACTICE and APPLY

Present Your Own Writing That Compares as a Speech

1. Write details on note cards.
2. Use graphs, maps, photos, or drawings to show what you are comparing.
3. Practice your speech with friends.
4. Present your speech in a loud and clear voice.

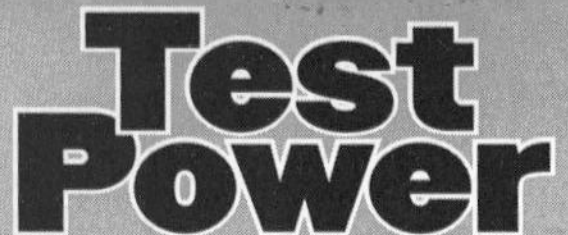

Writing Tests

TAAS

On a writing test, you are asked to write something in response to a prompt. Remember to read the prompt carefully. Look for key words and phrases that tell you what to write about and how to present your ideas.

Who will be the audience for this writing?

What words tell the kind of writing this will be?

What key word tells the purpose of this writing?

Prompt

Think about what you know about a horse and a zebra.

Write one or two paragraphs <u>for your teacher</u> describing these animals. Tell <u>how they are alike and how they are different</u>. Use details to <u>explain</u> your ideas.

How to Read a Prompt

Purpose Key words in a prompt will tell the purpose of the writing. The key word in this prompt is "explain." It tells you the purpose is to inform. When you explain something, you give your audience information, and you might do this in an entertaining way.

Audience A prompt may or may not tell you whom to write for. In this prompt, the words "for your teacher" tell you who your audience will be.

Writing That Compares The words "how they are alike and how they are different" tell you that this is writing that compares. Writing that compares looks at two topics and describes how they are alike and how they are different.

Test Tip
If you do not understand a prompt, read it again carefully.

How to Write to a Prompt

Here are some tips to remember when you are given a writing prompt.

Before Writing **Content/Ideas**	• Determine your writing purpose. • Know for whom you are writing. • Make a list of ways the two topics are alike and different.
During Writing **Organization/ Paragraph Structure**	• Write a good topic sentence. • Organize details in an order that makes sense. • Use comparing and contrasting words.
After Writing **Grammar/Usage**	• Take time to proofread your work. • Begin the first word of each sentence with a capital letter. • Use end marks and commas correctly. • Check your spelling. • Use the correct forms of irregular verbs.

Apply What You Learned

Always look for purpose, topic, and audience when you read a prompt on a writing test. Think about the best way to organize your ideas.

Prompt

Palms and pines are two kinds of trees.

Write two or three paragraphs about these trees for your teacher. Explain how the trees are alike and how they are different. Use details in your writing to help you compare the trees.

Unit 4 Review

Grammar and Writing Review

pages 240–241

Main and Helping Verbs

A. Write each sentence. Draw a line under each helping verb. Circle each main verb.

1. I was riding my bike in the backyard.
2. Trees have made our backyard shady.
3. My mom and I are watching one tree.
4. A mother bird is sitting in a nest.
5. The bird will sit on the eggs for a long time.

pages 242–243

Using Helping Verbs

B. Write each sentence. Choose the correct verb in ( ).

6. I (has, have) followed my dog outside.
7. Duke (has, have) dug a hole in the yard.
8. The children (has, have) watched the dog.
9. Yesterday, the dog (have, had) buried a bone.
10. Duke (had, have) chased a squirrel.

pages 244–245

Linking Verbs

C. Write each sentence. Draw a line under each linking verb. Circle each action verb.

11. My family hikes every Saturday.
12. I am happy in the woods.
13. One day we spotted an owl in a tree.
14. A large skunk blocked our path.
15. The skunk was not afraid of us.
16. We were all afraid of the skunk!
17. No one moved a muscle.
18. Four baby skunks followed the big skunk.
19. Dad laughed along with us.
20. Skunks are funny animals.

Unit 4 Review

pages 246–247

Using Linking Verbs

D. Write each sentence. Use the correct linking verb.

21. Spanish (is, are) my favorite subject.

22. Sarah and I (are, am) good students.

23. Spanish (is, are) fun.

24. The class (were, was) full the first day.

25. (Was, Were) you a classmate of ours?

pages 248–249

Mechanics and Usage: Commas in a Series

E. Write each sentence. Add commas where needed.

26. Randy Marcia and I did a report together.

27. Our report could be about the moon the sun or one of the planets.

28. First, we talked asked questions and made lists.

29. Then we looked at books videos and magazine articles.

30. We used pictures photos and diagrams in our report.

pages 252–255

Irregular Verbs

F. Write each sentence. Change each present-tense verb in ( ) to the past tense.

31. We (eat) breakfast early.

32. My dad (give) us cereal and milk.

33. Mom (say) she likes bagels.

34. I had (bring) out a bowl of fruit.

35. Julia (come) to the table.

36. Bobbie (do) the breakfast dishes.

37. Then the children (go) outside.

38. They (run) all the way to school.

39. The children (see) their friends.

40. School (begin) at 8:00 a.m.

Unit 4 Review

pages 256–257

Contractions With *Not*

G. Write each sentence. Use a contraction in place of the underlined words.

41. It <u>is not</u> hard to find an old log.

42. I <u>did not</u> know there was a log in the woods.

43. Carla <u>had not</u> looked under the log.

44. She <u>was not</u> afraid to lift up the log.

45. You <u>will not</u> believe how many insects you can find there.

pages 258–259

Combining Sentences: Verbs

H. Combine each pair of sentences. Use *and* to join the two predicates.

46. Corey raises dogs. Corey trains dogs.

47. Corey's dog Sparky hunts. Corey's dog Sparky fetches.

48. Sparky sits quietly. Sparky listens to Corey.

49. Corey speaks to Sparky. He gives a command.

50. The dog listens. The dog wags his tail.

pages 260–261

Mechanics and Usage: Apostrophes

I. Write the sentences. Add apostrophes as needed.

51. Luke doesnt have a bike.

52. Lukes brother gave him an old bike.

53. The old bikes tires were flat.

54. Luke didnt let those flat tires stop him.

55. Luke remembered his parents directions.

56. It wasnt long before Luke fixed the tires.

57. That boys friends came to watch.

58. His friends didnt know Luke could fix tires.

59. The children wont forget what they saw.

60. The childrens faces showed a look of surprise.

Unit 4 Review

pages 274–275

Vocabulary: Suffixes

J. Write each sentence. Circle the word that has a suffix. Then, write the suffix and its meaning.

61. The colorful stage set and props arrive.

62. A worker puts the stage set and props in place.

63. The audience waits patiently.

64. One actor steps onto the stage.

65. The applause seems endless.

pages 276–277

Composition: Writing Descriptions

K. Write the word or words in each sentence that tell how something looks, sounds, smells, tastes, or feels.

66. Annie and Amelia cook together in a cozy kitchen.

67. Dinnertime in their big kitchen is noisy and warm.

68. Annie tastes the thick, bubbly soup.

69. The girls think the soup is too salty.

70. Annie fries sweet peppers in a round pan.

pages 296–297

Proofreading Writing That Compares

L. 71.–80. Write the paragraphs correctly. Correct the spelling, punctuation, grammar, and capitalization mistakes. There are 10 mistakes.

Two dinosaurs that looked qiute a lot alike was the Tyrannosaurus and the Allosaurus. both dinosaurs ate meat and has large tooths

The Tyrannosaurus was actually much large than the allosaurus . The Tyrannosaurus weighed seven ton. The Allosaurus weigh only two or three tons.

Project File

PROJECT 1 A Research Report

A research report gives facts and information about a topic. Its purpose is to inform or explain. As you read the following research report, think about the information it contains.

Fossils: A Look into the Past

A fossil is the remains, or what is left, of a plant or animal that lived a long time ago. Over millions of years, the remains have turned into stone. Some fossils are 600 million years old.

There are many different kinds of fossils. In a few cases, whole animals, such as woolly mammoths, are preserved in ice or tar. In many cases, just the bones and teeth become fossils. Fossils also include shells, footprints, and eggs.

In 1923, the explorer Ray Chapman Andrews discovered dinosaur eggs in Mongolia. The fossils are at least 135 million years old. Like other fossils, the dinosaur eggs provide an interesting look into the past.

Write *the title.*

Introduce *your topic.*

Write questions *about your topic, such as "What is a fossil?" and answer them in the report.*

Begin *each paragraph with a topic sentence.*

Use supporting details *to explain each main idea.*

Include facts and information *you gathered in your research.*

Write a report What animal or plant interests you? Choose a topic. Read at least two books about your topic. Take notes.

Use your notes to write at least three paragraphs. Find photos to illustrate your article. You might download pictures from the Internet. Share your report with your classmates.

TIME FOR KIDS PHOTO ESSAY

PROJECT 2

An Article that Compares

Mt. Vesuvius and Mt. Pinatubo are both active volcanoes. But did you know that there are many volcanoes around the world that are inactive and do not erupt? Find more information about active volcanoes and inactive volcanoes from the Internet.

Different Volcanoes Pick two volcanoes you would like to write about, one active and one inactive. Write an article comparing these two different types of volcanoes.

Extra Practice

Main and Helping Verbs

A. Write the underlined verb in each sentence. Write *main verb* or *helping verb* next to it.

1. Our neighborhood is cleaning our park.
2. The parents will bring trash bags.
3. The children will collect the trash.
4. Mike has washed the benches.
5. Nick and Josh are pulling weeds.
6. Lisa and Keiko are sweeping the sidewalk.
7. Some people were building a new sign.
8. My dad has fixed the swing.
9. The girls have planted some flowers.
10. We will keep our park clean.

B. Write each sentence. Draw one line under each main verb. Draw two lines under each helping verb.

11. Our neighborhood is planning a block party.
12. Each family will make a booth.
13. Mr. Diaz has created a bean bag game.
14. Sammy and Juan are arranging the prizes.
15. My family will run a ring toss.
16. I am making the rings with rope.
17. The Santanas have finished a fruit stand.
18. Mrs. Santana was bringing the apples.
19. The boys were painting the sign.
20. Everyone will enjoy the games.

Using Helping Verbs

A. Write each sentence. Use the correct helping verb in ( ).

1. Dad (has, have) cooked a delicious meal.
2. We (had, has) asked Dad to make the meal.
3. I (have, has) helped to prepare the food.
4. You (have, has) eaten more than my brother.
5. My brother (had, have) eaten some grapes earlier.
6. My sisters (have, has) surprised us with a dessert.
7. My sisters (had, has) baked an apple pie.
8. Mom (have, has) tasted the pie.
9. She (had, have) saved room for dessert.
10. My brother and I (had, has) eaten too much.

B. Write each sentence. Use the correct form of the main verb in ( ).

11. The students have (visit, visited) an apple farm.
12. The farmer had (stack, stacked) boxes of apples.
13. The seeds have (form, formed) a star in the apple.
14. A worker has (pick, picked) some apples.
15. The workers have (pour, poured) the apples into a tub.
16. Some workers have (wash, washed) the apples.
17. They have (shine, shined) some apples.
18. The farmer has (slice, sliced) an apple.
19. We have (taste, tasted) the apples.
20. Many visitors had (walk, walked) through the orchard.

Grammar

Extra Practice

Linking Verbs

A. Write the underlined verb in each sentence. Write *linking verb* or *action verb* next to it.

1. The Nature Park is colorful in the fall.
2. The leaves change colors.
3. The leaves are orange, yellow, and brown.
4. The fallen leaves crackle under our feet.
5. The moss grows on the trees.
6. Many animals live in the park.
7. I hear the birds in the trees.
8. The mother bird is blue and gray.
9. I watch the squirrels.
10. The squirrels are so playful.

B. Write each sentence. Draw a line under each verb. Write *linking verb* or *action verb* to describe each verb.

11. The Nature Park is beautiful in the winter.
12. The snow covers the trees.
13. Everything is fresh and clean.
14. The air was cold and clear.
15. My hair was white with snowflakes.
16. My sister and I leave footprints in the snow.
17. I make a snow castle.
18. The snow castle is lovely.
19. My sister builds a snowman.
20. The snowman is big and round.

Using Linking Verbs

A. Write the underlined verb in each sentence. Write whether the subject is *singular* or *plural*.

1. My cousin is captain of the swim team.
2. He is a good swimmer.
3. Last year, he was the fastest swimmer on his team.
4. His teammates were proud of him.
5. I am proud of him.
6. The team's swimsuits are blue and white.
7. The swimmers are fine athletes.
8. They are ready to race.
9. The race is over quickly.
10. My cousin is the winner again.

B. Write each sentence. Use the correct verb in ( ).

11. Last week, my friends and I (was, were) at the lake.
12. The lake (was, were) very cold.
13. We (was, were) swimming in the lake.
14. Soon they (was, were) shivering from cold.
15. The lake (is, are) very calm after their swim.
16. I (am, are) tired after swimming in the lake.
17. My sister and I (is, are) at the pool today.
18. My brother (is, are) a good swimmer.
19. You (am, are) a better swimmer than my sister.
20. All my friends (is, are) good swimmers.

Grammar

Extra Practice

Commas in a Series

A. Write each sentence. Underline the words in a series. Circle the commas.

1. My father, sisters, and I went to a football game.
2. Teri, Olga, and Jamie know a lot about football.
3. I learned about touchdowns, touchbacks, and field goals.
4. Our favorite teams are the Bears, Broncos, and Cowboys.
5. The Broncos' colors are blue, orange, and white.
6. The quarterback caught, aimed, and threw the ball.
7. The team ran, blocked, and tackled the other team.
8. The players could catch, run, and throw well.
9. The cheerleaders, fans, and announcers enjoyed the game.
10. The trucks, vans, and cars left the parking lot.

B. Write each sentence. Add commas where they belong.

11. Ethan Bruno and Janel like basketball.
12. Bruno cheers stomps and claps for his favorite team.
13. Janel's favorite teams are the Bulls Jazz and Hornets.
14. The coaches watch pace and call plays for the teams.
15. Basketball players dribble pass and shoot the ball.
16. The basketball bounces soars and sinks into the net.
17. The fans shout scream and cheer for their team.
18. The team scored one two and three points.
19. The basketball player runs jumps and grabs the ball.
20. Our favorite team scores wins and celebrates.

Irregular Verbs

A. Write each sentence. Underline the irregular verb.

1. My family went to a campground.
2. The ranger had seen bears nearby.
3. We saw a big bear.
4. The bear had come for food.
5. The bear came too close.
6. We did nothing.
7. The ranger had gone home.
8. The bear ran into the forest.
9. We went into our tent.
10. I have seen enough bears.

B. Write each sentence. Change each present-tense verb in ( ) to the past tense.

11. Our family (see) some animals at the camp.
12. Most of the animals (run) away.
13. A duck (go) into the lake.
14. Two squirrels (come) close to us.
15. A deer (go) by our tent.
16. My mother (say) to stand still.
17. The deer (come) closer to us.
18. My brother (say) something.
19. The deer (run) away quickly.
20. I (see) many animals.

Extra Practice

More Irregular Verbs

A. Write each sentence. Underline the irregular verb.

1. The bicycle parade had begun in the morning.
2. Our family picnic began after the parade.
3. All of my relatives had brought food for the picnic.
4. Grandpa brought some fruit to the picnic.
5. Everyone ate plenty of food.
6. Our dog has eaten the scraps of food.
7. My cousin had grown two inches taller since last year.
8. My cousin has given me his old bike.
9. My dad gave his nieces stickers for their bikes.
10. Aunt Carmela sang the song "Bicycle Built for Two."

B. Write each sentence. Change each present-tense verb in ( ) to the past tense.

11. My mom and I (give) our neighbor a "Welcome" party.
12. The party (begin) at noon on Saturday.
13. We (eat) meatballs and pasta soup.
14. Our neighbor (bring) dessert for everyone.
15. My aunt (bring) flowers to the party.
16. Beautiful flowers (grow) in my aunt's garden.
17. My sister and I (give) our new neighbor a poem.
18. We (sing) our favorite songs.
19. Our new neighbor (begin) to feel at home.
20. Later, everyone (go) home.

Contractions With *Not*

A. Write the sentences. Write the words that make up each underlined contraction.

1. I haven't heard from my friend.
2. My friend hasn't written for a while.
3. My friend didn't send me a letter.
4. Maybe my letters haven't reached my friend.
5. I wonder if my friend didn't get to the mailbox.
6. Perhaps my friend doesn't have any stamps.
7. Maybe my friend isn't living at the same address.
8. I can't wait to get a letter from my friend.
9. I won't stop writing letters to my friend.
10. I haven't tried to call my friend yet.

B. Write each sentence. Change the underlined words to a contraction.

11. Our mail has not arrived yet.
12. I cannot wait for the mail.
13. The mail is not usually late.
14. The mail carrier was not feeling well.
15. I have not seen our mail carrier today.
16. Our mail carrier did not skip work.
17. Our mail carrier has not missed a day.
18. I do not want another mail carrier.
19. A mail carrier's job is not easy.
20. I hope she will not be sick for long.

Grammar

Extra Practice

Combining Sentences: Verbs

A. Write each sentence. Draw a line under the two predicates. Circle the word that joins the predicates.

1. Benito visited the museum and learned about space.
2. Benito saw pictures of the moon and touched some moon rocks.
3. The museum guide pointed to the sky and showed us some stars.
4. We looked through a telescope and studied the planets.
5. Benito opened a door and walked through a spaceship.
6. We talked with an astronaut and asked him questions.
7. The astronaut answered questions and told us about space.
8. Astronauts wear spacesuits and eat special foods.
9. Astronauts need special training and study hard.
10. We all enjoyed the museum and learned a lot about space.

B. Combine each pair of sentences. Use *and* to join the two predicates. Write the new sentence.

11. Astronauts travel in rockets. Astronauts explore space.
12. Astronauts landed on the moon. Astronauts placed a flag.
13. The crew trains hard. The crew faces many tests.
14. The crew enters the shuttle. The crew checks the controls.
15. The crew works together. The crew completes the checks.
16. The shuttle takes off. The shuttle uses lots of fuel.
17. The crew mends space stations. The crew fixes satellites.
18. Satellites orbit Earth. Satellites send information.
19. The crew finishes the job. The crew returns to Earth.
20. The crew is tired. The crew is glad to be home.

Apostrophes

A. Write each sentence. Underline the word that has an apostrophe. Write *P* if the word shows possession or *C* if the word is a contraction.

1. Mr. Caruso's class is interesting.
2. My sister doesn't understand her homework.
3. We sit at mother's desk to study.
4. I look over my sister's homework.
5. There weren't many mistakes in the homework.
6. The homework wasn't too hard.
7. My sister won't need much help with her homework.
8. I haven't finished my homework.
9. My brothers' homework is complete.
10. Our teacher checks my friend's homework.

B. Write each sentence. Change each word or words in ( ) to show possession or to show a contraction.

11. My friend and I went to my (teachers) story hour.
12. I enjoy listening to the (readers) voice.
13. She read my (brothers) favorite book.
14. The story is about some (pirates) treasure.
15. The story (is not) my favorite.
16. My favorite story (does not) have pirates.
17. I like the story about a (girls) adventure at sea.
18. My friend (did not) see the pictures.
19. My book (does not) have many pictures.
20. My friend and I (cannot) wait until the next story hour.

UNIT 5

Pronouns and Expository Writing

In this unit you will learn about pronouns. You will also learn about expository writing. Expository writing gives information about a topic.

Math Link *Why do crickets chirp? Do they tell the temperature? Read the facts and details below to draw your own conclusion.*

Crickets are animals whose body temperatures change with the temperature around them. On a hot day, crickets chirp so rapidly that it is hard to count the number of chirps. But on a cool day, crickets chirp much more slowly. We can then easily count the times they chirp.

Some people say they can use the number of chirps to find the exact temperature. That's not always possible. A cricket's chirping depends upon its age and health as well as on the temperature.

from ***Animal Fact/Animal Fable*** by Seymour Simon

Thinking Like a Writer

Expository Writing Expository writing uses facts and details to tell about a topic. Reread the passage.

- What information did you learn about crickets? Is this new information for you?

Pronouns The author used pronouns, such as *we*, *they*, *them*, and *its*. Read the passage again.

QUICK WRITE List the pronouns in each paragraph. Then, if you can, write the word that the pronoun replaces.

Pronouns

RULES

A pronoun is a word that takes the place of one or more nouns.

A pronoun must match the noun or nouns that it replaces.

Pam works alone. *Rick and Ed work together.*

She works alone. *They work together.*

THINK AND WRITE

Pronouns
How do you decide which pronoun to use? Write the answer in your journal.

A singular pronoun replaces a singular noun.

Ned lost a key. *He lost a key.*

A plural pronoun replaces a plural noun or more than one noun.

The children look for the key. They look for the key.

Singular Pronouns	*I, you, he, she, it, me, him, her*
Plural Pronouns	*we, you, they, us, them*

Guided Practice

Name the pronoun in each sentence. Tell if the pronoun is singular or plural.

EXAMPLE: He looks in one pocket. *He, singular*

1. We help Ned look for the key.
2. He has asked his friends for help.
3. I look on the floor.
4. They see the key in the lock.
5. Ned left it there by mistake.

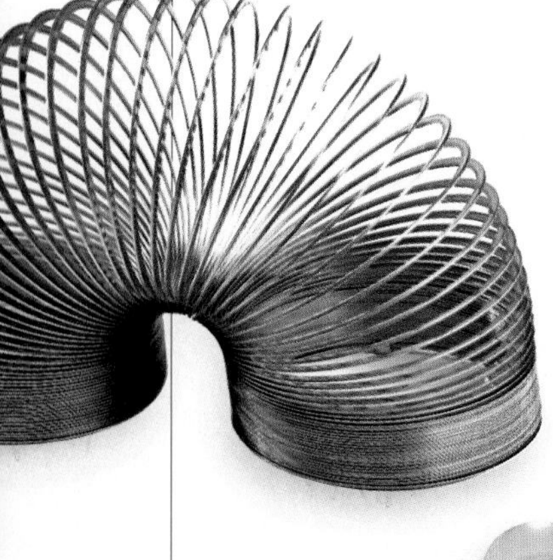

REVIEW THE RULES

- A pronoun is a word that replaces one or more nouns.

Grammar

More Practice

A. Write each sentence. Replace the underlined words with the correct pronoun in ( ).

6. The children found another key. (He, They)

7. What is the key used for? (it, them)

8. Ned, Kara, and I see a big box. (We, Them)

9. Does the box have a lock? (they, it)

10. Ned fits the key into the lock. (We, He)

11. Kara sees that the key fits. (You, She)

12. Kara and I open the box. (We, She)

13. Ned smiles at Kara and me. (us, her)

14. The box is full of old toys. (Them, It)

15. Kara and I play with the toys. (them, it)

Handbook
page 515

B. Spiral Review **Write each sentence. Draw one line under each singular noun. Circle any irregular verbs.**

16. Kara and I went home.

17. We opened the door.

18. The children saw boxes on a table.

19. Mom gave the gifts to Kara and me.

20. We shared them with Ned.

Extra Practice, page 388

Writing Activity A Sign

Make a sign announcing a toy sale. Organize your sign so people can easily get the facts they need. **APPLY GRAMMAR:** Use pronouns in your sign.

Grammar

Subject Pronouns

RULES

A subject pronoun is used as the subject of a sentence.

Singular subject pronouns: *I, you, he, she, it*
Plural subject pronouns: *we, you, they*

A subject pronoun must match the subject that it replaces.

singular subject	*plural subject*
Mom takes many pictures.	*Mom and Bob take pictures.*
singular subject pronoun	*plural subject pronoun*
She takes many pictures.	*They take pictures.*

THINK AND WRITE

Pronouns

How can you decide when to use a subject pronoun? Write your answer in your journal.

Guided Practice

Tell which subject pronoun would replace the underlined subject in each sentence.

EXAMPLE: Bob likes to look at the pictures. *He*

1. Dad likes the pictures, too.
2. The photographs are interesting.
3. Sue bought a photograph album.
4. The album has many pages.
5. Mom and I will fill the album.

REVIEW THE RULES

- Use a subject pronoun as the subject of a sentence.

More Practice

A. Write the sentences. Replace each underlined subject with a subject pronoun.

6. <u>Many pictures</u> are in the album.
7. <u>You and I</u> see all the baby pictures.
8. <u>Mom and Dad</u> have taken those pictures.
9. <u>Mom</u> left one picture out.
10. Where did <u>Dad</u> put the album?
11. <u>My brothers</u> laugh at the funny pictures.
12. <u>Ramon</u> has two pictures in the album.
13. <u>Sue</u> finds the missing photo.
14. <u>The photo</u> was in a box.
15. <u>The box</u> was in Mom's closet.

Handbook page 515

B. Spiral Review Write the sentences. Make the words in ( ) a contraction. Underline each plural subject.

16. The camera (does not) work.
17. It (is not) Mom's camera.
18. The children (do not) have any film.
19. They (were not) very happy.
20. (Can not) we get some film for Ramon?

Extra Practice, page 389

Writing Activity A Picture Caption

Write a caption for a favorite photograph. Choose your words carefully and tell something special about the picture. **APPLY GRAMMAR:** Use a subject pronoun in your caption. Circle the subject pronoun.

Grammar

Object Pronouns

RULES

Use an object pronoun after an action verb or words such as *for, at, of, with, in,* and *to*.

Singular object pronouns: ***me, you, him, her, it***
Plural object pronouns: ***us, you, them***

Object pronouns must match the words that they replace.

We will visit Grandma.

We will visit her.

Grandma waits for Mom and me.

Grandma waits for us.

Pronouns
Write how you decide when to use an object pronoun.

Guided Practice

Tell which object pronoun would replace the underlined word or words in each sentence.

EXAMPLE: Give the map to him. *it*

1. Mom will take the children on vacation.
2. Lucy asks Mom many questions.
3. Mom talks to Dad.
4. Mom hands Lucy and me a suitcase.
5. I'll put clothes in the suitcase.

REVIEW THE RULES

- Use an object pronoun after an action verb or after words such as *for, at, of, with, in,* and *to.*

Grammar

More Practice

A. Write each sentence. Replace the underlined word or words with an object pronoun.

6. Mom will take Lucy and me to Grandma's house.
7. I put the suitcases in the car.
8. I read the road signs for Mom.
9. Lucy reads the map.
10. I play the radio for Lucy and Mom.
11. Mom has trouble with a tire.
12. She drives to a gas station.
13. The owner talks to Mom, Lucy, and me.
14. The man fixes the tire for Mom.
15. She thanks the man for his help.

Handbook page 515

B. Spiral Review Combine each pair of sentences. Write the new sentence. Underline each subject pronoun.

16. We sing to Mom. We tell stories to Mom.
17. Cars pass us. Trucks pass us.
18. She stops for food. She stops for gas.
19. They drive for an hour. They finally arrive.
20. I run to Grandma. I give her a hug.

Extra Practice, page 390

Writing Activity A Word Game

Write directions for a word game you could play on a trip. Make sure the game rules are in the right order.

APPLY GRAMMAR: Use object pronouns and circle them.

Using *I* and *Me*

RULES

Use the pronouns *I* and *me* to write about yourself. Always write the pronoun *I* with a capital letter.

Use *I* in the subject of a sentence.

I went to school.

Use *me* after an action verb and words such as *for, in, into, to, with, by,* and *at.*

The teacher saw me.

Using I and Me
How can you decide where to use *I* or *me* in a sentence? Write your answer in your journal.

When you write about other people as well as yourself, name yourself last.

To help you decide whether to use *I* or *me* in a sentence, try the sentence without the other noun.

The teacher helps Dan and me.

The teacher helps me.

Guided Practice

Tell which pronoun to use in each sentence.

EXAMPLE: The teacher smiles at Dan and (I, me). *me*

1. (I, me) like the new school.
2. Dan and (I, me) want to make friends.
3. One student welcomes Dan and (I, me).
4. You and (I, me) walk into the gym.
5. The coach smiles at (I, me).

REVIEW THE RULES

- Use the pronouns *I* and *me* to write about yourself.
- Use *I* in the subject of a sentence and *me* after an action verb and words like *in, into, to, with, by,* and *at.*

Grammar

Handbook
page 515

More Practice

A. Write the sentences. Use the correct pronoun in ( ).

6. You and (I, me) play soccer.

7. Dan kicks the ball to (I, me).

8. Dan and (I, me) help win the game.

9. (I, me) feel so happy.

10. The team thanks you and (I, me).

11. Dan and (I, me) speak to the coach.

12. The students and (I, me) become friends.

13. The team makes (I, me) the captain.

14. Dan goes home with you and (I, me).

15. My family asks Dan and (I, me) about school.

B. Spiral Review Write each sentence. Replace underlined words with a pronoun. Circle each linking verb.

16. <u>Mr. Lee</u> is the math teacher.

17. He gives homework to <u>the students and me</u>.

18. <u>The homework</u> is about whole numbers.

19. <u>Dan and I</u> study together.

20. We give our homework to <u>Mr. Lee</u>.

Extra Practice, page 391

Writing Activity A Message

Write a message inviting a classmate to join you in a game. Messages are short, so choose your words carefully. **APPLY MECHANICS, USAGE:** Use *I* and *me* in your message.

Grammar REVIEW

Mixed Review

REVIEW THE RULES

- A **pronoun** is a word that takes the place of one or more nouns.
- A **pronoun** must match the noun that it replaces.
- Use a **subject pronoun** as the subject of a sentence.
- Use an **object pronoun** after an action verb or after words such as *for, at, of, with,* and *to.*
- Use the pronouns *I* and *me* to write about yourself. Use *I* in the subject of a sentence and *me* after an action verb and words such as *in, for, to, into, with, by,* and *at.*

QUICK WRITE

Pronouns
Make a list of all the pronouns you have learned.

Practice

A. Write each sentence. Write *S* above the subject pronouns. Write *O* above the object pronouns.

1. Greta showed me the storm clouds.
2. We looked at them together.
3. They filled the sky.
4. I asked her about lightning.
5. Greta saw it first.
6. Dad asked us to come inside.
7. I wanted to stay outside.
8. Dad told me about thunderstorms.
9. We watched the lightning.
10. It flashed across the sky.

B. Write each sentence. Replace the underlined words with a pronoun.

11. The rain poured down.
12. Raindrops beat against the windows.
13. Greta asked Dad about the storm.
14. Dad told Greta and me about thunder.
15. Then Greta and I saw a flash of lightning.
16. Greta was so scared.
17. Dad told Greta the storm was ending.
18. The rain fell lightly.
19. A rainbow appeared in the sky.
20. Greta, Dad, and I enjoyed the rainbow.

C. Challenge Write the following paragraph. Correct mistakes in the use of pronouns.

21.–25. Dad, Greta, and me saw a TV show about volcanoes. The film showed we how a volcano forms. They is quite a sight. Dad told Greta and I that he saw a real volcano in Hawaii. It amazed he.

Grammar REVIEW

Handbook page 515

Writing Activity An Article

Write an article about a storm you have seen. Remember that every detail should tell about the main idea.

APPLY GRAMMAR: Include pronouns in your article. Underline each pronoun you use.

Science Link

Grammar

Pronoun-Verb Agreement

RULES

A present-tense verb must agree with its subject pronoun.

Add *-s* or *-es* to most present-tense action verbs when you use the singular pronouns *he, she,* and *it.*

He gets a bike. She washes the bike.

Do not add *-s* or *-es* to an action verb in the present tense when you use the plural pronouns *we, you,* and *they,* or the singular pronouns *I* and *you.*

They get a bike. I wash the bike.

THINK AND WRITE

Pronouns

When do you add *-s* to an action verb if the subject is a pronoun? Write your answer in your journal.

Subject	Verb
he, she, it	Add *-s* or *-es* to verb.
I, we, you, they	Do not add *-s* or *-es*.

Guided Practice

Name the action verb in ( ) that agrees with the subject pronoun.

EXAMPLE: He (see, sees) the bike shop. *sees*

1. She (want, wants) a new bike.
2. We (walk, walks) to the bike shop.
3. You (look, looks) in the window.
4. He (point, points) to a large red bike.
5. I (like, likes) the big purple wheels.

REVIEW THE RULE

- A present-tense verb must agree with its subject pronoun.

More Practice

A. Write each sentence. Use the correct verb in ( ).

6. He (find, finds) an old bike.
7. It (need, needs) new handlebars and wheels.
8. I (get, gets) some tools for us.
9. You (put, puts) on new wheels.
10. They (fit, fits) just fine.
11. We (fix, fixes) the handlebars.
12. She (paint, paints) the bike bright colors.
13. I (tie, ties) a basket on the bike.
14. It (look, looks) as good as new.
15. We (give, gives) the bike to Maria.

Handbook
page 516

B. Spiral Review Write the sentences. Replace each subject with a pronoun. Combine the sentences.

16. Maria rides her bike. Maria pedals fast.
17. The bike goes slowly uphill. The bike races downhill.
18. Sam and I get our bikes. Sam and I join Maria.
19. Maria and Sam get tired. Maria and Sam go home.
20. Sam gets off his bike. Sam removes his helmet.

Extra Practice, page 392

Writing Activity Thank-You Note

Think about a time when someone did something nice for you. Write a thank-you note to that person. **APPLY GRAMMAR:** Use subject pronouns in your thank-you note and circle them.

Grammar

Possessive Pronouns

RULES

A possessive pronoun takes the place of a possessive noun. A possessive pronoun shows who or what owns something.

Al's favorite book	*the book's cover*
his favorite book	*its cover*

Use these possessive pronouns before nouns: *my, your, his, her, its, our, your, their.*

Your book is on the shelf.

Use these possessive pronouns alone: *mine, yours, his, hers, its, ours, theirs.*

That book is mine.

Pronouns

Write how you decide when to use a possessive pronoun.

Guided Practice

Tell which is the correct possessive pronoun in ( ).

EXAMPLE: That dictionary is (your, yours). *yours*

1. What is (your, yours) favorite story?
2. The tale about a lost bear is (her, hers).
3. He loses (her, his) way in the forest.
4. A friendly wolf comes to (his, their) rescue.
5. That new book is (my, mine).

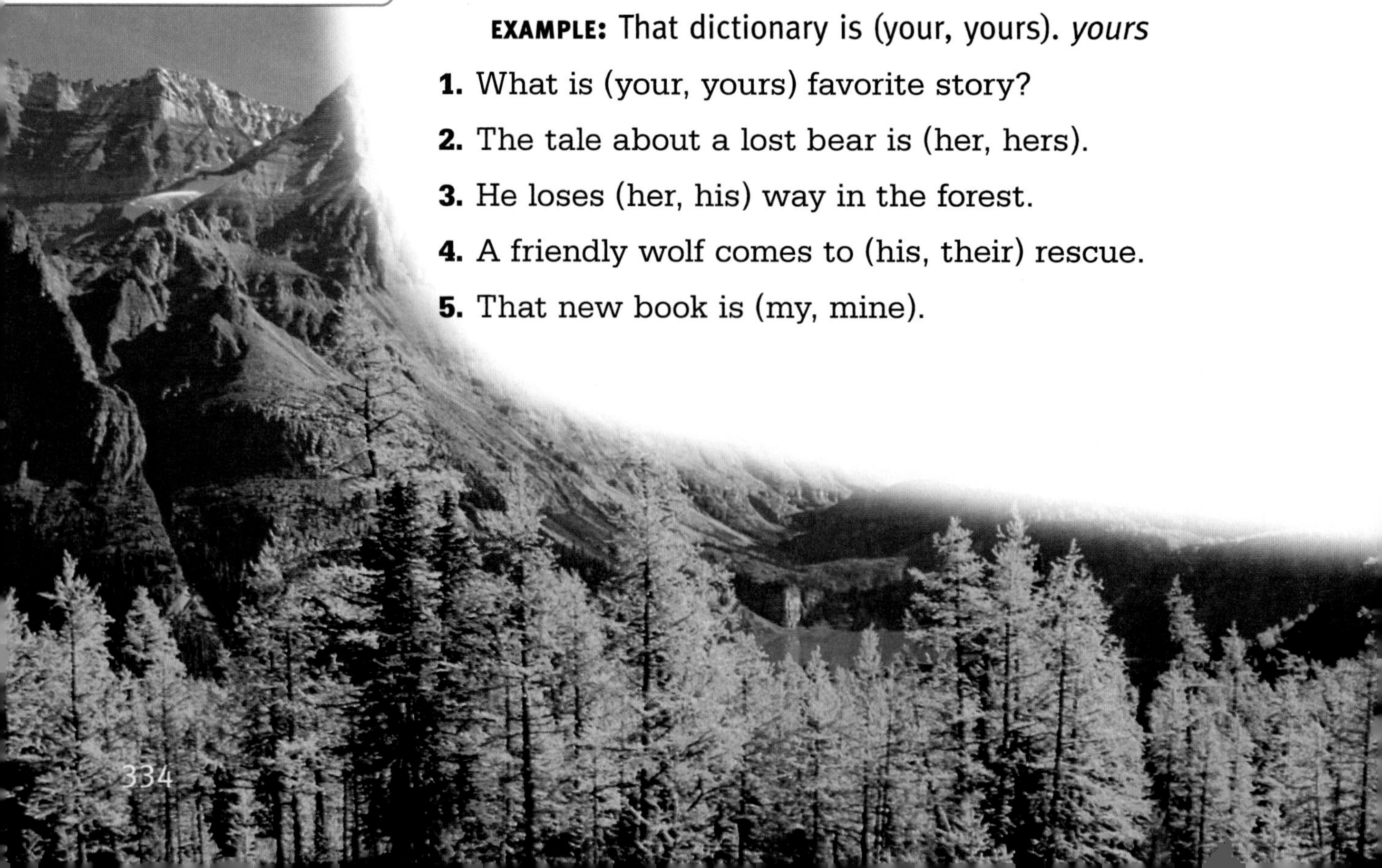

REVIEW THE RULES

- A possessive pronoun shows who or what owns something. It takes the place of a possessive noun.

More Practice

A. Write each sentence. Use the correct pronoun in ( ).

6. Is that storybook one of (our, ours)?
7. (My, Mine) favorite tale is an adventure story.
8. (Our, Ours) class has read the story.
9. The story is about a woman and (her, his) horse.
10. (Their, Theirs) home is out west.
11. I read the book to (our, ours) class.
12. You can read (yours, your) book now.
13. *Black Beauty* is a favorite book of (my, mine).
14. The book about a princess is (your, yours).
15. When did the princess ride that horse of (her, hers)?

B. Spiral Review Write each sentence. Circle each past-tense verb. Replace the underlined words with a possessive pronoun.

16. <u>Eric's</u> book is about bears.
17. He saw pictures of bears and <u>the bears'</u> cubs.
18. The mother bears brought the cubs out in the spring.
19. The baby bears think the forest is <u>the bears'</u>.
20. <u>A mother's</u> cubs will become big bears.

Extra Practice, page 393

Handbook
page 516

Writing Activity A Rule

Write a forest rule for bear cubs to follow. Make your rule specific.

APPLY GRAMMAR: Use possessive pronouns in your rule. Underline the possessive pronouns you use.

Social Studies Link

Grammar

Pronoun-Verb Contractions

RULES

A **contraction** is a shortened form of two words.

An **apostrophe (')** replaces letters that are left out in a pronoun-verb contraction.

We will see the kittens soon.
We'll see the kittens soon.

he's = he + is	they're = they + are	he'll = he + will
she's = she + is	I've = I + have	she'll = she + will
it's = it + is	you've = you + have	we'll = we + will
I'm = I + am	we've = we + have	you'll = you + will
you're = you + are	they've = they + have	it'll = it + will
we're = we + are	I'll = I + will	they'll = they + will

Pronoun-Verb Contractions

Why do writers use contractions? Write your answer in your journal.

Guided Practice

Name the contraction that could replace the underlined words in each sentence.

EXAMPLE: They are cute kittens. *They're*

1. They have grown well.
2. We have watched the mother cat.
3. She is a great mother.
4. Now we will find new homes for the kittens.
5. I will take one kitten home.

REVIEW THE RULES

- A contraction is a shortened form of two words. An apostrophe (') replaces letters that are left out.

More Practice

A. Write each sentence. Replace the underlined words with a contraction.

6. I am telling friends about the kittens.
7. He is making a kitten poster.
8. They are helping, too.
9. She is writing an ad.
10. We are working together.
11. I have found a home for one kitten.
12. He will live with Kate.
13. They will take Max and Tigger home.
14. You will take another kitten home.
15. Now it is quiet in the house!

B. Spiral Review Write the sentences. Circle helping and linking verbs. Underline subject pronouns.

16. The mother cat has curled into a ball.
17. Kate's kitten has disappeared.
18. It is not with the other kittens.
19. I have looked under Dad's chair.
20. We have seen the kitten's paw prints.

Extra Practice, page 394

Grammar

Handbook
page 517

Writing Activity An Advertisement

Write an ad to sell something or give something away. Plan your ad so it attracts and interests readers.

APPLY GRAMMAR: Use pronoun-verb contractions in your ad. Circle the contractions.

Grammar

Contractions and Possessive Pronouns

RULES

Do not confuse possessive pronouns with contractions.

The words it's, you're, and they're are contractions.

The words its, your, and their are possessive pronouns.

Contractions and Possessive Pronouns

Write how you can tell when to use an apostrophe.

Some possessive pronouns sound like contractions, but they are spelled differently. A contraction has an apostrophe. A possessive pronoun does not have an apostrophe.

Contraction	Possessive Pronoun
It's a horse.	The horse shook its head.
They're whales.	The ocean is their home.
You're getting a pet.	Your pet is a parrot.

Guided Practice

Name the contraction or possessive pronoun in each sentence.

EXAMPLE: You're good at solving riddles. *You're*

1. You're thinking of some animals.
2. They're such large animals.
3. Its nose is really a trunk.
4. Can we solve your riddle?
5. It's an elephant, of course.

REVIEW THE RULES

- The words *it's, you're,* and *they're* are *contractions*.
- The words *its, your,* and *their* are *possessive pronouns*.

Grammar

Handbook
pages 516–517

More Practice

A. Write each sentence. Choose the correct word in ( ).

6. (You're, Your) thinking of an animal.

7. (It's, Its) shaped like a horse.

8. (It's, Its) coat has black and white stripes.

9. I listen to (you're, your) clues.

10. (It's, Its) a zebra!

11. (You're, Your) going to guess now.

12. These animals have spots on (they're, their) bodies.

13. (You're, Your) guess is a giraffe.

14. No, (they're, their) big cats with spots.

15. Now (you're, your) guess is correct.

B. Spiral Review Write the sentences. Use the correct verb in ( ). Add an apostrophe where needed.

16. Mrs. Lee (tell, tells) her children a new riddle.

17. They (listen, listens) to their mothers riddle.

18. The riddles animal (is, are) small.

19. Its color (change, changes).

20. The childrens guesses (is, are) good.

Extra Practice, page 395

Writing Activity A Riddle

Write a riddle about an animal. Choose words that will help readers make a good guess.

APPLY MECHANICS, USAGE: Use possessive pronouns and contractions in your riddle.

Science Link

Grammar REVIEW

Mixed Review

REVIEW THE RULES

- A present-tense verb must agree with its subject pronoun.
- A possessive pronoun shows who or what owns something. It replaces a possessive noun.
- A contraction is a shortened form of two words. An apostrophe (') replaces the letters that are left out.
- Do not confuse possessive pronouns with contractions.

Pronouns

Write five sentences about your favorite game. Use possessive pronouns and pronoun-verb contractions.

Practice

A. Write the sentences. Use the correct verb in ( ). Write possessive pronouns correctly.

1. They (sit, sits) on the school steps.
2. The two children wait for they're friends.
3. She (read, reads) her book.
4. He looks through he's notebook.
5. They (wait, waits) quietly for a few minutes.
6. It (seem, seems) like a long time.
7. You (suggest, suggests) a game.
8. We (choose, chooses) a color to find.
9. Blue is mine color.
10. Yellow is your.

B. Write each sentence. Use a contraction for the words in ( ).

11. (She will) look for things that are red.

12. (I will) look for things that are blue.

13. (You have) spotted a yellow school bus.

14. (She has) pointed out a red car.

15. (I am) looking at the blue sky.

16. (You are) making a long list.

17. (You will) probably win the game.

18. (We will) count the items on our lists.

19. (I have) counted twenty items.

20. (We are) both winners!

Handbook
pages 516–517

C. Challenge Write the following paragraph. Correct mistakes in verbs, possessive pronouns, and contractions.

21.–25. Ours friend likes to play games. He lose him box of checkers. Its at you're house. We'll help him look for it.

Writing Activity **How-To Paragraph**

Write a paragraph that tells how to play a game. Remember to give instructions in the right order. **APPLY GRAMMAR:** Use possessive pronouns in your paragraph and circle them.

Common Errors with Pronouns

Sometimes writers make mistakes using pronouns. They may use subject and object pronouns in the wrong places. They may use a contraction instead of a possessive pronoun.

Common Errors	Examples	Corrected Sentences
Using an object pronoun as the subject of a sentence	Jack and me are at the library.	Jack and I are at the library.
Using a subject pronoun in the predicate of a sentence	Jack got a book for we.	Jack got a book for us.
Confusing a contraction with a possessive pronoun	It's cover is red.	Its cover is red.

Pronouns

How do you know whether to use a subject pronoun or an object pronoun? Write the answer in your journal.

REVIEW THE RULES

PRONOUNS

- Use a subject pronoun (*I, you, he, she, it, we, they*) as the subject of a sentence.
- Use an object pronoun (*me, you, him, her, it, us, them*) after an action verb or after a word such as *for, at, of, with,* or *to.*
- Use an apostrophe (') in a contraction but not in a possessive pronoun.

Practice

A. Read each sentence. Write the pronoun in each sentence.

1. Dad drove her to the mall.
2. They ate a salad for lunch.
3. The mall was too crowded for him.
4. He went outside to the car.
5. Its lights were still on!

B. Write each sentence. Choose the correct word in ( ).

6. (We, Us) wrote stories about animals.
7. Chantal and (I, me) wrote about snakes.
8. Maria does not like (they, them).
9. My story surprised Sarah and (she, her).
10. They think (it's, its) good.

C. Rewrite each sentence. Replace the incorrect pronoun in ( ) with the correct pronoun.

11. Jane and (me) like to look at stars at night.
12. Mom got a telescope for Jane and (I).
13. (Her) and Dad set the telescope in the yard.
14. (It's) tip pointed to the Big Dipper.
15. The stars looked bright to Jane and (we).

Troubleshooter, pages 498–499

Grammar
COMMON ERRORS

Handbook
pages 515–517

Writing Activity Write About a Picture

Find a photo of a friend or a relative. Think about where he or she is and what the person is doing. Then write about the picture.

APPLY GRAMMAR: Check the pronouns you used in your sentences. Make sure you used subject pronouns, object pronouns, and possessive pronouns correctly.

Mechanics and Spelling

TAAS

Directions

Read the passage and decide which type of mistake, if any, appears in each underlined section. Choose the correct answer. If there is no mistake, choose "No mistake."

Is the pronoun I written with a capital letter in every sentence?

Look for contractions with pronouns. Check to see if an apostrophe is needed.

Check the possessive pronouns. Remember, they do not have an apostrophe.

Sample

Last Saturday, I was painting a picture of a sunset. I used orange and yellow watercolors to start. <u>Next i wanted to add a few purple streaks</u>. **(1)** However, there was no purple color left in my pan of paints. Did I have to go to the store for purple paint? I didn't really want to stop painting. Then I got an idea. I mixed red and blue and got purple! <u>I think its a prettier purple</u> **(2)** than the one in the pan. Next <u>time you paint, try mixing you're colors</u>. **(3)**

1 ○ Spelling
○ Capitalization
○ Punctuation
○ No mistake

2 ○ Spelling
○ Capitalization
○ Punctuation
○ No mistake

3 ○ Spelling
○ Capitalization
○ Punctuation
○ No mistake

Test Tip
To catch mistakes, read the passage slowly and carefully.

Grammar and Usage

Directions

Read the passage and choose the word or group of words that belongs in each space.

Sample

Larry and Mary are twins. Today is __(1)__ birthday. The children's mother has planned a picnic for __(2)__. She has invited friends to come over this afternoon. Now this morning, it's raining. She talked with Larry and Mary.

She said, "We could have the picnic on another day. We could move the picnic inside the house. We could eat outside under umbrellas."

Both children said, "We want to eat outside." Mary said, "Larry and __(3)__ will help put up the umbrellas."

Look out for pronoun forms that show possession.

Be sure to use an object pronoun after an action verb or words such as for, at, of, with, *and* to.

Remember to use the pronoun I *in the subject of a sentence.*

1 ○ they
○ them
○ those
○ their

2 ○ he
○ she
○ they
○ them

3 ○ I
○ me
○ my
○ mine

TIME FOR KIDS Writer's Notebook

RESEARCH

When I write a report about animals, I start by looking in the **encyclopedia**. It has lots of information and great photos. The encyclopedia on CD-ROM even has sound effects, so I can tell my readers what the animals sound like!

WRITING WELL

When I write, I start by making an **outline**. I write my main ideas in the outline. As I write, I look back at the outline. It helps me stay on track!

USING WORDS

The words know and no are **homophones**. Homophones are words that sound the same but have different meanings and different spellings. Reed and read, and blue and blew are homophones. Can you think of others?

Read Now!

As you read the photo essay that follows, think about the main point of each of the four paragraphs. Then write a simple outline of the photo essay.

TIME FOR KIDS

PHOTO ESSAY

Trapped

Turning wild animals into pets is big business. It is also against the law.

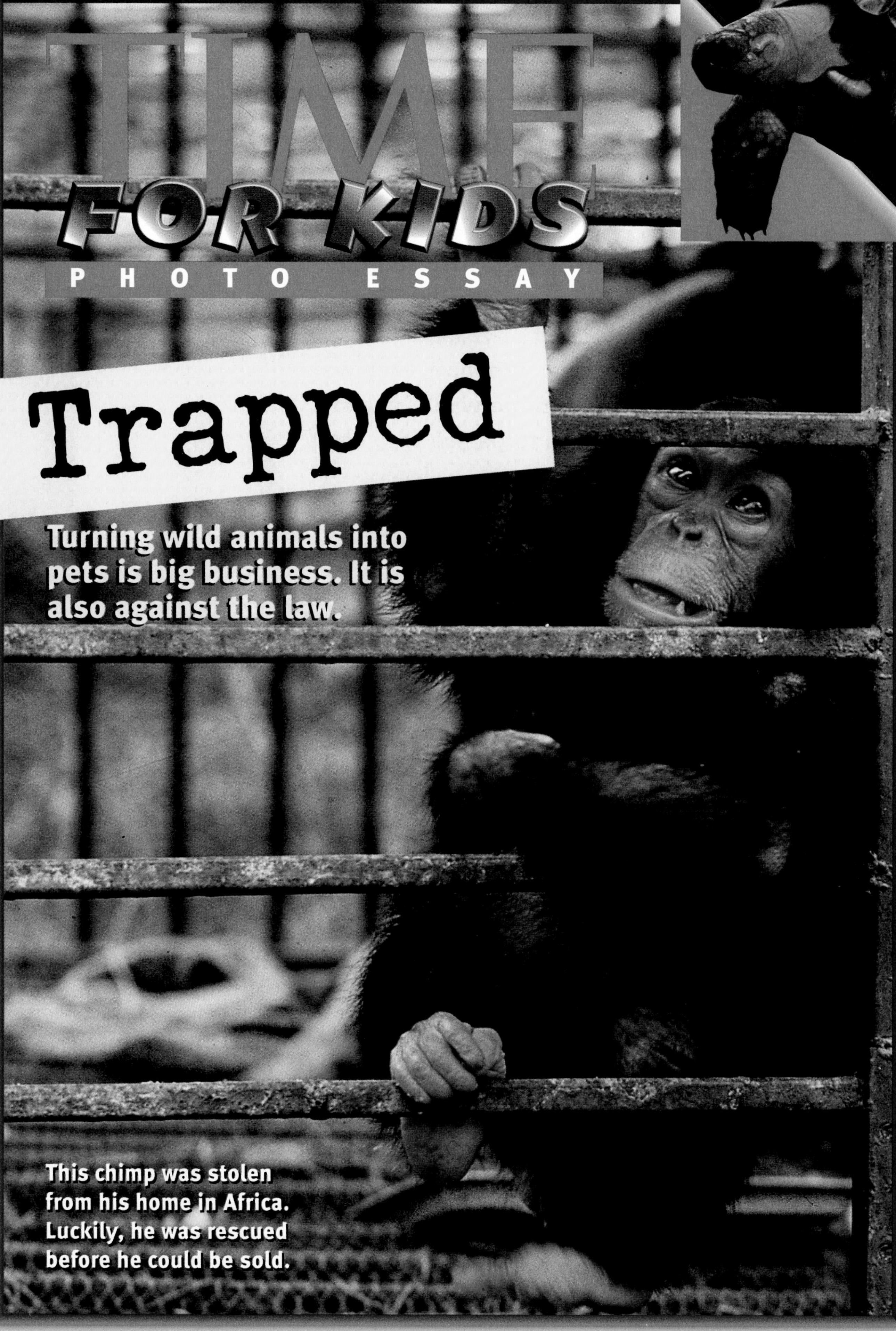

This chimp was stolen from his home in Africa. Luckily, he was rescued before he could be sold.

Stolen Animals

Bright green parrots are jammed into cages at a market in Mexico City. Brown snakes lie in bunches. Toucans squawk loudly. No wonder the animals seem unhappy. They were stolen from their homes in the wild. They are being sold for high prices to people who want them as pets.

"People collect rare pets like anything else—stamps, art, cars," says Craig Hoover. He works for a group called TRAFFIC. TRAFFIC keeps track of wildlife trade. "They want what no one else has."

It is against the law in many nations to sell many kinds of wild animals. What's more, many animals die when they are caught. And many more die when they are sent from one place to another.

So if you buy an unusual pet, always ask what country it came from. Make sure it is okay to own one. And make sure it's the kind of animal that will do well in your home.

Photo and Cover photo: Gerry Ellis/ENP Images

This Komodo dragon lives in Indonesia. Some people want Komodos for pets.

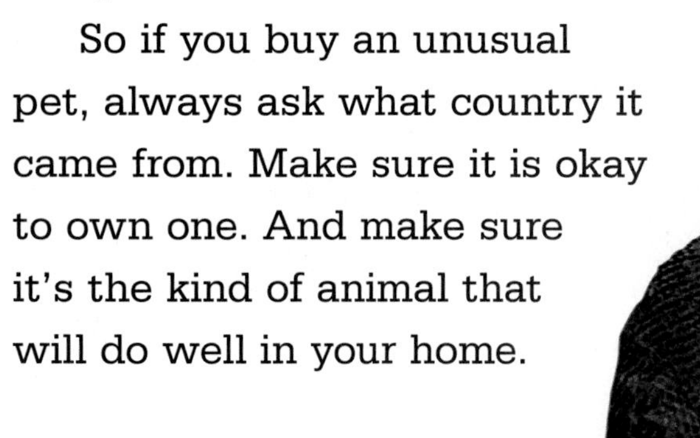

interNET CONNECTION Go to www.mhschool.com/language-arts for more information on the topic.

Michael Dick/Animals Animals

These yellow-shouldered parrots are for sale to visitors in Brazil.

The plowshare tortoise is found only in Madagascar, off the coast of Africa.

Write Now!

What unusual animal can you think of? Write to tell about it. If you need to find out specific information about the animal you choose, check the encyclopedia.

The Encyclopedia

An **encyclopedia** is a set of books that contains information about people, places, and things. Each book in an encyclopedia is called a volume. The volumes are arranged in alphabetical order.

The spine of each volume usually has a number and one or more letters. The numbers help you keep the volumes in order. The letter or letters show what topics are in the volume. The topics are in alphabetical order. Information about a person is listed by the last name.

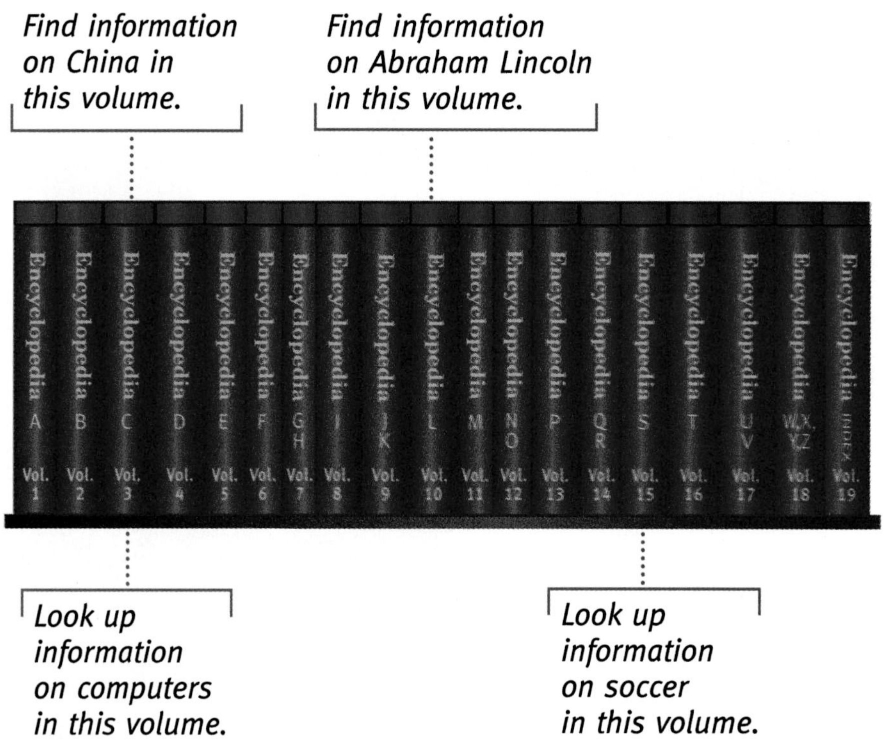

Find information on China in this volume.
Find information on Abraham Lincoln in this volume.
Look up information on computers in this volume.
Look up information on soccer in this volume.

An encyclopedia has an index. The index may be part of the last volume or may be in a separate volume. The index lists all the articles in the encyclopedia in alphabetical order. Each entry shows the volume number or letter and the pages of the article.

You can also use an encyclopedia CD-ROM. An encyclopedia CD-ROM contains all the information in a set of encyclopedias on a computer disk.

Search for your topic by typing in the key word. Some CD-ROMs give you a list of articles from which to choose. Select the article that looks best for your topic. Read the article on the screen or print it out.

Practice

A. Look at the set of encyclopedias on page 350. In what volume would you find an article on these topics?

1. Baseball
2. Swimming
3. Martin Luther King, Jr.
4. Helicopters
5. Dragons

B. Write how each of the encyclopedia aids helps you.

6. Volume numbers
7. Encyclopedia CD-ROM
8. Index
9. Letters on spines
10. Alphabetical order

*inter***NET** CONNECTION

Go to www.mhschool.com/language-arts **for more information on using the encyclopedia.**

Writing Activity Use an Encyclopedia

Use the encyclopedia to get information on a game or a hobby. Write a summary of the game or hobby. Use the summary to give a speech about the game or hobby to your classmates.

Vocabulary: Homophones

DEFINITION

Words that sound alike but have different spellings and different meanings are called **homophones**.

hi, high	hole, whole	see, sea
be, bee	rode, road, rowed	flour, flower
sun, son	to, two, too	would, wood
eye, I	nose, knows	right, write
blue, blew	horse, hoarse	there, their

Homophones

Why is it important to know which homophone is needed in your writing? Explain what might happen if you use the wrong spelling.

Look at the blue words in the paragraph below.

*Would your **son** and his friend like to visit a ranch in New Mexico in the summer? The **sun** is hot, and the air is dry. Mr. and Mrs. Ramos own a ranch **there**. The boys will see **their** wonderful animals.*

Practice

A. Write the sentences. Underline the homophone in each sentence that matches a homophone in the box.

hoarse four heard weak nose

1. Mr. Ramos knows a lot about animals.
2. He has two dogs and a horse.
3. He also has a herd of sheep.
4. The dogs help him care for the sheep.
5. Last week, they chased away a coyote.

B. Write the sentences. Correct homophone mistakes.

6. Won day some sheep got out.
7. There was a whole in the fence.
8. Several sheep went threw it.
9. Two were running down the rode.
10. The dogs brought them write back.

C. Grammar Link Write each sentence. Change the underlined words to subject or object pronouns. Use the correct homophone in ( ).

11. Lee and I visited the ranch this (weak, week).
12. Mrs. Ramos has a (pear, pair) of peacocks.
13. The male peacock has (some, sum) amazing feathers.
14. The feathers make a very beautiful (tale, tail).
15. She gave Lee and me a green and (blew, blue) feather.

Writing Activity A Paragraph

Write about an animal. Tell what is special about the animal. Use three homophones.

APPLY GRAMMAR: Underline the pronouns you use.

Composition: Outlining

Outlining is a good way to organize your ideas for writing. An outline lists main ideas and supporting details for one topic.

GUIDELINES

- **An outline is a way of organizing ideas.**
- **Write the topic at the top of the outline.**
- **List the main ideas you plan to include. Number each main idea with a Roman numeral, followed by a period.**
- **Under each main idea, list supporting details that help to develop that idea. Give each detail a letter.**
- **Ideas written in an outline do not need to be complete sentences. They can be words, phrases, or questions.**

Outlining

How can an outline help you plan your writing? Write your answer in your journal.

Read this outline for the first two paragraphs of a report about giraffes. Notice how the writer organizes the main idea and supporting details.

The main idea of the first paragraph is written next to the Roman numeral I.

Each supporting detail for that idea is indented and labeled.

Topic: Giraffes

I. Body features
    A. Long neck
    B. Patchy coat
    C. Knobby forehead
II. Places they live
    A. African grasslands
    B. Wildlife parks, zoos

Practice

A. Write each sentence. Should the detail be listed under the idea in the next box? Write *yes* or *no*.

Topic: Cactus Plants

I. How can they grow in hot, dry places?

1. Roots gather water quickly.
2. The desert is sandy.
3. Waxy skin keeps water in.
4. They can store water for a year or more.
5. Tumbleweeds live there, too.

B. Write one main idea for each outline topic.

6. Topic: Trees
7. Topic: Seasons
8. Topic: Transportation
9. Topic: Sports
10. Topic: Birds

C. Grammar Link Write each main idea or detail sentence. Change the underlined words to a pronoun.

11. <u>Maple trees</u> change color in the fall.
12. <u>Winter</u> is usually the coldest season.
13. <u>Swans, geese, and ducks</u> belong to the same family.
14. <u>Jackie Robinson</u> was a great baseball player.
15. Many people travel on <u>trains, buses, and planes</u>.

Writing Activity A Paragraph

Begin an outline for a familiar topic. Then write a paragraph about the first main idea in your outline. Use connecting words such as *because* and *so* in your paragraph.

APPLY GRAMMAR: Use pronouns to replace nouns that are repeated. Underline each pronoun you use.

Better Sentences

Directions

Read the passage. Some parts are underlined. The underlined parts may be one of the following:

- **Incomplete sentences**
- **Run-on sentences**
- **Correctly written sentences that should be combined**

Choose the best way to write each underlined part.

Do the sentences have any words that are the same?

Does the sentence have a subject and a predicate?

Sample

<u>Have you ever played soccer? Have you ever played basketball</u>(1)? Both sports have a special ball, but the rules for moving the ball are different. In soccer, unless you're the goalie, you mostly move the ball around on the field by kicking it.

<u>In basketball, you always use. Your hands to move the ball</u>(2). You might dribble it, pass it, or shoot it at the hoop. But you never kick it.

1 ○ Have you ever played, and soccer or basketball?

○ Have you ever played soccer or basketball?

○ Have soccer or basketball ever played?

2 ○ In basketball, you always use your hands to move the ball.

○ In basketball, you always move the ball.

○ In basketball, using your hands always moving the ball.

Test Tip
Check your answer by reading the underlined part again.

Vocabulary and Comprehension

TAAS

Directions

Read the passage. Then read each question that follows the passage. Choose the best answer to each question.

I wrote an article for our school newspaper about a problem in Ms. Washington's class: the noise. The students were trying to read. They were having a hard time. It was very noisy outside. Construction workers were putting up a building. Huge digging machines clanged loudly. Big dump trucks rumbled. Their brakes squeaked when they stopped. Tall cranes went beep, beep, beep each time they backed up. I ended my article with this question: "How can the students read when there is so much noise?"

Look for clues around the underlined word to help figure out what it means.

1 What is the main idea of the article?

- ○ Reading is important.
- ○ Noise is a problem.
- ○ Students solve problems.
- ○ Construction machines are big.

2 In this passage, the word brakes means—

- ○ pauses
- ○ bursts into pieces
- ○ parts that stop something from moving
- ○ parts that move things backward

Seeing Like a Writer

What information and ideas for writing do these pictures give you? Look at the details. How do they help you understand the point of each picture?

Red Carpet Landing by Gustavo Novoa.

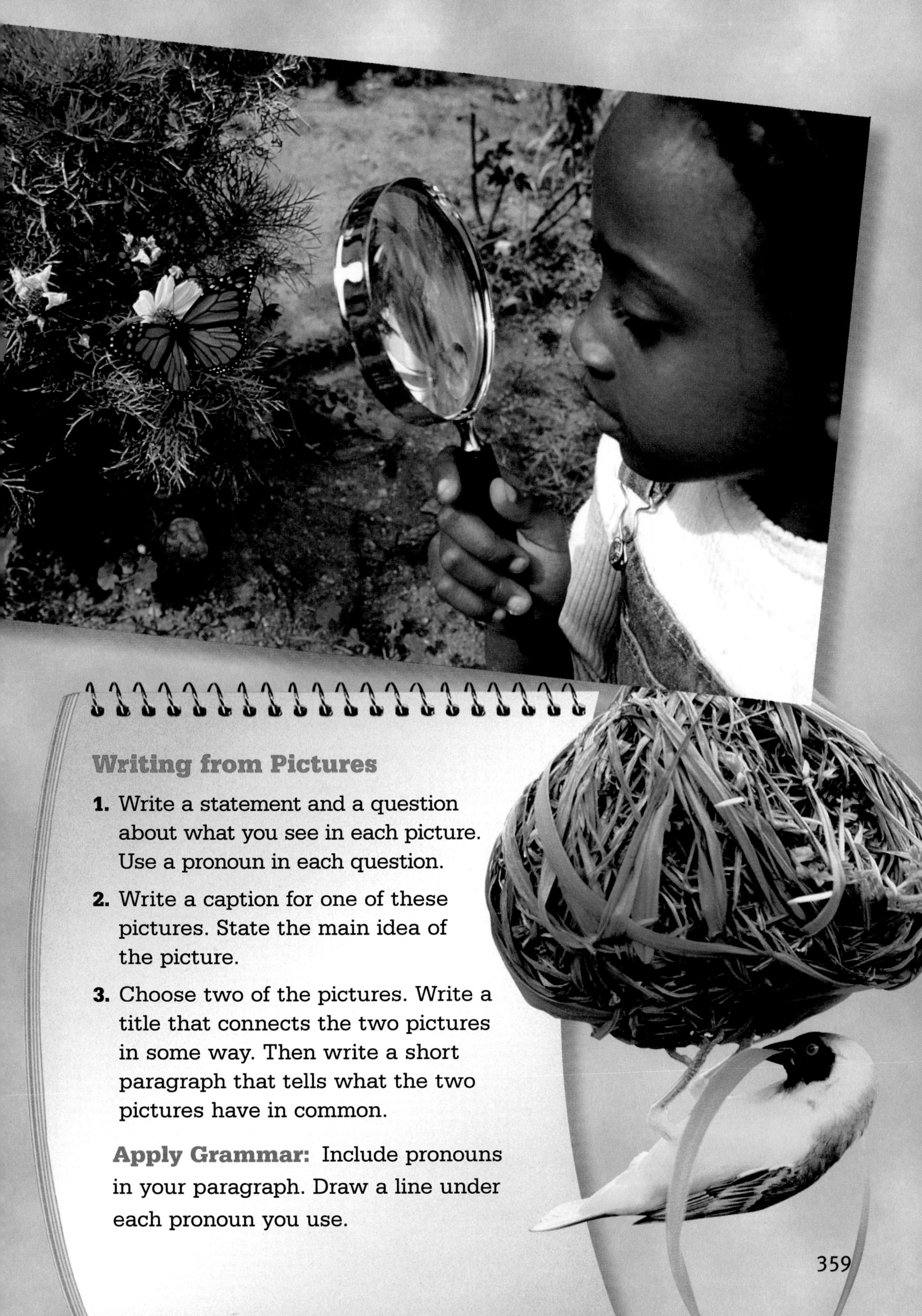

Writing from Pictures

1. Write a statement and a question about what you see in each picture. Use a pronoun in each question.
2. Write a caption for one of these pictures. State the main idea of the picture.
3. Choose two of the pictures. Write a title that connects the two pictures in some way. Then write a short paragraph that tells what the two pictures have in common.

Apply Grammar: Include pronouns in your paragraph. Draw a line under each pronoun you use.

Expository Writing

Purpose

How is expository writing different from a personal narrative? Write a short explanation.

Have you ever looked in different books and other sources to find information about a topic? Did you use that information to write a report? A report is expository writing. The purpose of expository writing is to share information about a topic.

Learning from Writers

Read the following examples of expository writing. What information is included? How is it organized? As you read, notice how each author connects ideas.

Clean as a Breeze

Whirling windmills have been used for energy in countries such as the Netherlands for hundreds of years. Today, windmills are popping up all over the U.S., Europe, and Asia. The modern windmills have lightweight blades that can catch more wind than ever before. They turn the wind into electricity.

One day, we will run out of coal and oil. But we will never run out of the energy we can get from the sun and the wind. Nancy Hazard says, "Energy from the sun and the wind is the key to the future."

— from "Pure Power!" in *Time for Kids*

How Frogs Live on Land and in the Water

Frogs are found in many places. They can live in water, on land, or even in trees. But all frogs start out in the water.

A frog begins as a tadpole that hatches from an egg. It lives underwater and breathes through gills like a fish. As the tadpole turns into a frog, it grows legs and lungs so it can live on land.

Although adult frogs have lungs, they take in most of the oxygen they need through their skin. Their skin can take oxygen from water or air. That is why they can live in water or on land.

—Suki Park

Practice and Apply

Thinking Like a Reader

1. What is the main idea of "Clean as a Breeze"?
2. According to "How Frogs Live on Land and in the Water," what do frogs need so they can live on land?

Thinking Like a Writer

3. How did the author of "Clean as a Breeze" support the main idea?
4. What sources might Suki Park have used to find facts about frogs?

5. **Reading Across Texts** Compare how each of the two examples draws a conclusion based on facts.

Features of Expository Writing

DEFINITIONS AND FEATURES

Expository writing gives information about a topic. Good expository writing:

- Introduces a **main idea** and supports it with details.
- **Summarizes information** from different sources.
- Uses **connecting words** to go from one idea to the next.
- **Draws a conclusion** based on the facts.

Main Idea

Reread "Clean as a Breeze" on page 360. What is the article about?

> Whirling windmills have been used for energy in countries such as the Netherlands for hundreds of years.

The opening sentence tells you that the article will be about using windmills for energy.

Summarizes Information

Good expository writing summarizes information from more than one source.

> Today, windmills are popping up all over the U.S., Europe, and Asia.

What sources might the writer have used for the information summarized in this sentence?

▶ Connecting Words

Words and phrases such as *because*, *as a result*, and *so* help readers connect related ideas in expository writing.

> One day, we will run out of coal and oil. But we will never run out of the energy we can get from the sun and the wind.

What connecting word did the author use?

▶ Draws a Conclusion

The author ends the article with this conclusion about the importance of wind power.

> Nancy Hazard says, "Energy from the sun and the wind is the key to the future."

What facts in the article support this conclusion?

PRACTICE and APPLY

Create a Features Chart

1. List the features of good expository writing.
2. Reread "How Frogs Live on Land and in the Water" by Suki Park on page 361.
3. Write one example of each feature in Suki's writing.
4. Write what you liked about Suki's report.

Features	Examples

Prewrite

Expository writing presents information about a topic. Writing a report gives you a chance to summarize and share what you have learned.

Purpose and Audience

The purpose for writing a report is to summarize factual information from different sources. It is also to share what you have learned with your audience.

Before you begin to write, think about your audience. Who will be reading your report? Write your report in a way that will interest your readers.

Audience

Write down what you need to remember about your audience as you plan and write your report.

Choose a Topic

Begin by **brainstorming** a list of topics that interest you. Choose something that your readers might like to learn about.

After choosing a topic, **explore ideas** by listing questions that your report will try to answer.

I explored my ideas by asking questions.

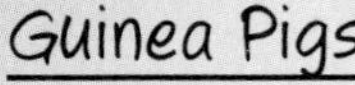

Guinea Pigs
What are they like?
What do they need?
What can you do with them?
Why do people like them?

Organize • Main Idea

Before you write a report, you need to narrow your topic. Your report should focus on just a few main ideas. To plan your report, you can use an outline. How did this writer organize the ideas from his list?

OUTLINE

Topic: Guinea Pigs

I. What are guinea pigs like?

II. What do guinea pigs need?

III. Why do people like guinea pigs?
  A. Guinea pigs are friendly and fun to watch and pet.
  B. They are small and easy to take care of.

Practice and Apply

Plan Your Own Report

1. Think about your purpose and audience.
2. Choose a topic.
3. Explore ideas about your topic.
4. Organize your ideas in an outline.

Checklist

Prewriting

- Have you thought about your purpose and audience?
- Have you chosen a topic and explored ideas about it?
- Have you made a list of ideas to include in your report?
- Are your ideas organized in an outline?
- What research do you need to do?

Writing PROCESS

Prewrite • Research and Inquiry

▶ Writer's Resources

When you write a report, you need to do some research to gather information. Make a list of your questions. Then decide what resources you need to answer your questions. Always use more than one resource.

What Else Do I Need to Know?	Where Can I Find the Information?
What do guinea pigs look like?	Use an encyclopedia.
What do guinea pigs eat?	Look in a telephone directory to find pet shops that sell guinea pigs.
Where can you keep them?	
What must the owner do?	

▶ Use an Encyclopedia

An encyclopedia is a good place to begin your research. Search for your topic on an encyclopedia CD-ROM by typing in key words. You will see a list of articles about your subject. Click on the article that you want to read.

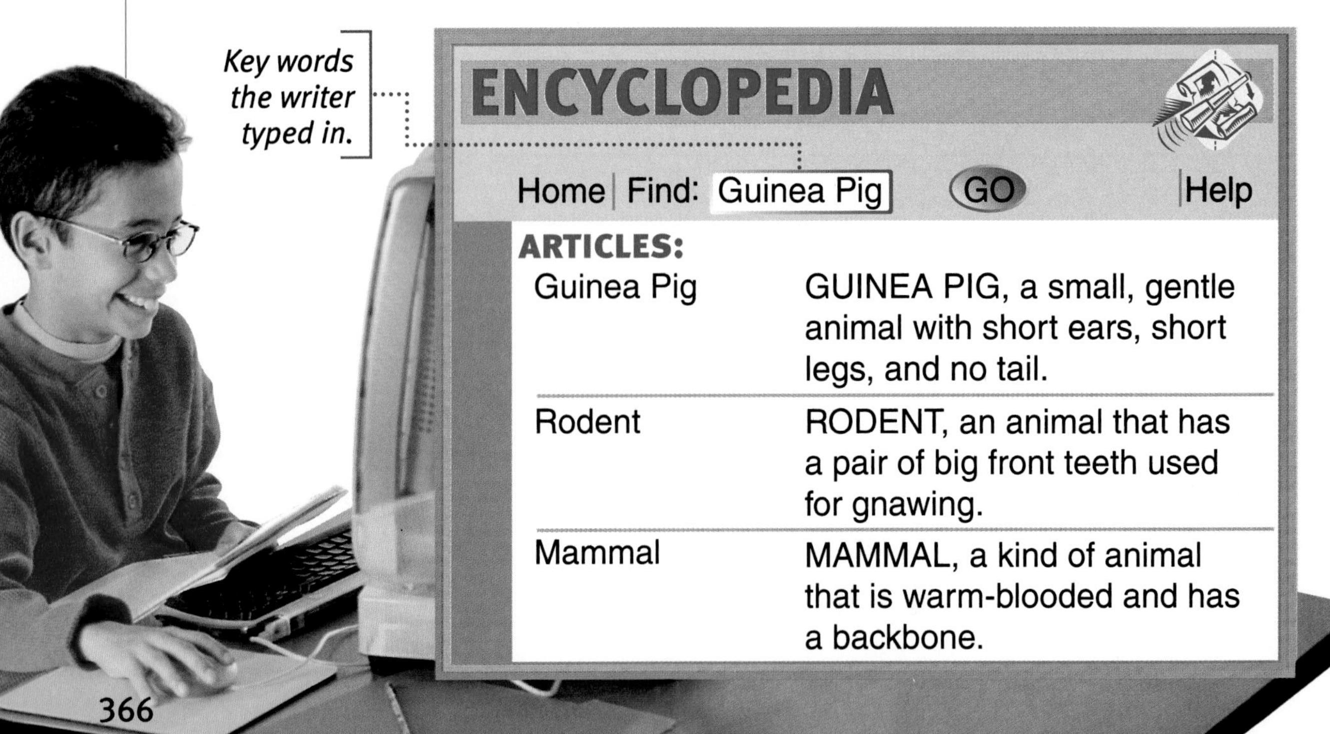

Key words the writer typed in.
ENCYCLOPEDIA
Home
Find: Guinea Pig
GO
Help
ARTICLES:
Guinea Pig
GUINEA PIG, a small, gentle animal with short ears, short legs, and no tail.
Rodent
RODENT, an animal that has a pair of big front teeth used for gnawing.
Mammal
MAMMAL, a kind of animal that is warm-blooded and has a backbone.

PREWRITE

DRAFT

REVISE

PROOFREAD

PUBLISH

▶ Use a Telephone Directory

A telephone directory gives the names, addresses, and phone numbers of people, businesses, and other resources. It is arranged in alphabetical order. You can find extra information about businesses in a section called The Yellow Pages.

▶ Use Your Research

Information gathered from your research goes into your outline. This writer added facts from his research. How did he change the outline?

I. What are guinea pigs like?
  A. many colors of fur; thick bodies, short legs
  B. make lots of noises, chew things

II. What do guinea pigs need?
  A. cage to live in
  B. vegetables and fruit; dry food; fresh water
  C. The owner must clean the cage and feed the guinea pig.

Handbook
pages 538–539

Checklist

Research and Inquiry

- Did you list your questions?
- Did you identify more than one resource?
- Did you take notes?

Practice and Apply

Review Your Plan

1. Look at your outline.

2. List questions you have about your topic.

3. Identify the resources you need to find answers.

4. Add the information you gather to your outline.

Writing PROCESS

Draft

Before you begin writing your report, review the outline you made. Think about making a paragraph for each main idea. Include details that support each main idea.

Main idea for first paragraph: What guinea pigs are like

OUTLINE

Topic: Guinea Pigs

I. What are guinea pigs like?
   A. many colors of fur; thick bodies, short legs
   B. make lots of noises, chew things

II. What do guinea pigs need?
   A. cage to live in
   B. vegetables and fruit; dry food; fresh water
   C. The owner must clean the cage and feed the guinea pig.

III. Why do people like guinea pigs?
   A. Guinea pigs are friendly and fun to watch and pet.
   B. They are small and easy to take care of.

Supporting details for first main idea.

Checklist

Drafting

- Does your report suit your purpose and audience?
- Have you given details to support your ideas?
- Have you summarized facts from more than one source?
- Have you drawn a conclusion based on the facts?

Look at how this writer used the ideas in his outline to write a first draft. He described guinea pigs in the first paragraph. He told about what they need in the second paragraph. In the third paragraph, he drew a conclusion based on the facts.

DRAFT

Guinea pigs are small, furry animals that come in many different colors. Guinea pigs have thick bodys and short legs. I think they're really cute. Guinea pigs can make a lot of noise.

Main idea of first paragraph

Supporting details further describe guinea pigs.

A pet guinea pig needs a cage to live in. It needs a food dish, a water bottle, and things to chew. guinea pigs need to eat fresh fruits or vegetables every day. It needs fresh water and dry food, too. The cage needs to be cleaned every week.

Main idea of second paragraph

Supporting details explain what guinea pigs need.

Guinea pigs are friendly and their not hard to take care of. Do you like feeding and petting small animals a guinea pig may be the pet for you!

Conclusion

PRACTICE and APPLY

Draft Your Own Report

1. Review your prewriting outline.
2. Summarize information from your research.
3. Draw a conclusion based on the facts.

TECHNOLOGY

Give your draft a name and a number. After you revise it, do a "save as" with the same name but a different number.

Revise

Elaborate

Reread your first draft. Are any important ideas or details missing? When you revise your report, you may need to elaborate by adding more details.

The details that the writer added tell the reader more about what this pet is like.

They squeak, squeal, whistle, and purr.
Guinea pigs can make a lot of noise.^

The writer added another detail to make this part more complete. When writing a report, you may need to learn new words that are special for your subject.

or hutch
A pet guinea pig needs a cage^ to live in.

Word Choice

When you write, it is important to choose your words carefully so that the reader will know exactly what you mean.

In a report, you need to find words that connect one idea to another.

Even though they are little,
^Guinea pigs can make a lot of noise.

CONNECTING WORDS

- but
- so
- at first
- later
- earlier
- however
- if so
- even though
- because of
- since
- as a result
- also

Better Sentences

As you are revising your draft, check your sentences to make sure they fit together well. Read your sentences aloud. How do they sound? Have you tried not to begin every sentence with the same subject?

You can use a pronoun to avoid repeating the same noun again and again.

> Guinea pigs are small, furry animals that come in many different colors. They ~~Guinea pigs~~ have thick bodys and short legs.

Handbook
page 515

Practice and Apply

Revise Your Own Report

1. Add details that will make your writing clearer and more interesting.
2. Use connecting words to lead your readers from one idea to the next.
3. Take out information that does not support your main ideas.
4. **Grammar** Should you use pronouns in place of some of the nouns in your report?

TECHNOLOGY

Some of your classmates may know word-processing tips or shortcuts. Ask them to share what they know.

Revise • Peer Conferencing

Exchange reports with a partner and read each other's first drafts. You may both be able to give each other some fresh ideas and suggestions.

Your topic interests me.

Your opinion doesn't belong in a report.

These details clearly tell me what it's like to take care of a guinea pig!

Guinea pigs are small, furry animals that come in many different colors. Guinea pigs have thick bodys and short legs. I think they're really cute. Guinea pigs can make a lot of noise.

A pet guinea pig needs a cage to live in. It needs a food dish, a water bottle, and things to chew. guinea pigs need to eat fresh fruits or vegetables every day. It needs fresh water and dry food, too. The cage needs to be cleaned every week.

Guinea pigs are friendly and their not hard to take care of. Do you like feeding and petting small animals a guinea pig may be the pet for you!

Conferencing for the Reader

- Did your partner include features of a report?
  - main idea and supporting details
  - summarizes information
  - connecting words
  - draws a conclusion
- Tell your partner what you like about the report, as well as what could be better.

Think about the comments and suggestions of your partner when you revise your report. This writer made some changes based on his partner's ideas.

PREWRITE

DRAFT

REVISE

PROOFREAD

PUBLISH

REVISE

Guinea Pigs

Guinea pigs are small, furry animals that come in many different colors. They ~~Guinea pigs~~ have thick bodys and short legs. ~~I think they're really cute~~. Even though they are little, Guinea pigs can make a lot of noise. They squeak, squeal, whistle, and purr.

A pet guinea pig needs a cage or hutch to live in. It also needs a food dish, a water bottle, and things to chew. guinea pigs need to eat fresh fruits or vegetables every day. It needs fresh water and dry food, too. The cage needs to be cleaned every week.

Guinea pigs are friendly and their not hard to take care of. Do you like feeding and petting small animals? If so, a guinea pig may be the pet for you!

Checklist

Revising

- Does your report suit your purpose and audience?
- Did you include enough details to support your main ideas? Did you choose words carefully?
- Do the sentences flow smoothly?
- Did you draw a conclusion based on the facts?

PRACTICE and APPLY

Revise Your Own Report

1. Have a partner read your report.

2. Take notes on your partner's comments.

3. Use your notes to improve your draft.

4. Add a title.

Proofread

Proofread your revised report to find and correct any mistakes in grammar and usage, mechanics, and spelling.

STRATEGIES FOR PROOFREADING

- Reread your revised report, each time looking for a different type of error. That way you will have a better chance of catching all mistakes.
- Read each sentence for correct capitalization.
- Reread each sentence for correct punctuation.
- Reread for correct use of possessive pronouns and contractions.
- Check each word for spelling mistakes.

Spelling

When a base word ends with a consonant followed by *y*, change the *y* to *i* when adding *-es*. (body = bodies)

REVIEW THE RULES

GRAMMAR

- A pronoun must match the noun it replaces. Use singular pronouns for singular nouns and plural pronouns for plural nouns.

MECHANICS

- Capitalize *I*.
- Refer to yourself last when writing about yourself and someone else.
- A contraction has an apostrophe (') to show missing letters.
- A possessive pronoun does not have an apostrophe.

Look at the proofreading corrections made on the draft below. What does the proofreading mark ^ mean? Why does the writer use this mark?

PROOFREAD

Guinea Pigs
^

Guinea pigs are small, furry animals that come in many different colors. ~~Guinea pigs~~ They have thick ~~bodys~~ bodies and short legs. ~~I think they're really cute.~~ Even though they are little, Guinea pigs can make a lot of noise. They squeak, squeal, whistle, and purr.

A pet guinea pig needs a cage or hutch to live in. It also needs a food dish, a water bottle, and things to chew. guinea pigs need to eat fresh fruits or vegetables every day. ~~It~~ They need~~s~~ fresh water and dry food, too. The cage needs to be cleaned every week.

Guinea pigs are friendly, and ~~their~~ they're not hard to take care of. Do you like feeding and petting small animals? If so, a guinea pig may be the pet for you!

PREWRITE

DRAFT

REVISE

PROOFREAD

PUBLISH

Checklist ✓

Proofreading

- Did you spell all the words correctly?
- Did you begin and end every sentence correctly?
- Does each pronoun match the noun it replaces?
- Are contractions and possessive pronouns written correctly?

PROOFREADING MARKS

- ¶ new paragraph
- ^ add
- ~ take out
- ≡ Make a capital letter.
- / Make a small letter.
- (sp) Check the spelling.
- ⊙ Add a period.

PRACTICE and APPLY

Proofread Your Own Report

1. Correct spelling mistakes and punctuation.
2. Use the correct pronoun.
3. Make sure contractions and possessive pronouns are written correctly.

Publish

Review your report one more time before you publish it. Using a checklist will help you focus.

Self-Check Expository Writing

- ❑ Who is my audience? Did I write in a way that will interest them?
- ❑ What is my purpose? Will the reader learn new facts about the subject?
- ❑ Did I narrow my topic?
- ❑ Did I use information from more than one source?
- ❑ Did I draw a conclusion based on the facts?
- ❑ Did I use pronouns in place of repeated nouns?
- ❑ Did I make sure that all pronouns matched the nouns they replaced?
- ❑ Did I write possessive pronouns correctly?

The writer used the checklist to review his report. Read "Guinea Pigs" and discuss it with your classmates. Was the piece ready to be published? Why or why not?

Guinea Pigs

by Raphael Garcia

Guinea pigs are small, furry animals that come in many different colors. They have thick bodies and short legs. Even though they are little, guinea pigs can make a lot of noise. They squeak, squeal, whistle, and purr.

A pet guinea pig needs a cage or hutch to live in. It also needs a food dish, a water bottle, and things to chew. Guinea pigs need to eat fresh fruits or vegetables every day. They need fresh water and dry food, too. The cage needs to be cleaned every week.

Guinea pigs are friendly, and they're not hard to take care of. Do you like feeding and petting small animals? If so, a guinea pig may be the pet for you!

Practice and Apply

Publish Your Own Report

1. Check your revised draft one more time.
2. Make a neat final copy.
3. Add some drawings or photographs.

TIP!

TECHNOLOGY

For your final report, choose a font size that is easy to read. Adjust your margins to make room for any drawings or photos you plan to use.

LISTENING

SPEAKING

VIEWING

PRESENTING

Present Your Expository Writing

Before you present your report, you need to plan and practice. Think of ways to make your presentation successful.

STEP 1

How to Explain Your Report

Strategies for Speaking Remember, your purpose is to give information to your audience. Try to help them understand the subject.

- On note cards, write down ideas and details.
- Make eye contact with your audience so they feel as if you are speaking to them.
- Do not speak too quickly. Your listeners need time to think about what you are telling them.

Listening Strategies

- Set a purpose. Are you listening to learn new information or to be entertained?
- Try to picture in your mind what the speaker is explaining.
- Don't interrupt. Save your questions for the end.
- Keep your eyes on the speaker. Let the speaker know you are paying attention.

Multimedia Ideas

You may want to show a video with your report. Check your library or media center for videos about your topic.

STEP 2

How to Show Your Report

Suggestions for Visuals You can make your presentation clearer and more interesting by adding visuals for your audience to look at as they listen.

- Photos or drawings can show your audience what you are explaining.
- A poster can help the audience follow facts as you present them.
- If possible, display real things. Remember to use large visuals.

STEP 3

How to Share Your Report

Strategies for Rehearsing The more you practice, the better you will feel when you present your report.

- Ask a friend to listen and make suggestions.
- Practice in front of a mirror.
- Practice pointing to your visuals and using any multimedia equipment you may need.

Viewing Strategies

- **Look carefully at the materials the speaker displays.**
- **Look for information that the speaker does not tell you.**
- **Read the labels on all visuals.**

PRACTICE and APPLY

Present Your Own Report

1. Write important ideas and details on note cards.
2. Illustrate your report with photographs, drawings, or real things.
3. Practice presenting your report in front of a friend or family member.
4. Make eye contact with your audience.

Writing Tests

TAAS

On a writing test, you will be asked to write something in response to a prompt. Read the prompt carefully. Look for key words and phrases that tell you what to write about and how to do your writing.

Sometimes a prompt names the audience for the writing.

Key words can tell the purpose of the writing.

There are clues that tell what kind of writing to do.

Prompt

Your teacher wants you to write a report about something you know about, such as a favorite person, animal, or activity. Choose a topic.

Write a paragraph that gives important information about the topic. Include facts that you have learned from your experience.

How to Read a Prompt

Purpose Look for key words in a prompt that will tell you the purpose of the writing. The key words "gives important information" tell you that the purpose of this writing is to inform.

Audience The words "your teacher" in this prompt tell you whom to write for.

Expository Writing The words "information about the topic" and "facts" tell you that this is expository writing. Expository writing gives information about a topic. It introduces a main idea and supports it with details.

Test Tip
If part of the test is not clear, try putting it in your own words.

How to Write to a Prompt

Read the following tips to help when you are given a writing prompt.

Before Writing **Content/Ideas**	• Look for words that tell your purpose. • Think about your audience. • Stick to facts and important information.
During Writing **Organization/ Paragraph Structure**	• Begin by writing a good topic sentence. • Support the main idea with details. • Use connecting words to go from one idea to the next in your expository writing.
After Writing **Grammar/Usage**	• Proofread your writing. • Check to see that you used pronouns and possessive pronouns correctly. • Use apostrophes correctly in contractions. • Use correct spelling.

Apply What You Learned

As you read a prompt on a writing test, be sure you understand the writing purpose and your audience. Think about the topic and what information you will include in your writing.

Prompt

Think about what you have learned in science about Earth.

Write a paragraph for your teacher giving information about Earth. Be sure to include facts.

Unit 5 Review

Grammar and Writing Review

pages 322–323

Pronouns

A. Write the sentences. Replace the underlined word or words with the correct pronoun in ( ).

1. The math test was on Friday. (He, It)
2. Some problems were hard. (They, She)
3. Everyone worked hard on the problems. (they, them)
4. Val was the first one finished. (It, She)
5. Bill and I needed more time for the test. (We, You)

pages 324–325

Subject Pronouns

B. Write the sentences. Replace the underlined word or words with a subject pronoun.

6. Ms. Levy gives the class a list of plants.
7. The students look for plants in a large field.
8. The field contains many different plants.
9. Many flowers are blooming in the field.
10. Sally and I check our list.
11. Sally finds two plants right away.
12. Jeff spots another plant on the list.
13. Lois and Ted find the most plants.
14. Soon the search is over.
15. The children take the bus back to school.

pages 326–327

Object Pronouns

C. Write the sentences. Replace the underlined word or words with the correct pronoun in ( ).

16. Mr. Ruiz took our class to the beach. (we, us)
17. We watched the seagulls. (they, them)
18. Cathy gave Pete her camera. (he, him)

19. Pete took a picture of Cathy. (she, her)

20. Then Cathy took a picture of Pete and a seagull. (him, them)

Mechanics and Usage: Using *I* and *Me*

pages 328–329

D. Write the sentences. Complete each sentence by adding *I* or *me*.

21. ________ was doing my homework.

22. My friend Jim phoned ________.

23. Jim asked, "Will you play ball with Ken and ________?"

24. "Ken and ________ will meet you at the park," Jim said.

25. ________ asked my mother if I could go.

26. My mother asked ________ about my homework.

27. My mother told ________ to finish my homework first.

28. Later, my brother and ________ went to the park.

29. Ken and Jim waved to Juan and ________.

30. Juan and ________ played ball with Ken and Jim.

pages 332–333

Pronoun-Verb Agreement

E. Write the sentences. Choose the correct verb in ( ).

31. We (play, plays) music after school.

32. I (hold, holds) my saxophone.

33. It (shine, shines) brightly.

34. Lin (take, takes) up her violin and bow.

35. They (lift, lifts) their flutes to their lips.

36. The conductor (raise, raises) his baton.

37. The children (look, looks) at the conductor.

38. You (drop, drops) your drumstick.

39. We (laugh, laughs) with you.

40. They (like, likes) our music.

Unit 5 Review

pages 334–335

Possessive Pronouns

F. Write each sentence. Choose the correct possessive pronoun in ( ).

41. That art project is (my, mine).

42. The students finished (their, theirs) reports.

43. John rewrote (his, her) report.

44. The science experiment is (your, yours).

45. (Our, Ours) class is having a book fair.

pages 336–337

Pronoun–Verb Contractions

G. Write the sentences. Use contractions.

46. My dad says we will see a volcano.

47. He is not exactly sure about the plans.

48. We are going with tour guides.

49. They are the only ones who can take visitors.

50. I am really excited!

51. It is an active volcano.

52. You have never seen anything like it!

53. You are invited to come with us.

54. My mom says she will take many pictures.

55. It will be a great trip!

pages 338–339

Mechanics and Usage: Contractions and Possessive Pronouns

H. Write each sentence. Choose the correct word in ( ).

56. Is this (your, you're) math homework?

57. Yes, (their, they're) math problems.

58. We helped Tess and Rick with (their, they're) math.

59. I think (its, it's) time for lunch.

60. (Your, You're) right about the time.

Unit 5 Review

pages 352–353

Vocabulary: Homophones

I. Write the sentences. Complete each sentence with the correct homophone in ( ).

61. (Hear, Here) is how to get rid of ants.

62. (By, Buy) an ant trap at the hardware store.

63. You may need to get (two, too) traps.

64. Set the traps in the (right, write) place.

65. I (no, know) the problem will be solved.

pages 354–355

Composition: Outlining

J. Read the paragraph. Use the information in the paragraph to complete the outline.

Butterflies and moths are two insects that are closely related to each other. Both have two pairs of wings covered with scales. Butterflies usually fly in the daytime, but most moths fly at night. Most butterflies are harmless, but many moths are pests.

66. I. Two Kinds of _______

67. A. _______

68. B. _______

69. II. How They Are _______

70. III. How They Are _______

pages 374–375

Proofreading Expository Writing

K. 71.–80. Write the paragraph correctly. Correct the punctuation, grammar, and spelling mistakes. Use capital letters correctly. There are 10 mistakes.

Simple machines work buy helping we move objects with less force. they includes the lever, inclined plane, wedge, and screw. Crowbars and shovels are examples of levers? Another names for inclined plain is ramp. Its one of the oldest kinds of simple machines. Knifes, axes, scissors, and needels are examples of wedges.

Project File

PROJECT 1 A Tall Tale

A tall tale tells about unusual characters and amazing events that could never happen in real life.

You will need to know the form for a tall tale when you write one in the next unit.

Paul Bunyan and Babe

Paul Bunyan was big and strong even as a baby. He destroyed a whole forest every time he rolled over. So his parents made a floating cradle for him and set it in the ocean. However, when Paul rocked in his cradle, he caused 75-foot-high waves! Four towns washed away.

*The **beginning** introduces a main character who has larger-than-life qualities and abilities.*

__Humor and exaggeration__ add interest to the tale.

Paul decided to go out west, where there was more room. With his giant ox, Babe, Paul became a logger. One day, Paul was floating a forest's worth of logs down the river. He came to a sharp curve in the river. Logs began to pile up in the river's bend. Soon there was a huge log jam! Not a log was moving.

*A **problem** tests the character's abilities.*

Paul studied the problem. Then he hitched Babe up to the river where it bent. With a mighty yank, Babe pulled that river straight! Soon the logs were floating again.

*In the **end**, the character uses his or her special abilities to solve the problem.*

Write a tall tale Think of a main character for a tall tale—a hero or heroine who can do unbelievable things. What problem might that main character face? How might he or she solve the problem? Now write about this character. Use humor and exaggeration to make the story fun to read.

PROJECT 2

A Report

The "Stolen Animals" article mentions animals that you may have seen at a pet shop or zoo. Choose one of these as a topic for a report. You might want to research on the Internet or in books.

Unusual Pets To prepare for your research, jot down questions such as: Where does the animal come from? What special needs does it have? Take notes to answer your questions. Then write your report using your research and your notes.

Extra Practice

Pronouns

A. Write the sentences. Underline each pronoun.

1. Do you hear Fritz meowing?
2. He is up in the tree.
3. Hans and Elsa called to him.
4. They hummed Fritz's favorite tune.
5. We listened to Hans and Elsa.
6. The kitten watched them.
7. Then Fritz looked at me.
8. Is he afraid of us?
9. I waved a tuna treat.
10. It brought Fritz down the tree!

B. Write each sentence. Replace the underlined word or words with the correct pronoun in ( ).

11. Miguel and Rosita pack for a vacation. (He, They)
12. Mother gave one suitcase to each child. (She, We)
13. The suitcases fill up fast! (It, They)
14. Miguel arranges shirts and jeans on one side. (He, We)
15. A softball and glove fit on the other side. (It, They)
16. Rosita puts her skates in with the clothes. (She, You)
17. The child can't close the bag. (him, it)
18. The children unpack Rosita's clothes. (She, They)
19. Rosita puts the skates in a backpack. (it, them)
20. Now the bag will close. (he, it)

Subject Pronouns

A. Write each sentence. Underline the subject pronoun.

1. We made a chart of our favorite fruit.
2. I drew a picture of a banana.
3. She found a photo of a basket of apples.
4. He drew a picture of some peaches and plums.
5. They painted bunches of grapes.
6. How will we arrange the pictures on the chart?
7. She pasted the fruit pictures in a circle.
8. He printed "Favorite Fruit" inside the circle.
9. It looks bright and colorful!
10. You will like our nice chart.

B. Write the sentences. Replace each underlined subject with a subject pronoun.

11. The children are making a birthday calendar.
12. Pablo and Ramon collect the names and dates.
13. Elsa creates the calendar on the computer.
14. Carl puts each name in the computer.
15. Angelo and Maria place each name on the right date.
16. The children want pictures on the calendar, too.
17. Ramon looks for the class photos.
18. The photos are kept in a box.
19. Carl scans each picture into the computer.
20. Elsa places a picture above each name.

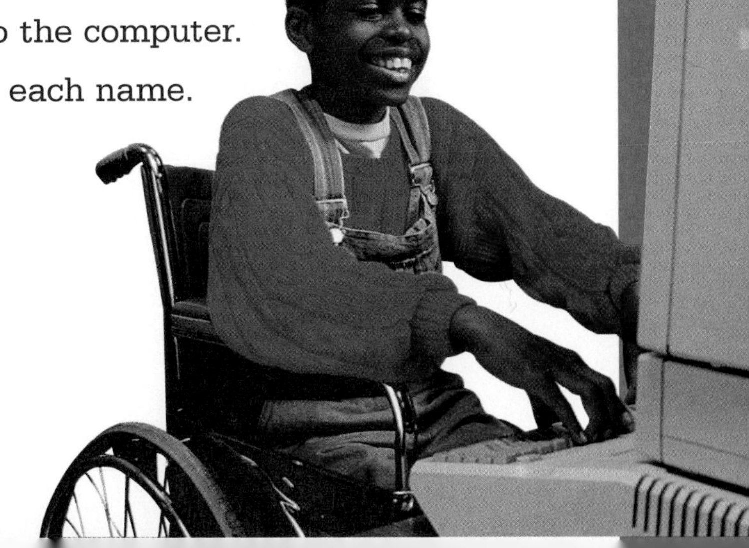

Extra Practice

Object Pronouns

A. Write each sentence. Underline the object pronoun.

1. Juan and Brigitte play tennis with us.
2. Gil and I face them across the net.
3. Brigitte throws the tennis ball to us.
4. Gil will hit the ball to them.
5. They will teach us.
6. Gil and I watch them carefully.
7. Gil hits it over the fence!
8. Juan throws it back.
9. Brigitte moves next to him.
10. Gil and I will not beat them.

B. Write each sentence. Replace the underlined word or words with an object pronoun.

11. Juan and Brigitte play soccer with Gil and me.
12. Brigitte kicks the soccer ball down the field.
13. Juan passes the ball to Brigitte.
14. Gil kicks the ball away from Juan and Brigitte.
15. Juan blocks Gil.
16. Gil runs in front of Juan.
17. Gil sees the goal and runs toward the goal.
18. I help Gil keep the ball from Brigitte.
19. I kick the ball right into the goal!
20. Juan and Brigitte thank Gil and me for a great game.

Using *I* and *Me*

A. Write the sentences. Write whether the underlined pronoun is *in the subject* or *in the predicate.*

1. I like my new school.
2. Today is a big day for me.
3. My new friend Eva takes me to the gym.
4. I sign up for the team.
5. Eva and I fill out a form.
6. I bring the form to the coach.
7. The coach smiles at Eva and me.
8. He will teach me the game.
9. The coach throws the ball to me.
10. I shoot the basketball into the basket.

B. Write the sentences. Use the correct pronoun in ( ).

11. Eva and (I, me) live near each other.
12. Eva and (I, me) walk to basketball practice together.
13. My mom takes Eva and (I, me) home after practice.
14. Eva and (I, me) are both forwards on the basketball team.
15. The coach helps Eva and (I, me) during practice.
16. Eva and (I, me) shoot baskets.
17. Many players will be on the team with Eva and (I, me).
18. Eva and (I, me) meet a new girl at basketball practice.
19. The coach and (I, me) help the new player shoot baskets.
20. The new girl will be on the team with Eva and (I, me).

Grammar

Extra Practice

Pronoun-Verb Agreement

A. Write each sentence. Use the verb in ( ) that agrees with the underlined subject pronoun.

1. He (borrow, borrows) some tools.
2. She (show, shows) Henri the broken wood.
3. We (give, gives) Henri some new pieces of wood.
4. He (mend, mends) the hole in the fence.
5. You (fix, fixes) the fence!
6. We (pack, packs) up the tools.
7. They (sweep, sweeps) the floor.
8. We (make, makes) him some lemonade.
9. I (thank, thanks) him for his help.
10. He (take, takes) a nap.

B. Write each sentence. Use the correct present-tense form of the verb in ( ).

11. He (find) old toys in the attic.
12. They (throw) out the broken toys.
13. She (keep) most of the toys.
14. We (need) a new home for these toys.
15. I (clean) the toys with soap and water.
16. Can you (fix) the broken toys?
17. We (paint) the toys many bright colors.
18. He (tie) a yellow bow around each toy.
19. They (place) the toys in a big box.
20. It (say) Toys for Kids on the outside of the box.

Possessive Pronouns

A. Write the sentences. Underline the possessive pronoun in each sentence.

1. Which is your favorite place?
2. My favorite place is the state of Texas.
3. Our family lives in Dallas.
4. The brick house on the street is ours.
5. Her house is behind those trees.
6. My best friend lived in a green house.
7. His family lives in Austin now.
8. They love its pretty lakes and green hills.
9. Their family will visit us.
10. He misses his old friends in Dallas.

B. Write each sentence. Use the correct possessive pronoun in ( ).

11. Mom and Dad packed (their, theirs) big suitcase.
12. (Our, Its) driving time was four hours.
13. The new van is faster than (their, theirs).
14. I followed the route on (his, its) map.
15. I left (my, mine) at home.
16. The city appears before (my, mine) eyes.
17. A river winds through (its, his) center.
18. Aunt Rosa's home is (our, ours) for this weekend.
19. (Its, Her) sister has a toy store in town.
20. (Their, Theirs) house is full of toys.

Grammar

Extra Practice

Pronoun-Verb Contractions

A. Write the sentences. Draw one line under the contraction in each sentence. Write the two words that make up each contraction.

1. We've put the mother and her puppies in a large box.
2. They're only two weeks old.
3. They've opened their eyes at last.
4. She's a good mother.
5. He's playing with the puppies.
6. We're taking turns watching them.
7. I've taken some pictures of the puppies.
8. I'll be happy that I did.
9. They'll grow very fast from now on.
10. You'll have to see the puppies soon!

B. Write each sentence. Replace the underlined words with the correct contraction.

11. <u>They are</u> old enough to leave now.
12. <u>You have</u> asked to keep one of the puppies.
13. <u>He is</u> the puppy with brown spots.
14. <u>You are</u> the first to ask for that puppy.
15. <u>I have</u> saved this puppy for you.
16. <u>We are</u> taking the puppy to the vet today.
17. <u>He will</u> give the puppy its shots.
18. <u>We will</u> have the puppy's fur washed and trimmed.
19. <u>I will</u> put the puppy on a leash for you.
20. I hope <u>you will</u> pick a good name for your pet.

Contractions and Possessive Pronouns

A. Write each sentence. Write *contraction* or *possessive pronoun* to describe each underlined word.

1. Their rabbits are cute.
2. They're always hungry.
3. I hope your grocery list includes more rabbit food.
4. You're going to need help with all those bags.
5. A rabbit uses its nose and eyes to find food.
6. It's a big bag of lettuce.
7. They're always asking for more food.
8. What is their favorite food?
9. You're supposed to feed them twice a day.
10. I like your friendly rabbits very much.

B. Write each sentence. Choose the correct word in ( ) to complete each sentence.

11. A good class depends on (its, it's) teacher and students.
12. (They're, Their) going to have a new art teacher this year.
13. (Its, It's) fun to teach art.
14. Most students like to share (they're, their) art.
15. (They're, Their) adding two more art classes.
16. (You're, Your) going to love Miss Jewel's art class.
17. Will you show me (you're, your) drawings?
18. (Its, It's) a good way to learn new ideas.
19. Some of (they're, their) drawings make me laugh.
20. (You're, Your) best ideas can come from sharing with others.

Theme Seeing All Sides

UNIT 6

Adjectives, Adverbs, and Writing a Story

In this unit you will learn about adjectives and adverbs. You will also learn how to write a story about characters and events.

Music Link *Reginald is the bat boy for his father's baseball team. In this part of the story, he plays his violin while he sits on the bench.*

I play *Swan Lake* the way I feel — sad and quiet. But I'm not clumsy with my violin. I'm careful, glancing only one time at the music I know by heart. In the last measure, I pull my bow slowly to hold the final note long.

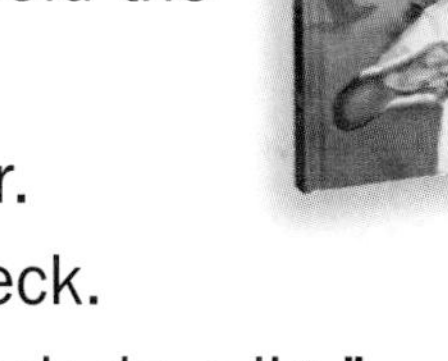

"That sure was somethin' pretty," says Mr. LaRue, the center fielder who is waiting on deck. "Kinda makes the hairs on the back of my neck do a jig."

As Mr. LaRue steps up to the plate, I start to play again. He lets the first pitch go past him but swings hard on the next.

from ***The Bat Boy and His Violin*** by Gavin Curtis

Thinking Like a Writer

Writing a Story A story tells about characters and events. Reread the passage.

- How do you think Reginald feels when Mr. LaRue gets a hit?

Adjectives and Adverbs The author used adjectives to describe nouns and adverbs to describe verbs in his writing. Read the passage again.

QUICK WRITE Write one adjective and its noun. Write one adverb and its verb.

Grammar

Adjectives That Tell *What Kind*

RULES

An adjective is a word that describes a noun. Some adjectives tell *what kind* of person, place, or thing the noun is.

Vicky read an interesting book about Marco Polo.

An adjective usually comes before the noun it describes.

Marco Polo had an exciting life.

Adjectives

How do adjectives help give the reader a clear picture? Write your ideas in your journal.

Guided Practice

Name the adjective and the noun it describes in each sentence.

EXAMPLE: Marco Polo went on a long trip.
Adjective: long Noun: trip

1. Marco Polo was a young boy in 1271.

2. Marco Polo lived in a beautiful city.

3. His father took him to faraway China.

4. The travelers crossed wide rivers.

5. The group climbed high mountains.

REVIEW THE RULES

- An adjective is a word that describes a noun.
- An adjective can tell *what kind*.

More Practice

A. Write each sentence. Underline each adjective. Circle the noun that the adjective describes.

6. The travelers reached a hot desert.
7. Strong camels carried them across.
8. The trip to China was a thrilling adventure.
9. The great ruler welcomed the travelers.
10. The people wore colorful clothes.
11. The palace had a pretty roof.
12. Gold tiles covered the roof.
13. People fed the hungry travelers.
14. Marco Polo liked the tasty food.
15. The men tasted strange spices.

B. Spiral Review **Write the sentences. Circle common nouns. Underline proper nouns. Add commas if needed.**

16. The ruler asked the travelers to stay.
17. Marco and his father stayed for many years.
18. Marco Polo finally left China.
19. The ruler gave gifts to Marco Polo.
20. Marco Polo brought home paintings silk and spices.

Extra Practice, page 470

Grammar

Handbook
page 518

Writing Activity A Supply List

What would you need for a trip to China? Write a list of supplies. Make sure the list is arranged in a logical way.
APPLY GRAMMAR: Circle each adjective in your list.

Social Studies Link

Grammar

Adjectives That Tell *How Many*

RULES

An adjective is a word that describes a noun. Some adjectives tell *how many*.

Four children went to the pet shop.

Few, many, and *several* are special adjectives that tell *how many*.

A few puppies played in the window.

Adjectives that tell *how many* come before the nouns they describe.

The children saw several parrots.

Adjectives
Write how you can decide when to use *few, many,* or *several.*

Guided Practice

Name the adjective and the noun it describes in each sentence.

EXAMPLE: Parrots can live for sixty years.
Adjective: sixty *Noun: years*

1. Erica said hello to one parrot.
2. The parrot said a few words.
3. The store had several snakes.
4. Two boys watched the snakes.
5. One snake was coiled up.

REVIEW THE RULES

- An **adjective** can tell *how many*. *Few, many,* and *several* are special adjectives that tell *how many*.

More Practice

A. Write each sentence. Underline each adjective that tells *how many*. Circle the noun that the adjective describes.

6. The shop had several cages of birds.
7. A few birds were singing.
8. Many fish swam in tanks.
9. The shop owner talked to one girl.
10. Carmen wanted to buy a few fish.
11. Carmen bought six goldfish.
12. One woman put the goldfish in a bag.
13. Tony taught two birds to speak.
14. Tony said three words over and over.
15. The birds spoke several times.

Handbook
page 518

B. Spiral Review Write each sentence. Use correct helping verbs and irregular verbs. Underline adjectives.

16. Lia were watching the sleepy lizards.
17. Two gray kittens was climbing a post.
18. One small mouse runned fast.
19. The children seen many wonderful pets.
20. They have buy a white mouse.

Extra Practice, page 471

Writing Activity A Shopping List

Write a shopping list of things to buy for a pet. Check your list for spelling errors.

APPLY GRAMMAR: Draw a line under adjectives that tell how many in your list.

Math Link

Grammar

Articles

RULES

Articles are special adjectives. The words *a, an,* and *the* are articles.

Use *a* before a singular noun that begins with a consonant.

a bird

Use *an* before a singular noun that begins with a vowel.

an egg

Use **the** before singular nouns and plural nouns.

the nest *the nests*

Articles
Write how you can decide when to use the article *a, an,* or *the.*

The articles *a, an,* and *the* can come before singular nouns. Only *the* can come before a plural noun. *The* is used to refer to a specific thing or group.

Jake's family went for a ride.

They looked at all the sights.

Guided Practice

Tell which article in ( ) is correct.

EXAMPLE: (A, The) flowers were in bloom. *The*

1. Jake saw (a, an) cactus.
2. (A, The) spines of the cactus were sharp.
3. Emily spotted (a, an) hole in the cactus.
4. (A, An) owl was living there.
5. (A, The) owl's eyes were huge!

REVIEW THE RULES

- **Articles** are the special adjectives *a, an,* and *the*.
- Use *a* before singular nouns that begin with a consonant. Use *an* with singular nouns that begin with a vowel.
- *The* comes before singular and plural nouns.

Grammar

Handbook
page 518

More Practice

A. Write the sentences. Use the correct article in ( ).

6. The family visited (a, an) lake.
7. Mr. Long rented (a, an) rowboat.
8. (An, The) oars were too heavy for Jake.
9. Mr. and Mrs. Long each used (a, an) oar.
10. (A, An) family of ducks swam by.
11. The male duck had (a, an) green head.
12. Three ducklings swam after (a, the) parents.
13. Emily saw (a, an) nest on the shore.
14. The nest had (a, an) egg in it.
15. Emily hoped (the, a) egg would hatch.

B. Spiral Review **Write the paragraph. Use the correct word in ( ).**

16.–20. The family got in (their, they're) blue car. They're going for (a, an) long ride. The shiny car raced (its, it's) engine. "Don't forget (the, an) new camera," Mom said. "(Its, It's) a great day for a ride!"

Extra Practice, page 472

Writing Activity A Description

Write a description of a special place you have visited. Choose vivid and exact words to paint a clear picture.

APPLY GRAMMAR: Draw a line under each article you use in your description.

Grammar

Adjectives That Compare

RULES

You can use adjectives to compare two or more nouns.

Add *-er* to an adjective to compare two nouns.

Add *-est* to compare more than two nouns.

Adjectives that compare are used to tell how things are alike or different.

The merry-go-round is slower than the Ferris wheel.

The roller coaster is the fastest ride in the park.

Adjectives That Compare

Write how you can decide whether to add *-er* or *-est* to an adjective to compare nouns.

Guided Practice

Name the correct adjective in ( ).

EXAMPLE: The bumper cars are the (rougher, roughest) ride of all. *roughest*

1. Is this the (tall, tallest) Ferris wheel of all?
2. Which ride in the park is the (long, longest)?
3. This line is (shorter, shortest) than that line.
4. That game is (harder, hardest) than this game.
5. Ted's prize is the (greater, greatest) of all.
6. The pond in the park is (bigger, biggest) than the one in the zoo.
7. Circus lights are the (brighter, brightest) lights of all.
8. Our car was (faster, fastest) than the train.
9. I saw a bird (smaller, smallest) than a robin.
10. Did you skate on the (wider, widest) lane of all?

REVIEW THE RULES

- Add *-er* to an adjective to compare two nouns.
- Add *-est* to an adjective to compare more than two nouns.

More Practice

A. Write the sentences. Use the correct adjective form.

11. The boat ride is (quiet) than the train ride.
12. The fun house is (dark) than a cave.
13. We heard the (loud) screams that day.
14. In the House of Mirrors, I looked (tall) than Mom.
15. The water slide is the (cool) ride I know.
16. The log ride is the (new) ride in the park.
17. Some rides are (wild) than others.
18. Nick won a prize as the (strong) boy of all.
19. The park lights are (bright) than stars.
20. The merry-go-round is the (old) ride in the park.

B. Spiral Review **Write the sentences. Circle singular nouns. Underline the adjectives and the nouns they describe.**

21. The carnival offers many amusements.
22. The child went on several rides.
23. Jane rode the carousel three times.
24. Pedro played a few games.
25. One worker handed out the prizes.

Extra Practice, page 473

Grammar

Handbook
page 519

Writing Activity A Postcard

Create a picture postcard of an amusement park ride. Write a message to a friend. Use interesting details.

APPLY GRAMMAR: In your message, include adjectives that compare. Circle them.

Art Link

Grammar

Spelling Adjectives That Compare

RULES

Some adjectives change their spelling when *-er* or *-est* is added.

When the adjective ends in a consonant sound and *y,* change the *y* to *i* and add *-er* or *-est*.

lucky *luckier* *luckiest*

When the adjective ends in *e,* drop the *e* and add *-er* or *-est.*

brave *braver* *bravest*

For adjectives that have a single vowel sound before a final consonant, double the final consonant and add *-er* or *-est*.

big *bigger* *biggest*

THINK AND WRITE

Spelling Adjectives That Compare

How can you remember the correct spelling of adjectives that compare? Write your answer in your journal.

Guided Practice

Tell the spelling of each adjective when you add *-er* or *-est*.

EXAMPLE: Add *-er.* Add *-est.*
pretty nice
prettier *nicest*

Add *-er.*

1. pale

2. thin

3. blue

4. fat

5. lazy

Add *-est.*

6. wet

7. busy

8. strange

9. heavy

10. small

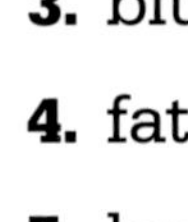

REVIEW THE RULES

- For adjectives ending in a consonant sound and *y*, change the *y* to *i* and add *-er* or *-est*.
- For adjectives ending in *e*, drop the *e* and add *-er* or *-est*.
- For adjectives that have a single vowel sound before a final consonant, double the consonant and add *-er* or *-est*.

Grammar

More Practice

A. Write the sentences. Add *-er* or *-est* to the adjective in ( ).

11. This parade is (big) than last year's parade.

12. The circus has the (funny) clowns in the world.

13. One clown has the (sad) face of all.

14. The lady clown has the (silly) hat of any clown.

15. That clown is (fat) than this clown.

16. Those horses are (white) than snow.

17. The drums are (noisy) than thunder.

18. The elephant is the (large) one I've seen!

19. That was the (nice) parade I've watched.

20. It was the (happy) day of my life.

Handbook
page 519

B. Spiral Review Write the paragraph. Add the correct article. Choose the correct pronoun in ( ).

21.–30. My sister and (I, me) watched ______ parade. (We, Us) saw ______ long line of elephants. ______ elephant winked at (we, us). (I, Me) laughed at ______ clowns. One clown gave (I, me) ______ balloon.

Extra Practice, pages 474–475

Writing Activity A Joke

Write a joke that compares two things. Pick just the right words to get the point of the joke across.

APPLY GRAMMAR: Circle the adjectives that compare.

Grammar

Using Commas

RULES

Use a comma after the name of a person being spoken to.

Carol, will you play with us?

Use a comma after words like *yes* and *no* when they begin a sentence.

Yes, I'll play with you.

When you read, commas tell you when to pause.

Bob, do you know this game?
No, I don't know how to play hopscotch.

Using Commas
How can you decide when to use commas? Write your answer in your journal.

Guided Practice

Tell where commas belong in each sentence.

EXAMPLE: Juan toss a stone into square 1.
Juan, toss a stone into square 1.

1. Carol hop into square 2.
2. Rosa can I use both feet?
3. No just hop on one foot.
4. Yes hop on all the squares but square 1.
5. Okay turn around and hop back.

REVIEW THE RULES

- Use a comma after the name of a person being spoken to.
- Use a comma after words such as *yes* and *no* when they begin a sentence.

Grammar

More Practice

A. Write each sentence. Add commas where they belong.

6. Ron let's play chain tag.

7. Bess how do you play the game?

8. First you tag another player.

9. Next that player links arms with you.

10. Ron and Bess do you both tag other players?

11. No only the first person tags people.

12. Yes you keep adding players to the chain.

13. Joe will you join the game?

14. Yes it sounds like fun.

15. Karen please start the game.

Handbook
page 528

B. Spiral Review Write the paragraph. Add commas and capital letters where needed.

16.–25. Tina and al play kickball soccer and dodge ball. Their last soccer game was on sept. 9 2001. The game took place in houston Texas. the next game will be in Atlanta georgia.

Extra Practice, page 476

Writing Activity A Conversation

Write a conversation between two children playing a game. Vary the sentences. Make them fun to read aloud. **APPLY MECHANICS AND USAGE:** Use the names of the people being spoken to. Circle the comma after each name.

Drama Link

Grammar
REVIEW

Mixed Review

REVIEW THE RULES

- An adjective is a word that describes a noun. It can tell *what kind* or *how many*.
- Add *-er* to an adjective to compare two nouns.
- Add *-est* to an adjective to compare more than two nouns.
- Some adjectives change their spelling when *-er* or *-est* is added.
- Use the article *an* before singular nouns that begin with a vowel. Use *a* before singular nouns that begin with a consonant. Use *the* before singular nouns and plural nouns.
- Use a comma after the name of a person being spoken to and after words such as *yes* and *no* when they begin a sentence.

Adjectives
Write five sentences using adjectives. Use adjectives that tell *what kind* and *how many*, and some that make comparisons with *-er* and *-est*.

Practice

A. Write each sentence. Underline each adjective. Circle the noun it describes.

1. James is painting a colorful picture.
2. Many animals are in the picture.
3. James painted a purple elephant.
4. A blue lion hides behind a bush.
5. Ms. Ling says it is a beautiful painting.
6. Polly paints several colors on paper.
7. Polly covers the paper with black crayon.
8. The girl scrapes off some of the top layer.
9. The bright paint shows through the drawing.
10. Ms. Ling hangs up the pretty picture.

B. Write the sentences. Complete each sentence with the correct article in ( ). Use commas where they belong.

11. Nina let me see (an, the) picture you're painting.

12. Ms. Ling may I make (a, an) picture with ink blots?

13. Yes here's (a, an) bottle of ink.

14. Paul do you have (a, the) scissors?

15. No but I have (a, the) paste.

16. Jean please give Luis (a, an) paintbrush.

17. Hank let Suzie have (a, the) clay now.

18. Lucy is that (a, an) alligator you're drawing?

19. Yes it's (a, an) animal that is hungry!

20. Luis isn't this (a, an) class that's fun?

Handbook
pages 518–519

C. Challenge Write the following paragraph. Correct mistakes in adjective forms.

21.–25. Carmen's statue is biggest than Lou's. Richie's work is messiest than Troy's. Harry's work is the neater of all. Josie's painting is the prettyest in the class. The children think Ms. Ling is the nicer teacher in the school.

Writing Activity Book Title

Write a good title for a book. Choose words that give the reader a clear idea of what the book is about.
APPLY MECHANICS AND USAGE: Use an adjective in your book title.

Grammar

Adverbs

RULES

An adverb is a word that tells more about a verb. Adverbs tell *how, when,* or *where* an action takes place.

> ***Yesterday we ate muffins.***

Adverbs can come before or after the verb in a sentence.

Where ——> ***Chris goes downstairs for a recipe.***
How ——> ***He reads the recipe carefully.***
When ——> ***Chris bakes muffins today.***

Adverbs

What does an adverb do? Write the answer in your journal.

Guided Practice

Name whether the underlined adverb tells *where, when,* or *how.*

EXAMPLE: Father beats the eggs lightly. *how*

1. Father walks downstairs.
2. He cooks breakfast quickly.
3. Father cracks two eggs easily.
4. He carefully mixes the batter.
5. Next, he pours the mix into a pan.

REVIEW THE RULES

- An **adverb** is a word that tells more about a verb. It tells *where, when,* or *how*.

More Practice

A. Write the sentences. Write what each underlined adverb tells about the verb.

6. Dad gladly cooks the pancakes.

7. Dad neatly stacks the pancakes.

8. Next, Dad sets the table.

9. He calls us downstairs.

10. Dad quickly leaves the room.

11. Our puppy Gus sits nearby.

12. I enter the kitchen eagerly.

13. I search everywhere for the pancakes.

14. The family sees pancake crumbs there.

15. We slowly follow the trail of crumbs.

Handbook
page 520

B. Spiral Review Write the paragraph. Make each underlined noun plural. Circle the adjectives.

16.–20. We see our puppy Gus eating the stolen pancake. Gus even licks up the leftover crumb. Pancakes are not for any hungry puppy. The children get the big box of dog food for Gus. Gus wags his tail to thank the helpful child.

Extra Practice, page 477

Writing Activity A Comic Strip

Create a comic strip about making pancakes. Let your personality show in your writing.
APPLY GRAMMAR: Use adverbs that tell *how, when,* and *where* in your comic strip. Circle each adverb.

Grammar

Adverbs That Tell *How*

RULES

Some adverbs tell *how* an action takes place.

Don enters the room quietly.

Adverbs that tell *how* usually end in *-ly.*

slow + -ly = slowly *I slowly climb into bed.*

quick + -ly = quickly *I quickly fall asleep.*

Adverbs

How do you know which adverbs tell *how*? Write the answer in your journal.

Guided Practice

Name the adverb that tells *how* in each sentence. Then name the verb it tells more about.

EXAMPLE: I wake up suddenly.
adverb that tells how: suddenly
verb it tells about: wake up

1. Shadows dance playfully on my walls.
2. I study them quietly.
3. The moonlight shines brightly.
4. The trees sway wildly.
5. I look out the window eagerly.

REVIEW THE RULES

- Some **adverbs** tell *how* an action takes place. Adverbs that tell *how* often end with *-ly*.

Grammar

More Practice

A. Write the sentences. Underline each adverb that tells *how*. Circle the verb it describes.

6. Footsteps tap loudly across the roof.
7. The children call their dad nervously.
8. Mr. Bond swiftly phones the police.
9. A policeman answers briskly.
10. The officer talks calmly to Mr. Bond.
11. A policewoman arrives quickly.
12. She shines a light directly on the roof.
13. Suddenly, a raccoon jumps to the ground.
14. The animal quickly disappears into the woods.
15. The family will rest safely, I think.

Handbook page 520

B. Spiral Review Write the sentences. Circle action verbs. Underline adjectives. Draw two lines under adverbs.

16. The noisy raccoon ran clumsily.
17. A large raccoon is bigger than a cat.
18. Raccoons eagerly hunt for food.
19. A raccoon is smarter than other animals.
20. Raccoons can climb tall trees easily.

Extra Practice, page 478

Writing Activity A Journal Entry

Write a journal entry about a decision you have made. Explain why you made that decision.

APPLY GRAMMAR: Use adverbs that tell *how* in your writing.

Grammar

Adverbs That Tell *When* or *Where*

RULES

Some adverbs tell *when* or *where* an action takes place.

The scuba divers arrive early.
The boat carries them far.

Adverbs
How can using adverbs make your writing clearer? Write the answer in your journal.

Here are some adverbs that tell *when* or *where*.

When		Where	
first	soon	there	ahead
always	early	outside	around
next	today	up	far
later	then	here	away
tomorrow	yesterday	nearby	everywhere

Guided Practice

Name the verb and the adverb in each sentence. Then tell if the adverb tells *when* or *where*.

EXAMPLE: I sail tomorrow.
Verb: sail   Adverb: tomorrow, tells when

1. The divers arrive early.
2. First, the divers prepare their supplies.
3. The boat pulls away.
4. Soon, the boat stops.
5. The captain drops the anchor here.

Grammar

REVIEW THE RULES

- Some adverbs tell *when* or *where* an action takes place.

More Practice

A. Write the sentences. Underline each verb. Circle each adverb. Write if the adverb tells *when* or *where*.

6. First, the divers put on wet suits.

7. Next, they get their safety vests.

8. Then, the divers lift their air tanks.

9. Finally, the divers leave the boat.

10. The divers swim down.

11. The leader of the group goes ahead.

12. The divers look around.

13. A school of fish swims nearby.

14. Red and yellow fish swim overhead.

15. Later, the divers take photos.

Handbook
page 521

B. Spiral Review Write each sentence in the past or future tense. Underline each adjective. Circle each adverb.

16. (past) Two angelfish (dart) ahead.

17. (past) The shiny fish (move) away.

18. (past) Suddenly, a giant octopus (appear).

19. (future) The fearful divers (return) immediately.

20. (future) Tomorrow, they (look) at the colorful fish.

Extra Practice, page 479

Writing Activity Story Summary

Write a summary of a story in which a character has an exciting experience. Write your opening sentence so it grabs the reader's attention.

APPLY GRAMMAR: Use adverbs that tell *when* or *where* in your writing.

Grammar

Combining Sentences: Adjectives and Adverbs

RULES

Two sentences that tell about the same person, place, or thing can be combined by adding an adjective to one sentence.

Gary goes on a treasure hunt. It is great.
Gary goes on a great treasure hunt.

Two sentences that tell about the same action can be combined by adding an adverb to one sentence.

Gary gets a map. He does that first.
First, Gary gets a map.

Adjectives and Adverbs

How can you tell when to combine sentences with adjectives and adverbs? Write the answer in your journal.

When you combine sentences, look for words that repeat.

Each person has a clue.
Each clue is different.
→ *Each person has a different clue.*

Guided Practice

Name the adjective or adverb in each pair of sentences. Combine each pair of sentences by adding an adjective or an adverb to one of the sentences. Write the new sentence.

EXAMPLE: Gary works with a group. It is small.
Adjective: small
Gary works with a small group.

1. The children talk. They talk excitedly.

2. They all look at the map. The map is old.

3. Gary reads a clue. It is the first clue.

4. The map shows a tree. It is a large tree.

5. They look for the tree. They look carefully.

REVIEW THE RULES

- Two sentences can be combined by adding an adjective or an adverb to one sentence.

Grammar

More Practice

A. Combine sentences by adding an adjective or adverb to one of the sentences in each pair. Write the new sentence.

6. Gary reads the clue. It is the second clue.

7. Gary points to the tree. Gary points quickly.

8. The group runs to the tree. The group runs eagerly.

9. A clue is under the tree. It is a big clue.

10. Pat reads the clue. Pat reads carefully.

11. The group takes 50 steps. They are giant steps.

12. The children look around. They look eagerly.

13. They find a sign. The sign is colorful.

14. The sign shows a clue. It is the final clue.

15. The group finds the treasure. The treasure was hidden.

Handbook page 521

B. Spiral Review Combine each pair of sentences. Add an adjective or an adverb to one sentence, or join two nouns.

16. Gary dug up the chest. The children dug up the chest.

17. Gary lifted the chest. He lifted the chest slowly.

18. The children saw the gold. The gold was shiny.

19. The children saw jewelry. The children saw coins.

20. They removed the treasure. It was valuable.

Extra Practice, page 480

Writing Activity Conversation

Write a conversation between people who have just discovered buried treasure. Make their words sound natural. **APPLY GRAMMAR:** Combine sentences in your writing by adding adverbs or adjectives.

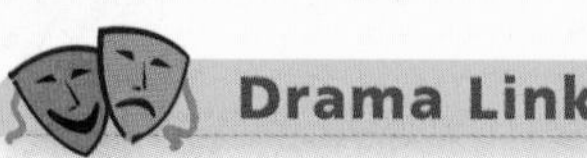

Drama Link

Grammar

Quotation Marks

RULES

Use quotation marks (“ ”) to show that someone is speaking. Quotation marks come at the beginning and end of a person's exact words.

Ling asked, “Do you know what origami is?”

Find the exact words the person says. Put quotation marks at the beginning and end.

“Origami is paper folding,” answered Al.
“It's so much fun to make!” Ling said.

Quotation Marks

How do quotation marks help the reader? Write the answer in your journal.

Guided Practice

Tell where the quotation marks belong in each sentence.

EXAMPLE: Origami is a Japanese art form, said Ling.
“Origami is a Japanese art form,” said Ling.

1. You don't need scissors, Ling told Al.
2. Ling said, All you need is paper.
3. The paper must be square, she added.
4. Have you ever tried origami? Ling asked.
5. No, I haven't, Al answered.

REVIEW THE RULES

- **Quotation marks** come at the beginning and end of the exact words a person says.

More Practice

A. Write each sentence. Add quotation marks.

6. Do you want to make a swan? Ling asked.
7. Al yelled, Yes!
8. First, get a square of paper, Ling said.
9. Then, fold it in half diagonally, she added.
10. Like this? Al asked.
11. That's perfect, Ling replied.
12. Ling said, Crease the fold.
13. Then, open it and turn it over, added Ling.
14. Fold two corners to the center, she said.
15. Al said, It looks like a kite now.

Handbook page 529

B. Spiral Review Write the sentences. Write the past form of each underlined verb. Add capital letters where needed. Circle each adverb that tells *when* or *where*.

16. Next, Ling <u>say</u>, "We're only half done."
17. Al and ling <u>begin</u> their work again.
18. Al <u>see</u> a swan there, not a kite.
19. Then, al <u>give</u> Ling a smile.
20. Later, Al <u>bring</u> the swan home.

Extra Practice, page 481

Writing Activity Character Sketch

Write a character sketch about someone who learned a lesson or something new. Use words that fit the character. **APPLY MECHANICS AND USAGE:** Use some words that the character said. Remember to use quotation marks.

Mixed Review

REVIEW THE RULES

- An adverb is a word that tells more about a verb.
- Some adverbs tell *how* an action takes place. Adverbs that tell *how* often end with *-ly.*
- Some adverbs tell *when* or *where* an action takes place.
- Two sentences can be combined by adding an adjective or an adverb to one sentence.
- Quotation marks come at the beginning and at the end of the exact words a person says.

Adverbs

Write five sentences using adverbs that tell *how*, *when*, and *where.*

Practice

A. Write each sentence. Draw one line under each verb and two lines under each adverb. Write *how, when,* or *where* to tell about each adverb.

1. People look proudly at the space shuttle.

2. They wait nervously for the blast-off.

3. People talk quietly among themselves.

4. Soon, the countdown begins.

5. The ground shakes violently.

6. Then, people become silent.

7. *Columbia* pulls away.

8. *Columbia* zooms overhead.

9. Everyone looks up.

10. Finally, people cheer.

B. Combine each pair of sentences by adding an adjective or an adverb to one of the sentences. Write the new sentence.

11. Eileen Collins is an astronaut. Eileen Collins is famous.

12. As a girl, she read about pilots. She read often.

13. Those pilots were famous. Those pilots were females.

14. Eileen read about some flights. They were dangerous.

15. The stories helped Eileen. They helped her greatly.

16. Eileen saved for flying lessons. She saved carefully.

17. Eileen dreamed about space flight. Eileen dreamed constantly.

18. Eileen set goals for herself. The goals were high.

19. Air Force pilot training changed her. It changed her forever.

20. Eileen Collins piloted the space shuttle. She did it proudly.

Handbook
pages 520–521

C. Challenge Write the sentences. Place quotation marks where they belong. Draw a line under each adverb.

21. I plan to be an astronaut, I said proudly.

22. I added hopefully, I'll be like Eileen Collins.

23. Did you hear the shuttle roar loudly? I asked.

24. I sure did, Jean quickly answered.

25. I'll be riding one someday! I exclaimed.

Writing Activity A News Report

Write a news report for a television broadcast about a space shuttle launch. Make sure your report is easy to read aloud and that it sounds interesting.

APPLY GRAMMAR: Draw a line under each adverb you use in your newscast.

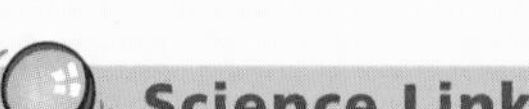

Common Errors with Adjectives

Writers sometimes make mistakes when using adjectives to compare people, places, or things. Study the two most common mistakes in the chart below.

Common Errors	Examples	Corrected Sentences
Using -er *or* -est *instead of* more *or* most	That flower is beautifuler than this flower.	That flower is more beautiful than this flower.
Using -er *or* -est *with* more *or* most	Mrs. Granger is the most nicest teacher I know.	Mrs. Granger is the nicest teacher I know.

Adjectives

How do you know when to use *more* and *most* to show comparison? Write the answer in your journal.

REVIEW THE RULES

ADJECTIVES THAT COMPARE

- For most short adjectives, add *-er* to compare two nouns and *-est* to compare more than two.
- For long adjectives, use *more* to compare two nouns and *most* to compare more than two.
- **Remember** When an adjective ends in a consonant and *y*, change the *y* to *i* before adding *-er* or *-est*.

  pretty + er = prettier

- **Remember** When a short adjective ends with a single vowel and a single consonant, double the consonant before adding *-er* and *-est*.

  big + est = biggest

Practice

A. Read each sentence. Write the adjective that compares.

1. My aunt's flower garden is the prettiest garden in town.
2. Her flowers are more colorful than her neighbor's flowers.
3. I think pink roses are the most beautiful of all.
4. This rosebud is tinier than the other buds.
5. The bud is smaller than my thumb.

B. Rewrite each sentence, using the correct form of the adjective in ( ).

6. I think I have the (great) family of all.
7. My parents are the (wonderful) people I know.
8. My dad is (young) than my friend's dad.
9. My brother is the (funny) kid at school.
10. Our dog is (interesting) than other dogs in town.

C. Write each sentence. Replace the incorrect adjective in ( ) with the correct form.

11. Today is the (most sunniest) day of all.
12. The sky is (more bluer) than the ocean.
13. Everyone seems (more happier) on sunny days.
14. Even my dog is (playfuler).
15. Frozen yogurt is (more tastier) on a warm day.

Troubleshooter, page 500

Handbook
page 519

Writing Activity — A Character Sketch

Tell about a family member or friend. Include at least two adjectives that make a comparison.

APPLY GRAMMAR: Be sure to use the correct form of each adjective you use.

Mechanics and Spelling

TAAS

Directions

Read the passage and decide which type of mistake, if any, appears in each underlined section. Choose the correct answer. If there is no mistake, choose "No mistake."

Remember, some adjectives that compare change their spelling when -er or -est is added.

Look for the name of a person being spoken to. Is a comma missing?

Be sure that quotation marks come at the beginning and end of a person's exact words.

Sample

Sal got a pet rabbit from an animal shelter. He picked the littleest one. (1) Sal learned that a rabbit's teeth continue to grow. He knew his rabbit would need to chew.

Sal named his rabbit Blackberry. He put Blackberry on the back porch. He put a cardboard tube, a cardboard box, and a grocery bag on the floor. His friend asked, "Sal why did you give Blackberry those things?" (2)

Sal said, Those are safe things for her to chew. (3)

1
- ○ Spelling
- ○ Capitalization
- ○ Punctuation
- ○ No mistake

2
- ○ Spelling
- ○ Capitalization
- ○ Punctuation
- ○ No mistake

3
- ○ Spelling
- ○ Capitalization
- ○ Punctuation
- ○ No mistake

Test Tip
Take your time and do your work carefully.

Grammar and Usage

Directions

Read the passage and choose the word or group of words that belongs in each space.

Sample

My brother's favorite insect is the cricket. He likes its chirping. My favorite insect is the firefly. I think fireflies are __(1)__ than crickets. There are no fireflies in our yard. I wanted to know why not, so I looked in __(2)__ encyclopedia. I learned that fireflies like long grass and an open field. Our grass is always cut very short. Our yard is small and filled with flower gardens.

My mother decided to call my grandparents. They invited us to watch fireflies at their house. We sat __(3)__ on their porch across from a field of long grass. Fireflies glowed all around us.

Adjectives with -er *are used to compare two things.*

Remember to use the article an *before singular nouns that begin with a vowel.*

Adverbs are used to tell how an action takes place.

1
- ○ pretty
- ○ prettier
- ○ prettiest
- ○ very pretty

2
- ○ a
- ○ am
- ○ an
- ○ and

3
- ○ quietly
- ○ quieter
- ○ quietest
- ○ quiet

TIME FOR KIDS Writer's Notebook

RESEARCH

RESEARCH

When I need a specific word to explain an idea, I look in the **thesaurus**. For instance, instead of using nice over and over, I look up nice in the thesaurus for words with similar meanings. Using different words makes my writing more interesting. What words can you think of that mean the same as nice?

COMPOSITION SKILLS

WRITING WELL

When I write, I make sure that my **beginning** tells clearly what I'll write about. Then I make sure that the **middle** gives all the details that my readers need, and that the **end** ties the information together. That way, I know my readers understand exactly what I want to say.

VOCABULARY SKILLS

USING WORDS

Many and few are **antonyms**. They are a pair of words with opposite meanings. Lovely and beautiful are **synonyms**. They are words with a similar meaning. Using antonyms and synonyms helps me say things in a new way.

Read Now!

As you read the photo essay, write down any pairs of antonyms and synonyms you find. (Read carefully! They may not be next to one another.)

TIME FOR KIDS

PHOTO ESSAY

VISIT A CAMEL LIBRARY!

A LIBRARY ON LEGS

In 1996, Wycliffe Oluoch was one lonely librarian. The library he runs in an area of Kenya has many books. But only a few people came to read them. Travel is tough in this dry, sandy part of East Africa. Roads are bad. Cars are few. "We had to find a way to reach the people because they were not coming to us," the librarian said.

Then Oluoch (All-wutch) had a big idea. If people couldn't go to the library, the library would come to them! He knew just the way to get over the hump of desert travel. The Camel Library was born.

"The camel is an ideal choice because it can go where cars cannot go," says Oluoch. Camels are widely used in this dry area because they store water in their hump. They need to drink only once a month. And camels can carry lots of books—up to 400 pounds. They also don't mind the stop and go of desert travel.

Each day for one week, the Camel Library brings books to a different town. Then the animal takes a week off. After that, it goes back to the same communities to pick up the books and deliver new ones.

*inter***NET** **CONNECTION** **Go to** www.mhschool.com/language-arts **for more information on the topic.**

Kids are thrilled when the library arrives.

With a camel looking on, students sit under a tree to enjoy their library books.

Write Now!

Write to tell about an animal doing something to help humans. You can either make up a story or write about a special animal that you know about.

Cover: Susan Ley/Animals,Animals
All other photos: Robert Maier/Animals Animals

Thesaurus

A **thesaurus** is a book of synonyms and antonyms. **Synonyms** are words that have almost the same meaning, and **antonyms** are words that have opposite meanings. A thesaurus can help you find the exact words you want to use to make your writing clearer and more interesting.

The words in a thesaurus are listed in alphabetical order. You look up words in a thesaurus as you would in a dictionary. If you looked up the words *laugh* and *little*, you would find these entries.

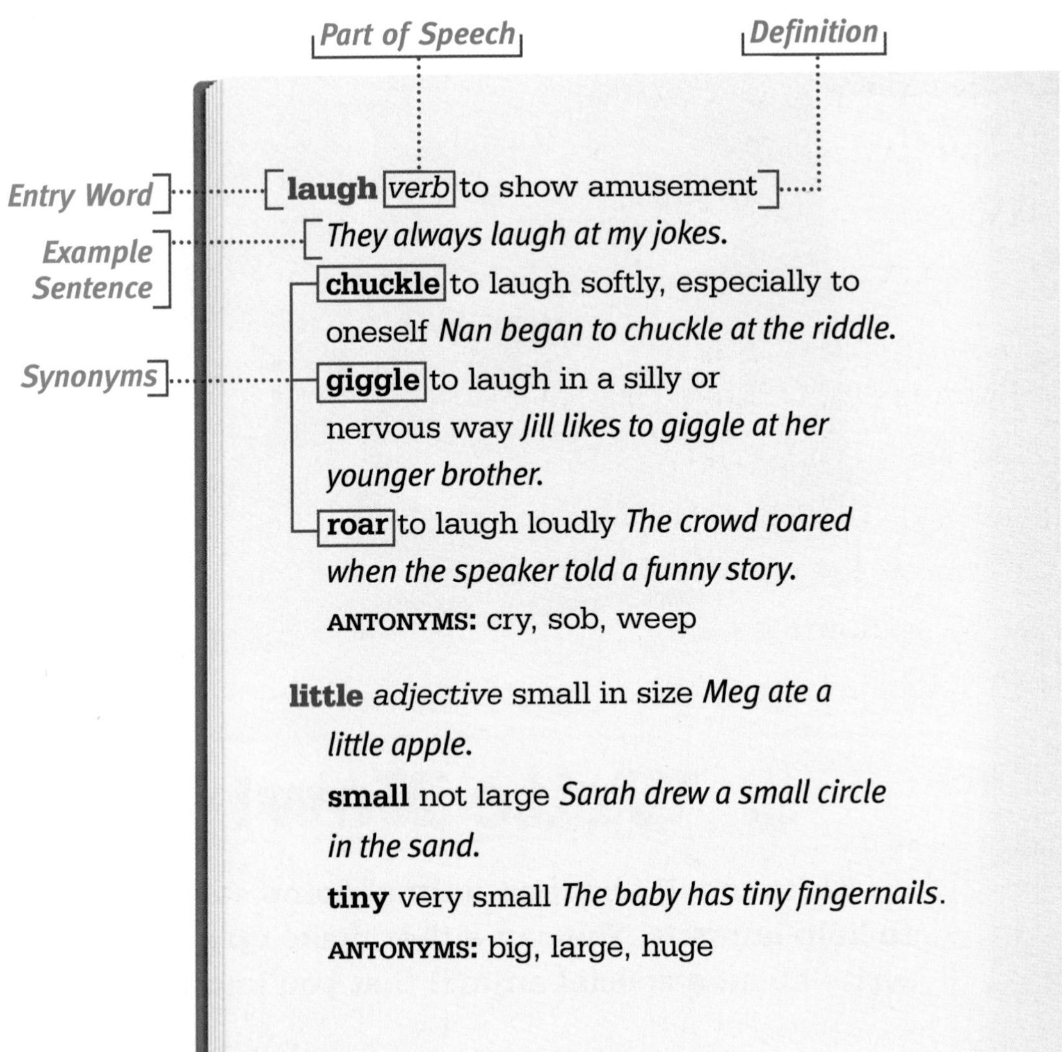

Part of Speech
Definition
Entry Word
Example Sentence
Synonyms
laugh *verb* to show amusement
They always laugh at my jokes.
chuckle to laugh softly, especially to oneself *Nan began to chuckle at the riddle.*
giggle to laugh in a silly or nervous way *Jill likes to giggle at her younger brother.*
roar to laugh loudly *The crowd roared when the speaker told a funny story.*
ANTONYMS: cry, sob, weep
little *adjective* small in size *Meg ate a little apple.*
small not large *Sarah drew a small circle in the sand.*
tiny very small *The baby has tiny fingernails.*
ANTONYMS: big, large, huge

Practice

A. Look at the sample entries on page 432. Use the entries to replace the underlined word in each sentence with a synonym. Write the sentence.

1. We laughed loudly at the funny clowns.
2. My sister and I laughed at the clown with the biggest feet.
3. The clown wore a huge flower on a little hat.
4. He carried a small bicycle that was too little to ride.
5. Even today, I laugh to myself thinking about the silly clowns.

B. Use the sample entries to write the answer to each question.

6. What are three synonyms for *laugh*?
7. What is the definition for *little*?
8. What are the antonyms for *laugh* and *little*?
9. What part of speech is *little*?
10. What are two synonyms for *little*?

Writing Activity Use a Thesaurus

Use the thesaurus on pages 556–569 to find three synonyms for the word **run**. Use the synonyms to write a paragraph about animals on the move.

Vocabulary: Synonyms and Antonyms

DEFINITION

- Synonyms are words that have the same or almost the same meaning.
- Antonyms are words that have opposite meanings.

Synonyms	Antonyms
big/large/huge	strong/weak
small/tiny/little	tall/short
pretty/beautiful/lovely	warm/cold
glad/happy/joyful	clean/dirty
fast/quick/swift	open/close

Synonyms and Antonyms

When might you use synonyms and antonyms? Write your answer in your journal.

Look at the blue words in the paragraph below. Which are synonyms? Which are antonyms?

Paul Bunyan was the most powerful man in America. He was so strong he could pick up a horse in one hand! Paul could jump over low hills. He could leap over high mountains.

Practice

A. Write each sentence. Replace each underlined word with the synonym in ( ).

1. Windwagon Smith was smart. (clever, famous)
2. Smith had unusual ideas. (actions, thoughts)
3. The man made a wagon with a sail. (cart, ship)
4. The wind would make the wagon go. (breeze, calm)
5. The wagon went too fast! (slowly, quickly)

B. Write the sentences. Replace each underlined word with a synonym or antonym from the box.

many	cruel	bags	long
tall	kind	little	traveled

6. Johnny Appleseed lived a short time ago. (antonym)
7. He wandered around planting trees. (synonym)
8. Johnny carried sacks of apple seeds with him. (synonym)
9. People were often mean to Johnny. (antonym)
10. Johnny planted few trees. (antonym)

C. Grammar Link Write each sentence. Circle the word that is an antonym of the underlined adjective or adverb.

11. Babe was a huge ox with little ears.
12. Babe's horns were smooth, but his tongue was bumpy.
13. Babe was gentle, but he could be rough.
14. The ox snorted quietly and roared loudly.
15. Babe was brave when other oxen were afraid.

Writing Activity A Postcard

Write a postcard from a place Johnny Appleseed visited. Use two pairs of synonyms and antonyms.

APPLY GRAMMAR: Include adjectives that tell what kind in your postcard. Draw a line under each adjective.

Composition: Beginning, Middle, End

All good writing has a beginning, a middle, and an end. The beginning of a story tells what it will be about. The middle of a story tells what happens. The end of a story tells how everything turns out.

GUIDELINES

- The **beginning** of a story tells who the story is about and when and where the story takes place.
- The **middle** develops the story events, actions, and problems.
- The **end** tells how everything turns out in a way that makes sense.

THINK AND WRITE

Beginning, Middle, and End

Why is it important for a story to have a clear beginning, middle, and end? Write your answer.

Read this story. Notice how the writer develops the beginning, the middle, and the end.

An interesting beginning grabs the reader's attention.

Pecos Bill, old cowhands say, invented roping. He had a rope that stretched across the state of Texas. That rope got him into tons of trouble.

The middle of the story tells a clear sequence of events.

Pecos Bill roped everything he saw. The first time he saw a train, he thought it was a strange animal. He threw his rope over it and hauled it in!

A good ending gives readers a feeling of completeness.

Pecos Bill got quite a surprise when the conductor yelled out, "This is a train, not a cow!" From that day on, Pecos Bill only roped cattle.

Practice

A. Write the sentences. Write *beginning* or *end* to tell where each sentence would go in a story.

1. Annie Oakley was the most famous woman in the West.
2. Finally, Johnny Appleseed went back home.
3. Since that day, no one ever saw the bear again.
4. One year there was no rain, and the river dried up.
5. Things changed when Giant George arrived in Texas.
6. At last, his work was finished.
7. Sue's first boat ride was one she would never forget.
8. Mighty Mike Fink was the king of the riverboats.
9. That is how the Rocky Mountains were built.
10. By morning, the boat was loaded and on its way.

B. Write a good beginning for each of these topics.

11. The Giant Squash
12. The Great Bike Race
13. How the Town Was Saved
14. A Day to Remember
15. Monty Moves a Mountain

C. Grammar Link Combine each pair of sentences by adding an adjective or an adverb to one. Write the new sentence.

16. Paul's ox was named Babe. Babe was powerful.
17. Paul ate fifty pancakes. They were blueberry pancakes.
18. Paul threw his lasso. He threw it high.
19. Paul pulled down a giant tree. He pulled it quickly.
20. The tree came down. It fell smoothly.

Writing Activity A Character Sketch

Write a character sketch. Say where you might use each detail—at the beginning, middle, or end of a story.

APPLY GRAMMAR: Use adjectives that compare in your character sketch and underline them.

Better Sentences

Directions

Read the passage. Some parts are underlined. The underlined parts may be one of the following:

- **Incomplete sentences**
- **Run-on sentences**
- **Correctly written sentences that should be combined**

Choose the best way to write each underlined part.

Check to see if the sentence expresses a complete thought.

Is the sentence written correctly? Correct run-on sentences.

Sample

There's an unusual pig in Nebraska. Heard of a pig called Speed? **(1)** Speed is the fastest pig in the world! She has won every pig race there is. Speed has 2,184 ribbons and 673 silver cups. Last week, she entered the Great Nebraska Automobile Race. Speed didn't bother with a car. She just hoofed it that is, she used her hoofs. **(2)** It was an exciting event.

1
- ○ Have you ever heard of a pig called Speed?
- ○ Have you ever heard of a pig? Called speed?
- ○ A pig called Speed you ever heard of it?

2
- ○ She just hoofed it and used her hoofs.
- ○ She just hoofed it. That is, she used her hoofs.
- ○ She just hoofed it that is. She used her hoofs.

Test Tip
Read each answer choice before choosing the best one.

Vocabulary and Comprehension

TAAS

Directions

Read the passage. Then read each question that follows the passage. Choose the best answer to each question.

Sample

High-Flying Annie was a clever woman. She invented a remarkable flying machine. It was an extraordinary invention. High-Flying Annie called her machine a carcopter. It was a car that could fly in the air like a helicopter. Annie drove her new carcopter across America. Sometimes she parked on the roofs of tall buildings. Sometimes she parked on a cloud.

Is there an antonym or a synonym to help you figure out what the word means?

1 What feature tells you this is a tall tale?

- ○ All events are real.
- ○ All events are impossible.
- ○ Some events are real and some are impossible.
- ○ The events are told in an order that makes sense.

2 In this passage, the word extraordinary means—

- ○ clever
- ○ large
- ○ remarkable
- ○ ordinary

Seeing Like a Writer

Look closely at the pictures. Imagine that one of the pictures is telling a story. Where and when does the story take place? What happens?

Neptuna's Fantasy (detail) by Jane Wooster Scott.

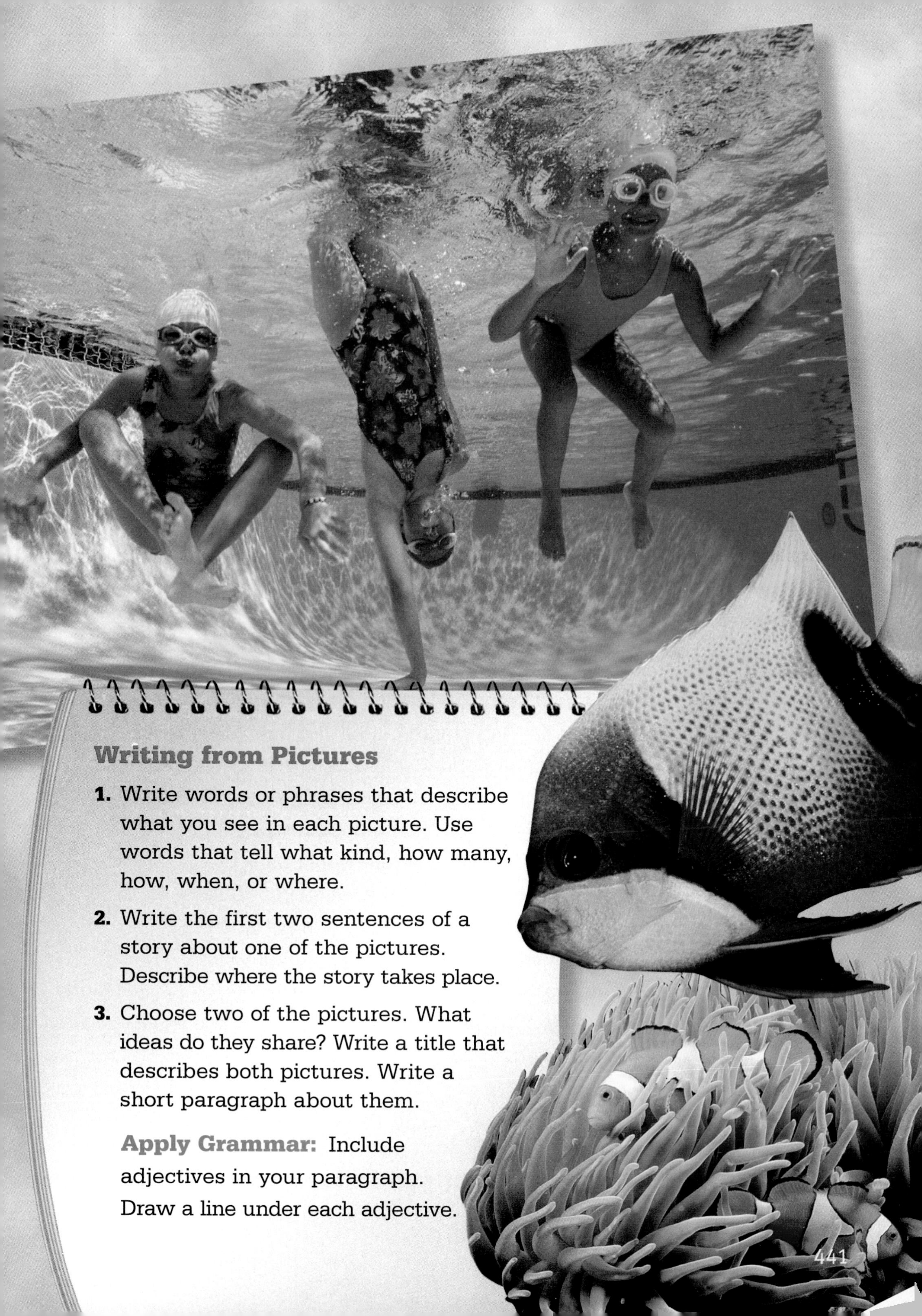

Writing from Pictures

1. Write words or phrases that describe what you see in each picture. Use words that tell what kind, how many, how, when, or where.
2. Write the first two sentences of a story about one of the pictures. Describe where the story takes place.
3. Choose two of the pictures. What ideas do they share? Write a title that describes both pictures. Write a short paragraph about them.

Apply Grammar: Include adjectives in your paragraph. Draw a line under each adjective.

A Story

A story can be about anyone and anything. When you write a story, you can use your imagination to create interesting, entertaining characters and events. Your story can tell how the characters solve their problems.

Purpose

Why do you think people write stories? Why do you think other people like to read them? Write a brief explanation.

Learning from Writers

Read the following examples of stories. What events do the writers describe? As you read, look for problems the characters must solve.

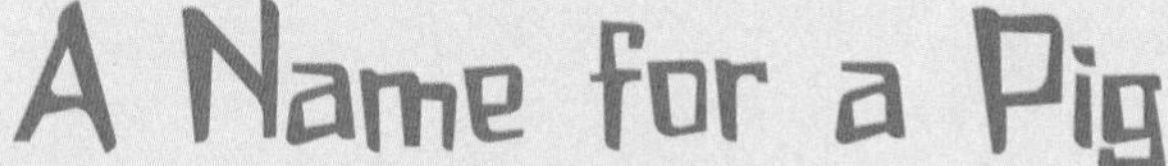

A Name for a Pig

The children ran out to the road and climbed into the bus. Fern took no notice of the others in the bus. She just sat and stared out of the window, thinking what a blissful world it was and how lucky she was to have entire charge of a pig. By the time the bus reached school, Fern had named her pet, selecting the most beautiful name she could think of.

"Its name is Wilbur," she whispered to herself.

She was still thinking about the pig when the teacher said, "Fern, what is the capital of Pennsylvania?"

"Wilbur," replied Fern, dreamily. The pupils giggled. Fern blushed.

—E. B. White, from *Charlotte's Web*

The Thinking Cap

Max's big sister was so smart that she could do her homework just by looking at it. Max wasn't like that. He had to work and work.

"Put on your thinking cap," everyone told him.

"I wish I had a thinking cap," said Max sadly as he walked home from school.

Just then, Max saw a red hat on the path.

He picked up the hat and put it on. "I have 500 meters left to go," he thought. How strange! He hardly knew what a meter was!

Max wore the hat home. His mother was cooking. "If you double that recipe, you'll need 3 1/2 cups of flour," said Max. His mother dropped her spoon.

Max wore the hat to school. In no time, his teacher saw that Max should graduate and go to college. At graduation, people wore black caps with tassels. Max wore his red hat.

— Robbie Clifford

Practice and Apply

Thinking Like a Reader

1. Name an event from the beginning, middle, and end of E. B. White's story.

2. How was Max's problem solved in "The Thinking Cap"?

Thinking Like a Writer

3. How did E.B. White get you interested in reading his story from beginning to end?

4. How did the author of "The Thinking Cap" present the problem and solution?

5. Reading Across Texts How are the characters in the two stories alike and different?

Features of a Story

DEFINITIONS AND FEATURES

Stories can be make-believe or real. A good story:

- Has an interesting **beginning, middle, and end.**
- Has a **plot** with a problem that needs to be solved.
- Has **characters** who make things happen and a **setting** where the action takes place.
- Uses **describing words** to tell about the characters, setting, and events.

Beginning, Middle, and End

The beginning of a story tells what the story will be about. The middle of the story tells what happens. The end of the story tells how everything turns out. Reread "A Name for a Pig" on page 442.

> The children ran out to the road and climbed into the bus. Fern took no notice of the others in the bus.

How does this beginning grab your attention?

Plot

The events of the plot show the character's problem and how it is solved.

> By the time the bus reached school, Fern had named her pet, selecting the most beautiful name she could think of.

This solution may make you wonder what name Fern has chosen for her pet.

▶ Characters and Setting

The people in a story are called characters. The setting is where a story takes place. The sentence below introduces the main character of "A Name for a Pig" and shows how she is feeling.

> Fern took no notice of the others in the bus. She just sat and stared out of the window, thinking what a blissful world it was and how lucky she was to have entire charge of a pig.

Where is Fern? What is she feeling?

▶ Describing Words

To help readers form a clear picture in their minds of story characters, settings, and events, writers use describing words such as adjectives and adverbs.

> "Wilbur," replied Fern, dreamily.

What describing word did the author use to show how Fern replied?

PRACTICE and APPLY

Create a Features Chart

1. List the features of a good story.
2. Reread "The Thinking Cap" by Robbie Clifford on page 443.
3. Write one example of each feature in Robbie's writing.
4. Write what you thought was the funniest part of Robbie's story.

Features	Examples

Writing PROCESS

Prewrite

A story can be make-believe or real. Writing a story lets you use your imagination and be creative.

Purpose and Audience

The purpose of writing a story is to express your ideas and entertain your audience.

Before writing, you need to think about your audience. Who will be reading your story? How will you present your ideas to your readers?

Choose a Topic

Begin by **brainstorming** a list of topics. Remember that there are many kinds of stories. From your list, choose a topic that would make an enjoyable story for your readers.

After you have chosen a topic, **explore ideas** about characters, a setting, a story problem, and events you might include in your story. This writer decided to write a tall tale about a character who is larger than life and can do amazing things.

THINK AND WRITE

Audience

How can you give your audience a clear picture of your characters? Write your ideas in your journal.

Here is how I explored my ideas.

My character is a giant woman.
She's very strong and powerful.
Too big for her home
Needs a bigger place to live
Lives in Texas
Can lasso things with her rope
Can walk across state in a few minutes
Changes size of the state

Organize • Beginning, Middle, and End

A good story has a beginning, middle, and end. The writer introduces the main character and a problem in the beginning. In the middle, the writer shows how the character tries to solve the problem. Then the writer tells what happens at the end. To plan your story, you can use a story map.

PREWRITE
DRAFT
REVISE
PROOFREAD
PUBLISH

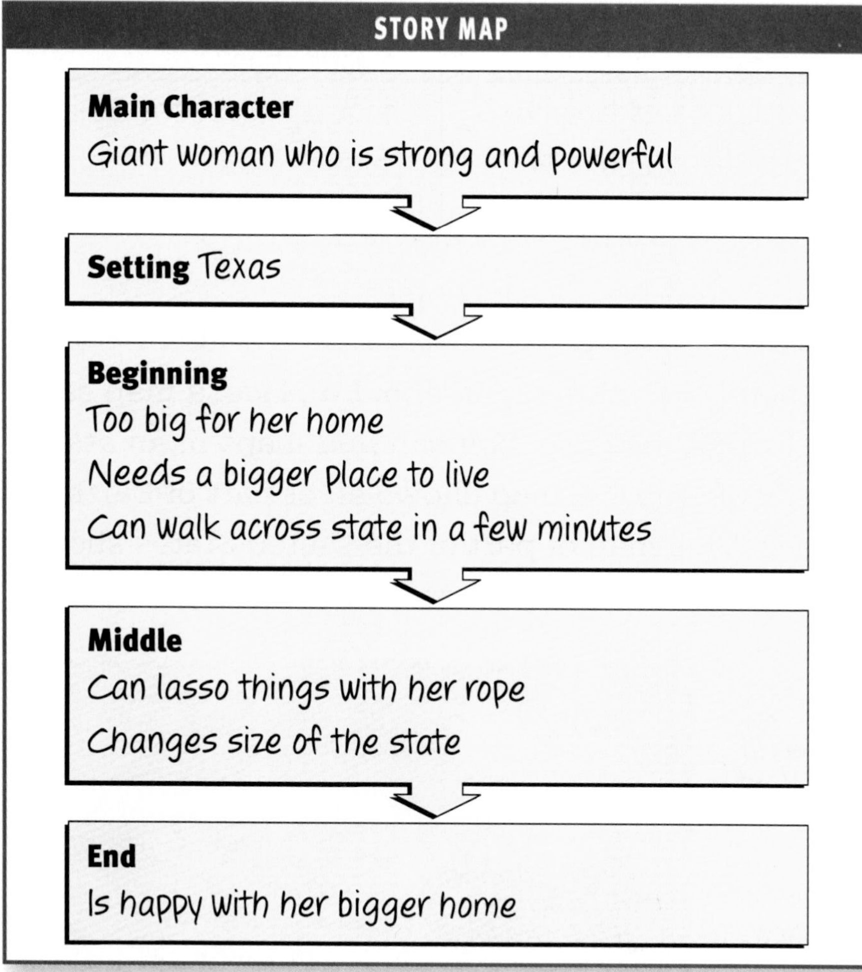

STORY MAP
Main Character
Giant woman who is strong and powerful
Setting Texas
Beginning
Too big for her home
Needs a bigger place to live
Can walk across state in a few minutes
Middle
Can lasso things with her rope
Changes size of the state
End
Is happy with her bigger home

Checklist ✓

Prewriting

- Have you thought about your purpose and audience?
- Have you decided what type of story to write and chosen a topic?
- Have you thought about characters, setting, and a story problem?
- Are your ideas organized in a chart that tells the beginning, middle, and end of your story?
- Do you need to do any research?

Practice and Apply

Plan Your Own Personal Narrative

1. Decide on a type of story.

2. Brainstorm and explore story ideas.

3. Organize your ideas.

Prewrite • Research and Inquiry

▶ Writer's Resources

You may have to do research to get more information for your story. First, make a list of questions you have. Next, decide what resources you can use to find the answers.

What Else Do I Need to Know?	Where Can I Find the Information?
What does Texas look like?	Check a map of the United States.
What words can I use to describe my character?	Look in a thesaurus.

▶ Study a Map

If you need information about a place, a map can be a helpful resource. You can find maps in an *atlas*, or book of maps. A map shows all or part of Earth's surface. This map of part of the United States shows what Texas and some other states look like.

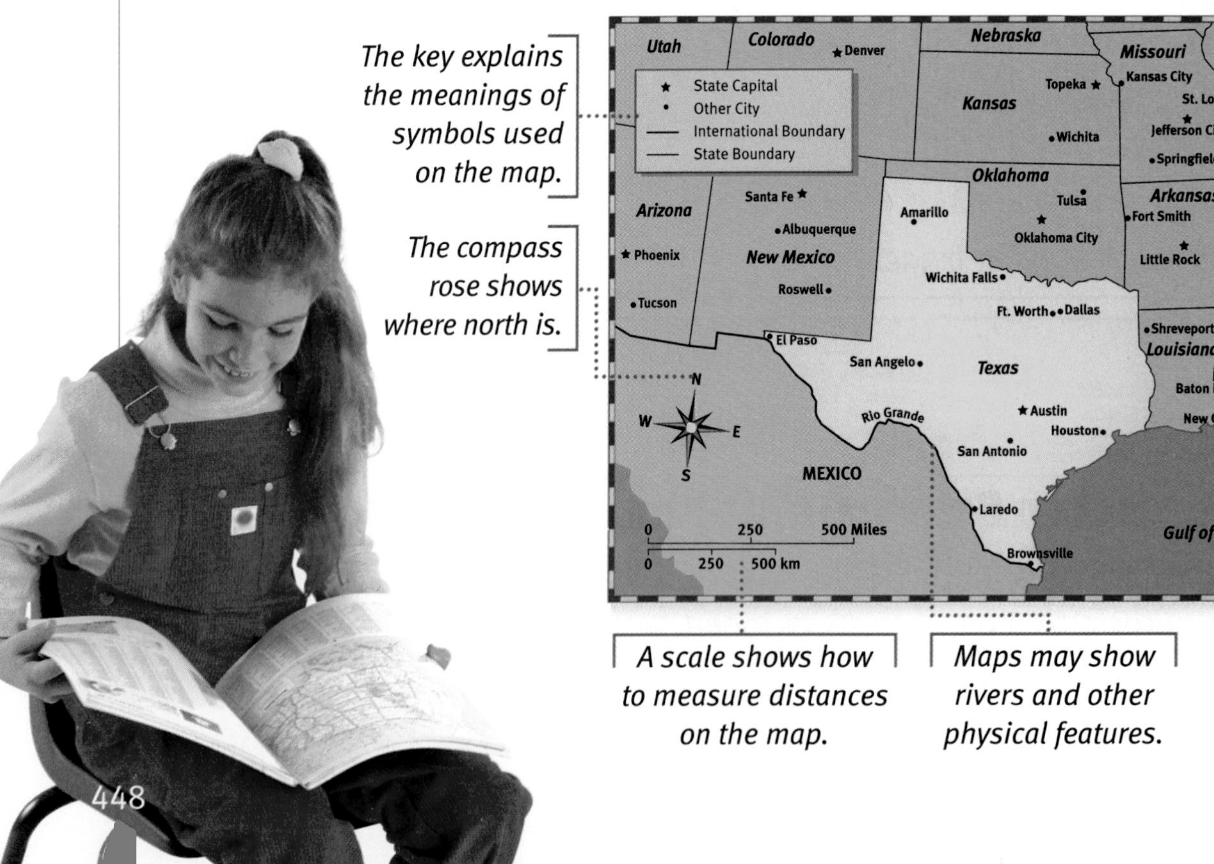

The key explains the meanings of symbols used on the map.

The compass rose shows where north is.

A scale shows how to measure distances on the map.

Maps may show rivers and other physical features.

▶ Use a Thesaurus

A thesaurus is a special kind of dictionary that lists synonyms, or words that have almost the same meaning. It also lists antonyms, which are words with opposite meanings. You can use a thesaurus when you don't want to use the same word over and over.

Use Your Research

You can include in your story map new information gathered from your research. This writer learned important information from studying a map and using a thesaurus. How did she change her story map?

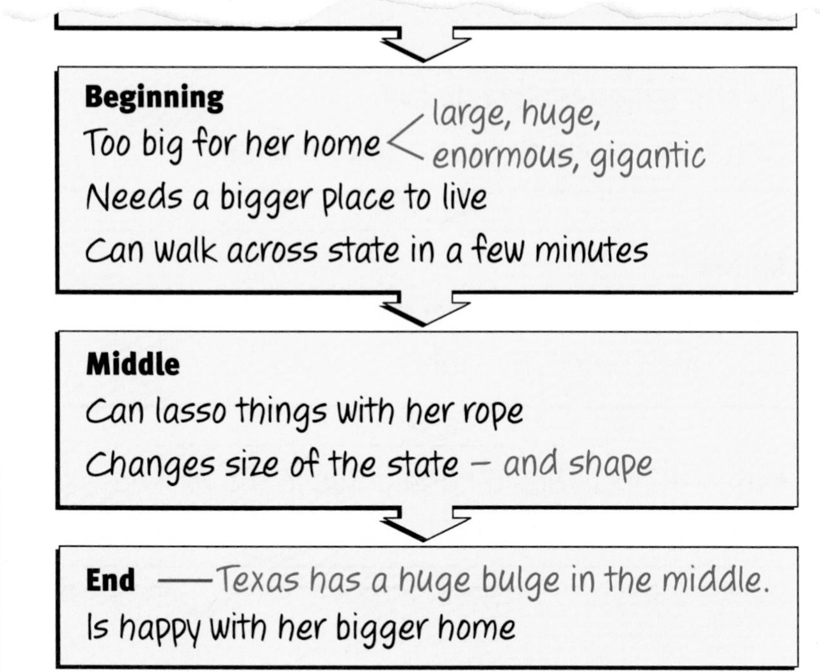
Beginning
Too big for her home < large, huge, enormous, gigantic
Needs a bigger place to live
Can walk across state in a few minutes
Middle
Can lasso things with her rope
Changes size of the state – and shape
End — Texas has a huge bulge in the middle.
Is happy with her bigger home

Handbook
pages 540–541

Checklist ✓

Research and Inquiry

- Did you list questions about your topic?
- Did you identify resources to use?
- Did you take notes?

Practice and Apply

Review Your Plan

1. Look at your prewriting chart.
2. List questions you have about your topic.
3. Identify the resources you will need to use.
4. Add new information you gather to your chart.

Writing PROCESS

Draft

Before you begin writing your story, review the story map you made. Think about making a paragraph for each part of the story.

STORY MAP

Main Character
Giant woman who is strong and powerful

Setting Texas

Beginning
Too big for her home < large, huge, enormous, gigantic
Needs a bigger place to live
Can walk across state in a few minutes

Middle
Can lasso things with her rope
Changes size of the state – and shape

End —Texas has a huge bulge in the middle.
Is happy with her bigger home

First paragraph: Introduces the character and her problem

Second paragraph: How the character solves the problem

Third paragraph: What happens at the end

Checklist

Drafting

- Does your story fit your purpose and audience?
- Did you introduce the characters at the beginning?
- Does your story have a plot with a problem that needs to be solved?
- Have you written an interesting beginning, middle, and end?
- Did you include details that will help readers picture what is happening?

Look at how this writer used the ideas in her story map to write a draft.

PREWRITE
DRAFT
REVISE
PROOFREAD
PUBLISH

DRAFT

Too-Tall Tilly lived in Texas. Too-Tall Tilly was almost as big as Texas. She had a big horse, too. She was so large that she could walk across the whole state in a few giant steps.

This state is too small for me, Too-Tall Tilly said. So she tied a rope around one side of the state. She yanked and pulled. That side of the state stretched and stretched. Then Too-Tall Tilly leaped to the other side of the state. She tied the rope to it and yanked and pulled. that side of the state stretched out, too. Too-Tall Tilly kept stretching the state. It's big enough for me now, she shouted. And that is why Texas has a huge bulge in the middle.

The main character is introduced and described at the beginning.

The problem that needs to be solved is stated.

Plot events in the middle tell how the character solves her problem.

The story ends in an interesting way.

TECHNOLOGY

When you write on the computer, remember to save your work often. Give your document a name that will help you remember what it is about and when it was written.

Practice and Apply

Draft Your Own Story

1. Review your prewriting chart.
2. Write about a problem that needs to be solved.
3. Give your story a beginning, middle, and end.

Writing PROCESS

Revise

Elaborate

You can improve your writing by elaborating. When you elaborate, you add important ideas and details that may be missing from your writing. When you revise your story, you may need to add more details to create a picture for the reader.

The writer added a detail that explains why Texas is important to her tall tale.

> , which is a big state
> Too-Tall Tilly lived in Texas^.

The next detail the writer added helps the reader understand what happened to the state.

> Soon Texas was the size it is today.
> Too-Tall Tilly kept stretching the state.^

Word Choice

When you write, choosing just the right words for your topic and audience is important.

In a story, you need to use colorful, interesting words to describe settings, characters, and actions.

> This state is too small for me, Too-Tall Tilly
> grumbled glumly
> ~~said~~.^

DESCRIBING WORDS

huge
floppy
swift
funny
delicious
cheerful
loudly
eagerly
slowly
carefully
brightly
rapidly

Better Paragraphs

As you revise your draft, check your paragraphs to make sure each paragraph contains just one main idea. Details in the paragraph should support that main idea.

Sometimes you may need to move sentences from one paragraph to another.

She was so large that she could walk across the whole state in a few giant steps. ^

This state is too small for me, Too-Tall Tilly ~~said~~ grumbled glumly.

TECHNOLOGY

Use the FIND AND REPLACE feature when you want to replace a word that you have used several times in your draft.

PRACTICE and APPLY

Revise Your Own Story

1. Add details or information that will make your writing clearer or more interesting.
2. Use colorful and exact words that will create a clear picture for the reader.
3. Take out information that is not necessary.
4. **Grammar** Can you combine two sentences that tell about the same person, place, or thing by adding an adjective to one of the sentences?

Writing PROCESS

Revise • Peer Conferencing

Give a copy of your first draft to a partner to read. Read your partner's draft. You may be able to offer each other some fresh ideas.

Too-Tall Tilly lived in Texas. Too-Tall Tilly was almost as big as Texas. She had a big horse, too. She was so large that she could walk across the whole state in a few giant steps.

This state is too small for me, Too-Tall Tilly said. So she tied a rope around one side of the state. She yanked and pulled. That side of the state stretched and stretched. Then Too-Tall Tilly leaped to the other side of the state. She tied the rope to it and yanked and pulled. that side of the state stretched out, too. Too-Tall Tilly kept stretching the state. It's big enough for me now, she shouted.

And that is why Texas has a huge bulge in the middle.

What does Too-Tall Tilly look like?

This part about the horse isn't necessary.

Good ending for a tall tale!

Conferencing for the Reader

- Are features of a story included in your partner's draft?
  - an interesting beginning, middle, and end
  - a plot with a problem
  - characters who make things happen
  - describing words
- Tell what you like about the draft.

PREWRITE

DRAFT

REVISE

PROOFREAD

PUBLISH

When you revise your story, think about the suggestions your partner made. This writer made some changes based on her partner's ideas.

REVISE

Too-Tall Tilly lived in Texas. Too-Tall Tilly was almost as big as Texas. ~~She had a big horse, too.~~ She was so large that she could walk across the whole state in a few giant steps.

This state is too small for me, Too-Tall Tilly ~~said~~.

So she tied a rope around one side of the state. She yanked and pulled. That side of the state stretched and stretched. Then Too-Tall Tilly leaped to the other side of the state. She tied the rope to it and yanked and pulled. that side of the state stretched out, too. Too-Tall Tilly kept stretching the state. It's big enough for me now, she shouted. And that is why Texas has a huge bulge in the middle.

(Revisions written in: "Too-Tall Tilly"; ", which is a big state"; "She had broad shoulders and strong arms."; "grumbled glumly"; "Soon Texas was the size it is today."; "happily")

Checklist

Revising

- Does your story suit your purpose and audience?
- Do you need to elaborate on any part of your story?
- Does your story have a clear beginning, middle, and end?
- Did you use colorful words?
- Do the sentences flow smoothly when read aloud?
- Did you add a title?

PRACTICE and APPLY

Revise Your Own Story

1. Take notes on your partner's comments.
2. Use your notes to improve your draft.
3. Add a title.

Writing PROCESS

Proofread

After you have revised your story, you should proofread it. You need to correct any errors in mechanics, grammar and usage, and spelling.

TECHNOLOGY

Do you sometimes forget to indent paragraphs? Word processing programs usually let you set margins so that the first line of a paragraph indents automatically.

STRATEGIES FOR PROOFREADING

- **Reread your revised story, each time looking for a different type of mistake. You'll have a better chance of catching all the errors.**
- **Check each sentence for correct capitalization.**
- **Reread for correct end punctuation.**
- **Look for quotation marks at the beginning and end of a person's exact words.**
- **Check for spelling mistakes.**

REVIEW THE RULES

GRAMMAR

- An adjective is a word that describes a noun. An adjective tells *what kind* or *how many.*
- An adverb tells more about a verb. Some adverbs tell how an action takes place. Some adverbs tell when or where an action takes place.

MECHANICS

- Use a comma after the name of a person being spoken to.
- Use a comma after words such as *yes* and *no* when they begin a sentence.
- Use quotation marks at the beginning and end of a person's exact words.

Look at the proofreading corrections made on the draft below. What does the proofreading mark ¶ mean? Why does the writer use this mark?

PROOFREAD

Too-Tall Tilly
, which is a big state
Too-Tall Tilly lived in Texas. Too-Tall Tilly was
She had broad shoulders and strong arms.
almost as big as Texas. ~~She had a big horse, too.~~

She was so large that she could walk across the whole state in a few giant steps.

grumbled glumly
"This state is too small for me," Too-Tall Tilly ~~said~~.

So she tied a rope around one side of the state. She yanked and pulled. That side of the state stretched and stretched. Then Too-Tall Tilly leaped to the other side of the state. She tied the rope to it and yanked and pulled. that side of the state stretched out, too. Too-Tall Tilly kept stretching the
Soon Texas was the size it is today. happily
state. "It's big enough for me now," she shouted.

¶And that is why Texas has a huge bulge in the middle.

PREWRITE
DRAFT
REVISE
PROOFREAD
PUBLISH

Checklist ✓

Proofreading

- Did you spell all words correctly?
- Did you begin each sentence with a capital letter?
- Did you indent each paragraph?
- Did you use quotation marks correctly?

PROOFREADING MARKS

- ¶ new paragraph
- ^ add
- take out
- ≡ Make a capital letter.
- / Make a small letter.
- (SP) Check spelling.
- ⊙ Add a period.

Practice and Apply

Proofread Your Own Story

1. Correct spelling mistakes.
2. Use quotation marks where needed.
3. Indent paragraphs.

Writing PROCESS

Publish

Before you publish, review your story one more time. A checklist can help you.

Self-Check Story

- ❑ Who is my audience? Did I write about something that will interest them?
- ❑ What is my purpose? Will readers be entertained?
- ❑ Did I write an interesting beginning, middle, and end?
- ❑ Does my plot have a problem to be solved?
- ❑ Did I choose good describing words and details to tell about the characters, setting, and events?
- ❑ Do I like the sound of my story when I read it aloud? Do the sentences flow smoothly?
- ❑ Did I proofread and correct all mistakes?

The writer used the checklist to review her story. Read "Too-Tall Tilly" and discuss the writer's published piece. Was it ready to be published? Discuss why or why not.

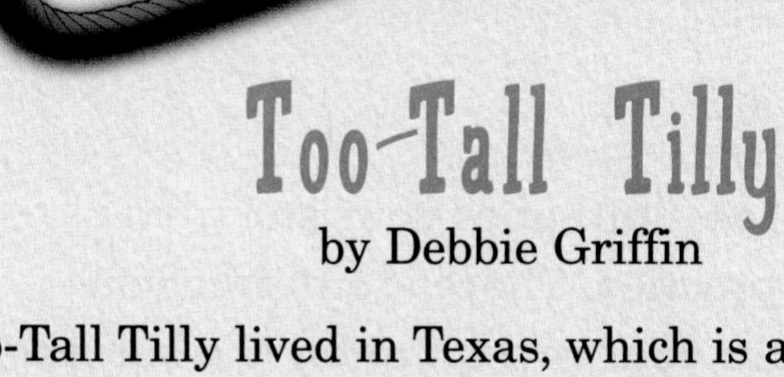

Too-Tall Tilly

by Debbie Griffin

Too-Tall Tilly lived in Texas, which is a big state. Too-Tall Tilly was almost as big as Texas. She had broad shoulders and strong arms. She was so large that she could walk across the whole state in a few giant steps. "This state is too small for me," Too-Tall Tilly grumbled glumly.

So she tied a rope around one side of the state. She yanked and pulled. That side of the state stretched and stretched. Then Too-Tall Tilly leaped to the other side of the state. She tied the rope to it and yanked and pulled. That side of the state stretched out, too. Too-Tall Tilly kept stretching the state. Soon Texas was the size it is today. "It's big enough for me now!" she shouted happily.

And that is why Texas has a huge bulge in the middle.

Practice and Apply

Publish Your Own Story

1. Check your revised draft one last time.

2. Make a neat copy of your draft.

3. Add a border, pictures, or a cover.

TIP!

Handwriting

When you make your final copy, leave some space between the title and the rest of the story. Remember to indent the first line of each paragraph.

LISTENING
SPEAKING
VIEWING
PRESENTING

Present Your Story

To make a good presentation of your story, you need to plan and practice. There are things you can do to make sure your presentation is a success.

Listening Strategies

- **Be clear about your purpose for listening. Are you listening to be entertained or for new information?**
- **Try to picture in your mind what the speaker is describing.**
- **Listen politely. Don't talk or move around the classroom.**

STEP 1

How to Tell Your Story

Strategies for Speaking When you present a story, your purpose is to entertain your listeners. Try to make your story sound funny, scary, or exciting.

- Use gestures and facial expressions to help you tell about actions and feelings.
- Use a tone of voice that matches the mood of the story.
- Speak clearly and loudly enough so that everyone can hear you.

Multimedia Ideas

You may want to play sound effects as you tell your story. Try to find sounds on the Internet or play a sound-effects recording. You might even tape-record the sound effects yourself!

STEP 2

How to Show Your Story

Suggestions for Visuals You can make your presentation more interesting by adding visuals.

- Create a collage or a poster to draw your audience into the story.
- Acting out parts of the story can bring it to life for your audience.
- If it is important to know where something happened, show a map or diagram.

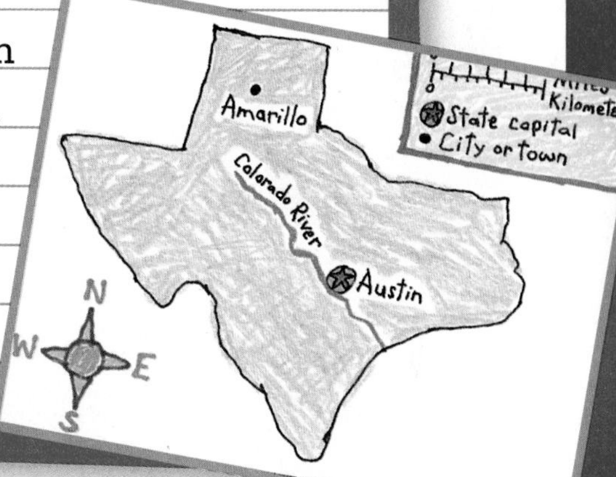

STEP 3

How to Share Your Story

Strategies for Rehearsing The more you practice, the more comfortable you will feel when you make your presentation.

- Practice in front of a mirror.
- Ask a friend to listen to you and make suggestions.
- Rehearse your presentation in front of family members. Ask them for comments.

Viewing Strategies

- **Look carefully at the speaker and at any visual displays.**
- **The speaker's gestures and facial expressions may help you enjoy the story.**
- **Visuals may help you follow the story events.**

Practice and Apply

Present Your Own Story

1. Use gestures and facial expressions.
2. Create drawings or maps.
3. Rehearse your presentation in front of a mirror.
4. Answer questions about your story.

Test Power

TAAS

Writing Tests

On a writing test, you are asked to write one or more paragraphs in response to a prompt. Remember to read the prompt carefully. Look for key words and phrases that describe the topic and explain how you should present your ideas.

Sometimes a prompt will not tell who the audience will be.

Look for words that tell the purpose of the writing.

Look for words that are clues to the kind of writing.

Prompt

A brother and sister were playing in their yard. A frog quietly hopped up to them and started talking.

Write a funny story telling all about what happened after that.

How to Read a Prompt

Purpose There are key words in a prompt that tell you the purpose of your writing. In this prompt, the key words "funny story" tell you that the purpose will be to entertain. The purpose of some stories is to inform or influence as well as entertain.

Audience When a prompt does not tell you whom to write for, think of your teacher as your audience.

A Story When you write a story, you tell about the characters, setting, and events. The words "all about what happened" mean that you write what happened at the beginning, in the middle, and at the end. The words "brother and sister" and "frog" tell you the characters in the story. The words "their yard" tell you the setting.

Test Tip
Plan what you want to say before you begin to write.

How to Write to a Prompt

Remember these tips when you are given a writing prompt.

Before Writing **Content/Ideas**	• Figure out your writing purpose. • Think about your audience. • Make notes about story characters, setting, and plot.
During Writing **Organization/ Paragraph Structure**	• When you are writing a story, write an interesting beginning, middle, and end. • Tell what your characters do to make things happen. • Use words that describe.
After Writing **Grammar/Usage**	• Always proofread your writing. • Use adjectives and adverbs to describe the characters, the setting, and the events. • Use quotation marks around the exact words characters say. • Spell all words correctly.

Apply What You Learned

Read a prompt on a writing test to find out what kind of writing you will do. Think about the purpose and the audience. Think about the kind of writing. Plan the order of events in your writing.

Prompt

A friendly and curious cat decides to visit everybody in an apartment building.

Write a story telling about the people the cat meets and what happens.

Unit 6 Review

Grammar and Writing Review

pages 398–399

Adjectives That Tell *What Kind*

A. Write the sentences. Draw one line under each adjective that tells *what kind*. Draw two lines under the noun that the adjective describes.

1. Kareem taught his puppy a new trick.
2. The boy held up a long stick.
3. The playful puppy jumped up.
4. Kareem threw the stick across the green lawn.
5. The frisky pup raced after the stick.

pages 400–401

Adjectives That Tell *How Many*

B. Write the sentences. Draw one line under each adjective that tells *how many*. Draw two lines under the noun that the adjective describes.

6. Angie learned several games this summer.
7. One game was called Giant Steps.
8. A few children stood in a row.
9. The leader told Angie to take three steps.
10. Angie took five steps by mistake.

pages 402–403

Articles

C. Write the sentences. Complete each sentence with the correct article in ( ).

11. (A, An) elephant is not a good pet.
12. Even (a, an) baby elephant is very big.
13. The elephant might break (the, an) couch.
14. An elephant would eat all (a, the) peanuts.
15. (A, An) cat would make a better pet.

pages 404–405, 406–407

Adjectives That Compare

D. Write the sentences. Complete each sentence with an adjective that compares. Use the correct form of the adjective in ( ).

16. Kiki is the (smart) of my three parakeets.

17. Kiki is a (dark) blue than Coco.

18. Coco is (big) than Lulu.

19. Lulu is the (pretty) of all the birds.

20. I taught Kiki the (fine) tricks of all.

pages 408–409

Mechanics and Usage: Using Commas

E. Write the sentences. Use commas correctly.

21. Dara let's plant the seeds.

22. Suzie do you have the flower seeds?

23. No I have some vegetable seeds.

24. Jim did you buy any seeds?

25. Yes here are the seed packets.

pages 414–415

Adverbs That Tell *How*

F. Write the sentences. Draw a line under each adverb that tells *how*. Draw two lines under the verb it describes.

26. Lou suddenly lifted his head.

27. Something had softly scratched the door.

28. The boy walked bravely across the room.

29. Lou opened the door slowly.

30. A dog sat quietly on the steps.

Unit 6 Review

pages 416–417

Adverbs That Tell *When* or *Where*

G. Write the sentences. Draw a line under each verb. Draw two lines under each adverb. Then write if the adverb tells *when* or *where*.

31. We boarded the airplane early.

32. We placed our bags overhead.

33. Soon, the pilot spoke to us.

34. Then, the plane flew.

35. Green islands appeared ahead.

pages 418–419

Combining Sentences: Adjectives and Adverbs

H. Combine each pair of sentences. Add an adjective or an adverb to the first sentence. Write the new sentence.

36. Becky heard a squawk. The squawk was loud.

37. Becky ran to the window. Becky ran quickly.

38. The bird sat on the fence. The bird was noisy.

39. The bird spread its wings. Its wings were colorful.

40. Becky laughed at the bird. Becky laughed happily.

pages 420–421

Mechanics and Usage: Quotation Marks

I. Write the sentences. Write quotation marks where they belong in each sentence.

41. Do you like to climb mountains? asked Kelly.

42. I've never climbed a mountain, answered Mack.

43. Now is your chance! exclaimed Kelly.

44. What do I need? asked Mack.

45. You'll need a backpack, replied Kelly.

Unit 6 Review

pages 434–435

Vocabulary: Synonyms and Antonyms

J. Write each sentence. Circle the word that is a synonym or antonym of the underlined word.

46. Dan saw a gigantic animal with huge ears.

47. The animal had a thick trunk and a skinny tail.

48. The animal's eyes were tiny in its giant head.

49. The scary beast made a frightening noise.

50. Dan turned quickly and walked speedily away.

pages 436–437

Composition: Beginning, Middle, and End

K. Write the sentences in an order that makes sense.

51. The tortoise moved slowly, so the hare stopped to rest.

52. While the hare rested, the tortoise kept going.

53. Once, a tortoise and a hare had a race.

54. In the end, the tortoise won the race.

55. Before the race, the hare bragged about winning.

pages 456–457

Proofreading a Story

L. 56.–65. Write the story correctly. There are 10 mistakes.

One summer, people complained loud about the heat. the sun got very upset and said, If you don't like my warm rays, I wont shine anymore."

The earth became darker and coldest. Then people beged the sun to come back.

"Sun we'll be happy with whatever you give us," the people promised. So the sun shone again People still complaned when it was hot or cold, but they did it quiet so the sun wouldn't hear.

Project File

PROJECT 1 A News Article

A news article presents facts about events that have just happened. It answers five questions about the events: *Who? What? When? Where? How?*

You will need to know the form for a news article when you write one in the next unit.

Girl's Goat Gets the Gold!

Headline Grabs the attention of the reader.

June 1, 20_ _ Joanne Ware's goat took top prize at the Center School pet show on Wednesday. Principal Harold Stein presented the gold medal to the student. He remarked, "Your goat has it all — looks and good manners, too!"

Dateline Gives the date of the article.

The Center School looked like a zoo last Wednesday. Dozens of pets arrived in cages and fish tanks. Students led dogs and cats around on leashes. There were birds, rabbits, hamsters, and pet mice. Other than the barks, meows, squeals, and other noises, the show was peaceful. Most of the animals behaved well, and no pets got loose.

Everyone said the pet show was a huge success. As for the winning goat, all she said was, "Maaa."

Facts Cover Who? What? When? Where? How?

Write a news article What exciting events happened recently in your school or town? Choose an event, such as a parade or visit by a famous person, and think about the answers to these questions: *Who? What? When? Where? How?* List your answers.

Describe the event for the school newspaper. Be sure to include the details you listed.

PROJECT 2

A Comic Strip

Wycliffe Oluoch's camel has probably had some interesting adventures bringing books to village children in Kenya. Imagine one special adventure the camel has crossing the desert with a load of books.

Book Tour Now, turn your idea into a comic strip that tells the story. Include captions or speech balloons to tell what happens in each panel of the comic strip.

Grammar

Extra Practice

Adjectives That Tell What Kind

A. Write each sentence. Write the adjective that describes each underlined noun.

1. China is a huge country.
2. There are high mountains in parts of China.
3. There are dry deserts in the north.
4. Rice is a favorite food in the south.
5. In the north, wheat is a popular grain.
6. Northern China has cold winters.
7. Southeastern China has warm weather.
8. Bicycles fill the noisy streets of the cities.
9. Trains and boats carry people and useful goods.
10. Visitors go to the famous places.

B. Write each sentence. Draw one line under each adjective. Draw two lines under the noun that the adjective describes.

11. Camels are helpful animals.
12. They carry heavy loads.
13. The animals have strong legs.
14. They are interesting creatures.
15. We enjoy the bumpy ride on a camel.
16. Camels have long eyelashes.
17. The eyelashes protect a camel's big eyes.
18. Hungry camels eat hay and grain.
19. They like to drink cool water.
20. Camels store food and water in their large humps.

Adjectives That Tell How Many

A. Write the sentences. Write the adjective in each sentence that tells how many.

1. The farmer has many animals.
2. The pig has seven piglets.
3. Two goats play in the field.
4. A few roosters crow loudly.
5. Several hens have laid eggs.
6. One hen has chicks.
7. The farmer owns many sheep.
8. Several lambs stay by their mothers.
9. The busy farmer milks five cows.
10. A few ducks swim in the big pond.

B. Write each sentence. Draw one line under each adjective that tells how many. Draw two lines under the noun that the adjective describes.

11. Many children go into the red barn.
12. There are brown saddles on three horses.
13. Several children ride the gentle horses.
14. The happy children ride for fifteen minutes.
15. The tired horses rest for a few hours.
16. One horse has black spots.
17. Five girls go to the pretty pond.
18. The girls see a few ducks.
19. There are two white ducks on the pond.
20. Rachel feeds one hungry duck.

Extra Practice

Articles

A. Write the sentences. Draw a line under the article or articles in each sentence.

1. An oak tree grew by the pond.
2. The roots of an oak tree go deep into the ground.
3. The branches of the tree spread out wide.
4. Birds build nests in the tree.
5. An owl makes its home in the tree.
6. A swing hangs from one branch of the tree.
7. My father made the swing with a tire.
8. My friends and I enjoy playing on the swing.
9. We collect the acorns that drop from the oak tree.
10. We play in the leaves in the fall.

B. Write the sentences. Complete each sentence with the correct article in ( ).

11. Our family went to (a, the) Animal Park.
12. We saw (a, the) animals in their own habitats.
13. I enjoyed watching (a, an) elephant eat peanuts.
14. My brother enjoyed (the, a) African adventure ride.
15. We ate lunch by (the, a) ape's cage.
16. Mother packed (a, an) sandwich for each of us.
17. After lunch we shared (an, a) orange.
18. We took (a, an) tram across the Animal Park.
19. Dad took a photo of (a, an) alligator.
20. The alligator had (a, an) long tail.

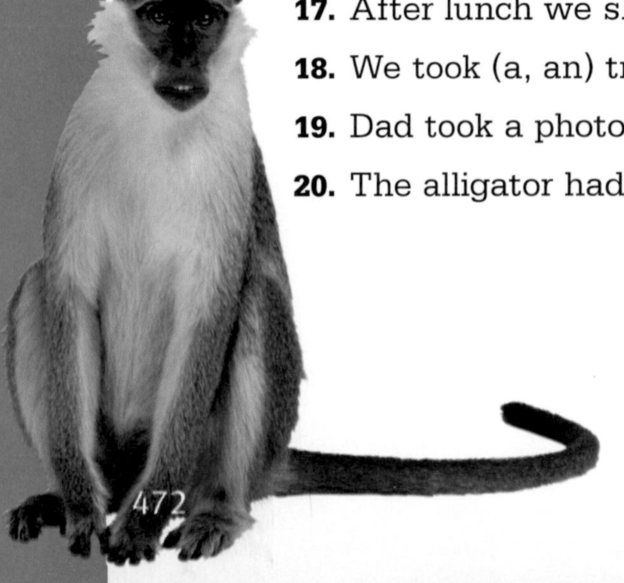

Adjectives That Compare

A. Write the sentences. Use the correct adjective in ( ).

1. The (greater, greatest) zoo of all is the Animal Park.

2. This park is the (newer, newest) zoo in our state.

3. The Animal Park is (smaller, smallest) than the city zoo.

4. The grass is the (greener, greenest) in town.

5. The safari ride is the (longer, longest) ride in the park.

6. The animal cages seem (taller, tallest) than the cages at other zoos.

7. The water in the pond is the (cleaner, cleanest) of all.

8. The elephants are (louder, loudest) than the lions.

9. The bears are (quieter, quietest) than the monkeys.

10. The workers at the park are the (kinder, kindest) people.

B. Write the sentences. Use the correct form of the adjective in ( ).

11. We had the (smart) guide in the Animal Park.

12. The lion keeper is the (strong) worker in the park.

13. The guide gave us the (clear) information.

14. Do you know which animal is the (fast) of all?

15. A cheetah is (fast) than a lion.

16. The snake is one of the (long) animals.

17. The giraffe is the (tall) animal.

18. The spider is one of the (small) animals.

19. A lion is (short) than an elephant.

20. The tortoise has a (long) life than many animals.

Grammar

Extra Practice

Spelling Adjectives That Compare

A. Write each sentence. Look at the underlined adjective. Circle the letter that is changed, doubled, or dropped when *-er* or *-est* is added. Write the correct spelling of the adjective when the ending in ( ) is added.

1. The weather for this year's field day is sunny. (-er)
2. Last year, the weather was cloudy. (-er)
3. The track was wet last year. (-er)
4. Blue Ridge School has the big playing field. (-est)
5. Our school has the nice pool. (-est)
6. The swim lanes are wide. (-er)
7. The swimmers think the water is icy today. (-er)
8. The other team's basketball players are big. (-er)
9. Most of our football players are heavy. (-er)
10. The speedy runners are the girls. (-est)
11. The tiny skater won a medal. (-est)
12. The thin soccer player kicked a goal. (-est)
13. The bike riders are safe with helmets. (-er)
14. Your school has the noisy fans. (-est)
15. The wise judges give the medals. (-est)

B. Write the sentences. Add *-er* or *-est* to the adjective in ( ). Use the correct spelling.

16. Our family went to a carnival on the (busy) day of the summer.

17. My brother Antonio is often the (lucky) one in the family.

18. Antonio found the (speedy) line for the ride.

19. We went on the (big) Ferris wheel I've ever seen.

20. I was (brave) than my brother.

21. My sister Anna was (happy) on the roller coaster.

22. The house of mirrors was the (scary) place.

23. We saw the (funny) circus act.

24. A clown was wearing the (baggy) outfit in the show.

25. The (silly) clown gave each of us a bunch of balloons.

26. Antonio's balloons were (big) than mine.

27. At lunch, I got a (tiny) hamburger than Antonio did.

28. Antonio got the (hot) bag of popcorn.

29. My sister ate the (juicy) apple of all.

30. My brother and sister are the (fine) people I know.

Grammar

Extra Practice

Using Commas

A. Write each sentence. Underline the word that is followed by a comma.

1. Mom, can I make a sandwich?
2. Yes, you can eat lunch now.
3. Katie, would you help me please?
4. Sure, I will get the bread to make a sandwich.
5. Okay, I will get the peanut butter and jelly.
6. Katie, you can spread the peanut butter on the bread.
7. No, I have never had peanut butter and jelly on toast.
8. Yes, the sandwich is delicious.
9. Orlando, would you like your sandwich on toast?
10. No, I would like my sandwich untoasted.

B. Write each sentence. Add a comma where it is needed.

11. Sydney do you know sign language?
12. Yes my cousin taught me sign language.
13. Okay let me show you the alphabet in sign language.
14. Carlos now let me show you how to sign words.
15. Reggie let's practice signing whole sentences.
16. Marie you are learning sign language quickly.
17. Sydney do you speak any other languages?
18. No I only speak English and American Sign Language.
19. Okay I will teach you to speak Spanish.
20. Carlos I can't wait to learn Spanish.

Adverbs

A. Write each sentence. Write whether the underlined adverb tells *where*, *when*, or *how*.

1. The campers sleep <u>peacefully</u>.
2. The stars twinkle <u>brightly</u>.
3. Shooting stars sail <u>quickly</u> across the sky.
4. The moon shines <u>overhead</u>.
5. The forest animals fall asleep <u>quietly</u>.
6. An owl hoots <u>softly</u>.
7. The sun rises <u>early</u>.
8. Birds sing <u>nearby</u>.
9. The campers <u>slowly</u> awaken.
10. <u>Now</u> the stillness of the forest disappears.

B. Write each sentence. Underline the adverb. Write whether it tells *where*, *when*, or *how*.

11. Soon the campers will go on a hike.
12. Always take water on a hike.
13. The water bottles are kept here.
14. Fill your bottles completely.
15. Everyone packs for a hike carefully.
16. The trail leads there.
17. The hikers walk slowly.
18. They look down.
19. Hikers need breaks often.
20. The campers return safely.

Grammar

Extra Practice

Adverbs That Tell How

A. Write each sentence. Underline the adverb that tells how.

1. The wind blows gently.
2. The clouds move quickly.
3. The storm starts wildly.
4. The rain falls rapidly.
5. The hail bounces noisily against the roof.
6. The thunder crashes loudly.
7. Suddenly, the storm stops.
8. The clouds disappear swiftly.
9. The sun shines brightly.
10. The rainbow stretches beautifully across the sky.

B. Write each sentence. Draw one line under the adverb that tells how. Then draw two lines under the verb it describes.

11. The sun shines directly on the lake.
12. The lake sparkles brightly.
13. The fish jump high.
14. My friend and I sit quietly on the dock.
15. We anxiously wait.
16. My fishing pole moves suddenly.
17. A fish blindly takes the bait.
18. I quickly grab the fishing line.
19. A small fish hangs helplessly on the fishing hook.
20. I carefully free the fish.

Adverbs That Tell When or Where

A. Write each sentence. Write if the underlined adverb tells *where* or *when*.

1. The divers finished the training yesterday.
2. Today, they will make their first dive.
3. All the divers arrived early.
4. First, they checked their air tanks.
5. The divers then boarded the boat.
6. The boat took them out to sea.
7. Soon, they will arrive at the diving spot.
8. Another boat floats nearby.
9. The divers go into the water now.
10. The swimmers look around.

B. Write the sentences. Draw a line under each verb. Draw two lines under each adverb that tells *where* or *when* the action takes place.

11. Alex will dive first.
12. Next, Tara dives.
13. Franklin jumps there.
14. Soon, Alex is breathing easily.
15. He swims down.
16. Tara sees him underwater.
17. Franklin dives last.
18. Finally, the other divers follow.
19. The pleased instructor waits nearby.
20. Later, the happy divers describe their dives.

Grammar

Extra Practice

Combining Sentences: Adjectives and Adverbs

A. Combine each pair of sentences by adding the underlined adjective or adverb to one sentence. Write the new sentence.

1. The children gather around the piñata. They are excited.
2. The piñata is full of prizes. The piñata is colorful.
3. The children swing the bat. They swing the bat hard.
4. The piñata does not break. The piñata is tough.
5. My brother misses the piñata. My brother is big.
6. My cousin hits the piñata. My cousin hits it harder.
7. The prizes spill on the floor. The floor is messy.
8. The children dive for the prizes. The children dive quickly.
9. Everyone loves the prizes. The prizes are great.
10. The children play with the prizes. They play happily.

B. Combine each pair of sentences by adding an adverb or adjective to one sentence. Write the new sentence.

11. The children play a game. They play it next.
12. My mother plays the music. She plays it loudly.
13. Everyone marches around the chairs. There are ten chairs.
14. The music stops. It stops suddenly.
15. The children rush for a chair. The children are eager.
16. I find a chair. The chair is free.
17. My brother finds a chair. My brother's chair is nearby.
18. The boy waits for the music. He is laughing.
19. The game will end. It will end soon.
20. My brother wins the game. The game is difficult.

Quotation Marks

A. Write each sentence. Underline the exact words being said.

1. "Does anyone want to go swimming?" Mother asked.
2. "We will go swimming," my sister and I answered.
3. "Loni, get the towels," Mother said.
4. "I will get the sunscreen," I offered.
5. "I will make some lunch," Mother added.
6. "Can we have turkey sandwiches?" my sister asked.
7. Mother replied, "Yes."
8. "I'm ready now," my sister shouted.
9. "So am I," I said.
10. "Let's go!" we exclaimed.

B. Write each sentence. Add quotation marks where they are needed.

11. It is a nice day for swimming, Mother said.
12. Don't go out too far, Mother warned.
13. We won't, my sister and I promised.
14. Do you want to race? my sister asked.
15. No running! the lifeguard yelled.
16. Mother, watch me swim, I called.
17. Mother called back, You are doing great!
18. I cannot hear you, I shouted.
19. You are doing great, my mother repeated.
20. Let's come to the pool again tomorrow, my sister said.

Grammar

Cumulative Review

Unit 1 Sentences

A. Write each sentence correctly. Add capital letters, end marks, and commas where needed.

1. summer days are warm and the sun shines brightly
2. what beautiful roses Mom grows in summer
3. do you swim every day
4. we studied the sun hot gases make the sun bright
5. don't ever look directly at the sun

B. Write each sentence. Draw one line under the subject and two lines under the predicate.

6. The squirrels gathered nuts last fall.
7. All the leaves fell from the trees.
8. Snow covers the ground in winter.
9. Mr. Romano will feed the winter birds.
10. The birds will eat from feeders.

Unit 2 Nouns

A. Write the plural form of each singular noun.

11. story
12. fox
13. child
14. mouse
15. pumpkin
16. bakery
17. bench
18. house
19. cherry
20. wish

B. Write each sentence. Write the proper nouns and abbreviations correctly. Add apostrophes where needed. Combine the two sentences that have repeated words.

21. A vet will attend the taft schools "Petmania."

22. The vets name is dr brown.

23. Students will introduce their pets. Teachers will introduce their pets.

24. All the pets names will be posted.

25. The principal, ms chavez, will be one of the judges.

Unit 3 Verbs I

A. Write each item correctly. Add capital letters and commas where needed. Use the correct verb in ( ). Combine the two sentences that have repeated words.

26. dear grandpa

27. I (like, likes) living in Fort Worth Texas.

28. Please (come, comes) to our holiday parade on July 4 2002.

29. My school band always (march, marches). My school band always (play, plays) music.

30. your grandson
Ramon

B. Write each sentence. Change the underlined verb to the tense shown in ( ).

31. Yesterday Dad and I <u>pick</u> apples. (past)

32. My shiny red apple <u>taste</u> so good! (past)

33. We <u>carry</u> a big basket of apples to our car. (past)

34. Tomorrow Dad and I <u>cook</u> applesauce. (future)

35. Then we <u>give</u> some of the applesauce to our neighbor. (future)

Cumulative Review

Unit 4 Verbs II

A. Write each sentence. Use the correct form of the verb in ( ). Write *H* above each helping verb, *M* above each main verb, and *L* above each linking verb.

36. Anita and Sumi (is, are) at the swimming pool.

37. Their instructor (is, are) teaching them a new stroke.

38. They (have, has) learned four strokes in all.

39. Sumi (have, has) taken diving lessons, too.

40. She (was, were) an eager beginner!

B. Write each sentence. Change each present-tense verb in ( ) to the past tense.

41. My little brother (begin) to learn about the computer.

42. He (go) to computer class for two weeks.

43. He (say) the class was fun.

44. Mom and Dad (give) him new software.

45. The computer program (sing) a song about the alphabet.

C. Write each sentence. Change the words in ( ) to a contraction or a possessive noun, or add commas.

46. (Parents teachers and students) attended the fair.

47. Tom's project showed a (butterflys) life cycle.

48. We watched a movie by (Ana Bill and Maria).

49. The three (judges) final decision was a surprise.

50. My favorite project (did not) win a prize.

Unit 5 Pronouns

A. Write each sentence. Replace the underlined word or words with a subject or object pronoun.

51. Ruth and Abbey play basketball.

52. Ruth is the team's best player.

53. Mr. Tang coaches the basketball team.

54. The players listen closely to Mr. Tang.

55. The coach helps the players.

B. Write each sentence. Write the correct verb in ( ).

56. She (get, gets) a package of seeds.

57. They (prepare, prepares) the soil in the garden.

58. He (plant, plants) the seeds six inches apart.

59. They (water, waters) their plants every day.

60. I (enjoy, enjoys) the beautiful flowers.

C. Write each sentence. Choose the correct word in ( ).

61. (They're, Their) presenting a play next week.

62. Caroline and (I, me) practice our parts.

63. Pick up (your, you're) tickets at the box office.

64. People will come to see Caroline and (I, me).

65. (It's, Its) a big day for both of us.

66. (My, Mine) parents are coming to see the play.

67. I don't know if (her, hers) parents are coming.

68. I know Caroline will be pleased if (they, them) attend.

69. After you see the play, tell (I, me) how you like it.

70. (We'll, Well) be anxious to hear from you.

Grammar

Cumulative Review

Unit 6 Adjectives, Adverbs, and Quotation Marks

A. Write each sentence. Choose the correct form of the adjective or article in ( ). Draw a line under the noun it describes.

71. I like (hot, hottest) pizza.

72. We have (a, an) cutter to cut it.

73. Is your crust (thick, thicker) than mine?

74. This is the (spicier, spiciest) topping I've ever tasted.

75. Karl likes (an, the) salad.

B. Write the sentences. Combine pairs of sentences that have repeated words. In your sentences, draw one line under each verb and two lines under each adverb.

76. We planned our trip. We planned it eagerly.

77. Today, we packed the van.

78. We carefully loaded the big suitcases under the small ones.

79. Everyone cheerfully shared the job. The job was big.

80. Now the trip begins!

C. Write each sentence. Use commas and quotation marks correctly.

81. Maria I finished my painting, I said.

82. Yolanda asked, Will you frame it?

83. Yes I already have a frame, I said.

84. Please may I show it to Ms. Lee? Maria asked.

85. Ms. Lee smiled and said, I like the colors!

Troubleshooter

Contents

Correcting Sentence Fragments

- A sentence is a group of words that expresses a complete thought.
- A sentence fragment is a group of words that does not express a complete thought.

Problem 1

A sentence fragment that does not have a subject

Sentence Fragment: *Came for Greg today.*

Who or what came for Greg today?

Solution 1

Who or what is the subject of the sentence. You must add a subject to each sentence fragment to make it a complete sentence.

Sentence: *A letter came for Greg today.*

Problem 2

A sentence fragment that does not have a predicate

Sentence Fragment: *Greg's family.*

What about Greg's family?

Solution 2

The part of a sentence that tells what the subject does or is is called the predicate. You must add a predicate to the sentence fragment to make it a complete sentence.

Sentence: *Greg's family invited Carlos for a visit.*

Problem 3

A fragment that does not have either a subject or a predicate

Sentence Fragment: *From Argentina.*

Who is this about? Who is from Argentina?

Solution 3

A complete sentence must tell who or what. It must tell what the subject does or is. You must add a subject and a verb to make the sentence fragment a complete sentence.

Sentence: *Carlos is from Argentina.*

Practice **Rewrite the sentence fragments correctly. Add a subject, a predicate, or a subject and a predicate.**

1. Carlos speaks Spanish. Is the main language of Argentina.
2. Carlos also speaks English. He and his friends.
3. Greg speaks a little Spanish. Many new words from Carlos.
4. Carlos and his friends play soccer. Play soccer, too.
5. Greg writes back to Carlos. All about his last game.

For more help, see Sentences on pages 2–3, Subjects in Sentences and Predicates in Sentences on pages 12–15, and Handbook pages 502–504.

Correcting Run-on Sentences

- A sentence is a group of words that expresses a complete thought.
- A run-on sentence joins together two or more sentences that should be written separately.

Problem 1

Two sentences joined with no punctuation between them

Run-on Sentence: *Cats make great pets they are funny and lovable.*

What are the two ideas in the run-on sentence?

Solution 1

You can correct a run-on sentence by separating two complete ideas into two sentences.

Two Sentences: *Cats make great pets. They are funny and lovable.*

Problem 2

Two sentences joined with only a comma

Run-on Sentence: *I held the cat in my lap, he slept all the way home.*

Where should the word *and* go to join the two ideas?

Solution 2

Add *and* to correct the sentences. You also need to use a comma before *and* to join them.

Compound Sentence: *I held the cat in my lap, and he slept all the way home.*

Problem 3

Three or more sentences joined with *and*

Run-on Sentence: *Our cat fetches like a dog and he pounces on paper and pretzels are his favorite snack.*

What are the three ideas in this run-on sentence?

Solution 3

When three or more sentences are joined by *and*, you need to break them into shorter sentences.

Shorter Sentences: *Our cat fetches like a dog. He pounces on paper. Pretzels are his favorite snack.*

Practice Rewrite each run-on sentence correctly.

1. I have a new book about cats Mom bought it yesterday.
2. I read some of the book last night, it is really interesting.
3. The book has many helpful hints and it tells the history of cats and it gives amazing facts.
4. A cat named Ma lived 34 years, a tabby cat named Joseph weighed 48 pounds.
5. I will finish the book soon then you can borrow it.

For more help, see Combining Sentences on pages 16–17, Correcting Run-on Sentences on pages 18–19, and Handbook page 504.

Troubleshooter

Confusing Plurals and Possessives

- A plural noun names more than one person, place, or thing.
- A possessive noun is a noun that shows who or what owns or has something.

Problem 1

Using an apostrophe in a plural noun

Incorrect: *My friend's spot a nest in a tree.*

Does a spot belong to one friend?

Solution 1

Take out the apostrophe to correct a plural noun.

Correct: *My friends spot a nest in a tree.*

Problem 2

Leaving out the apostrophe in a possessive noun

Incorrect: *A hornets nest is made from chewed-up wood.*

Does one or more than one have something?

Solution 2

A singular possessive noun shows what one person, place, or thing has. You need to add an apostrophe (') and an *-s* to a singular noun to make it possessive.

Correct: *A hornet's nest is made from chewed-up wood.*

Problem 3

Putting the apostrophe in the wrong place in a plural possessive noun

Incorrect: *Hornets are gardener's friends.*

Ask yourself: "Does the plural of *gardener* add *s*?"

Solution 3

Add an apostrophe to make most plural nouns possessive.

Correct: *Hornets are gardeners' friends.*

Practice Rewrite the sentences. Write any incorrect plural nouns and possessive nouns correctly.

1. Hornets are related to yellow jackets. Both insects' build nests the same way.
2. Yellow jackets sometimes build in gophers' holes. Empty field mices' holes are good, too.
3. Hornets' markings are yellow or white. Yellow jackets stripes are yellow and black.
4. Al's book has many photographs. The books title is *Bees, Wasps, and Other Insects*.
5. The photographers' names are Jason and Ann Lee. What is the authors name?

For more help, see Plural Nouns on pages 80–85, Singular Possessive Nouns and Plural Possessive Nouns on pages 92–95, and Handbook pages 505–506.

Lack of Subject-Verb Agreement

- A verb in the present tense must agree with its subject.
- Do not add *-s* or *-es* to a present-tense verb when the subject is plural.

Problem 1

Using a plural verb with a singular subject

No Agreement: *Mom look over her plans for a garden.*

What is *Mom*, a singular subject or a plural subject?

Solution 1

When the subject of a sentence is one person or thing, the verb must tell about one person or thing. Add *-s* or *-es* to a present-tense verb to make the subject and verb agree.

Agreement: *Mom looks over her plans for a garden.*

Problem 2

Using a singular verb with plural subject or *I* or *you*

No Agreement: *My sisters goes to the garden center for seeds.*

How can the verb agree with its subject?

Solution 2

When the subject of a sentence is more than one person or thing or *I* or *you*, you do not need to add *-s* or *-es* to a present-tense verb.

Agreement: *My sisters go to the garden center for seeds.*

Problem 3

Using a singular verb when a subject has two nouns joined by *and*

No Agreement: *Lisa and my little sister Ellie plants the seeds.*

How many nouns are in the subject?

Solution 3

When the subject of a sentence has two nouns joined by *and*, you do not add *-s* or *-es* to a present-tense verb. Take out *-s* or *-es* to make the subject and verb agree.

Agreement: *Lisa and my little sister Ellie plant the seeds.*

Practice **Rewrite the sentences correctly. Make the subject and verb in each sentence agree.**

1. Everyone cleans up. Even Fuzzer help.
2. Lisa and Ellie put away the hand tools. Dad and Mom rewinds the hose.
3. I put away the shovel. Then you empties the wheelbarrow.
4. Two weeks pass by. Tiny plants finally pops up through the soil.
5. My family and I water and weed the garden. Before long Lisa, Ellie, and I picks vegetables.

For more help, see Present-Tense Verbs and Subject-Verb Agreement on pages 162–165 and Handbook pages 509 and 511.

Incorrect Verb Forms

- An irregular verb has a special spelling to show the past tense.
- Some irregular verbs have a special spelling when used with the helping verb *have*.

Problem 1

Forming the past tense of an irregular verb incorrectly

Incorrect: *My friend Anna comed to New York with us.*

Is *come* an irregular verb?

Solution 1

Some verbs are irregular. You do not add *-ed* to show actions in the past. Use the special forms of the irregular verbs.

Correct: *My friend Anna came to New York with us.*

Problem 2

Using incorrect irregular verb form for past tense

Incorrect: *We seen many interesting sights.*

Which sounds right: "We seen" or "We saw"?

Solution 2

For irregular verbs, you do not add *-ed* to show actions in the past. You need to use the special forms of the irregular verbs.

Correct: *We saw many interesting sights.*

Problem 3

Using incorrect irregular verb form for past with *have*

Incorrect: *I have never saw the Statue of Liberty before.*

Should *have, has,* or *had* go with *saw* or *seen?*

Solution 3

The helping verb *have* helps the main verb tell about an action. You know that some irregular verbs change their spelling in the past tense and when they are used with the helping verb *have.* Change the verb form to the one used with *have.*

Correct: *I have never seen the Statue of Liberty before.*

Practice **Rewrite the sentences. Use the correct verb forms.**

1. Our class had to do oral reports. I done mine on our trip to New York.
2. I finished my scrapbook just in time. I bringed it to school.
3. Rita asked about the Statue of Liberty. Mike said he seen it last summer.
4. Have you been to New York City? Have you saw the Statue of Liberty?
5. Everyone liked my report. I sayed , "I'm glad."

For more help, see Helping Verbs on pages 242–243, Irregular Verbs and More Irregular Verbs on pages 252–255, and Handbook pages 512 and 514.

Troubleshooter

Incorrect Use of Pronouns

- A pronoun must match the noun or nouns that it refers to.
- A subject pronoun is used as the subject of a sentence.
- An object pronoun is part of the predicate.
- Do not confuse possessive pronouns with contractions.

Problem 1

Using object pronouns as subjects

Incorrect: *Her and I enjoyed playing the piano.*

How does the sentence sound without *and I*?

Solution 1

Replace the object pronoun with a subject pronoun. Subject pronouns include *I, you, he, she, it, we,* and *they.*

Correct: *She and I enjoyed playing the piano.*

Problem 2

Using subject pronouns in the predicate

Incorrect: *Scales are easier for me than for she.*

Is *she* used as the subject or as the object?

Solution 2

Replace the subject pronoun with an object pronoun. Object pronouns include *me, you, him, her, it, us,* and *them.*

Correct: *Scales are easier for me than for her.*

Problem 3

Confusing contractions and possessive pronouns

Incorrect: *You're mother's lesson is on Monday.*

Can you say "You are" instead of "You're"?

Solution 3

A possessive pronoun shows who or what owns something. A pronoun-verb contraction is a shortened form of a pronoun and a verb. It has an apostrophe.

Correct: *Your mother's lesson is on Monday.*

Practice Rewrite the sentences. Write the pronouns, contractions, and possessive pronouns correctly.

1. We have our first recital soon. Mom and me are nervous.
2. Mrs. Lowski said, "You're ready." She added, "So is you're mother."
3. I played my piece for Dad and my sister. Him and her really liked it.
4. Then Mom played for Dad, Patty, and me. She made they and me proud.
5. My friends say they're coming. Their proud of me.

For more help, see Subject Pronouns and Object Pronouns on pages 324–327, Using *I* and *Me* on pages 328–329, Contractions and Possessive Pronouns on pages 338–339, and Handbook pages 515 and 517.

Incorrect Use of Adjectives

- You can use adjectives to compare two or more nouns.
- Add *-er* to an adjective to compare two nouns.
- Add *-est* to compare more than two nouns.

Problem 1

Forming adjectives that compare incorrectly

Incorrect: *Is the Nile River the longer river in the world?*

Are you comparing two or more than two?

Solution 1

Count how many people, places, or things you are comparing. Then add *-er* or *-est*.

Correct: *Is the Nile River the longest river in the world?*

Practice Rewrite each sentence. Write the adjectives that compare correctly.

1. Is the Rocky Mountain range longest than the Appalachian Mountain range?
2. Is Asia, North America, or Africa the world's greater continent of all?
3. Is the Pacific Ocean deepest than the Atlantic Ocean?
4. Is the Atacama Desert in Chile the drier place on Earth?
5. Where is the world's older capital city of all?

For more help, see Adjectives that Compare on pages 404–405, and Handbook page 519.

Handbook

Contents

Grammar

Mechanics and Usage

Build Skills

Writing

Handbook

RULE 1 pages 2–3

Sentences

- A **sentence** is a group of words that expresses a complete thought. It begins with a capital letter.

  Tomas has an interesting hobby.

- A **sentence fragment** is a group of words that does not express a complete thought.

  Collects rocks. (needs a subject)
  One large gray rock. (needs a predicate)

Practice **Write each group of words that is a sentence.**

1. Looks through the rock pile.
2. Tomas sorts the rocks into boxes.
3. Some people collect rocks.
4. Labels each rock.
5. Many museums have rock collections.

RULE 2 pages 4–5, 6–7

Types of Sentences

- When you write or talk, you use different kinds of sentences.

Type of Sentence	Example
A **statement** tells something. It ends with a period.	*You can grow plants in a window box.*
A **question** asks something. It ends with a question mark.	*Should I water the plants every day?*
A **command** tells someone to do something. It ends with a period.	*Don't give the plants too much water.*
An **exclamation** shows strong feeling. It ends with an exclamation mark.	*What a lot of work a garden is!*

Practice **Write the sentences. Then write *statement*, *question*, *command*, or *exclamation* to tell what type of sentence each is.**

1. Plant some peppers in the garden.
2. Where can we get seeds?
3. I'll order seeds from this catalog.
4. Don't plant the seeds too close together.
5. What a great garden we'll have!

Subjects in Sentences

- Every sentence has two parts. The subject of a sentence tells what or whom the sentence is about. The subject of a sentence can be more than one word.

  Seeds travel in different ways.
  Dandelion seeds are carried by the wind.

Practice **Write the sentences. Draw a line under the subject of each sentence.**

1. Some plants have seeds with little hooks.
2. The hooks cling to an animal's fur.
3. The animal carries the seeds to another place.
4. Birds eat fruit and drop the seeds.
5. These seeds grow into plants.

RULE 4

pages 14–15

Predicates in Sentences

- Every sentence has a subject and a **predicate**. The predicate tells what the subject does or is.

  Ralph Samuelson invented water skis.
  Ralph was eighteen years old.

Practice **Write the sentences. Draw a line under the predicate of each sentence.**

1. Ralph worked with snow skis.
2. The skis were too narrow.
3. The young inventor made wide skis from boards.
4. A fast boat pulled Ralph across the water.
5. Crowds cheered at the sight.

RULE 5

pages 16–17

Combining Sentences

- Two sentences with similar ideas can be **combined** using a comma and the word *and*. This kind of sentence is called a **compound sentence**.

  It is a clear night, and the stars are bright.

Practice **Write each pair of sentences as one sentence. Use a comma before *and* when you join the sentences.**

1. The earth turns. Stars rise and set like the sun.
2. The teacher sets up a telescope. Students aim it at the stars.
3. Everyone looks closely. Doug finds the North Star first.
4. The moon glows. The stars shine.
5. Amber found a special star. She made a wish.

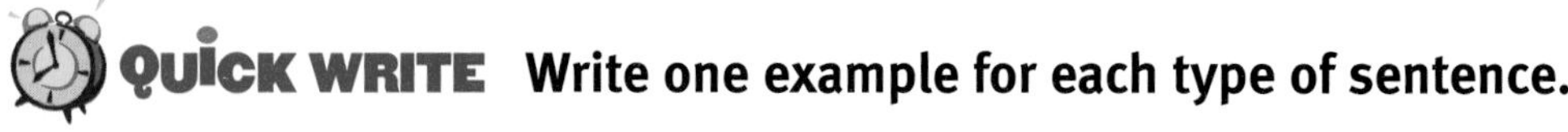

QUICK WRITE **Write one example for each type of sentence.**

RULE 1
pages 78–83

Nouns, Singular and Plural

- A **noun** names a person, place, or thing.
- A **singular noun** names one person, place, or thing. A **plural noun** names more than one.
- Add *-s* to form the plural of most singular nouns.
- Add *-es* to form the plural of singular nouns that end in *s, sh, ch,* or *x*.
- To form the plural of nouns ending in a consonant and *y*, change the *y* to *i* and add *-es*.

cow cows bush bushes party parties

Practice Write the sentences. Use the plural form of the noun in ( ).

1. Many (family) visit Florida in the winter.
2. The weather is warm in most (month).
3. Florida has beautiful (beach).

RULE 2
pages 84–85

More Plural Nouns

- Some nouns have special plural forms.

Those men fed three geese.

- A few nouns have the same singular and plural forms.

Many moose and deer live in the woods.

Practice Write the sentences. Use the plural form of the noun in ( ).

1. Those two (woman) are dentists.
2. The dentists take care of people's (tooth).
3. One girl plays with two stuffed (sheep).

RULE 3
pages 86–87

Common and Proper Nouns

- A common noun names any person, place, or thing.

  The girl went to the zoo.

- A proper noun names a special person, place, or thing. A proper noun begins with a capital letter.

  Ellen went to the Bronx Zoo.

Practice **Write the sentences. Write *common* or *proper* under each underlined noun.**

1. The London Zoo had an elephant named Jumbo.
2. The giant animal came from Africa.
3. P. T. Barnum bought the huge beast.
4. The man brought the elephant to the United States.
5. Jumbo amazed people in New York.

RULE 4
pages 92–95

Singular and Plural Possessive Nouns

- A possessive noun is a noun that shows who or what owns or has something. Add an apostrophe (') and an *s* to a singular noun to make it possessive.

  Dan's friend Edna likes apples.

- Add an apostrophe (') to make most plural nouns possessive.

  Those trees' apples are ripe.

- Add an apostrophe (') and an *s* to form the possessive of plural nouns that do not end in *-s*.

  The children's baskets are full.

Practice **Write the sentences. Use the possessive form of the noun in ( ).**

1. Apple trees grow on (Dan) farm.
2. Apple (growers) work is hard.
3. The (men) job is to pick apples.
4. Apples are many (people) favorite fruit.
5. (Edna) favorite apples are green.

RULE 5

pages 96–97

Combining Sentences: Nouns

- Two **sentences can be combined** by joining two nouns with ***and***. Leave out the words that repeat.

Guy wanted a tree house. Pete wanted a tree house.
*Guy **and** Pete wanted a tree house.*

Practice **Write each pair of sentences as one sentence. Use the word *and* to join two nouns.**

1. Guy looked for some wood. Pete looked for some wood.
2. Guy brought a hammer. Guy brought nails.
3. Pete found a ladder. Pete found rope.
4. Guy climbed an old maple tree. Pete climbed an old maple tree.
5. The boys' mother helped. The boys' father helped.

QUICK WRITE **Write five sentences with singular and plural possessive nouns.**

Handbook

RULE 1

pages 160–161

Action Verbs

- An action verb is a word that shows action.

  Ray climbs the ladder.

- Some action verbs tell about actions that are hard to see.

  Ray thinks about the work.

Practice **Write each sentence. Draw a line under the action verb.**

1. Ray and his friends paint houses.
2. The painters wear white coveralls.
3. Brett stirs a can of paint.
4. Marjorie cleans her brush.
5. Ray brushes paint on the wall.

RULE 2

pages 244–245

Linking Verbs

- An action verb is a verb that shows action. A linking verb does not show action. It connects the subject to the rest of the sentence. The verb *be* is a common linking verb. It has special forms in the present tense and in the past tense.

  Present-tense forms of *be*: *are, is, am*
  Past-tense forms of *be*: *were, was*

Practice **Write the sentences. Draw a line under each verb. Write *linking verb* or *action verb* to describe each verb.**

1. The school bus was late.
2. We worried about the bus.
3. The bus driver is sorry.
4. An accident caused a traffic jam.
5. Now I am late for school.

RULE 3

pages 162–163

Present-Tense Verbs

- The tense of a verb tells when the action takes place.
- A verb in the present tense tells what happens now.

  Gary collects seashells.

- Add *-s* to most singular verbs in the present tense.
- Add *-es* to verbs that end in ***sh, ch, ss, s, zz,*** or ***x***.
- Change *y* to *i* and add *-es* to verbs that end with a consonant and y.

  looks *fixes* *worries*

Practice **Write each sentence. Use the correct form of the verb in ( ).**

1. Gary (walk) along the beach.
2. The boy (search) for shells.
3. A big wave (wash) some shells onto the sand.
4. Gary (hurry) to find more shells.
5. The boy (drop) one shell.

Past-Tense Verbs

- A past-tense verb tells about an action that has already happened. Add *-ed* to most verbs to form the past tense.

  Last night, it snowed.

- Change the *y* to *i* before adding *-ed* if the verb ends with a consonant and *y*.
- Drop the *e* and add *-ed* to verbs that end with *e*.
- Double the consonant and add *-ed* to verbs that end with one vowel and one consonant.

  try tried smile smiled plan planned

Practice Write the sentences. Use the past tense of the verb in ( ).

1. In the morning, snow (cover) the ground.
2. The weather (surprise) us.
3. No one (expect) snow in October!
4. Les and I (grin) at each other.
5. We (bundle) ourselves in warm clothes.
6. Then we (hurry) outside.
7. Les and I (pile) snow into a big mound.
8. We (pack) the snow into a fort.

Future-Tense Verbs

- A future-tense verb tells about an action that is going to happen. Use the special verb *will* to write about the future.

  Next year, Cara will go to Rome.

Practice **Write the sentences. Write the verb in the future tense.**

1. Cara and her family fly in a big plane.
2. The family tours the city.
3. Cara takes many pictures.
4. Cara sees old ruins.
5. Everyone buys presents for friends back home.

RULE 6

pages 164–165

Subject-Verb Agreement

- **A present-tense verb must agree with its subject.**

  Two children gather ***pink flowers.***

- **Do not add *-s* or *-es* to a present-tense verb when the subject is plural or *I* or *you*.**

Practice **Write the sentences. Use the correct form of the present-tense verb in ( ).**

1. Terry and I (place) flowers on the table.
2. Grandma (thread) two large needles with string.
3. Terry (poke) the needle through each flower.
4. Both of us (work) carefully.
5. We proudly (wear) our flower necklaces.

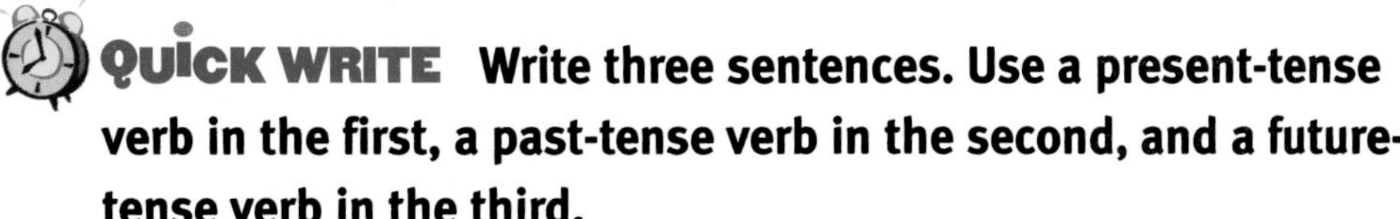

QUICK WRITE **Write three sentences. Use a present-tense verb in the first, a past-tense verb in the second, and a future-tense verb in the third.**

Main and Helping Verbs

- Sometimes a verb can be more than one word. The main verb tells what the subject does or is.

  Jess is visiting his uncle's ranch.

- The helping verb helps the main verb show an action.

  Jess is visiting his uncle's ranch.

- Use the helping verbs *has, have,* and *had* to help main verbs show an action in the past. In sentences with helping verbs, both the main verb and the helping verb must agree with the subject.
- Use *has* with a singular subject and *he, she,* or *it.*
- Use *have* with a plural subject and *I, you, we,* or *they.*
- Use *had* with a singular or plural subject.

Practice **Write the sentences. Draw one line under each main verb. Draw two lines under each helping verb.**

1. Jess had flown to Texas in a jet.
2. Uncle Bob is raising cattle.
3. Jess has helped his uncle every summer.
4. This summer Jess is helping Uncle Bob again.
5. Uncle Bob and Aunt Rita have met Jess at the airport.

Contractions with *Not*

- A contraction is a shortened form of two words.
- An apostrophe (') shows where one or more letters have been left out.

Practice **Write the new sentences. Write the words that make up each contraction.**

1. I can't find my book.
2. It isn't in the bookcase.
3. I don't know where to look.
4. Didn't you see the book?
5. I haven't looked in my room.

RULE 9 pages 258–259

Combining Sentences: Verbs

- You can join two sentences with the same subject by combining the predicates. Use *and* to join the predicates of two sentences that have the same subject.

Laura loved science. Laura studied the stars.
Laura loved science and studied the stars.

Practice **Write each pair of sentences as one sentence. Use the word *and* to join the predicates.**

1. Nina loved space. Nina wanted to be an astronaut.
2. The space program needed astronauts. The space program accepted Nina.
3. The shuttle lifted off. The shuttle flew to the space station.
4. Nina lived in the space station. Nina stayed six months.
5. The scientists did experiments. The scientists carried out projects.

RULE 10 pages 252–255

Irregular Verbs

- An irregular verb has a special spelling to show the past tense. Some irregular verbs have a special spelling when used with the helping verb *have*.

Present	Past	Past with *have*, *has*, or *had*
begin	began	begun
bring	brought	brought
come	came	come
eat	ate	eaten
do	did	done
give	gave	given
go	went	gone
grow	grew	grown
run	ran	run
say	said	said
see	saw	seen
sing	sang	sung

Practice **Write the sentences. Change each present-tense verb in ( ) to the past tense.**

1. Lil and Beth (go) to the movies.
2. The girls (run) all the way.
3. Beth (do) not want to be late.
4. Lil (see) her friend Maria at the movie.
5. Maria had (bring) her brother with her.

QUICK WRITE **Write five sentences with irregular verbs in the past tense.**

RULE 1
pages 322–323

Pronouns

- A **pronoun** is a word that takes the place of one or more nouns.

  Nora plays soccer. She plays soccer.

Practice **Rewrite each sentence. Replace the underlined word or words with the correct pronoun in ( ).**

1. The children run after the ball. (They, He)
2. Nora kicks the ball toward the goal. (she, it)
3. Lennie cheers when Nora scores. (I, He)
4. Nora waves at Meg and me. (us, them)
5. Will our team win the game? (you, we)

RULE 2
pages 324–327

Subject Pronouns and Object Pronouns

- A **subject pronoun** is used as the subject of a sentence.

  Singular subject pronouns: *I, you, he, she, it*
  Plural subject pronouns: *we, you, they*

- Use an **object pronoun** after an action verb or words such as *for, at, of, with,* and *to*.

  Singular object pronouns: *me, you, him, her, it*
  Plural object pronouns: *us, you, them*

Practice **Write the sentences. Replace the underlined word or words with a subject pronoun or an object pronoun.**

1. Carl told Mark and me about his hobby.
2. Coin collecting interests Carl.
3. Carl showed his coins to Jill.
4. Jill and Carl have pictures of coins.
5. Jill gave a coin book to Mark.

RULE 3

pages 332–333

Pronoun-Verb Agreement

- A present-tense action verb must agree with its subject pronoun.
- Add *-s* to most action verbs in the present tense when you use the pronouns *he, she,* and *it*.
- Do not add *-s* to an action verb in the present tense when you use the pronouns *I, we, you,* and *they*.

He picks blueberries. I pick blueberries.

Practice Write the sentences. Complete each sentence with the correct verb in ( ).

1. We (bring, brings) some blueberries home.
2. They (taste, tastes) sweet.
3. You (make, makes) blueberry jam.
4. It (smell, smells) wonderful!
5. I (eat, eats) some bread and jam.

RULE 4

pages 334–335

Possessive Pronouns

- A possessive pronoun takes the place of a possessive noun. It shows who or what owns something.

Walt's game is fun. His game is fun.

- These possessive pronouns are used before nouns: *my, your, his, her, its, our, their*.

That is their computer.

- These possessive pronouns can stand alone: *mine, yours, his, hers, its, ours, theirs*.

Is that yours?

Practice **Write the sentences. Draw a line under each possessive pronoun.**

1. The computer is his.
2. My computer screen changes color.
3. Her fingers are on the keyboard.
4. You can play your computer game.
5. When did you get that game of yours?

RULE 5 pages 336–337

Pronoun-Verb Contractions

- A contraction is a shortened form of two words. There are many pronoun–verb contractions.
- An *apostrophe* (') replaces missing letters.

he's = he + is; he + has
she's = she + is; she + has
it's = it + is; it + has
I'm = I + am
you're = you + are
we're = we + are
they're = they + are
I've = I + have
you've = you + have

we've = we + have
they've = they + have
I'll = I + will
he'll = he + will
she'll = she + will
we'll = we + will
you'll = you + will
it'll = it + will
they'll = they + will

Practice **Write each sentence. Replace the underlined words with a contraction.**

1. She is my sister.
2. He is a friend of mine.
3. They are my cousins.
4. We are part of a large family.
5. It is a family with many children.

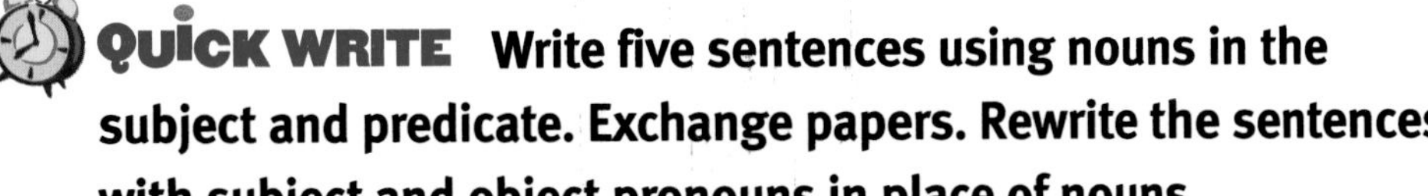

QUICK WRITE Write five sentences using nouns in the subject and predicate. Exchange papers. Rewrite the sentences with subject and object pronouns in place of nouns.

RULE 1

pages 398–401

Adjectives That Tell What Kind or How Many

- An adjective is a word that describes a noun.
- Some adjectives tell *what kind* of person, place, or thing the noun is.

  The moon shines in the dark sky.

- Some adjectives tell *how many*.

  Three men enter the spaceship.

- *Few, many,* and *several* are special adjectives that tell *how many*.

  Many people watch the launch on TV.

Practice **Write the sentences. Draw one line under each adjective that tells *how many* or *what kind*.**

1. One man counts off to blastoff.
2. The long trip begins.
3. Two astronauts step onto the moon.
4. Astronauts study the rocky surface of the moon.
5. Few people have made this trip!

RULE 2

pages 402–403

Articles

- Articles are special adjectives. The words *a, an,* and *the* are articles.
- Use *a* before singular nouns that begin with a consonant.
- Use *an* before singular nouns that begin with a vowel.
- Use *the* before singular nouns and plural nouns.

Practice **Write the sentences. Complete each sentence with the correct article in ( ).**

1. Rusty and I play in (the, an) park.
2. I throw (a, an) ball, and Rusty chases it.
3. Rusty brings (a, an) apple back to me!
4. I tell Rusty to get (an, the) ball.
5. Rusty is (a, an) very silly dog!

RULE 3

pages 404–407

Adjectives That Compare

- You can use adjectives to compare nouns.
- Add *-er* to an adjective to compare two nouns.
- Add *-est* to compare more than two nouns.
- Some adjectives change their spelling when *-er* or *-est* is added.
- When the adjective ends in a consonant sound and y, change the *y* to *i* and add *-er* or *-est.*
- When the adjective ends in *e*, drop the *e* and add *-er* or *-est.*
- For adjectives that have a single vowel before a final consonant, double the final consonant and add *-er* or *-est.*

Practice **Write the sentences. Add *-er* or *-est* to the adjective in ( ).**

1. Dolphins are (small) than killer whales.
2. A crocodile is (big) than an alligator.
3. A sea turtle is (heavy) than a snapping turtle.
4. Whale sharks are the (large) of all fish.
5. Some whales eat the (small) of all fish.

QUICK WRITE **Write five sentences with adjectives that compare.**

RULE 1

pages 412–413

Adverbs

- An adverb is a word that tells more about a verb. Adverbs tell *how, when,* or *where* an action takes place.

Yesterday, dark clouds swiftly moved overhead.

Practice **Write *how, when,* or *where* to show what each underlined adverb tells about the verb.**

1. Thunder rumbled loudly.
2. Lightning flashed brightly.
3. Next, rain poured from the clouds.
4. I ran inside.
5. Then I dried myself off.

RULE 2

pages 414–415

Adverbs That Tell How

- Some adverbs tell *how* an action takes place.
- Adverbs that tell *how* often end with *-ly*.

The dog barked loudly.

Practice **Write the sentences. Draw a line under each adverb that tells *how*. Draw two lines under the verb it describes.**

1. A stray dog walked slowly into town.
2. Mr. Stacy petted the dog gently.
3. The dog wagged his tail excitedly.
4. Mr. Stacy kindly adopted the dog.
5. The dog quickly answered to his new name.

Adverbs That Tell When or Where

- Some adverbs tell *when* or *where* an action takes place.

Practice **Write the sentences. Draw a line under each verb. Circle each adverb. Write if the adverb tells *when* or *where*.**

1. Vera lost her bike today.
2. The bike disappeared from inside.
3. Vera looked for the bike outdoors.
4. Later, Vera called Wally.
5. Soon, Wally arrived at Vera's house.

Combining Sentences: Adjectives and Adverbs

- Two sentences that tell about the same person, place, or thing can be combined by adding an adjective to one sentence.

  Sylvie heard a noise. It was a loud noise.
  Sylvie heard a loud noise.

- Two sentences that tell about the same action can be combined by adding an adverb to one sentence.

  The trash can fell. It fell noisily.
  The trash can fell noisily.

Practice **Add an adjective or adverb to one of the sentences in each pair. Write the new sentence.**

1. Sylvie opened the door. She opened it quickly.
2. A raccoon was in the can. The raccoon was fat.
3. The raccoon ran. It ran swiftly.

QUICK WRITE **Write five sentences using adverbs that tell *how, when,* or *where*.**

Abbreviations

Abbreviations are used in informal writing. An **abbreviation** is the shortened form of a word and usually begins with a capital letter and ends with a period.

Titles

- You can abbreviate titles before a name.

Ms. Rose *Mrs. Gordon* *Mr. Martinez* *Dr. Wong*

Practice **Write each abbreviation correctly.**

1. ms Inez Vasquez
2. dr Ellen Right
3. mrs Karen Inagaki
4. mr Thomas Hale
5. dr Ed Jones

Days of the Week

- You may abbreviate the days of the week.

Sun. Mon. Tues. Wed. Thurs. Fri. Sat.

Months of the Year

- You may abbreviate most months of the year.

Jan. Feb. Mar. Apr. Aug. Sept. Oct. Nov. Dec.

- Do not abbreviate the months *May, June, July.*

Practice **Write each abbreviation correctly.**

6. tues
7. august
8. Sat
9. jan
10. november
11. Fri
12. apr
13. thursday
14. Wed
15. feb.

States

- In informal writing and on envelopes you may use United States Postal Service Abbreviations for the names of states.

Alabama	AL	Kentucky	KY	North Carolina	NC
Alaska	AK	Louisiana	LA	North Dakota	ND
Arizona	AZ	Maine	ME	Ohio	OH
Arkansas	AR	Maryland	MD	Oklahoma	OK
California	CA	Massachusetts	MA	Oregon	OR
Colorado	CO	Michigan	MI	Pennsylvania	PA
Connecticut	CT	Minnesota	MN	Rhode Island	RI
Delaware	DE	Mississippi	MS	South Carolina	SC
District of Columbia	DC	Missouri	MO	South Dakota	SD
Florida	FL	Montana	MT	Tennessee	TN
Georgia	GA	Nebraska	NE	Texas	TX
Hawaii	HI	Nevada	NV	Utah	UT
Idaho	ID	New Hampshire	NH	Vermont	VT
Illinois	IL	New Jersey	NJ	Virginia	VA
Indiana	IN	New Mexico	NM	Washington	WA
Iowa	IA	New York	NY	West Virginia	WV
Kansas	KS			Wisconsin	WI
				Wyoming	WY

Practice **Write the U.S. Postal Service abbreviation for each of the following states.**

1. Hawaii
2. Utah
3. Alabama
4. Michigan
5. Vermont
6. Iowa
7. Oregon
8. Louisiana
9. North Dakota
10. Texas

Handbook

Capitalization

First Word in a Sentence

- Capitalize the first word in a sentence.

  Spiders have eight legs.

- Capitalize the first word of a direct quotation. A quotation is the exact words of a person speaking.

  José said, "Insects have six legs."

Letters

- Capitalize all words in a letter's greeting.

  Dear Robin, *Dear Mr. Henderson,*

- Capitalize the first word in the closing of a letter.

  Yours truly, *Your friend,* *Sincerely,*

Practice **Write each item. Use capital letters correctly.**

1. dear aunt juana,

2. "do you like spiders?" asked Louis.

3. some people are afraid of spiders.

4. Tina said, "spiders catch harmful insects."

5. very truly yours,

Proper Nouns: Names and Titles of People

- Capitalize names and initials that stand for names.

  Joan Cohen *T. R. Sullivan*

- Capitalize titles or abbreviations of titles when they come before the names of people.

  Aunt Ada *Mr. Westly* *Mayor Gomez*

- Capitalize the pronoun *I*.

  My parents and I had a great vacation.

Practice **Write the sentences. Use capital letters correctly.**

1. Our family visited uncle chet on his ranch.
2. Mom and i rode horses for the first time.
3. I helped aunt ida clean the stalls.
4. The vet, dr. brand, treated a sick horse.
5. My uncle's neighbor is named k. c. whitby.

Proper Nouns: Names of Places

- Capitalize the names of cities, states, countries, and continents.

  Boston *Florida* *China* *Africa*

- Capitalize the names of geographical features.

  Pacific Ocean *Loon Mountain* *Mojave Desert*

- Capitalize the names of streets and highways.

  Grand Avenue *Route 66*

- Capitalize the names of buildings and bridges.

  Museum of Modern Art *Sears Tower* *Brooklyn Bridge*

- Capitalize the names of stars and planets.

  Rigel *Altair* *Saturn* *Mars*

Practice **Write the sentences. Use capital letters correctly.**

6. Mark drove to florida last week.
7. Mark enjoyed visiting miami beach.
8. The atlantic ocean was bright blue.
9. Mark took route 1 to the end.
10. The trip over seven-mile bridge was exciting.

Other Proper Nouns

- Capitalize the names of schools, clubs, and businesses.

Frontier School | *4H Club*
Apex Computers | *Rice Oil Company*

- Capitalize the days of the week, months of the year, and holidays. Do not capitalize the names of the seasons.

Friday *July* *Presidents' Day* *spring*

- Capitalize abbreviations.

Dr. *Mrs.* *Ave.* *Rte.* *Mt.*

- Capitalize the first, the last, and all important words in the title of a book, poem, song, short story, film, and newspaper.

Robots on the Loose! | "April Rain"
"The Alphabet Song" | "Harry's Cat"
Star Wars | *Washington Post*

Practice **Write the sentences. Use capital letters correctly.**

1. My class at deerfield school is reading a book called *all the presidents*.
2. Our teacher, ms. Choi, showed the film *famous presidents*.
3. Next monday is presidents' day.
4. This holiday comes in february.
5. Today's *deerfield recorder* has a story about president kennedy.

Punctuation

End Marks for Sentences

- A period (.) ends a statement or command.

  There are seals on the ice.
  Hand the field glasses to me.

- A question mark (?) ends a question.

  Do you see any walruses?

- An exclamation mark (!) ends an exclamation.

  Wow, that is a huge walrus!

Periods for Abbreviations

- Use a period to show the end of an abbreviation.

  Mrs. *Rd.* *Conn.*

- Use a period with initials.

  P. T. Barnum *L. C. Cox*

Practice **Write the sentences. Add end marks and periods where they are needed.**

1. Mr Shapiro took out his camera
2. Can you get a picture of the baby seals
3. Please don't alarm the seals
4. What a wonderful sight this is
5. How many seals do you see

Commas in Letters

- Use a comma between the names of cities and states.

  Dallas, Texas *Chicago, Illinois*

- Use a comma between the day and the year in dates.

  July 4, 2001 *October 17, 1836*

- Use a comma after the greeting and closing in a letter.

  Dear Grandma, *Yours truly,*

Practice **Add commas where they are needed.**

1. Trenton New Jersey
2. January 1 2002
3. Your friend
4. Dear Uncle Al
5. Kent Ohio

Commas in Sentences

- Use a comma to separate words in a series.

  The media center has videos, tapes, and CDs.

- Use a comma after the words *yes* and *no* when they begin a sentence.

  Yes, I have read that book.

- Use a comma after the name of a person being spoken to.

  Jill, are you going to the library?

Practice **Add commas where they are needed.**

6. Donna Hal and Kathy are at the library.
7. Hal do you want books on animals?
8. No I want books on baseball soccer and hockey.
9. Donna did you find what you wanted?
10. Yes I found poems stories and novels.

Apostrophes

- Use an apostrophe (') with nouns to show possession.
- Add an apostrophe and an *s ('s)* to singular or plural nouns that do not end in *s*.

boy's bat *Tina's ball* *men's caps*

- Add an apostrophe (') to plural nouns ending in *s*.

games' scores *players' uniforms*

- Use an apostrophe (') in contractions to show where a letter or letters are missing.

doesn't *we're* *you've* *I'm*

Practice **Write the possessive form of the noun in ( ). Write the contraction of the two words in ( ).**

1. Baseball (is not) (Jake) favorite game.
2. (I have) gone to all of my (friends) games.
3. Some (children) parents (are not) at the game.

Quotation Marks

- Use quotation marks at the beginning and at the end of the exact words a person says.

"Have you seen my hamster?" asked Sarah.

Practice **Add quotation marks where they are needed.**

4. The hamster can't have gone far, said Ned.
5. Sarah said, I've looked everywhere.
6. There's my hamster! Sarah cried.

Italics or Underlining

Underline or use *italics* for the title of a book, movie, magazine, or newspaper.

<u>The Cloud Book</u> *The Lion King*

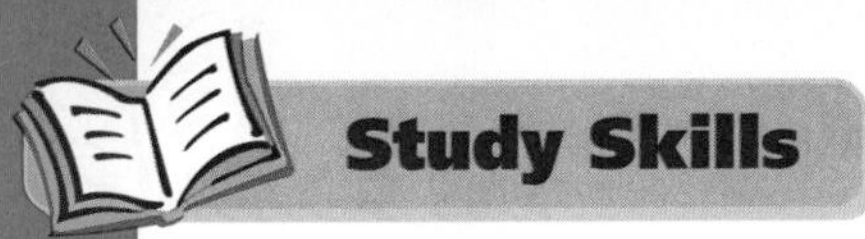

Dictionary

DEFINITIONS

- A dictionary is a book that gives the definitions, or meanings, of words.
- Entry words are the words that are explained in a dictionary. All the words are in alphabetical order.
- Often, a word may have more than one meaning. Each meaning of a word is numbered in a dictionary.
- An example sentence shows one way to use the entry word.
- Guide words at the top of each page show the first and last entry words on the page.
- The part of speech tells how the word can be used in a sentence as a noun, verb, adjective, and so on.

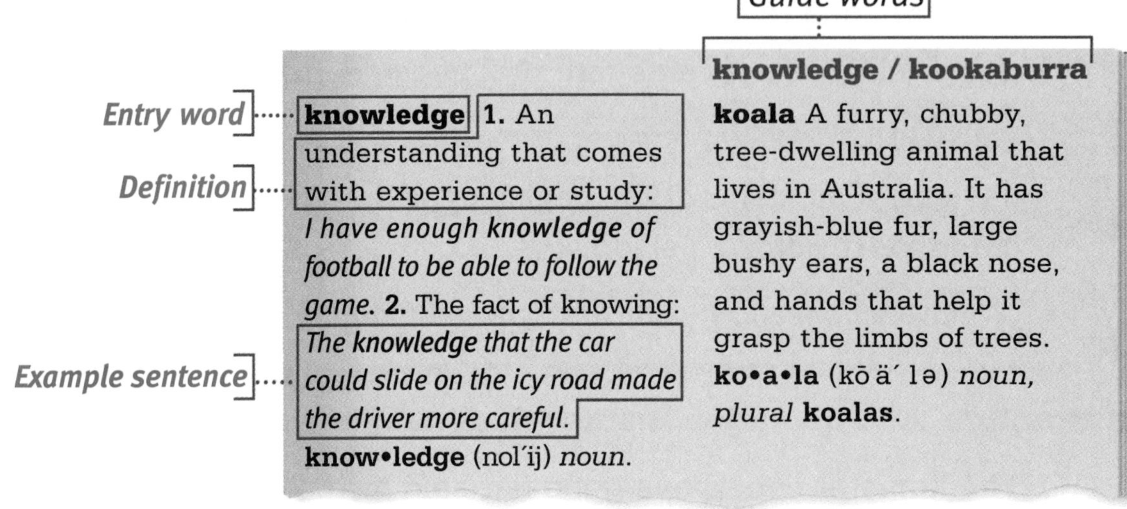

Practice Answer the questions about the dictionary.

1. What are the two guide words on the page?
2. Is *koala* a noun or a verb?
3. What are two meanings of the word *knowledge*?
4. What is the last word on this page?
5. Would the word *knot* come before or after this page?

Card Catalog

DEFINITIONS

- The card catalog contains information about all of the books in the library.
- Each book has a title card, an author card, and a subject card.
- The call number helps you find the book on the shelves.

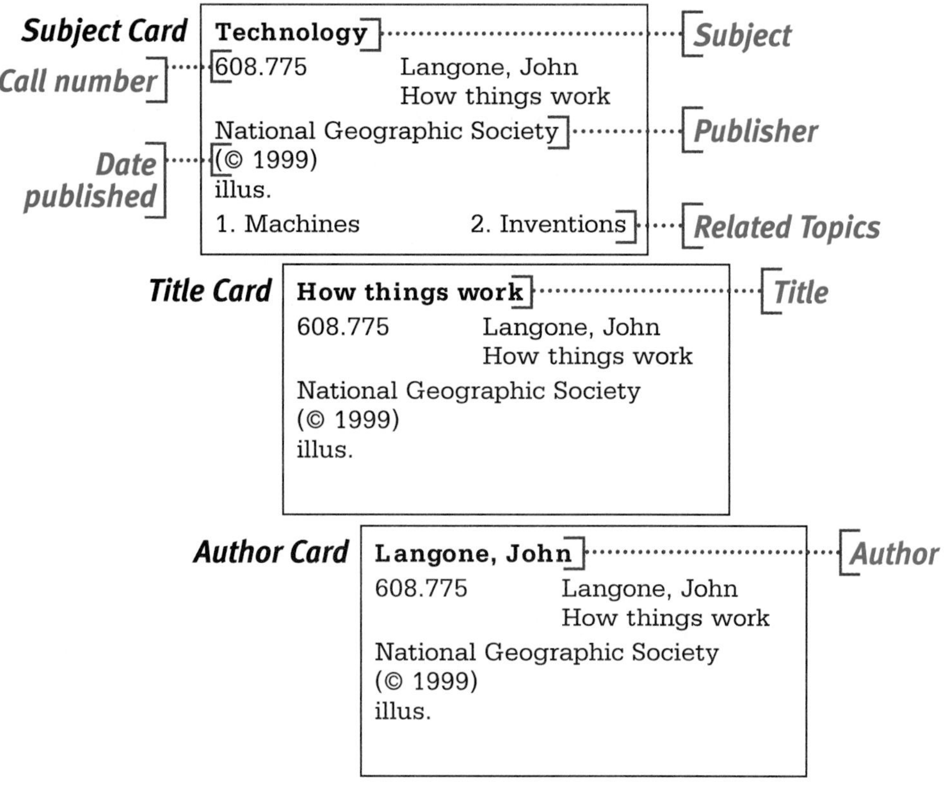

Practice **Use the cards above to answer these questions.**

1. What is the title of John Langone's book?
2. What is the call number of this book?
3. If you wanted to find a book about machines, which type of card would you use?
4. If you knew the author's name but not the title, which type of card would you use?
5. If you knew the book's title, which type of card would you use?

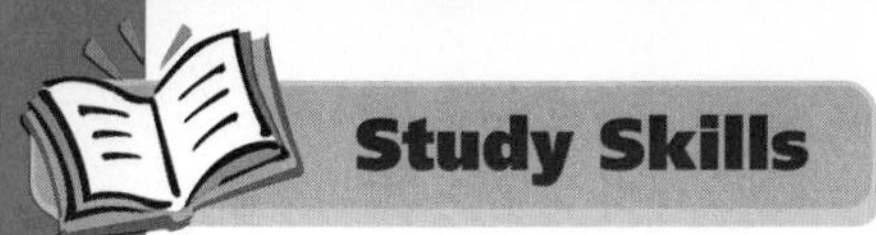

Parts of a Book

DEFINITIONS

- The **title page** of a book tells the title of the book, the author's name, and the illustrator's name.
- The **table of contents** lists the **titles** and **beginning page numbers** of all the chapters or parts of the book.
- The **index** at the back of a book lists all the important **topics** in alphabetical order.

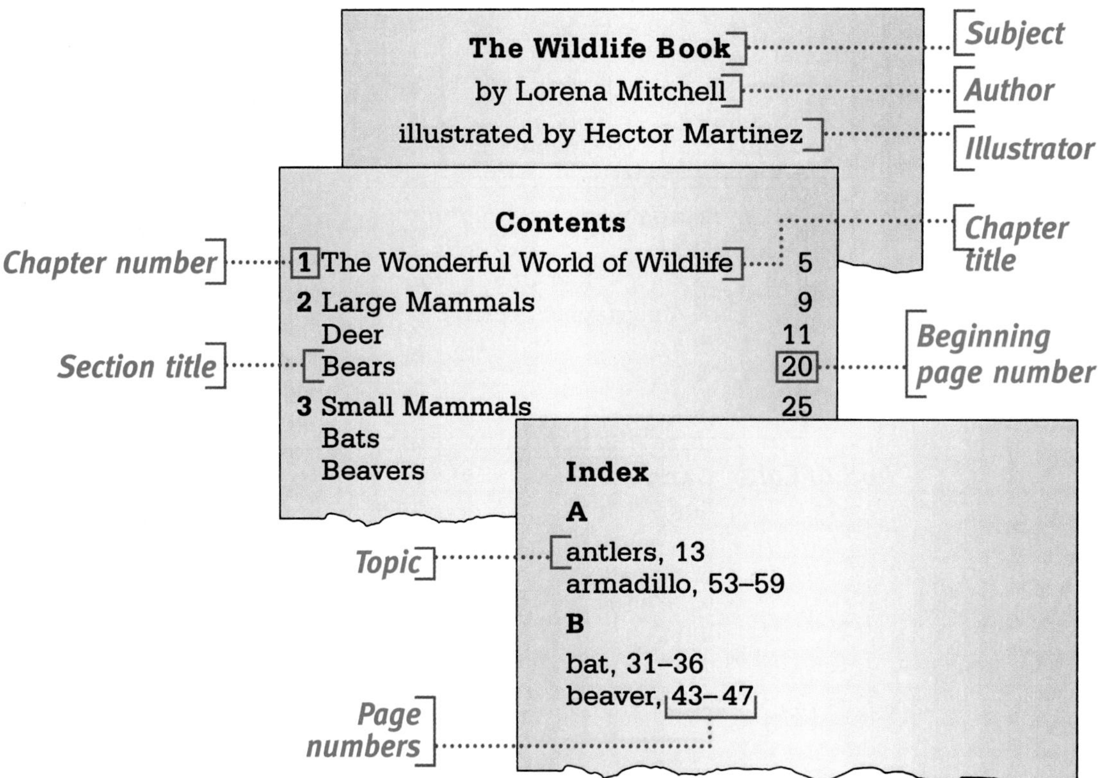

Practice **Use the title page, table of contents, and index above to answer the following questions.**

1. Who is the author of *The Wildlife Book*?
2. What is the title of Chapter 2 of the book?
3. On what page does the subtopic titled "Bears" begin?
4. On what pages can you find information about armadillos?
5. On what pages would you find information about beavers?

Note-taking and Summarizing

DEFINITIONS

- **When you read articles for information, you can take notes on the main idea and the important details.**
- **You can use your notes to write a summary. A summary tells in a few sentences the main idea and the important details.**

Zebras

Zebras are members of the horse family. They look like horses, but they have white and black or dark brown stripes. No zebra has exactly the same stripes as another.

A zebra's stripes help confuse its enemies. A hungry lion may see the stripes, not the zebra.

Notes

part of horse family
stripes—white and black or dark brown
no stripes the same
zebra's stripes protect it

Summary

Zebras belong to the horse family. The zebras' stripes help hide them from their enemies. All zebras have stripes. No two patterns are the same.

Practice Read the article, the notes, and the summary. Then answer the following questions.

1. What is the article about?
2. What is the main idea of the last paragraph?
3. To what family do zebras belong?
4. What color are a zebra's stripes?
5. Why is the summary shorter than the article?

Handbook

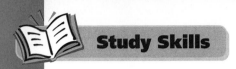

Library Catalog Menu

DEFINITIONS

- In most libraries, the catalog, or PAC (Public Access Catalog), is on the computer.
- All books are listed by author, title, and subject.
- Click on the menu to start your search.
- Type in the key words, names, or titles in the search field.

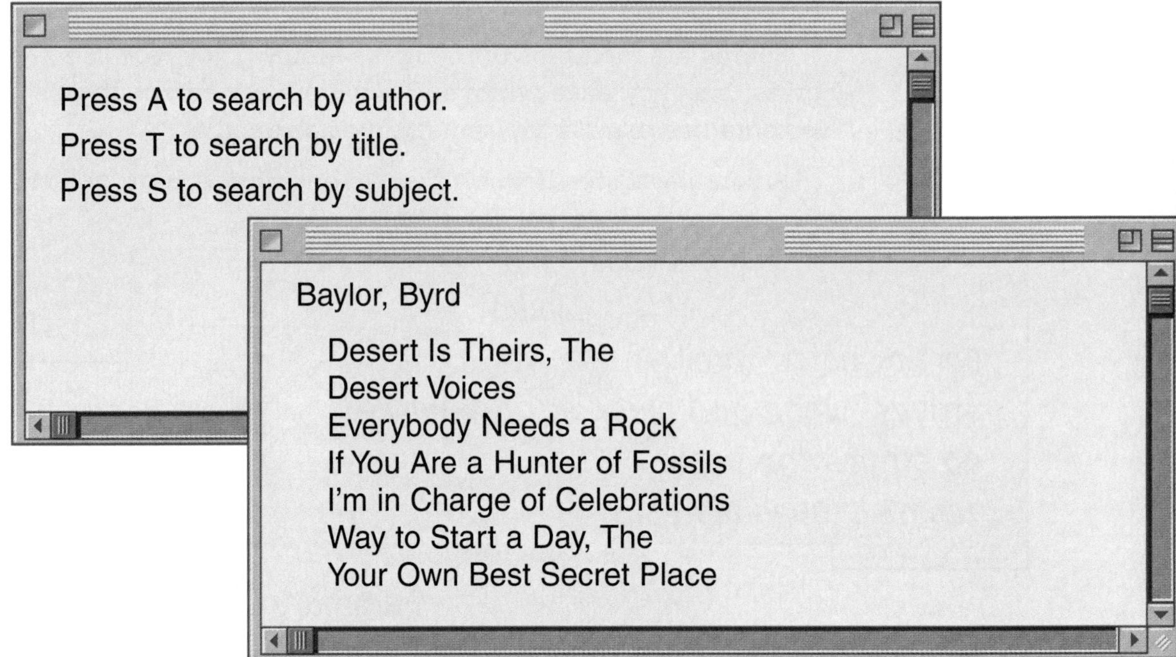

Press A to search by author.
Press T to search by title.
Press S to search by subject.
Baylor, Byrd
Desert Is Theirs, The
Desert Voices
Everybody Needs a Rock
If You Are a Hunter of Fossils
I'm in Charge of Celebrations
Way to Start a Day, The
Your Own Best Secret Place

Practice Use the computer screens above to answer the following questions.

1. If you were looking for books on a specific subject, how would you start your search?
2. What would you type in the search field to find books by an author whose name you know?
3. If you knew the title of the book, but not the author's name, how would you start your search?
4. If you wanted to find a book titled *The Cloud Book,* how would you start your search?
5. How did the person find a list of books by Byrd Baylor?

Periodicals

DEFINITIONS

- Magazines and newspapers are called periodicals. They are good sources for up-to-date information.
- Magazines often cover many topics. Some magazines are about a single topic. Magazines may be published once a week or once a month.
- Newspapers contain local, state, national, and world current events. Most newspapers are published every day.
- Your library may have a guide to periodicals that will lead you to newspaper or magazine articles on a topic.

Practice Look at the newspaper and magazine covers. Think about the kind of information you could find in each. Then write the name of the one that you might use to find the following stories or information.

1. the score of yesterday's baseball game in Middletown
2. an article about camping equipment
3. "Basketball Stars of Tomorrow"
4. "How to Build a Bookcase"
5. "Tango—the New Dance Craze"

Graphs

DEFINITIONS

- A **graph** is a diagram that shows the relationship between two or more things. You can use a graph to compare information.
- A **line graph** shows changes or differences over a period of time. It uses lines to join points that stand for numbers.
- A **bar graph** compares facts. It uses bars that go across or up and down.
- A **circle graph** compares parts of a whole. You can compare the sizes of the parts into which the circle is divided.

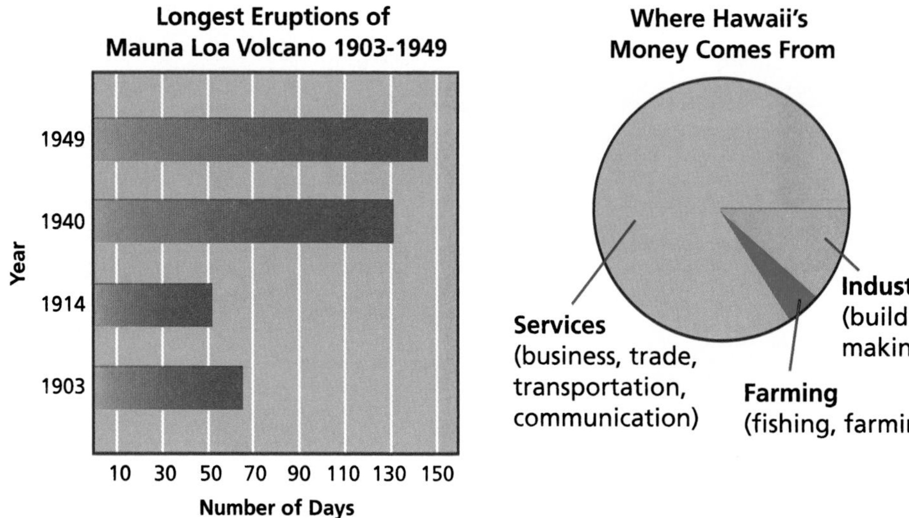

Practice **Use the graphs above to answer the questions.**

1. How many years does the bar graph show?
2. When was the longest eruption of Mauna Loa?
3. Was there a longer eruption in 1914 or in 1903?
4. According to the circle graph, what are the three ways that Hawaii makes money?
5. Where does most of Hawaii's money come from?

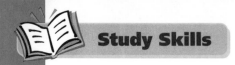

Internet: Online Search

DEFINITIONS

- The Internet is a system that lets computers all over the world talk to each other. It can help you research a topic.
- A search engine is a tool that searches the Internet for Web sites on your topic.
- A Web site is a page or series of pages with information on a topic. To find a Web site on your topic, do a key word search by typing in a subject.

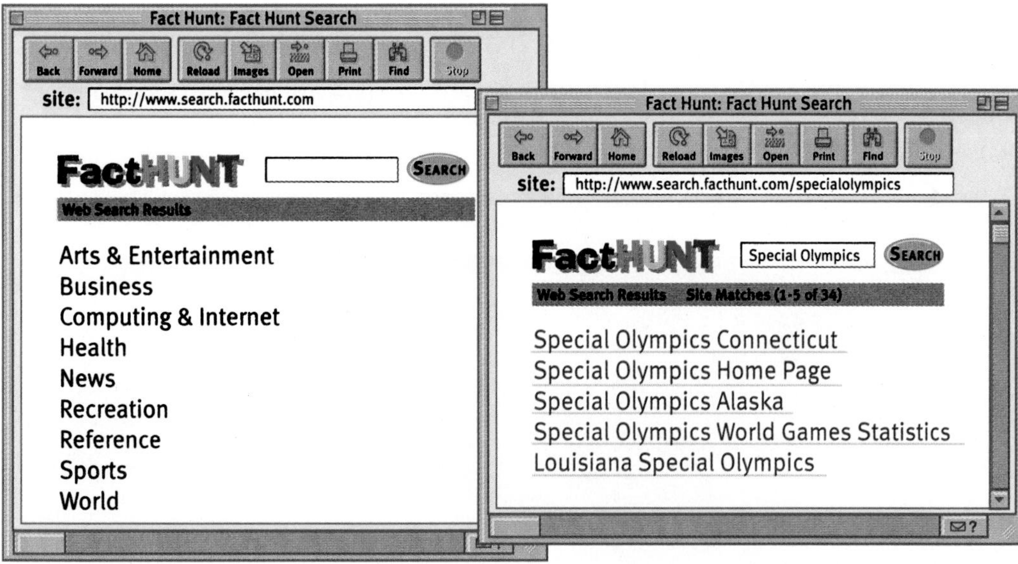

Practice Use the computer screens above to answer the following questions.

1. Which search engine was chosen?
2. What is the topic of the search?
3. How many Web sites did the search find?
4. What Web address might you click on to find out more about the Special Olympics in Alaska?
5. Which Web site might have more general information about the Special Olympics?

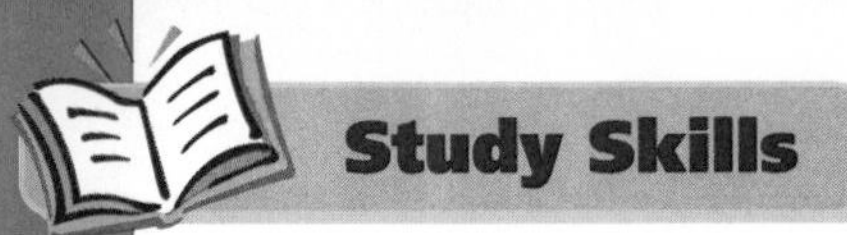

Encyclopedia

DEFINITIONS

- An **encyclopedia** contains articles about people, places, things, and events.
- **Articles** in an encyclopedia often answer these questions: *Who? What? Where? When? Why? How?*
- The articles are arranged in **alphabetical order** in books called *volumes*.
- Each **volume** is labeled with a number and one or more letters that stand for the beginning letters of the subjects in the volume.
- **Key words** name subjects that you might find in an encyclopedia. Look up key words in the *index* to research your subject.

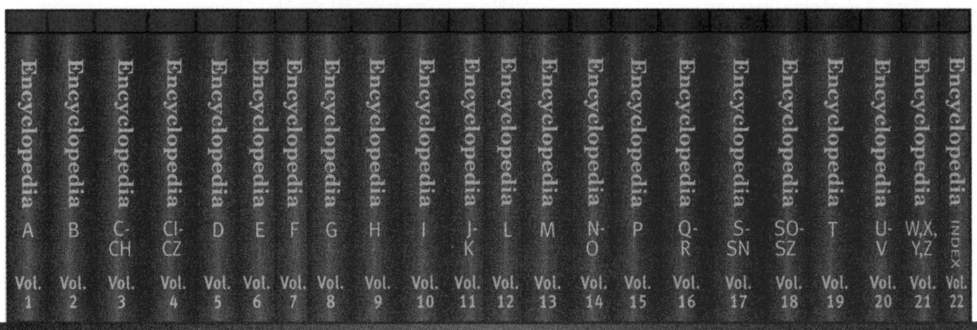

Practice **Write the key word or words that you would look up in an encyclopedia to find information about each subject. Then write the letter or letters of the volume in which you would find each key word.**

1. George Washington's birthplace
2. an elephant's trunk
3. holidays in Japan
4. important dates in California history
5. how volcanoes are formed

Telephone Directory

DEFINITIONS

- The **telephone directory** is a list of names, addresses, and telephone numbers.
- The **White Pages** list the names of people and companies in ABC order.
- The **Yellow Pages** list the names of different types of businesses. Within each group, businesses are listed in ABC order.
- **Emergency numbers** for police, ambulance, and fire department are found at the front of the telephone directory.
- **Guide words** at the top of each page give the first and last names on the page.

HEALTH CLUBS

Family Fitness Center
197 Federal St., Greenfield 555-1023
Karate for Kids
40 Bank Row, Conway 555-4139

► **Hospitals**

County Hospital
8 Valley View Dr., Conway 555-3295
West Medical Center
35 Lee Rd., Greenfield 555-5775

Dorman—Dumont

Dorman, Eric 47 Gothic St., Amherst . . .555-9521
Dougherty, Kay & David
148 Wells St., Greenfield. 555-3384
Dove's Nest Restaurant
35 Amberton Rd., Sunderland. 555-7168
Downey, Henry T 3 Elm Terr., Conway . . .555-8050
Dumont Country Store
221 Hendrick Ave., E. Hampton. 555-6579

Practice Use the telephone directory pages above to answer the following questions.

1. What is Eric Dorman's telephone number?
2. What is the address of Karate for Kids?
3. What number would you call for the Family Fitness Center?
4. What is Henry Downey's address?
5. What number would you call for the County Hospital?

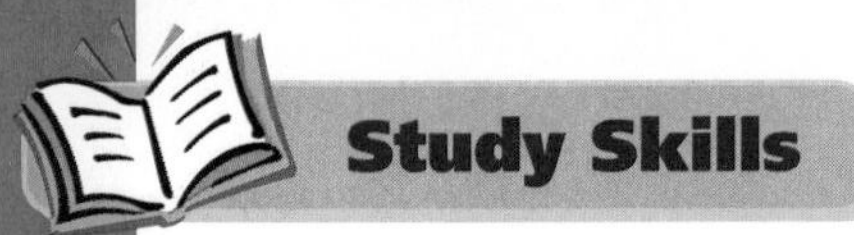

Thesaurus

DEFINITIONS

- A thesaurus is a book that gives synonyms for many common words. Synonyms are words that have the same or almost the same meaning.
- The words in a thesaurus are listed in alphabetical order.
- Under each entry word is a list of synonyms, their definitions, and a sample sentence.
- Some entries also have antonyms, words with opposite meanings.

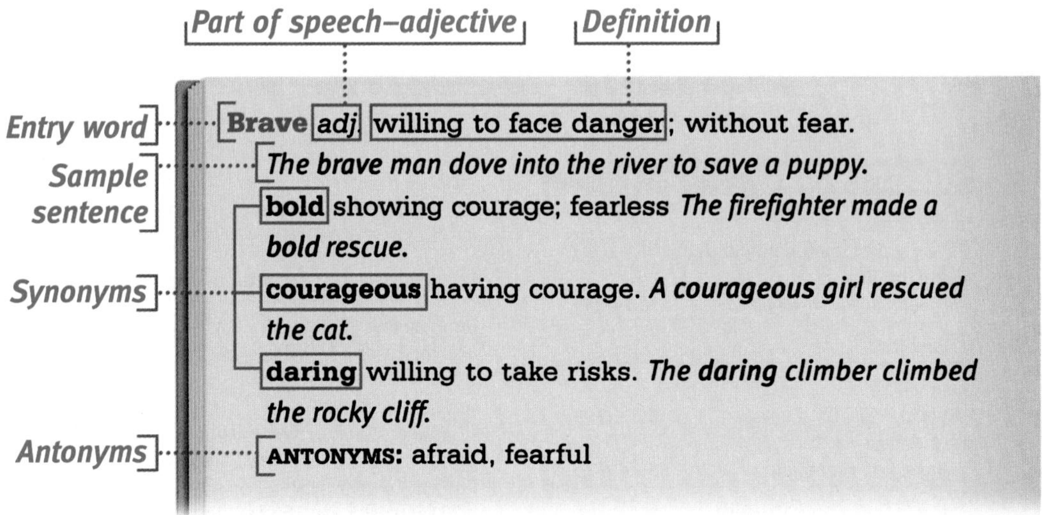

Part of speech–adjective
Definition
Entry word
Sample sentence
Synonyms
Antonyms
Brave adj. willing to face danger; without fear.
The brave man dove into the river to save a puppy.
bold showing courage; fearless The firefighter made a bold rescue.
courageous having courage. A courageous girl rescued the cat.
daring willing to take risks. The daring climber climbed the rocky cliff.
ANTONYMS: afraid, fearful

Practice Use the thesaurus entries above to answer the following questions.

1. What are the synonyms for *brave*?
2. Which synonym means "willing to take risks"?
3. What synonym would you use to describe someone who acts without fear?
4. What is the definition of *courageous*?
5. What antonyms are given for the word *brave*?

Map/Atlas

DEFINITIONS

- A map is a drawing that shows all or part of Earth's surface.
- The compass rose on a map shows direction.
- A map has pictures on it called symbols. The key explains the meaning of the symbols.
- The scale bar shows how distances on the map relate to distances in the real world.
- An atlas is a book of maps.
- The index of an atlas shows the page numbers of all the maps in the atlas.

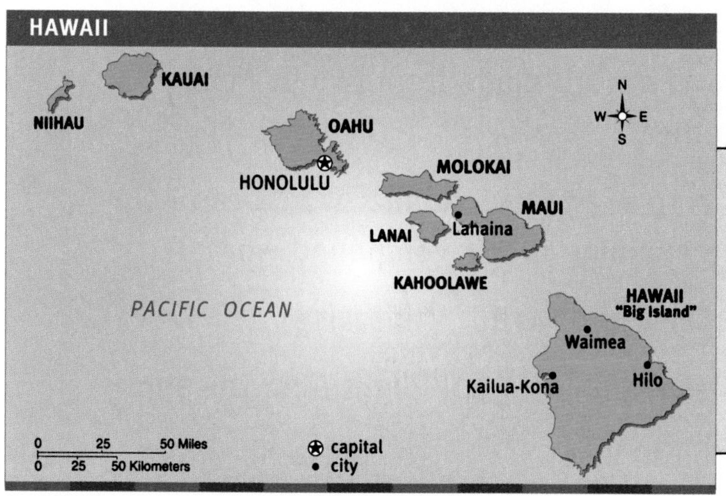

INDEX

Havasu, Lake, Ariz. 211 J2
Havasupai IR, Ariz. 211 D7
Haverhill, Mass. 41 B9
Hawaii 281
Hawaii (Island), Hawaii 281 K25
Hays, Kans. 179 D8
Haystack Mountain, Vt. 53 T4

Practice Use the map and index above to answer the following questions.

1. What is the capital of Hawaii?
2. In what direction from Maui is Lanai, east or west?
3. What are the names of two cities on the island of Hawaii (the Big Island)?
4. Is the island of Lanai north or south of Molokai?
5. On what page of this atlas can you find the map of Hawaii?

Vocabulary

RULE 1

pages 32–33

Time-Order Words

- A time-order word or phrase tells when things happen and in what order.
- Time-order words help you tell about events in order.

Time-Order Words and Phrases

first	after	now
next	before	as soon as
then	while	tomorrow
later	this morning	last year
last	yesterday	long ago

RULE 2

pages 112–113

Compound Words

- A compound word is a word made from two or more words joined together.
- Knowing the meaning of the two smaller words can help you figure out the meaning of the compound word.

Two Words	Compound Word	Meaning
sun + light	sunlight	light from the sun
bird + house	birdhouse	a house for a bird
sea + shell	seashell	a shell from the sea
paint + brush	paintbrush	a brush for paint
hand + made	handmade	made by hand
note + book	notebook	a book for notes
bath + tub	bathtub	a tub for a bath
snow + ball	snowball	a ball made of snow
sail + boat	sailboat	a boat with a sail

RULE 3
pages 190–191

Prefixes

- A prefix is a word part that is added to the beginning of a word.
- A prefix changes the meaning of a word.

Prefix	Meaning	Example
un-	not, the opposite of	*untie*
re-	again, back	*rebuild*
dis-	not, the opposite of	*disappear*
pre-	before	*preschool*

RULE 4
pages 274–275

Suffixes

- A suffix is a word part that is added to the end of a base word.
- A suffix changes the meaning of the base word.

Suffix	Meaning	Example
-er	person who	*manager*
-or	person who	*spectator*
-less	without	*careless*
-able	able to be	*readable*
-ly	in a certain way	*suddenly*
-ful	full of	*hopeful*

RULE 5

pages 352–353

Homophones

- Words that sound alike but have different spellings and different meanings are called **homophones**.
- You must use **context** to figure out which spelling of a homophone is correct.

Homophones	
hi	high
be	bee
sun	son
eye	I
blue	blew
hole	whole
rode	road, rowed
to	two, too
nose	knows
horse	hoarse
see	sea
flour	flower
would	wood
right	write
there	their

RULE 6

pages 434–435

Synonyms and Antonyms

- **Synonyms** are words that have the same or almost the same meaning.
- **Antonyms** are words that have opposite meanings.

Word	Synonym	Antonym
big	large	small
cold	icy	warm
strong	firm	weak
glad	happy	unhappy
fast	quick	slow
below	under	above
dark	dim	bright
friend	pal	enemy
let	allow	deny
ask	question	answer
like	love	dislike
laugh	giggle	cry

Problem Words

The English language includes some confusing words that are often used incorrectly. The following charts will help you understand how to use these words in the correct way.

Words	Correct Usage	Correct Usage
bad/badly	*Bad* is an adjective used to describe a noun. It means "the opposite of good." *That fruit left a bad taste in my mouth.*	*Badly* is an adverb that tells "how" about a verb. It means "in a bad way." *He tied the knot badly because he rushed.*
beside/besides	*Beside* means "next to." *Kim sat beside me at the play.*	*Besides* means "in addition to." *Besides art and math, she likes music best.*
can/may	*Can* means "be able to." *Most foxes can run very fast.*	*May* means "be permitted to." *Each student may borrow three books.*
good/well	*Good* is an adjective used to describe a noun. *We had a good time at the zoo.*	*Well* is usually an adverb. It describes a verb by telling "how." *Sara's soccer team played well and won.*
in/into	*In* means "inside." *Are your books in your book bag?*	*Into* means "moving to the inside of." *I put the quarter into my piggy bank.*
its/it's	*Its* is a possessive pronoun. *Its* does not have an apostrophe. *The dog wagged its tail.*	*It's* is a contraction for "it is." The apostrophe takes the place of the *i* in *is*. *It's a cold, rainy day.*

Words	Correct Usage	Correct Usage
lay/lie	*Lay* means "to put something down." *Lay the books gently on the table.*	*Lie* means "to rest on something." *My cat likes to lie on a soft pillow.*
loose/lose	*Loose* means "not tight." *My little sister has a loose tooth.*	*Lose* means "to be missing something." *Did Sam lose his notebook?*
set/sit	*Set* means "to put in a certain place." *Mom set the dish on the counter.*	*Sit* means "to be seated." *Let's sit here and watch the game.*
than/then	*Than* means "compared to." *My brother's bike is newer than mine.*	*Then* means "after that." *Ali did her homework and then played outside.*
their/they're	*Their* is a possessive pronoun that means "belonging to them." *Lee and Lin showed us their shell collection.*	*They're* is a contraction for "they are." *They're ready to sing the new song.*
your/you're	*Your* is a possessive pronoun that means "belonging to you." *Is your birthday this month?*	*You're* is a contraction for "you are." *You're so funny when you tell a joke.*

QUICK WRITE Create your own chart of problem words. Include words from this chart or other words you sometimes get confused. Write sentences to help you remember how to use the words correctly.

Easily Confused Words

Some words are easily confused because they are spelled in a similar way or because they sound alike. These words have different meanings, so you need to be sure you use the correct one.

all ready already	breath breathe	desert dessert	hour our	picture pitcher	tired tried
an and	close clothes	ever every	lay lie	quiet quite	wander wonder
any more anymore	cloth clothe	farther further	loose lose	share sure	weather whether
any way anyway	costume custom	for four	marry merry	than then	were where
bean been	dairy diary	hear here	of off	though through	your you're

Frequently Misspelled Words

For many writers, some words are hard to spell. You can use this list to check your spelling.

a lot	brother	enough	I'm	often	they
again	brought	every	instead	once	thought
against	busy	family	let's	outside	together
all right	buy	favorite	library	people	tomorrow
already	caught	finally	listen	probably	trouble
always	certain	first	live	really	upon
answer	charge	found	love	receive	we'll
around	country	friend	many	rhyme	we're
balloon	cousin	guess	might	said	when
because	different	half	minute	school	while
before	does	happened	neighbor	since	won't
believe	dollar	have	ninety	straight	word
bicycle	done	heard	nothing	surprise	work

Common Homophones

Homophones are words that sound the same but are spelled differently and have different meanings. ***Blew*** and ***blue*** are examples of homophones.

ad add	dear deer	I eye	one won	sail sale	wait weight
ate eight	fair fare	its it's	pail pale	son sun	way weigh
bare bear	flour flower	knew new	peace piece	tail tale	weak week
beat beet	for four	know no	plain plane	their there they're	wear where
blew blue	hear here	knows nose	right write	threw through	who's whose
buy by	heard herd	made maid	road rode	to too two	wood would
cent sent	hole whole	meat meet			your you're

Spelling Rules and Strategies

1. When words end in silent ***e,*** drop the ***e*** when adding an ending that begins with a vowel. ***(like + ed = liked)*** When adding an ending that begins with a consonant, keep the silent ***e***. ***(nice + ly = nicely)***
2. When a base word ends with a consonant followed by ***y,*** change the ***y*** to ***i*** when adding any ending except endings that begin with ***i. (try + es = tries; try + ing = trying)***
3. When a base word ends with a vowel followed by ***y,*** do not change the ***y*** when adding suffixes or endings. ***(key + s = keys)***
4. When a one-syllable word ends in one vowel followed by one consonant, double the consonant before adding an ending that begins with a vowel. ***(stop + ing = stopping)***
5. The letter ***q*** is always followed by ***u. (quick, quite)***
6. No English words end in ***j, q,*** or ***v.***
7. Add ***-s*** to most words to form plurals or present-tense verbs. Add ***-es*** to words ending in ***x, z, s, sh,*** or ***ch. (fork + s = forks; dish + es = dishes; glass + es = glasses)***
8. To make plurals of words that end with one ***f*** or ***fe,*** you often need to change the ***f*** or ***fe*** to ***v*** and add ***-es. (wolf + es = wolves)***
9. When the /s/ sound is spelled ***c, c*** is always followed by ***e, i,*** or ***y. (trace, city, bicycle)***
10. When /j/ is spelled ***g, g*** is always followed by ***e, i,*** or ***y. (gentle, giant, gym)***
11. Short vowels are followed by ***dge.*** Long vowels are followed by ***ge. (edge, cage)***
12. If the /ch/ sound immediately follows a short vowel in a one-syllable word, it is spelled ***tch.*** There are a few exceptions in English: ***much, such, which,*** and ***rich.***

Use these strategies to help you become a better speller.

1. Learn common homophones and make sure you have used the correct homophone in your writing.
   They ate ***their*** lunch. They sat over ***there.***
   It's a pretty cat. ***Its*** name is Bell.
2. Think of a word you know, such as a rhyming word, that has the same spelling pattern as the word you want to spell. ***(play, day, gray)***
3. Use words that you know how to spell to help you spell new words: ***(glad + snow = glow)***
4. Make up clues to help you remember the spelling. ***(u and i build a house; a piece of pie; the principal is your pal)***
5. Think of a related word to help you spell a word with a silent letter or a hard-to-hear sound. ***(sign–signal; relative–related)***
6. Divide the word into syllables. ***(mul ti ply)***
7. Learn to spell prefixes and suffixes you use often in writing.
8. Look for word chunks or smaller words that help you remember the spelling of the word. ***(hippopotamus = hippo pot am us)***
9. Change the way you say the word to yourself to help with the spelling. ***(knife = /ke nif/; beauty = /be e u te/)***
10. Think of times you may have seen the word in reading, on signs, or in a textbook. Try to remember how it looked. Write the word in different ways. Which one looks correct? ***(~~adress~~, ~~addres~~, address)***
11. Keep an alphabetical Personal Word List in your Spelling Journal. Write words you often have trouble spelling.
12. Become familiar with the dictionary and use it often.

Poem

A **poem** is a special kind of writing that uses word pictures to explain, describe, or tell a story. Poems often use rhyme, rhythm, and the sounds of words to "paint a picture" of an idea or a subject.

The Merry-Go-Round

The merry-go-round
whirls round and round
in giant circles on the ground.

And the horses run
an exciting race
while the wind blows music in your face.

Then the whole world spins
to a colored tune
but the ride is over much too soon.

— Myra Cohn Livingston

In poetry, a group of lines is called a ***stanza****. This poem has three stanzas.*

This line helps readers picture what a rider on a merry-go-round hears and feels.

Poetry often ***rhymes****. In this poem, the second and third lines in each stanza end with the same sound.*

Poetry often has a ***rhythm****. Read aloud to hear the sound pattern in a poem.*

GUIDELINES FOR WRITING A POEM

- Choose something fun or interesting to write about.
- You might choose to capture a special moment or feeling.
- Think about the pictures you want to create with words. Decide if you want to use rhyme, rhythm, and the sounds of words.
- Write as many stanzas and lines as you want.
- Give your poem a title.

Practice **Pretend that you have been named the official town poet. Write and illustrate a poem about what is best about your town.**

Business Letter

A **business letter** is a formal letter that is written to a person or a company. You can write a business letter to persuade or to inform. You can also write one to ask for something or to apply for a job.

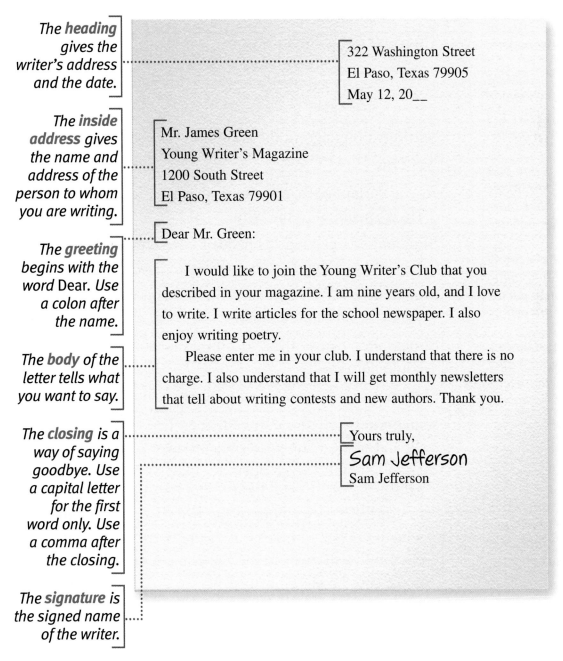

*The **heading** gives the writer's address and the date.*

322 Washington Street
El Paso, Texas 79905
May 12, 20__

*The **inside address** gives the name and address of the person to whom you are writing.*

Mr. James Green
Young Writer's Magazine
1200 South Street
El Paso, Texas 79901

*The **greeting** begins with the word* Dear. *Use a colon after the name.*

Dear Mr. Green:

*The **body** of the letter tells what you want to say.*

I would like to join the Young Writer's Club that you described in your magazine. I am nine years old, and I love to write. I write articles for the school newspaper. I also enjoy writing poetry.

Please enter me in your club. I understand that there is no charge. I also understand that I will get monthly newsletters that tell about writing contests and new authors. Thank you.

*The **closing** is a way of saying goodbye. Use a capital letter for the first word only. Use a comma after the closing.*

Yours truly,

*The **signature** is the signed name of the writer.*

Sam Jefferson
Sam Jefferson

Practice Write a business letter to one of your favorite authors. Tell the author what you like about his or her writing. Ask one or two questions.

Handbook

Play

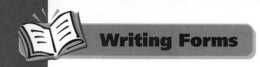

A **play** is a story that is written to be acted out on a stage for an audience. In a play, characters use words (called dialogue) and actions to tell the story.

A play has a cast of characters.

The setting is when and where the play happens.

An act is one part of a play. Many plays have more than one act.

Stage directions at the beginning of an act tell about the action.

The dialogue is written after each character's name.

Stage directions in () tell how characters speak and act.

The Elves and the Shoemaker

Characters: **Shoemaker**
Shoemaker's Wife
Elf 1
Elf 2

Setting: Long ago in the shop of a poor shoemaker.

Act One

As the curtain rises, the shoemaker is at his bench. He is speaking to his wife.

Shoemaker (shaking his head) I have enough leather for only one pair of shoes. What are we going to do?

Shoemaker's Wife It's late. Go to bed now. We will worry about money tomorrow.

Shoemaker I'm so tired. If only I had someone who could help me.

Shoemaker's Wife We can't afford to hire anyone.

Shoemaker You go on to bed, dear. I'm going to stay up and work. (The wife goes offstage.) I'm so tired. I can't keep my eyes open. I... (The shoemaker falls asleep. Suddenly, the light in the fireplace begins to grow. Elf 1 steps out of the fireplace, turns and whistles. Elf 2 tumbles out of the fireplace. The elves carefully walk over to the Shoemaker and check to make sure he is still asleep.)

Practice **Write the first act of a play. You can base your play on a favorite story or folktale.**

Editorial

An **editorial** is a newspaper article. It gives the writer's opinion of an event, a situation, or a problem. Editorials appear on the editorial page of a newspaper.

The title of an editorial is called a ***headline****.*

The subject of this editorial is a ***current situation*** *at school.*

The writer gives ***reasons*** *why she thinks her opinion is correct.*

A Soccer Field for Our School

Why doesn't our school have a soccer field? I think we need one. We have a nice playing field for baseball. We even have a track for running. But no one has built a field for soccer. If our school had a soccer field, we could start a school soccer team. Also, people in our town could use the field for soccer games on the weekend. There is room behind the cafeteria for a field.

Why don't we build one soon?

Jennifer Felner

The writer states her ***opinion****.*

The writer uses facts to ***persuade*** *readers.*

The ***writer's name*** *is given at the end of the editorial.*

GUIDELINES FOR WRITING AN EDITORIAL

- Choose a subject that is important to you.
- Give your opinion and reasons for your opinion.
- Use facts to help persuade your readers.
- Write a title that could be used in the newspaper as a headline.

Practice Write an editorial for your school, town, or city newspaper. Think of an event, a situation, or a problem. Write about your opinion or what you think needs to be changed.

Thesaurus

What Is a Thesaurus?

A **thesaurus** is a collection of synonyms for many common words. It gives more exact words to make your writing more interesting. Take the word *fast* in this sentence:

A fast horse galloped across the field.

If you check the thesaurus, you will also find: *quick, rapid, speedy, swift*. The following entries in a thesaurus will help you find a more exact word than *fast*.

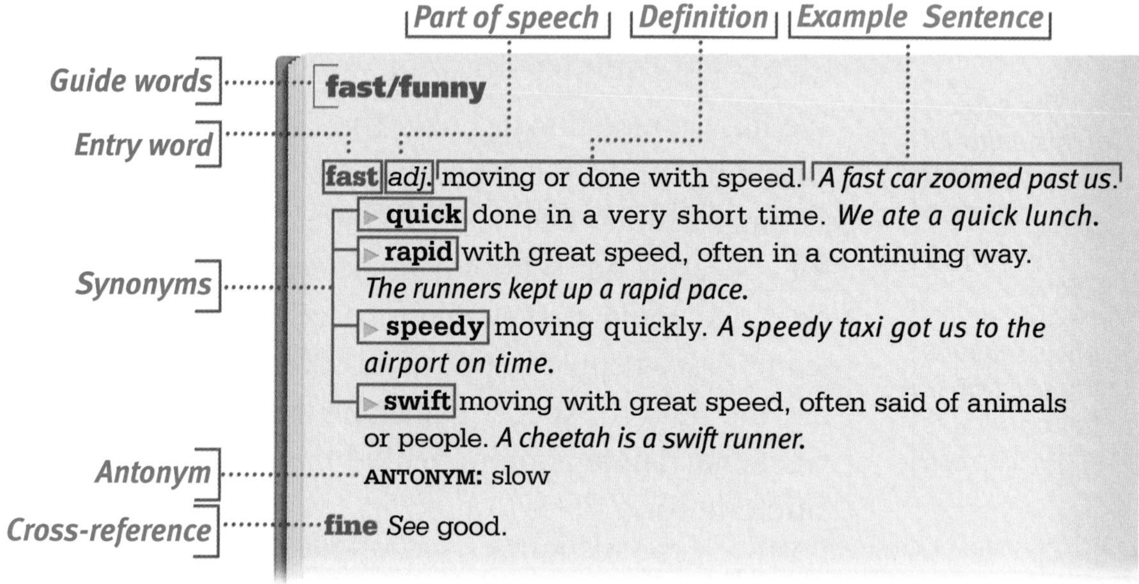

Part of speech
Definition
Example Sentence
Guide words
Entry word
Synonyms
Antonym
Cross-reference
fast/funny
fast adj. moving or done with speed. A fast car zoomed past us.
quick done in a very short time. We ate a quick lunch.
rapid with great speed, often in a continuing way. The runners kept up a rapid pace.
speedy moving quickly. A speedy taxi got us to the airport on time.
swift moving with great speed, often said of animals or people. A cheetah is a swift runner.
ANTONYM: slow
fine See good.

DEFINITIONS AND FEATURES

- The guide words at the top of each page show the first and last words on that page.
- The word *fast* is the entry word. Entry words are arranged alphabetically in a thesaurus.
- The part of speech is given for each entry. *Fast* is an adjective.
- A definition tells what the entry word and each synonym mean.
- An example sentence shows how each entry word and each synonym can be used.

Practice **Look up the entry for the word *quiet*. Then answer the following questions.**

1. What are the guide words on the page?
2. What is the part of speech of the entry word *quiet*?
3. Which synonyms have almost the same meaning as *quiet*?
4. Write a new example sentence for the word *calm*.
5. Which of the following words would you find on the page with the guide words *bright/delicious*: *big, clean, brave, empty, dark, cold?*

- **Synonyms** are words that have the same or almost the same meaning.
- There may be different **shades of meaning** among the synonyms listed within a single entry. Look at the **definitions** and **example sentences** with each word.
- At the bottom of some entries you will find **antonyms**, or words that have the opposite meaning from the entry word.
- **Cross-references** show other words that you can look up. For example, under the entry word ***large***, you will find the cross-reference "***See*** big." This means that when you look up *big*, the word *large* will be listed.

Practice **Write the sentences. Use the thesaurus to replace each underlined word with a more exact word.**

1. The <u>brave</u> skier zoomed down the mountain.
2. Don painted a <u>great</u> picture.
3. The <u>smart</u> girl solved the puzzle quickly.
4. <u>Bright</u> stars filled the night sky.
5. The <u>little</u> mouse peeked through a hole.

Poem

Practice **Words used in a poem need to be descriptive and exact in meaning. Find a better word in the thesaurus for each of the underlined words in the poem below.**

One very nice day,
I met along the way
A really big man and his little dog.
Both had funny caps on
That nodded in the wind as they walked on.

Business Letter

Practice **Exact words make the meaning of a business letter clear. Replace the underlined words in the letter below with more specific synonyms from the thesaurus.**

Ms. Janet Addams, Producer
Kids on Kids, Network Television
555 Second Avenue
New York, NY 10016

Dear Ms. Addams:

I like watching your program because it shows what kids can do.

I have a good idea for the program. My friend Lily uses a wheelchair, but she is a good dancer! In her group, some dancers can walk and some can't. Don't you think a program about Lily's group would be nice?

Sincerely,

Amy Beth Glasthal

Amy Beth Glasthal

Play

Practice When you write a play, you want to use just the right words. Rewrite this part of a play below. Replace underlined words with descriptive, interesting, and exact words from the thesaurus.

Little Mouse Bells the Cat

Scene 1

Narrator: Snarl, the mean cat, has all the mice feeling scared. Snarl crawls up and snatches their food and little treasures. The mice talk about the problem.

Little Mouse: I dislike that cat. If only we could hear Snarl coming, we could hide.

Old Mouse: Once we thought about putting a bell around his neck. It was too hard to do, though.

Little Mouse: Snarl is always stealing from us. That gives me a good idea! Give me a bell and some ribbon. (She ties the bell around her neck with the ribbon.) Now I'll go find Snarl and test my smart plan.

QUICK WRITE Write an editorial on a topic you feel strongly about. You may want to write about getting more computers for your school. Or you might write about saving an endangered animal. Whatever your topic, use the thesaurus to find the exact words to get your ideas across.

above *prep.* over or higher than. *The kite flew **above** the trees.*

▶ **over** in a place or position higher than. *Clouds drifted over the city.*

ANTONYMS: *See* below.

alike *adj.* like one another. *No two snowflakes are exactly alike.*

▶ **same** like another in every way. *The twins always dress in the same way.*

▶ **similar** having many qualities that are the same. *These two coats are similar.*

ANTONYM: different

allow *See* let.

angry *adj.* feeling or showing anger. *Her mean remark made me angry.*

▶ **furious** extremely angry. *I was furious when I saw the mess.*

▶ **mad** feeling or showing anger; angry. *I was mad at myself for losing my notebook.*

ask *v.* to put a question to. *Ask your parents if you can come to my party.*

▶ **demand** to ask forcefully. *She demanded an immediate apology.*

▶ **inquire** to seek information by asking questions. *Please inquire at the front office.*

▶ **plead** to make a sincere request. *I pleaded with my parents to let me go to the game.*

▶ **question** to try to get information. *Our teacher questioned us about our homework.*

▶ **request** to ask or ask for. *They requested permission to leave early.*

ANTONYM: answer

awful *adj.* causing fear, dread, or awe; very bad. *The hurricane damage was awful.*

▶ **dreadful** very frightening; very bad; awful. *We thought the movie was dreadful.*

▶ **horrible** causing or tending to cause horror. *What a horrible sight!*

▶ **terrible** causing fear or terror; very bad; awful. *The volcano erupted with a terrible roar.*

▶ **unpleasant** not pleasant. *Camping in the rain was an unpleasant experience.*

beautiful *adj.* full of beauty; having qualities that are pleasing. *What a beautiful sunset!*

▶ **attractive** pleasing to the eye. *The store has an attractive entrance.*

▶ **lovely** beautiful in a comforting way. *This is a lovely day.*

▶ **pretty** pleasing or attractive, often said of something small or dainty. *What pretty flowers these are!*

ANTONYMS: ugly, unattractive

believe *v.* to feel sure that something is true, real, or worthwhile. *I believe that George Washington was a great president.*

▶ **imagine** to suppose; guess. *I don't imagine we'll have a picnic if it rains.*

▶ **suppose** to believe; guess. *I suppose I'll finish my homework soon.*

▶ **think** to have or form an opinion, belief, or idea. *I think we should go home before it gets dark.*

below *prep.* lower than in place, rank, or value. *The small plane flew below the clouds.*

▶ **beneath** lower than; under. *Leaves fell onto the ground beneath the tree.*

▶ **under** in or to a place lower than. *The letter was under a pile of books.*

ANTONYMS: *See* above.

big *adj.* of great size. *A hippo is a big animal.*

▶ **enormous** much greater than the usual size. *An enormous whale swam by.*

▶ **giant** very large. *A redwood is a giant tree.*

▶ **gigantic** like a giant; huge and powerful. *A gigantic crane easily lifted the truck.*

▶ **huge** extremely big. *That elephant is huge!*

▶ **large** of great size; big. *A Great Dane is a large dog.*

ANTONYMS: *See* little.

brave *adj.* willing to face danger; without fear. *The brave man dove into the river to save a puppy.*

▶ **bold** showing courage; fearless. *The firefighter made a bold rescue.*

▶ **courageous** having courage. *A courageous girl rescued the cat.*

▶ **daring** willing to take risks. *The daring climber climbed the rocky cliff.*

▶ **fearless** without fear. *The fearless explorer entered the thick jungle.*

ANTONYMS: afraid, fearful

bright *adj.* filled with light; shining. *The sun was so bright that I put on sunglasses.*

▶ **brilliant** shining or sparkling with light. *The stars' light is brilliant on a clear night.*

▶ **glittering** sparkling. *Lucy's costume was covered with glittering sequins.*

▶ **glowing** shining. *The glowing candle gave off a soft light.*

▶ **shiny** gleaming brightly. *Dad gave me a shiny new quarter.*

ANTONYMS: dark, dull

clean *adj.* free from dirt. *Max took the clean clothes out of the washing machine.*

▶ **pure** not stained, dirty, or mixed with anything else. *We drank pure water from a spring.*

▶ **spotless** absolutely clean. *His new shirt was spotless.*

ANTONYMS: dirty, filthy

cold *adj.* having a low temperature; lacking warmth. *We shivered in the cold air.*

▶ **chilly** uncomfortably cool. *The day was rainy and chilly.*

▶ **freezing** extremely cold. *The snowy weather was freezing.*

▶ **icy** very cold. *An icy wind blew across the frozen lake.*

ANTONYMS: *See* hot.

cry *v.* to shed tears. *The baby started to cry.*

▶ **sob** to cry with short gasps. *He began to sob when his balloon flew away.*

▶ **weep** to show grief, joy, or other strong emotions by crying. *She began to weep when she heard the good news.*

dark *adj.* having little or no light. *With no moon, it was a very dark night.*

▶ **dim** having or giving little light; not bright. *There was only a dim light in the hall.*

▶ **shady** darker than the surrounding area. *We sat in a shady part of the yard.*

ANTONYM: light, bright

delicious *adj.* pleasing to the taste or smell. *The spaghetti sauce smelled delicious.*

▶ **flavorful** tasting good; full of flavor. *The apple was juicy and flavorful.*

▶ **tasty** pleasing to the sense of taste. *I had a tasty salad for lunch.*

dislike *v.* to have a feeling of not liking. *I dislike spinach.*

▶ **hate** to have very strong feelings against; dislike very much. *I hate losing a game!*

empty *adj.* having nothing or no one in it. *Mom washed out the empty vase.*

▶ **blank** not written or printed upon; unmarked. *One side of the paper was blank.*

▶ **vacant** containing no one or nothing; empty. *The parking lot is vacant.*

ANTONYM: full

far *adj.* a long way off; not near. *Our house is far from the city.*

▶ **distant** extremely far. *The cruise ship sailed to a distant island.*

ANTONYMS: close, near

fast *adj.* moving or done with speed. *A fast car zoomed past us.*

▶ **quick** done in a very short time. *We ate a quick lunch.*

▶ **rapid** with great speed, often in a continuing way. *The runners kept up a rapid pace.*

▶ **speedy** moving quickly. *A speedy taxi got us to the airport on time.*

▶ **swift** moving with great speed, often said of animals or people. *A cheetah is a swift runner.*

ANTONYM: slow

fine *See* good.

friend *n.* a person one knows well and likes. *Kareem is my best friend.*

▶ **buddy** a close friend. *Warren has been my buddy since first grade.*

▶ **companion** a person or animal who often goes along with another person. *My dog is my constant companion.*

▶ **pal** a close friend. *My pal Theo and I play every day after school.*

ANTONYM: enemy

funny *adj.* causing laughter. *We chuckled at the funny joke.*

▶ **amusing** causing smiles of enjoyment or laughter. *Tia's amusing story made me smile.*

▶ **comical** causing laughter through actions. *My dog looked comical in a silly hat.*

▶ **entertaining** interesting; amusing. *We found the movie entertaining.*

▶ **humorous** making people laugh. *We saw a humorous movie about a talking cat.*

good *adj.* above average in quality. *That was a good book.*

▶ **excellent** extremely good. *Swimming is excellent exercise.*

▶ **fair** somewhat good; slightly better than average. *He got a fair grade on the spelling test.*

▶ **fine** of high quality; very good. *Our class is doing a fine job in science.*

▶ **terrific** extremely good; wonderful. *Juanita had a terrific idea.*

▶ **wonderful** very good; excellent. *I had a wonderful dinner last night.*

ANTONYMS: bad, poor

great *adj.* of unusual quality or ability. *Jackie Robinson was a great ballplayer.*

▶ **remarkable** having unusual qualities. *He has a remarkable voice.*

▶ **superb** of greater quality than most. *She is a superb violinist.*

halfway *adv.* to or at half the distance. *Tad fell halfway through the race.*

▶ **midway** in the middle; halfway. *Your house is midway between Sam's and mine.*

happy *adj.* having, showing, or bringing pleasure. *The happy children laughed out loud.*

▶ **cheerful** showing or feeling cheer or happiness. *The cheerful boy whistled as he walked.*

▶ **glad** feeling or expressing joy or pleasure. *Maria was glad to see her friend.*

▶ **joyful** very happy; filled with joy. *Eric was joyful when he heard the good news.*

ANTONYMS: *See* sad.

hard *adj.* not easy to do or deal with. *Cutting wood is hard work.*

▶ **difficult** hard to do; requiring effort. *These math problems are difficult.*

▶ **tough** difficult to do, often in a physical sense. *Firefighters have a tough job.*

ANTONYM: easy

hot *adj.* having a high temperature; having much heat. *The sun is hot.*

▶ **fiery** as hot as fire; burning. *The leaves burned in a fiery blaze.*

▶ **warm** somewhat hot; not cold. *My mittens kept my hands warm.*

ANTONYMS: *See* cold.

idea *n.* a picture or thought formed in the mind. *Pedro had an idea for a new invention.*

▶ **thought** a product of thinking; an idea or opinion. *What are your thoughts on this problem?*

large *See* big.

laugh *v.* to show amusement. *Everyone laughed at the silly clowns.*

▶ **chuckle** to laugh softly, especially to oneself. *Taro began to chuckle at the joke.*

▶ **giggle** to laugh in a silly or nervous way. *Those children giggle at everything.*

ANTONYMS: cry, sob, weep

let *v.* to give permission to. *My dad will let me go fishing.*

▶ **allow** to give permission to. *The town does not allow swimming in the pond.*

▶ **permit** to allow someone to do something. *Mrs. Casey will permit us to leave early.*

ANTONYMS: deny, forbid, refuse

like *v.* to enjoy something; to feel affection for someone or something. *I like to play soccer.*

▶ **admire** to have affection and respect for someone. *Tina admires her teacher.*

▶ **enjoy** to take pleasure in doing something. *Tranh enjoys solving puzzles.*

▶ **love** to like something a lot; to have great affection for someone. *Carrie loves her dog.*

ANTONYMS: *See* dislike.

little *adj.* small in size. *A pebble is a little stone.*

▶ **small** not large. *A mouse is a small animal.*

▶ **tiny** very small. *The baby has tiny fingers.*

ANTONYMS: *See* big.

look *v.* to see with one's eyes. *Look at the colorful butterfly.*

▶ **glance** to look quickly. *I glanced at the page and shut the book.*

▶ **peer** to look closely. *I had to peer to read the fine print.*

▶ **scan** to look at closely and carefully. *The astronomer scanned the sky to find the comet.*

▶ **stare** to look at for a long time with eyes wide open. *It's not polite to stare at people.*

loudly *adv.* in a loud way. *The doorbell rang loudly.*

▶ **noisily** in a loud, harsh way. *The children's shoes clattered noisily on the tile floor.*
ANTONYMS: quietly, silently

many *adj.* consisting of a large number. *Dara has many books about animals.*
▶ **numerous** a great many. *We have ridden the subway numerous times.*
▶ **several** more than a few but fewer than many. *Our team won several games this year.*
ANTONYM: few

mean *adj.* without kindness or understanding. *It is mean to tease people.*
▶ **cruel** willing to cause pain or suffering. *It is cruel to hurt an animal.*
▶ **nasty** very mean. *That was a nasty thing to say.*
▶ **selfish** concerned only about oneself. *He is too selfish to share his toys.*
▶ **spiteful** filled with bad feelings toward others. *They sometimes act in a spiteful way.*
▶ **unkind** not kind; cruel. *Your unkind words hurt my feelings.*
ANTONYMS: *See* nice.

nice *adj.* agreeable or pleasing. *We had a nice time at the zoo.*
▶ **gentle** mild and kindly in manner. *The lioness is gentle with her cubs.*
▶ **kind** friendly; good-hearted. *It was kind of you to send me a card.*
▶ **pleasant** agreeable; giving pleasure to. *I had a pleasant visit with my grandmother.*
▶ **sweet** agreeable. *Debbie is so sweet with her baby brother.*
ANTONYMS: *See* mean.

old *adj.* having lived for a long time. *This pine tree is old.*
▶ **ancient** very old; from times long past. *The museum has some ancient pots from Mexico.*
▶ **elderly** rather old. *Our elderly neighbor swims every day.*
ANTONYMS: new, young

quiet *adj.* with little or no noise. *A library is a quiet place.*
▶ **calm** free of excitement or strong feeling; quiet. *The ocean is calm today.*

▶ **peaceful** calm; undisturbed. *The garden is a peaceful place to sit.*

▶ **silent** completely quiet; without noise. *The crowd was silent when the concert began.*

▶ **still** without sound; silent. *Be still and listen to the teacher.*

ANTONYMS: loud, noisy

right *adj.* free from error; true. *Jeff gave the right answers on the test.*

▶ **accurate** without mistake. *Erin's math was accurate.*

▶ **correct** agreeing with fact or truth. *Our coach showed us the correct way to hold a bat.*

▶ **exact** very accurate; completely correct. *Lorenzo knew the exact number of stamps in his collection.*

ANTONYMS: wrong, mistaken

sad *adj.* feeling or showing unhappiness or sorrow. *Della was sad when her friend moved away.*

▶ **depressed** feeling low; sad. *We were depressed when we could not find our dog.*

▶ **miserable** extremely unhappy. *He felt miserable when he lost the race.*

▶ **unhappy** without happiness or joy; sad. *I was unhappy when summer ended.*

ANTONYMS: *See* happy.

say *v.* to make known or express in words. *What did Abdul say about the ballgame?*

▶ **speak** to utter words; talk. *The baby can't speak yet.*

▶ **talk** to say words; speak. *Jess talked to Mel on the phone.*

scared *adj.* afraid; alarmed. *I felt scared when I smelled smoke.*

▶ **afraid** feeling fear, often for a long time. *My dog is afraid of thunder.*

▶ **fearful** filled with fear. *The hikers were fearful of losing their way.*

▶ **frightened** scared suddenly. *I was frightened when I heard a strange noise.*

▶ **terrified** extremely scared; filled with terror. *He is terrified of heights.*

small *See* little.

smart *adj.* intelligent; bright; having learned a lot. *Juan is a smart boy.*

▶ **clever** mentally sharp. *Jerry is clever at solving puzzles.*

▶ **intelligent** able to learn, understand, and reason. *Mei-ling is intelligent enough to figure out the answer.*

▶ **wise** able to know or judge what is right, good, or true. *The wise woman knew who was telling the truth.*

strange *adj.* unusual; out of the ordinary. *An emu is a strange bird.*

▶ **odd** different; not ordinary. *The doll's hair was an odd shade of green.*

▶ **weird** strange or odd, in a frightening or mysterious way. *The movie had a weird plot.*

strong *adj.* having much power, force, or energy. *The strong man lifted the huge box.*

▶ **mighty** having great power. *Paul Bunyan was a mighty man.*

▶ **powerful** having great power. *This big truck has a powerful engine.*

ANTONYMS: *See* weak.

surprised *adj.* feeling sudden wonder. *Nell was surprised when she saw us.*

▶ **amazed** overwhelmed with wonder or surprise. *Everyone was amazed by Jed's magic tricks.*

▶ **astonished** greatly surprised; shocked. *Grace was astonished when she won the contest.*

thin *adj.* not fat. *A greyhound has a long, thin body.*

▶ **lean** with little or no fat. *Jogging gave her a lean look.*

▶ **skinny** extremely thin. *It is not healthy to be too skinny.*

▶ **slender** not big around; thin. *He is tall and slender.*

▶ **slim** thin, in a good or healthy way. *Exercising helps my dad stay slim.*

ANTONYMS: chubby, fat, plump

unusual *adj.* not usual, common, or ordinary; rare. *It is unusual for it to rain in the desert.*

▶ **rare** not often seen, happening, or found. *A double rainbow is a rare sight.*

▶ **uncommon** not usually found or seen. *Bears are an uncommon sight in these woods.*

ANTONYMS: common, ordinary, usual

very *adv.* to a great extent. *The water is very cold.*

▶ **considerably** to a large or important degree. *A bus is considerably bigger than a car.*

▶ **extremely** greatly or intensely. *I was extremely happy with my perfect score on the test.*

▶ **quite** completely. *We were quite pleased by the news.*

walk *v.* to move or travel on foot. *I walk to school every day.*

▶ **march** to walk with regular steps. *The band will march in the parade.*

▶ **shuffle** to drag the feet when walking. *The children shuffled through the dry leaves.*

▶ **stride** to walk with long steps. *Ella can stride along rapidly.*

▶ **stroll** to walk in a relaxed, slow way. *Let's stroll around the mall.*

want *v.* to have a desire or wish for. *Lauren wants to be a doctor someday.*

▶ **desire** to wish for; long for. *Anne desires a horse more than anything.*

▶ **long** to want very much. *I long to see my old friends again.*

▶ **wish** to have a longing or strong desire for. *Mac and Tracy wish they could go skiing.*

weak *adj.* not having strength, force, or power. *The light is too weak to read by.*

▶ **feeble** not strong; weak. *The sick puppy was too feeble to stand up.*

▶ **frail** lacking in strength; weak. *This old chair is too frail to hold a person.*

▶ **powerless** without power; helpless. *The mouse was powerless in the cat's claws.*

ANTONYMS: *See* strong.

whole *adj.* having all its parts; entire. *Is that the whole set of cards?*

▶ **complete** having the full number of; whole. *Jack has a complete set of trains.*

▶ **entire** with nothing left out. *Did you eat the entire salad?*

▶ **total** being all there is; making up the whole. *Kim paid the total amount of the bill in pennies.*

ANTONYM: incomplete.

Index

Index

Index

Index

Index

Index

ACKNOWLEDGMENTS

(continued from page ii.)

Cover Design and Illustration: Robert Brook Allen
Cover Photo: Steve Starr/Stock, Boston

ILLUSTRATION CREDITS: Daniel DelValle: 301, 378, 459, 461. Lou Pappas 301.

PHOTO CREDITS: Animals Animals: Zig Leszczynski 376; Robert Maier 136; Patti Murray 147; Richard Sobol 9. Art Resource: Fine Art Photographic Library, London/Art Resource, NY 280. Beaura Ringrose 57, 215. Bob Daemmerich Photo Inc. 98. Nina Berman/Sipa 185E. Bruce Coleman Inc.: Erwin and Peggy Bauer 434; Jane Burton 189, 320; J-C Carton 363; John Elk III 71; A Kerstitch 417; R. Kopfle 172; Larry Lipsky 96; James Montgomery 398-9; Hans Reinhard 353; Michael S. Renner 33; Lee Rentz 42; John Shaw 97; Kim Taylor 137; Larry West 122. Christie's Images: Diego Rivera 118. Corbis: Morton Beebe 73; Peter Johnson 80; Catherine Karnow 386; Daphne Kinzler 4; Buddy Mays 68; Jeffry W. Myers 171. Corel: Al Greening 84-5. Lori Cross/Nuckols Farm Elementary School 185J, M. Brian Diggs/AP 185L. David R. Frazier Photolibrary: 90, 437; John Cancalosi 308; D. Cavagnaro 57; Chuck Dresner 433; Wayne Lankinen 273; Pat O'Hara 334-5. Fotograf Hans-Olof Utsi: Lars Thulin 238. FPG International: 310; Ken Chernus 209; Larry Grant 326; Ken Reid 412; A. Schmidecker 468. Gamma Liaison: Bill Greenblatt 249. Grant Heilman Photography: Gemma Giannini 453; Larry Lefever 371. Phillip Greenberg for Time for Kids 185G, I. Courtesy Hillside Intermediate School 185B, C. Hutchings Photography: T3, T4, T10, T13, T14, T17, 44, 46, 52, 56, 58, 115, 124, 126, 132, 136, 138, 161, 169, 177, 197, 202, 204, 210, 214, 216, 257, 258, 262, 286, 288, 294, 298, 300, 364, 366, 372, 376, 378, 409, 446, 448, 454, 458, 460. Index Stock Imagery 7, 10, 83. Index Stock Photography Inc.: 296, 332, 411; Melanie Carr 214; Frank Siteman 227. International Stock 56. Freddi Jacobi 185P. Bill Kostroun/AP 185N. Steve Liss for Time for Kids 185A, S. Lawrence Migdale: 1, 51, 199, 275, 361, 389, 443. Macmillan/McGraw-Hill 340. Mike Mullen/San Gabriel Valley Newspaper/AP 185H. MMSD: 215; Bob Randall 329. Monkmeyer Conklin: 89; McCutchen 8; Paras 157; Frank Siteman 173; Gerard Smith 253; Ullman 255; Van Etten 317. NASA 111, 422. Panoramic Images: BO Brännhage 148; Karalee Griffin 277; O. Grunewald 67; Tom Jelen 260; Jack Krawczyk 244-5; Neil Meyerhoff 176-7, 352; Richard Sisk 312-3, 458-9; Thomas Winz 8,324; Koji Yamashita 418. Peter Arnold Inc.: Fred Bavendam 441; Bios (A. Compost) 441; John Cancalosi 402; Michael Gunther 377; Clyde H. Smith 99; Erika Stone 471. Photo Edit: Nancy Sheehan 98; Bill Bachmann 407, 425; Cindy Charles 414; Myrleen Ferguson 401; Tony Freeman 88, 246, 256; Robert Ginn 281; Dennis MacDonald 333; Felicia Martinez 162, 168, 226, 421; Tom McCarthy 343; Michael Newman 113, 259, 323, 359; Johnathan Nourok 283; A. Ramey 20, 469; B.W. Stitzer 263; David Young-Wolff 93, 121, 163, 248, 311, 410, 420. Photo Researchers, Inc.: 31; Bill Bachmann 149; Mark Burnett 274; Scott Camazine and Sue Trainor 131; Ken Cavanagh 225; Tim Davis 444; Gregory G. Dimijian 119; R. Ellis 285; J.A. Hancock 174; Walter E. Harvey 137; Bruce M. Herman 435; Tom Hollyman 470; Richard Hutchings 230; Adam Jones 78-9; John Kaprielian 128; Jeff Lepore 299; Michael Lustbader 94; Renee Lynn 11, 293; Raphael Macia 475; Jerry McCormick-Ray 156; Lawrence Migdale 15, 405; Mug Shots 476; Kenneth Murray 403; Rod Planck 238; Frans Rombout 377; Blair Seitz 341; Peter Skinner 481; Mark Smith 150; K. Stranton 69; George Turner 113; Larry West 228. PhotoDisc: 3, 47, 57, 74, 85, 154, 193, 231, 233, 243, 315, 322, 392, 416, 459, 470, 472. Photolibrary: David R. Frazier 2. Picturequest 407. Richard Haynes 396. Richard T. Nowitz: Richard T. Nowitz 408. Robert Winslow 23. Karl Ronstrom/Reuters 185O. Ann States/SABA 185D, Q. Stock • Boston: Bob Daemmerich 178; Gayna Hoffman 18; William Johnson 139; Lawrence Migdale 5; A. Ramey 69; Frank Siteman 4, 6, 13, 16, 21, 43, 66, 87, 92, 100, 119, 153, 170, 174, 178, 247, 327, 394, 416, 477. SuperStock: Gustavo Novoa 358; Jane Wooster Scott 440. The Bridgeman Art Library: Luis Graner Arrufi 42. The Curtis Publishing Company: Norman Rockwell 196. The Granger Collection: The Image Bank: Barros And Barros 333; Rockwell Kent 387. The Image Works: Bill Bachmann 281; Bob Daemmerich 43, 265; Townsend P. Dickinson 31; Esbin-Anderson 155, 250; Granitsas 151; Jeff Greenberg 404; Randy Jolly 233; Lisa Krantz 240; C. W. McKeen 32; Ellen Senisi 152. The Jackson Citizen Patriot 185F. The Stock Market: 81; Paul Barton 82, 101, 160; Ed Bock 390, 393; Mark Cooper 391; Jon Feingersh 167, 261; Zefa Germany 339, 473; Charles Gupton 14, 319; John Henley 175; Michael Heron 179; Gary Landsman 41; Mark M. Lawrence 423; Lester Lefkowitz 76; Bob Lewine 251; Don Mason 322, 322-3; Roy Morsch 388; Gabe Palmer 79; Chuck Savage 413; Norbert Schafer 351; Ariel Skelley 75, 254, 324, 325; Tom Stewart 164, 165, 187; David Stoecklein 19; David Woods 193. Tony Stone Images: 359; Brian Bailey 70; Gay Bumgarner 228, 316-7; Peter Cade 35; Laurie Campbell 174; Ray Corra 435; Daniel J. Cox 415; Tim Davis 336; Tony Dawson 335; Bruce Foster 200; Penny Gentieu 59; Chip Henderson 190; Alan Hicks 166; Frans Lanting 400; Renee Lynn 337, 338; Kevin R. Morris 91; Dennis O'Clair 441; David Olsen 331; Donovan Reese 252; Frank Siteman 241; Rob Talbot 355; D&K Tapparel 479; Bob Thomas 328; Arthur Tilley 242; Nick Vedros 419; John Warden 73, 86; Stuart Westmorland 417; Art Wolfe 298, 299; David Woodfall 17. Uniphoto Picture Agency: 197; Cheryl A. Ertelt 12. Visuals Unlimited: Barbara Gerlach 95; John Gerlach 224; Maslowski 137; Glenn M. Oliver 112; David Sieren 309.